SCC LIBRARY

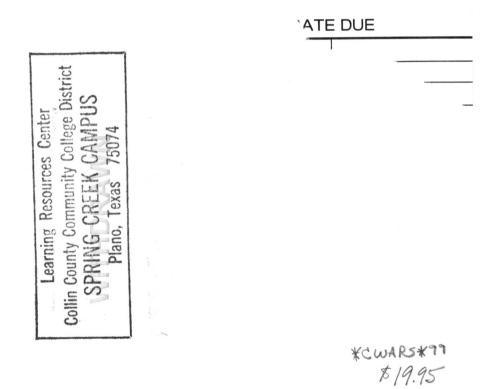

CULTURE
WARS

CULTURE
WARS

Documents from
the Recent Controversies
in the Arts

Edited by
RICHARD BOLTON

NEW PRESS
New York

Acknowledgments

A book of this scope could not have been completed without the help of a great many people. Special thanks must go to the staff of the Washington Project for the Arts, particularly Debra Singer, who, besides coauthoring the chronology in this volume, provided invaluable research assistance and advice. Thanks must also go to David Hildebrand, Bettina Bell, Danielle Saba, Megan Teare, Rachel Hubbs, and Michael Albo of the WPA, as well as to John Moore, and of course, Jock Reynolds. Norton Dodge provided crucial financial support for the project in its early phase, as did Betsy Frampton of the Glen Eagles Foundation. Thanks also to Chris Morrison, Travis Smalls, and Susan Lubowsky at the National Endowment for the Arts; to Charlotte Murphy and Penny Boyer at the National Association of Artists' Organizations; to Christine Lenchow and Elaine Kingsbury at People for the American Way; to Chip Berlet and Margaret Quigley at Political Research Associates; and to the Congressional Arts Caucus. Finally, I want to express my gratitude to Allison Gamble of the New Arts Examiner, for her consistent support and incisive criticism; and to Gretel Huglin, who was indispensable as an assistant during the final stages of this book.

Illustrations 309

Preface

Philip Brookman

On June 14, 1989, *The Washington Post* reported that the Corcoran Gallery of Art in Washington, D.C., had canceled their planned exhibition of *Robert Mapplethorpe: The Perfect Moment*. According to the *Post*, the museum's trustees had abruptly changed their agenda to avoid becoming involved in a growing political debate over the sexual content of the artist's work. Apparently, they feared that the exhibition would jeopardize the upcoming congressional reauthorization of the National Endowment for the Arts (NEA), a federal agency that had partially funded the show. Their decision changed the course of arts funding in 1990s.

At the time, I was working as a curator at Washington Project for the Arts, a nonprofit, experimental gallery in the nation's capital. I had been following closely the political debates over arts funding and content, and the specific controversies that were beginning to engulf the art world. The country was moving into an election year, and certain politicians seemed ready to exploit a handful of artists and their work in order to capture the attention of the electorate. These artists, who had received NEA funding, directly or indirectly, had struck a raw nerve in Congress and in some segments of the public: federal money, it was thought, should not support the creation and exhibition of ideas that questioned the status quo.

Between 1985 and 1990, artists were increasingly confronted by government agencies and special interest groups for creating work that some considered to be obscene, pornographic, blasphemous, politically motivated, or degrading of national symbols. Those artists — whose work addressed specific social issues such as war, economics, racism, environmental concerns, immigration, multiculturalism, gender representations, sexuality, and AIDS — and by extension their sponsors (the NEA, state arts councils, foundations, museums, and so on), were criticized in Congress and the national media for the content of their outspoken work. For example, Representative Richard Armey (R–Tex.), a vociferous critic who tried to eliminate the NEA, admonished the agency in 1985 for funding gay-oriented literary journals. In response, the arts community began to question congressional criticism, arguing that any attempt to legislate the content of work that qualified for federal funding was tantamount to censorship. Armey's response: "This is not a matter of censorship, it is a matter of judgement, of values."[1] Arguments about symbolic speech and public morality politicized the issue of arts patronage.

Less than four years later, the NEA again came under attack from members of Congress, and from a handful of confrontational religious groups, led by Reverend Donald Wildmon, executive director of the American Family Association (AFA) in Tupelo, Mississippi. The AFA sent mass mailings to Congress, the media, and to several hundred thousand constituents, in which they complained of alleged NEA abuses of taxpayers' money for funding artists like Robert Mapplethorpe, Andres Serrano, David Wojnarowicz, and Karen Finley. Questioning the merits of an NEA fellowship to the photographer Serrano,

Senator Alfonse D'Amato (R–N.Y.) exclaimed, "This is not a question of free speech. This is a question of abuse of taxpayers' money."[2] As the debate continued, the issues of free speech, censorship, and legislative control of arts funding were continually invoked by Congress and by the national arts community.

When the NEA was first chartered in 1965, care was taken to remove legislators from determining in any way the aesthetic directions of the agency, in part by implementing procedures to remove Congress and the NEA bureaucracy from infringing on artistic freedom. Grants were to be given on the basis of artistic quality. A democratic system of peer review panels was put in place to assist the agency in determining funding for artists and projects. In its report on Public Law 89-209 — the National Foundation on the Arts and Humanities Act of 1965, which initially authorized creation of the NEA — the Senate required that "in the administration of this act there be given the fullest attention to freedom of artistic and humanistic expression."[3] The NEA was originally created in this spirit of open inquiry and experimentation.

Nonetheless, the escalation of disharmony between artists, government funders, lobbyists, and other arts patrons during the late 1980s and early 1990s arose from issues far more complex than the debates over federal funding for the arts. Artists were certainly challenged for the content of their work and the ideologies their work represented. These disputes, though, were not limited to funded artists; rather, they represent various ideological disagreements over the content of documentary and feature films, television programming, novels, poetry, magazines, student newspapers, and the freedom to voice political dissent in public. Many forms of cultural expression were being probed and certain qualifying limitations to these expressions were proposed or implemented by government agencies, special interest groups, or the courts. This was the climate in which *Robert Mapplethorpe: The Perfect Moment* became a monument on the nation's cultural battlefield.

When I came into work at Washington Project for the Arts the morning after the Corcoran Gallery canceled the Mapplethorpe exhibition, Jock Reynolds, then executive director of WPA, asked me right away if I had heard what happened — it was all over the news — and if I had any thoughts about it. I said, "We should hang the show here at WPA. We have the space in Washington and people have a right to see it." It seemed like the obvious thing to do. "Well, I've already called Philadelphia [the Institute of Contemporary Art, University of Pennsylvania] to see if it's possible," Jock responded. In our minds, the immediate question was one of freedom of expression, an idea that would become a principal point of contention for artists and politicians throughout the country.

By coincidence, WPA had six weeks during the summer with no exhibitions scheduled in our galleries, to prepare for a big project opening in the fall. After a unanimous show of support from the board of directors and some seat-of-the-pants fund-raising, it was announced publicly that the exhibition would open in our own small exhibition space in downtown D.C. on July 21, 1989. At the time, we had little understanding of what this decision would mean in the months and years to come. The implications became clearer as calls and letters came in from around the country, offering help or criticism for the seemingly simple act of exhibiting an artist's photographs. Battle lines were being drawn.

As the media gathered and people chose sides, I began to understand that, on a larger scale, we were witnessing an attempt to regulate not only the content of NEA-funded art and exhibitions but also the kind of work that artists would make, thus the kind of cultural expression to which the public would be exposed. Decision-making at the Corcoran Gallery had already been affected, and storm clouds were gathering at other prominent institutions. Less than one year later, the Mapplethorpe exhibition would be the focus of a landmark court case, when Cincinnati's Contemporary Art Center and its director Dennis Barrie were indicted on, and later acquitted of, obscenity and child pornography charges.

With an international spotlight focused on a few photographs, *Robert Mapplethorpe: The Perfect Moment* opened in Washington, D.C., to great reviews and record crowds. Visitors were struck by the artist's technical mastery of his craft and the beauty he found in making portraits of flowers and of the people he had known. At each venue where it was shown, the exhibition was received in a similar way. The controversial, sexually explicit photographs from Mapplethorpe's *X-Portfolio*, which depicted a gay subculture of which Mapplethorpe was a part, were but a fraction of the works on view; they were isolated on a table in a separate room so viewers could see the exhibition without confronting them if they chose not to. Since these were the pictures that caused all the trouble, signs were posted to let people know what was there. We improvised tickets to handle the long lines that formed every day, sometimes stretching around the block. In a video documentary about Mapplethorpe, who had died earlier that year, he explained his work to large audiences every day. The longest lines, though, were those snaking through the galleries as crowds waited patiently for hours to view the *X-Portfolio*.

In twenty-five days almost fifty thousand people came to see Mapplethorpe's work for themselves. There was a sense in the crowd that this was a historic moment and not to be missed. Fewer than two dozen complaints were received from across the country. One telling comment came from a guest who exclaimed, "I've been here four times already and this show disgusts me more each time I see it." Yet thousands of people showed their overwhelming support for the exhibition and for their right to view it, through their attendance, comments, and financial contributions. This heightened public awareness helped to combat an increasingly homophobic atmosphere generated by the debate over Mapplethorpe's images.

During WPA's presentation of *Robert Mapplethorpe: The Perfect Moment* we began to compile an archive of reference materials pertinent to the subjects of censorship, arts funding, and freedom of expression. These materials included news clippings, books, magazines, photographs, videotapes, testimony, and government documents. As our archive grew, writers, journalists, researchers, and students interested in these topics began to use it for reference. When artist and writer Richard Bolton wanted access to our materials, I asked him to help organize them so the archive would be easily accessible to everyone. He suggested that we undertake additional research and begin to compile a useful reference guide to the principal issues of controversy in the arts during the late 1980s and early 1990s. As an artist-in-residence, Rick worked closely with WPA's staff for almost two years as we watched these events unfold.

The materials in this book focus on the cultural issues and arguments surrounding the complex and problematic 1989–1990 reauthorization of the NEA and other issues related to government censorship and symbolism. Because these issues and events are volatile and constantly changing, and the arguments on both sides are so impassioned and divisive, we decided to present a broad selection of articles, editorials, and detailed discussions, supplemented with examples of key legislation, congressional arguments, and testimony regarding the roles and functions of the NEA. Also included is an introductory essay by the editor, which discusses some of the ways in which culture, religion, morality, and politics have informed the debate over the content and funding of the arts, as well as an annotated chronology of related events from 1962 through 1990. These contributions help to situate the controversies surrounding government funding of the arts in the context of broader attempts by government to regulate culture.

---

1. *The Washington Post*, September 12, 1985, p. C1.
2. Quoted in *Congressional Record*, Senate, May 18, 1989.
3. *A Report to Congress on the National Endowment for the Arts*, September 1990.

CULTURE
WARS

Introduction
Richard Bolton

On May 18, 1989, Senator Alphonse D'Amato tore up a reproduction of *Piss Christ*, a photograph by artist Andres Serrano, and threw the pieces to the floor of the U.S. Senate. "This so-called piece of art is a deplorable, despicable display of vulgarity," he exclaimed to his fellow legislators. D'Amato went on to complain that this very artist had received funding for his work from the National Endowment for the Arts (NEA). "Incredible," he grumbled. "What a disgrace."

So began a vocal two-year battle between politicians and artists over the budget and reauthorization of the NEA. On the surface, this controversy may seem like much ado about nothing — a partisan clash over a tiny bit of the federal budget, a brouhaha of muddled arguments and confusing legislation. Nothing could be more mistaken. The clash over government funding was much more than an argument over art; it was a debate over competing social agendas and concepts of morality, a clash over both the present and the future condition of American society. This anthology aims to describe the struggle as broadly as possible, providing both an understanding of the battle over the NEA and the larger context of the fight.[1]

Throughout, there seemed to be as many view-points about the issues at hand as there were participants in the debate. But two positions have remained central to the controversy. Liberals generally argue that any attempt to restrict the work of the NEA would ultimately violate the First Amendment rights of artists. Content restrictions proposed for grants to artists were seen as censorship, pure and simple, as part of a larger plan to control artists politically. "The freedom to create art is a form of free speech protected by the First Amendment," argued the National Association of Artists' Organizations, one of the leading advocacy groups. "Those who receive public funds deserve the freedom to create...regardless of its possible interpretation by some as disagreeable or offensive" ("Statement Regarding Censorship," p. 63). Congress, it was said, has no right to interfere in the Endowment; the NEA's decision-making process, based in peer review, is sound, and has produced many successes over the years.

Conservatives, on the other hand, define the issue as one of government sponsorship rather than censorship. They argued that Congress has the responsibility to spend tax dollars wisely, and that placing restrictions on Endowment money is a reasonable exercise of that responsibility. Provocative art, it was argued, is a bad candidate for federal funding, since this kind of art seems to insult the taxpayers. Senator D'Amato stated the point definitively:

> If this is what contemporary art has sunk to...some may want to sanction that, and that is fine. But not with the use of the taxpayer's money. This is not a question of free speech. This is a question of abuse of taxpayer's money. If we allow this group of so-called art experts to get away with this...then we do not deserve to be in office. (*Congressional Record*, May 18, 1989, p. 28)

In short, those on the Left want to join the issues of censorship and sponsorship, and those on the Right want to separate them. "However divided individuals are on matters of taste, freedom is in the interest of every citizen," wrote philosopher and art critic Arthur C. Danto. "The taxpayer supports the freedom to make and show art, even when it is art of a kind this or that *individual* finds repugnant" ("Art and Taxpayers," p. 96). Representative Dana Rohrabacher, the leader of the anti-NEA faction in the House, saw it another way: "Artists can do whatever they want on their own time and with their own dime" (*Congressional Record*, Sept. 13, 1989, p. 101). Restrictions on the NEA would make the agency "hostage to every crank, ideologue and God botherer in America...[creating] a loony parody of cultural democracy in which everyone becomes his or her own Cato the Censor," wrote critic Robert Hughes ("A Loony Parody of Cultural Democracy," p. 90). But Senator Jesse Helms thought otherwise: "I do not propose that Congress 'censor' artists. I do propose that Congress put an end to the use of federal funds to support outrageous 'art' that is clearly designed to poison our culture" ("It's the Job of Congress to Define What's Art," p. 100).

Warring groups found a touchstone early in the conflict in the so-called Helms amendment. This amendment, attached to an appropriations bill that provided the NEA with its annual budget, aimed to limit severely the kinds of art that could receive funding. The amendment, as originally proposed by Senator Helms, denied funding to "indecent" art depicting sadomasochism, homoeroticism, children, or the sex act itself, as well as art "denigrating" any person's religion, nonreligion, race, creed, sex, handicap, age, or national origin. Had the amendment passed into law as proposed, it would have allowed the government to withhold funding from art critical of almost any subject (see *Congressional Record*, July 26, 1989, p. 73).

The profound shortcomings of this legislation were evident to many, including members of Helms' own party. In a speech to the Senate, Republican Senator John Danforth discussed a range of important works of literature — including *Tom Sawyer, The Color Purple,* and works by William Shakespeare — that would have violated the Helms amendment and would have been denied funding (see *Congressional Record*, Sept. 29, 1989, p. 104). Yet in spite of legislators' skepticism, a version of the amendment still became law. In the end, elected officials seemed more worried about how a vote for the NEA would look to the "folks back home." Democratic Senator Patrick Leahy frankly discussed this problem during the Senate debate, describing the thirty-second political commercial that would inevitably be aimed at any senator voting against the Helms amendment:

> Senator So-and-So voted for pornography tonight. Senator So-and-So wants to waste taxpayers' dollars so that you do not have enough money to buy your home. He wants that money to go to producing pornographic pictures of children, or people performing...unnatural sex acts.[2]

Senator Helms seemed to make such a threat himself during the debate: "If senators want the Federal Government funding pornography, sadomasochism, or art for pedophiles, they should vote against my amendment."

The final statute — Public Law 101-121 — was a diluted version of the Helms amendment based on *Miller* v. *California*, the Supreme Court decision that stands as the legal definition of obscenity. Some legislators thought such an approach was appropriate; artists, as citizens, are subject to the *Miller* ruling whether they receive NEA funding or not. But, as Stephen Rohde and other lawyers pointed out, the wording of Public Law 101-121 differed enough from the Miller standard to invite wide interpretation and abuse (see "Art of the State," p. 194). In the end, the law satisfied no one. Conservatives continued to lobby for stricter measures, and artists were outraged that the law existed at all. And when, in an attempt to carry out the law, the NEA began asking grantees to sign statements promising not to produce obscene works with government funds, many grantees, considering the pledge to be a form of illegal prior restraint, forfeited their money rather than sign (see "Letter to John Frohnmayer," p. 171, and "Letter to Joseph Papp," p. 173). Eventually, the NEA pledge failed a challenge in court, and it was dropped from grant requirements the next year. But a point had been made: government officials, when pressured by conservative activists, were indeed willing to harass artists. It was something that neither side was likely to forget.

What was at stake in this debate for conservatives? Many found in the artworks under question proof that artists were trying to introduce a progressive agenda into society, an agenda based upon multiculturalism, gay and lesbian rights, feminism, and sexual liberation. For conservatives, this meant that artists were engaged in antisocial activity — challenging the family, traditional religious beliefs, and the existing structure of power. The government, it was felt, should not fund antisocial activity, whether it was Serrano's *Piss Christ* (seen to be antireligious), Robert Mapplethorpe's homoerotic works (antifamily), or Artists Space's *Witnesses* exhibition (thought to be antifamily, antigovernment, *and* antireligious).

One of the most considered expressions of this view-point came from Republican Senator Slade Gorton. In his remarks "On the Official Funding of Religious Bigotry," Gorton argued that the government really should not fund the arts at all. "The state must confine itself to its own interests, and art must be free. Neither subsidy nor censure are appropriate, for the state, with its unrivalled power, must not take sides in purely symbolic disputes." The government could not support work like Serrano's *Piss Christ* because to do so would be to take sides in a religious dispute. "Is there anyone in this body who will stand to declare that Americans should subsidize religious bigotry? Is there anyone who will declare that this [work by Serrano] is not religious bigotry?" Support for this work, he concluded, would violate the separation of church and state upon which our government is based (see *Congressional Record*, May 31, 1989, p. 33).

Many disagreements can be raised here. Gorton (along with almost every other critic of Serrano's work) never considered that *Piss Christ* might be a work that interrogates religion rather than insults it. Gorton also seemed to feel that the interests of the state were self-evident, and clearly had nothing to do with art — surely this is arguable. He also ignored the frequency with which the state takes sides in disputes over symbols: Congress has in fact debated the meaning of the flag and the pledge of allegiance, as well as Salman Rushdie's *The Satanic Verses* and Martin Scorsese's *The Last Temptation of Christ*. Nevertheless, his position is a thoughtful one, and few other arguments on the Right were as sophisticated.

Critic James Cooper (one of the few who would not allow his editorials to be reproduced in this volume) was the source of many of the more influential, and less reasonable, arguments. Early on, he worked to rally the Right, complaining that conservatives had spent the last decade allowing art to be destroyed, watching "as one sacred symbol after another was savaged by an elitist cabal hellbent on laying waste to American cultural values." According to Cooper, now that the controversy over *Piss Christ* had revealed this cabal for all to see, conservatives had to go on the attack, and work to "produce an alternative culture that is morally and aesthetically superior."

> We need a cultural and moral renaissance to lift us out of the soup of corruption and crime into which we have fallen. At stake is the future of American culture — and perhaps America itself.[3]

He echoed these views in several other essays published during the debate, complaining, for example, that modern art had become "the purveyor of a destructive, degenerative, ugly, pornographic, Marxist, anti-American ideology." He called on American artists to

> establish an alternative agenda whose priority is the restoration of beauty, harmony, and order in the arts.... Conservatives have an opportunity to celebrate the values that have enabled America to prevail over the century-long challenge of fascism and communism. Five thousand years of Eastern and Western art serve as inspiration.[4]

Cooper's arguments are a good example of the way in which conservatives attempted to use the NEA debate to promote "traditional American values," which, for conservatives, bore a striking resemblance to their own agenda — patriotic, profamily, prochurch, antigay.

Columnist Patrick Buchanan, quite influenced by Cooper's editorials, issued a call to arms for this agenda. "The hour is late," he warned. "America needs a cultural revolution in the '90s as sweeping as its political revolution in the '80s" ("Losing the War for America's Culture?" p.31). In fact, many conservative attacks on the NEA seemed like tailor-made propaganda for their larger cause. Polemic ruled the day, and the demagoguery evident in many editorials was shocking. The prize for extremism must go to the *Washington Times*, our capital's conservative newspaper, which argued that Serrano's supporters were "aesthetic cretins" and that Serrano was forcing the public to "subsidize his perversions"; the paper even warned of "wacked-out aesthetes who smear their bodily fluids over mainstream American beliefs and values" ("Urine the Money," p. 103). The *Times* compared artists to pigs, and their work to excrement:

> If artists are going to pig out at the public trough, they have to expect that taxpayers who pick up the tab for their swill might want to keep an eye on what

the artists give in return. If it's as offensive as what Mr. Mapplethorpe and Mr. Serrano excrete...people who appreciate real beauty are entitled to flush the products of their imaginations down the nearest drainpipe. ("Mapplethorpe Agonistes," p. 39)

Patrick Buchanan's blunt remarks, which appeared in the *Washington Times*, were central to the debate, quoted with approval by the Right and with disbelief by the Left. As the NEA debate progressed, Buchanan found more and more proof of the corruption of American society. In a May 1989 editorial, he implicated artists in the spiritual decline of the country:

America's art and culture are, more and more, openly anti-Christian, anti-American, nihilistic.... While the right has been busy winning primaries and elections...the left has been quietly seizing all the commanding heights of American art and culture. ("Losing the War for America's Culture? p. 31)

The subsequent controversy surrounding Mapplethorpe's work gave Buchanan an opportunity to decry homosexuality, widely cited by conservatives as another factor in the country's decline:

Barbarism! The precise word, as we observe journalistic yahoos hailing poor, pathetic Robert Mapplethorpe for having photographed, for their amusement, the degraded acts by which he killed himself. What's to be done? We can defund the poisoners of culture, the polluters of art; we can sweep up the debris that passes for modern art outside so many public buildings; we can discredit self-anointed critics who have forfeited our trust. ("Pursued by Baying Yahoos," p. 86)

Buchanan again attempted to tie together art and homosexuality in an editorial on *Witnesses*, the controversial NEA-funded exhibition on the subject of AIDS. Buchanan accused both the gay community and the arts community of suffering "from an infantile disorder":

The gays yearly die by the thousands of AIDS, crying out in rage for...medical research to save them from the consequences of their own suicidal self-indulgence.... What does the "arts community" want?...To be honored and subsidized by a society they appear to loathe. Like spoiled children, our artists rant and rail at us; then cry "repression" and "censorship" when we threaten their allowance. ("Where a wall is needed," p. 137)

The discussion in the *Washington Times* about Mapplethorpe brought out the worst in conservative commentators, many of whom fell even lower than Buchanan. Judith Reisman, for example, accused Mapplethorpe of being a Nazi. Fascist art and Mapplethorpe's photographs, it seemed to Reisman, shared many characteristics: both were homoerotic, both glamorized "dominance...'supermen,' sadism and 'child nudes.' " Reisman also accused Mapplethorpe of being a child molester. In making his portrait of a child (*Honey, 1976*), he is said to have responded like "thousands of other child molesters/pornographers before and after him.... The photo advertises the availability of the child (and, by extension, all children) for photographic assault and rape."

7

Reisman concludes her editorial with a bizarre image of the photographer, a mélange of details from several of his self portraits. Mapplethorpe is described as "a child-molesting-rectum with a bull-whip implant, at the ready with his tommy gun" ("Promoting Child Abuse as Art," p. 56).

And as if this wasn't enough, the *Times* also published an editorial by Richard Grenier in which the writer imagines discovering Mapplethorpe's dead body and setting it on fire. The act is ironically justified as self-expression:

> Expressing myself in the constitutional way that makes us so different from...Stalin's Russia...and Deng Xiaoping's China.... I'd burn the guy up.... If I wanted to do more than win over the Supreme Court, and craved the support of the entire intellectual community, I'd set fire to this Mapplethorpe, and not just as self-expression, but as performance art.... And I'd do my darndest to get a $15,000 grant from the National Endowment for the Arts, like Andres Serrano. ("A Burning Issue Lights Artistic Ire," p. 44)

Editorials, of course, do not a revolution make. But conservatives have been doing much more than talk. Buchanan's call for a conservative cultural revolution may have sounded like a new and startling idea, but political and religious activists had been trying to foment this revolution since the beginning of the Reagan era. Writer Carole Vance has pointed out that "the desire to eliminate symbols, images and ideas they do not like from the public space is basic to contemporary conservatives' and fundamentalists' politics about sexuality, gender and the family" ("The War on Culture," p. 106).

The Reverend Donald Wildmon has been one of the most dedicated religious activists of the last decade, and a close look at his work reveals much about the conservative cultural project. Wildmon first came to many people's attention through his role in the NEA debate, but he had previously campaigned for many years against an array of television programs, films, and other works of popular culture. In the early 1980s, Wildmon collaborated with the Reverend Jerry Falwell to create the Coalition for Better Television; in recent years he has operated the American Family Association (AFA), which has an annual budget of $5 million and a newsletter received by about 400,000 people.[5]

Wildmon's strategy — attacking NEA funding and otherwise setting the stage for economic censorship — was consistent with his past actions against the patrons of popular culture. Wildmon has made frequent and dramatic use of the consumer boycott, threatening those advertisers that support works he considers offensive. Wildmon hopes that, under threat of a boycott, advertisers will begin to use their patronage to regulate (that is, censor) works of culture. Wildmon's first success came in 1981, when, after threatening to boycott Proctor and Gamble, he convinced the company, the largest advertiser on television, to withdraw their support for dozens of programs. The reverend has since led campaigns against the sponsors of such television programs as *The Thorn Birds* (in which a Catholic priest breaks a vow of chastity), *Saturday Night Live* (too many uses of the word "penis"), and a never-aired ABC show called *Adam and Yves* (a program about a gay couple). When the patrons prove inaccessible, Wildmon aims his efforts at those who disseminate culture. For example, Wildmon organized a boycott of Holiday Inn because the company made televised pornography available to motel patrons. (Congress adopted this same tactic during the NEA debate, punishing two exhibition spaces — the Southeastern Center for Contemporary Art (SECCA) in Winston-Salem, and the Institute of Contemporary Art (ICA) in Philadelphia — for hosting controversial works of art.) Wildmon has also worked in partnership with the government, testifying before the 1985 Meese Commission on Pornography, discussing a boycott his organization was planning of 7-Eleven convenience stores for selling pornography. The commission followed up his testimony by sending a letter — of dubious legality — to 7-Eleven, stating that a certain "witness" had named the company as a distributor of pornography. The commission requested that the company "respond" to the charge. Intimidated, many of the stores removed the magazines.

In recent years, Wildmon has broadened his attacks, going after more visible targets. He led a nationwide boycott against *The Last Temptation of Christ* (only in a "twisted mind," he said, could such a "weak, insecure, mentally deranged Jesus" exist), and also convinced Pepsi to cancel a $5 million commercial contract with Madonna (he was disturbed about her "open sexuality," and her "blatantly offensive" music video *Like A Prayer)*. He even persuaded CBS to remove a 3½-second scene from the cartoon *Mighty Mouse* (Mighty Mouse, shown sniffing a flower, was actually sniffing cocaine, according to the reverend). And, as many artists know, he helped initiate the attack on the NEA, informing Congress about *Piss Christ* (see "Letter Concerning Serrano's *Piss Christ*," p. 27). Since that time, Wildmon has devoted significant energy to his attacks upon the Endowment and upon various artists (see "Is This How You Want Your Tax Dollars Spent?" p. 150).

What does Wildmon believe is at stake in his work? He says that he is "involved in a great spiritual struggle for the heart and mind and soul of our society. It's very much a cultural battle.... It has taken fifty years or longer to reduce our culture to its present sorry state. We are just beginning to swing the pendulum back the other way." The "other way" is toward the values at "the base of Western civilization.... Our Republic is the result of the Founders' efforts to put into a political frame of reference the ideals of Jesus Christ."[6] This struggle is "not with an enemy from beyond our shores," but with one "inside our borders."[7] Wildmon believes that "anti-Christian TV executives" and others are trying to replace "Christian values with their own secular-humanist values."[8] Liberals from such groups as the People for the American Way, the ACLU, NOW, and Planned Parenthood are trying to destroy the "nation's moral and spiritual fibre," and "if good people don't get involved in increasing numbers, we will go by the way of Rome and others."[9] Wildmon echoed these views in a 1984 editorial, claiming that "if they had their way, consumer groups, intellectuals, blacks and feminists would run our society, while Christians and the military would have very little influence."[10]

These prejudices have grown even more overt in recent years. During his boycott of *The Last Temptation of Christ*, he informed the readers of *USA Today* of the Jewish background of the studio president that released the film, and claimed that, by boycotting the film, Christians could counteract the influence of such people. "Only when it becomes profitable will Hollywood stop crucify-

9

ing our Lord."[11] One of his top goals for 1989 was to force the cancellation of television programs that "promote the homosexual lifestyle and portray practicing homosexuals in a positive light."[12] Wildmon found these same threats — heathens and homosexuals — at work in the art world. Regarding the former, he argued that "the bias and bigotry against Christians, which has dominated television and movies for the past decade or so, has now moved over to the art museums" ("Letter Concerning Serrano's *Piss Christ*," p. 27). An AFA press release on the NEA described the latter: "The exhibit of photographs by Mapplethorpe, a homosexual who died of AIDS earlier this year, contains homoerotic photos that are nothing less than taxpayer funded homosexual pornography" ("Press Release on the NEA," p. 71).

Reverend Wildmon has an ideological partner in Senator Jesse Helms, the most prominent anti-NEA legislator. In a recent promotional letter written for Jerry Falwell, Senator Helms warned that "the homosexual 'community,' the feminists, the civil libertarians, the pro-abortionists, the flag burners and many other fringe political groups are more active than ever in promoting their dangerous anti-family and anti-American agendas" ("Letter to Jerry Falwell," p. 306). Helms responded to Wildmon's call to arms against *Piss Christ* with a similar fundamentalist disgust. In his first Senate speech on the NEA, he had this to say about Andres Serrano: "He is not an artist. He is a jerk. And he is taunting the American people.... And I resent it" (*Congressional Record*, May 18, 1989, p. 28).

Helms's broad agenda is also revealing, for his views place him in the extreme Right of the Republican Party. A few examples: The Senator tried to prevent Martin Luther King Jr's birthday from becoming a national holiday, declaring that the civil rights leader was a communist. He has attempted to remove amnesty provisions for illegal aliens from immigration legislation. Helms supported Roberto d'Aubuisson's failed campaign for the presidency of El Salvador (d'Aubuisson has been linked to the death squads in that country), and he extended sympathies to Chilean President Augusto Pinochet after violence against Chilean citizens by Pinochet's military forces drew worldwide criticism. He has previously organized other efforts to control expression: for example, he and other conservatives once tried to buy CBS television so that Helms could fire Dan Rather and "end the liberal bias" of the network. Helms has been a frequent advocate of restrictive legislation in the area of sexuality. He is a key player in the movement to make abortion illegal, and he has proposed compulsory AIDS testing as well as a mandatory quarantine for people infected with HIV. He led a successful effort to deny federal AIDS funds to groups "advocating" homosexuality (for example, the Gay Men's Health Crisis). Helms, along with many other right-wing activists, sees legislative action against the NEA as being in consonance with these other positions.

In short, behind conservative arguments about government support for the arts could be found extraordinarily repressive social and political goals. Yet conservatives often portrayed themselves as the champions of community values — as the voice of the people. Reverend Wildmon has been particularly fond of this strategy. The AFA press release included in this volume is typical: according to Wildmon, the NEA claims that "artists" such as Mapplethorpe and Serrano are an elite group of people, superior in talent to the working masses, who deserve to be supported by...tax dollars imposed on the working people of America.... Truck drivers, factory workers, carpenters, and sales clerks are all artists, but the government doesn't force taxpayers to give them $171 million a year to support their art.... We ask that the Senate stop all funding to the National Endowment for the Arts, or provide equal funding for all other groups of artists — carpenters, brick masons, truck drivers, sales clerks, etc. ("Press Release on the NEA," p. 71)

Commentator Robert Samuelson provided another version of this argument. In an editorial about the NEA, he complained that government subsidies for culture only benefit higher-income people. He concluded, then, that programs such as PBS's *MacNeil/LehrerNewshour* should not receive any government subsidies.

It's a superb program, but what public purpose does it serve? Can anyone claim there isn't enough news? My guess is that its audience consists heavily of news junkies, who read newspapers and magazines, and watch CNN. The program doesn't inform the uninformed but better informs the well-informed. ("Highbrow Pork Barrel," p. 94)

A populist argument? Perhaps. But Samuelson's conclusion — that all government subsidies for public communication should cease — is certainly not a populist one, for how would this help inform the larger population? In the end, the editorial is simply another attack on the "liberal" media, a favorite target of conservatives.

It is of more than passing interest that "populist" conservatives, while rejecting "high culture" in the name of the masses, also detest the popular culture — television, music, and film — commonly shared by these same masses. And in matters of policy, conservative activists and officials have consistently opposed government programs that would benefit the typical worker. Conservatives opposed any raises in the minimum wage for almost a decade, and supported many antiunion actions (the destruction of the air traffic controllers union, for example). By and large, recent conservative administrations have offered little educational assistance, job training, or health care to working people. Seen in this light, conservative "working-class" concern over arts funding seemed nothing more than a convenient strategy to tap popular resentment of wealth and privilege, while directing this resentment toward an entirely different agenda.

Conservatives do not seem to worry about the inequities of American society because they believe that our economic system is full of democratic possibilities — the marketplace is held up as a direct reflection of popular will. This unshaking belief in free enterprise was applied to the NEA debate by Senator Helms, who stated that "no artist has a preemptive claim on the tax dollars of the American people; time for them, as President Reagan used to say, 'to go out and test the magic of the marketplace'" (*Congressional Record*, July 26, 1989, p. 73). His statement asserts that the marketplace is innately good; left alone, it will provide moral guidance and create social harmony. This philosophy must be contrasted with the ways that conservatives have in fact manipulated the marketplace in recent years, subsidizing such institutions as defense companies and the savings and loan industry, while removing the "safety net" for the poor, the homeless, the unemployed. Such social harmony as we have has not been achieved through a "free-enterprise system" at all, but through considered attempts to increase inequality by adding to the power of some groups while marginalizing and isolating others. The attack on the NEA was also informed by this strategy. One might even choose to see the attack as an extension of the conservative attack on the welfare state — in this case with subsidies to "perverts" being the issue, rather than the subsidies to the poor.

Conservatives know that the subsidized, nonprofit art world is of vital importance to artists. Government subsidy helps to free artists from the pressures of the marketplace, and this helps create a space where alternative views of the world can be articulated. This situation is feared precisely because it gives the artist independence, and, furthermore, some means to critically examine the marketplace, and its social and ethical underpinnings. Restrictions on the nonprofit world can only force artists to become more dependent on the marketplace. The result is a privatization of art production that reduces encounters between critical artists and the public.

Ironically, one of the central figures in the NEA controversy, Robert Mapplethorpe, was quite successful in the marketplace. By the logic of conservatives, Mapplethorpe's success should make him a great popular artist, one that reflects the will of the people, who are said to vote with their wallets. It is even more ironic that the controversies surrounding Mapplethorpe's work have increased its market value. Conservatives may trust the marketplace to be a stabilizing force in society, but the marketplace continues to place great value on transgression. To put it another way, sex still sells. Because of this, many conservatives refuse to endorse the marketplace wholeheartedly. The evangelical Right, in particular, has grave misgivings; its members regularly warn of the marketplace's corrupting influences, and mount boycotts to purge the entertainment industry, for example, of its sins.

The arguments of political and religious conservatives did not exhaust the range of conservative thinking on the NEA. Cultural conservatives, primarily those critics associated with the *New Criterion*, also had much to say. Samuel Lipman, its publisher, and Hilton Kramer, its editor, argued from the perspective of self-proclaimed elitists, art-world insiders (Lipman once served on the NEA's National Council) who want to restructure the production and patronage of high culture in the United States. Both are suspicious of art within the marketplace; further, both seem suspicious of most things popular and common. Lipman, for example, has frequently complained that the audience for art "is being destroyed by well-meaning attempts to expand it." He supports government funding for the arts, but only if this money is used to support "a real academy — one that represents the institutionalization of tradition."[13] In Lipman's view, the arts have been debased by their popularization. While approving of "the great expansion in American artistic life which took place from the Great Depression to the end of the 1950s, aided by the great post-World

12

War II expansion of college education," he despairs of culture produced since the 1960s, a time when

> the inflation of publicity and glamour had begun to make the arts in America into another branch of Broadway and Hollywood. Led by the sexual revolution of the 1960s, the cry of pleasure was everywhere in the air, and the forces of seriousness and reflection were in full flight. The consequence of these society-wide developments was a gathering tendency to see the arts as entertainment and artists as entertainers.[14]

This tendency is said to affect us to this day. "The greatest art, just as the greatest civilization, is the heritage of all,"[15] according to Lipman, but the public must be up to the challenge of this art. Otherwise,

> in the sadly half-educated and apathetic center of American life, the ideal of leadership in art and learning bids fair to become at best the advocacy of genteel diversions and at worst the provision of fodder for the voracious maw of a debased popular culture.[16]

Lipman brought this perspective to the NEA debate. He had commented on the Endowment early in the 1980s, when he contributed to an evaluation of the agency that was published in the Heritage Foundation's *Mandate for Leadership*. This report, which served as a blueprint for the first Reagan administration, criticized the NEA for undertaking an "unwise expansion" in its attempt to reach an "unsophisticated mass public," and recommended that the Endowment work instead to preserve "the integrity of great art." According to the report, the NEA had grown

> more concerned with politically calculated goals of social policy than with the arts it was created to support. To accomplish goals of social intervention and change...the Endowment...serve[s] audiences rather than art, vocal constituencies rather than individually motivated artistic impulses.[17]

During the 1989–1990 debate, Lipman sustained these various arguments. For instance, he saw in Mapplethorpe's work evidence of a decadence that was "everywhere, from high art to popular culture"; he warned that the government should avoid this decadence and concentrate instead on "the championing of the great art of the past" ("Say No to Trash," p. 41). He argued that the problems with the NEA could be attributed to the lack of a clear national cultural policy. Since the Endowment has no detailed public declaration of purpose, he argued, arts administrators could invent any purpose that suited them. The consequence: administrators began to argue (falsely, for Lipman) that the Endowment's function was to make controversial grants, thus reducing "not only the NEA but art itself to being the handmaiden of anger, violence, and social upheaval." For Lipman, this meant that although no official cultural policy existed, an unspoken agenda was being implemented by vocal constituencies controlling the NEA, an agenda of affirmative action, multiculturalism, and disruptive avant-gardism. We should "refuse to abandon public life to those

13

hostile to cultural traditions, and social norms, by which we continue to define — and defend — ourselves" ("Backward and Downward with the Arts," p. 214).

Hilton Kramer, the editor of the *New Criterion*, echoed many of Lipman's points, but took a more moralistic tone. Like other conservatives, Kramer was particularly disturbed by Mapplethorpe's work. He claimed that this work represented the larger danger to society posed by homosexuals. Disturbed that the men photographed by Mapplethorpe were "rendered as nothing but sexual — which is to say, homosexual — objects," Kramer allowed that "as long as they [Mapplethorpe's photographs] remained a private taste, they could not...be seen to be a threat to public decency." But the willingness of some to make these images public, and the willingness of the NEA to fund the dissemination of these images, revealed for Kramer the art world's inability to recognize the fact

> that not all forms of art are socially benign.... Certain forms of popular culture have a devastating effect on the moral sensibilities of the young. Well, it is no less true that certain forms of high culture are capable of having something other than a socially desirable impact on the sensibilities of young and old alike. ("Is Art above the Laws of Decency?" p. 51)

This "attempt to force upon the public the acceptance of the values of a sexual sub-culture that the public at large finds loathsome" was indicative of the art world's and the NEA's "sentimental" attachment to the notion of the avant-garde, "the idea that art is at its best when it is most extreme and disruptive." In a direct-mail letter for the *New Criterion*, Kramer puts his argument more bluntly: "Do you sometimes have the impression that our culture has fallen into the hands of the barbarians?" he asks potential subscribers ("There Is Only One Magazine," p. 259).

It is important to recognize that although Lipman and Kramer have gone to great lengths to separate themselves from the conservative hoi polloi, in the end the views they express are very similar to those of Wildmon and Helms. Both schools of conservative thought — what we might call the populist and the elitist, or, using Robert Hughes's distinction, the paleo- and neoconservatives — claim that the NEA has fallen into the hands of subversive agents (liberals and radicals bent on social intervention and change). The NEA, and in a broader sense, all contemporary artists, are accused of undermining the morality of the United States, of spreading corruption and disrespect for authority and institutions.

Did the attack on the arts represent "the will of the people"? Were the repressive policies proposed by conservatives widely desired? It may be impossible to answer these questions, for we must first ascertain whether the public truly speaks through its legislators. The belief that the American government mirrors the will of the people, or, to be less generous, that the agendas of elected officials reflect the greater good, assumes that the American political process is accessible to everyone. But as the arguments sketched above suggest, the outrage over the NEA was *not* fueled by popular rebellion. Most of the public had never heard of Mapplethorpe or Serrano prior to the controversy, and they did not seem to get very exercised about them once they had.

Broad claims about the will of the people can be made by conservatives precisely because many mechanisms for public participation have been dismantled over the last decade. Conservatives have in fact presided over the development of *non*participatory democracy in the United States. Controls on public expression and discussion, not to mention the rise of expensive and negative political campaigns, have alienated more and more people from the political process. With only 60 percent of the voting-age public registered to vote (and not all of these registrants voting), our government can barely be said to be representative. Generally, the gap between the average American and access to the political system has widened; the distance between the rich and the poor has also increased, as have disparities in education. In spite of their attempts to portray themselves as "populist," a conservative ruling elite in the United States was strengthened and even glamorized during the 1980s.

In fact, the success of politicians in recent years has *not* depended on their ability to sustain and engage a diverse public; instead success depends on a politician's ability to create an image of a mandate. Democracy now proceeds through the manipulation of "perception," rather than through extensive citizen participation. In other words, politicians no longer need to represent the public interest if they can *construct* a "public interest" through the exercise of power. As the spectrum of opinion in society and in the media narrows, with the diversity within the public arena ignored, the views of those in power *become* representative. It is thus only in the context of a concerted effort to control the expression of political and moral differences that conservatives are able to portray themselves as populists. This strategy succeeded in many policy battles in the 1980s, and conservatives assumed it would succeed again during the NEA debate.

In their debate, opponents of the NEA practiced a political strategy developed by anticommunists in the 1950s: accuse those with whom you disagree of sedition and immorality; but first, marginalize this opposition, and limit its access to public communication. Although the United States has historically claimed a commitment to public communication and access to information, the actual fact of this commitment varies from era to era. The 1980s marked a particularly low point in public communication, as the government consciously worked to limit access. David Stockman, President Reagan's first budget director, once noted that the success of conservatism would depend not on "budget policy, or economic policy, but [on] whether we can change the habits of the political system."[18] This is a telling remark, for the Reagan administration did indeed set out to change the habits of the system, and the control of information was key to their strategy. Attempts to restrict government funding for the arts came at the end of a decade of efforts to limit the public exchange of ideas.

Although these efforts are too numerous to describe here fully, some knowledge of them is needed if the attack on the NEA is to be understood within a larger political context.[19] Some pertinent examples: The Immigration and Nationality Act of 1952 (known as the McCarran-Walter Act) was dusted off and used to deny entrance to the United States to novelist Gabriel García Márquez, playwright Dario Fo, author Farley Mowat, and other foreign writers. The government tried to deport author Margaret Randall (a U.S.-born Mexican

15

citizen) because, it was claimed, her writings advocated world communism. The Foreign Agents Registration Act of 1938 was used as a rationale to label as "propaganda" several Canadian films, including a prize-winning antinuclear film; as a result, the name of every individual who received these films had to be filed with the government. A 1981 Presidential Order that gave the CIA and the FBI new authority to conduct domestic surveillance resulted most bizarrely in the FBI's "Library Awareness Program," in which librarians were asked to spy on researchers who were "foreign" or who were working on sensitive topics. New controls on scholarly and scientific research were implemented. Hundreds of thousands of government employees were asked to sign nondisclosure agreements subjecting their public statements to official review for the rest of their lives. Lie detector and drug tests were considered for federal employees. The Reagan administration even modified the rules governing nonprofit groups, making it more difficult for them to speak out on public issues.

In the communications industry, the deregulation of broadcasting made broadcasters less responsible to the public; no longer were the airwaves considered to be public resources, with owners as trustees of these resources. Restrictions on commercial advertising fell by the wayside, as did regulations governing children's programming. President Reagan vetoed the "Fairness Doctrine," the rule requiring balanced treatment of controversial issues by broadcasters. Restrictions on media ownership were loosened, and the resulting concentration of media monopolies further diminished the spectrum of ideas and voices heard in the public sphere.

Direct moves were made to silence the press. The government developed new ways to "organize" journalists during the invasions of Grenada and Panama, so controlling the reporting of these military actions, effectively turning journalists into government mouthpieces. During the Gulf War, the government succeeded in controlling the news outright — so successfully, in fact, that a number of news organizations tried to sue the government over this issue.

Into this repressive atmosphere the attack on the arts was born. Looking once again at the demagoguery that characterized the crisis (which continues to this day), and recognizing that the communication system in our country stymies true debate and analysis, it becomes clear how the attack on the arts went as far as it did. Most of the public was informed about the NEA debate through the exaggerated statements of legislators, activists, and editorialists, and through one-line "summaries" of the works and artists in question slipped into the evening news. Many politicians turned these failings in the public realm to their advantage. An unspoken agreement seemed to exist among politicians and conservative activists: public communication should not aim to facilitate the discussion of this, or any other, complex issue; instead it should aim to stimulate, enrage, and entertain through stereotypes tailored for each occasion. The art world found it difficult to contest the Right's exaggerated pronouncements, and found it impossible otherwise to negotiate the closed system of public communication. Unable to reduce their arguments to soundbites, artists saw their work shorn of its complexity and placed in the service of reactionary agendas.

Of course, even if the communication environment was less prejudiced, and one *could* determine the will of the majority, the majority cannot be counted on to defend controversial speech. That is why we have the First Amendment — to protect the views of the minority. Our Constitution gives dissent a central role in our democratic system, acknowledging that it is actually in the best interests of the community if the majority does not rule absolutely. Free speech is meant to keep the citizenry and the government honest, and so encourage the decentralization of power. Dissent, from Left and Right alike, is counted on to maintain the open, changeable civic life necessary for democracy.

Such faith in the First Amendment informed the government's approach to the NEA in the past. When the agency was established, President Lyndon Johnson stressed the importance of facilitating artistic speech while limiting government interference:

> We fully recognize that no government can call artistic excellence into existence. It must flow from the quality of the society and the good fortune of the nation. Nor should any government seek to restrict the freedom of the artist to pursue his calling in his own way. Freedom is an essential condition for the artist, and in proportion as freedom is diminished so is the prospect of artistic achievement.
>
> But the government can seek to create conditions under which the arts can flourish; through recognition of achievements, through helping those who seek to enlarge creative understanding, through increasing the access of our people to the works of our artists, and through recognizing the arts as part of the pursuit of American greatness. That is the goal of this legislation.[20]

A specific policy of noninterference was written into the National Foundation on the Arts and Humanities Act of 1965, the law creating the NEA. The legislation stated that support for the arts was indeed a government responsibility:

> The practice of art and the study of the humanities requires constant dedication and devotion and...while no government can call a great artist or scholar into existence, it is necessary and appropriate for the Federal Government to help create and sustain not only a climate encouraging freedom of thought, imagination, and inquiry, but also the material conditions facilitating the release of this creative talent. (20 U.S.C. 951 [5])

The law also required the following:

> In the administration of this Act no department, agency, officer, or employee of the United States shall exercise any direction, supervision, or control over the policy determination, personnel, or curriculum, or the administration or operation of any school or other non-Federal agency, institution, organization, or association. (20 U.S.C. 953 [c])

Many legislators, Republican as well as Democratic, worried that the Endowment would be dominated by politics, and this policy of noninterference provided one solution. A second solution was found in the establishment of a grant review system based on panels composed of art-world peers. The Senate committee overseeing the Endowment's 1968 reauthorization remarked on the success of both of these solutions: "By helping sustain that climate of freedom and by meticulously refraining from any interference...[the Endowments have] reassured even those who were skeptical in 1965 when the National Foundation on the Arts and Humanities Act was being initially considered."[21]

In the past, there have been small controversies over projects that have received Endowment funding. For example, in 1974 a one-word poem ("L-I-G-H-G-H-T") funded by the Endowment created a stir, and in 1984 there were questions about a production of *Rigoletto* thought to be anti–Italian-American. But argument over these and several other works did not undermine the Endowment's policy of noninterference. The more recent attacks on the policy can be traced to the 1985 reauthorization hearings, in which there were questions raised by Republican Representative Dick Armey of Texas over homo-erotic poems funded through the NEA's literature program. Armey described to the Congress his shock over these poems: "I sat in my office with seven young, virile men, and not one of us could read several of these poems aloud, they were that bad."[22] The resulting debate served as a dress rehearsal for the 1989-1990 controversy: an amendment was even proposed that would have required panelists to reject projects that "in the context with which they are presented, in the expert's view, would be patently offensive to the average person and lack serious literary or artistic merit."[23] This amendment, the first attempt to apply obscenity law to Endowment grants, was finally rejected.

Ironically, conservatives themselves have expressed the importance of pro-tecting the process of the NEA from politics. Although the Heritage Foundation's *Mandate for Leadership* voiced many complaints about the NEA's social agenda, the report insisted that "because art does not move in obedience to social dictates...it must be granted an existence independent from the pro-claimed social goals of the state; accordingly, it must be funded for its own sake, rather than for any presumed economic or propaganda benefits."[24] Unfortu-nately, as soon as the Right gained power, this position was conveniently forgotten, and conservatives began to argue for increased government control.

Ideally, when the government guarantees a forum for free speech, it will not discriminate between the viewpoints expressed in that forum. Broadcasting's "Fairness Doctrine" provides a good example of this philosophy: designed to broaden debate by providing the underdog, liberal or conservative, with access to the television audience, the Fairness Doctrine was informed by an absolute reading of the First Amendment — the more speech, the better. This same understanding can be seen in Congress's plan for the NEA. Against such a background, it could indeed be said that any move to eliminate the NEA would be considered an attack on an institutionalized venue of open speech, and so an act of censorship. A lesser act — restricting the speech of grantees, or otherwise controlling speech through economic means — could be considered a more covert form of the same censorship. The Helms amendment, and Public Law 101-121, both of which declared certain subject matter to be off limits, promoted viewpoint discrimination, and so promoted censorship. As First Amendment lawyer Kathleen Sullivan pointed out, "the First Amendment applies whether the Government is wielding its checkbook or its badge" ("A Free Society Doesn't Dictate to Artists," p. 211).

The NEA's policy of noninterference does not mean that the grant selection process is completely neutral. Since peer panels are drawn from the art world, these panels will reflect many of its preoccupations. But artists and others on NEA panels don't always hold the same values, or agree with one another; still, one could probably say the art world as a whole is fairly liberal. The possible ideological influences this might introduce into the panel process are to be balanced by the rigorous evaluation of the quality of the artwork itself. Of course, criteria for quality are themselves ideological at some level, so the issue of "objectivity" in the grant process is a thorny one. No matter who is running the NEA, disagreements about meaning and quality will be present. The real issue is whether one can identify in the NEA grant process a clear attempt to implement an ideological agenda by judging work on viewpoint alone. This does not seem to have been the case. Each person on a review panel arrives with his or her own ideas about quality, beauty, content, and meaning, and each panel must struggle to make fair decisions. A policy of noninterference acknowledges both the difficulty and importance of this task; in the end, peer-panel review is far less capricious than decision-making by lone officials or irate politicians.

Furthermore, a policy of noninterference is consistent with the way the government facilitates speech in other areas. The government's role in free speech is often portrayed as merely passive — the government simply allows free speech to occur. But if our democracy is to function fully, the government must also *guarantee* free speech, providing opportunities for public communication just as it provides opportunities for education. In truth, our government often intervenes to guarantee free speech, supporting viewpoints that might otherwise go unheard, and spending tax dollars in the process. This has been done in many different ways: by restricting monopolies in the field of communications, by providing access on public airwaves to competing opinions, by providing public funding to political candidates, by bestowing tax-exempt status on a variety of nonprofit organizations and churches.

Given all that has occurred with respect to censorship over the last decade, and particularly given the NEA debate itself, it is difficult to believe that the NEA has been overrun by liberals and other "vocal constituencies." Certainly the Endowment's policy of noninterference has allowed many progressive works of art to be funded; conservatives have focused on these grants and have claimed that they are typical. But there was very little defense of a progressive agenda during the NEA controversy; instead, most of the agency's defenders emphasized the ways in which the NEA has improved the status quo rather than challenged it. Most emphasized its role in sustaining history and tradition. NEA chair John Frohnmayer's testimony to Congress was typical. He noted that the Endowment provided "continuity to those core institutions which, through their continued excellence, preserve and enhance our cultural heritage"; the NEA thus guaranteed "the training, the discipline, and the artistry of our dancers, our musicians, and our painters." He emphasized as well the Endowment's role in sustaining rural and Native American cultures (see "Statement to House Sub-committee on Postsecondary Education," p. 154).

Few spokespeople came directly to the defense of experimental artists and art forms. Commentators instead offered a straight First Amendment defense for the funding of this work, arguing that, while they too were disgusted by the art in question, they supported the right of the artist to be disgusting. Some commentators gave support to the *idea* of the socially concerned artist, but in a very general way. The words of Representative Ted Weiss provide an example: "Artists are society's watchers, critics, and champions. They speak the unspeakable, even if it manifests itself in horrifying, untidy, or esoteric matters" ("Statement to House Subcommittee on Postsecondary Education," p. 166). Conservatives assumed otherwise, but progressive artists got the very clear message that the NEA did not want to be a partner to social change.

This was not the only lesson learned by progressive artists. The NEA controversy not only revealed many things about conservatism, it also created many doubts about the role of art — particularly political art — in American society. Art critic Eleanor Heartney felt that the crisis revealed a fundamental social irresponsibility among artists:

> Having long absolved itself of any real moral or social responsibility, the art world is in a poor position to take the high ground now.... If we want to convince society that freedom of artistic expression really matters, we are first going to have to start believing it ourselves. ("Social Responsibility and Censorship," p. 140)

Heartney complained that the art world was distracted by commercialism and trendy obscurity, and that it was not really interested in developing a more socially engaged practice.

The issue is a complex one, but if the art world is indeed cut off from participation in public life, it is important to ascertain whether artists have contributed to this problem. Artists may have been hurt by the collapse of public communication in the United States, but how have they responded? As Heartney suggests, many have withdrawn into their own success, either commercial or academic. Others, though, have attempted to challenge the prejudices — the racism, homophobia, and sexism — that seem endemic to American society. When this art has been attacked by conservatives, it has (understandably so) been automatically defended by progressives. But if critical art is to gain anything from the NEA debate, its prevailing presumptions and strategies must be reexamined.

One of the central controversies in the NEA debate involved a catalog essay for the *Witnesses* exhibition at Artists Space in New York City. This essay, written by artist David Wojnarowicz, attacked many public figures who have publicly opposed homosexuality, or who have stood in the way of AIDS research and education. In his essay, Wojnarowicz offered a now-infamous description of Cardinal John O'Connor as a "fat cannibal from that house of walking swastikas up on Fifth Avenue," and he remarked vengefully that in his ungoverned imagination he could "douse Helms with a bucket of gasoline and set his putrid ass on fire" and "throw Rep. William Dannemeyer off the Empire State Building" ("Postcards from America: X-rays from Hell," p. 126). Obviously, these sentences did not sit well with NEA opponents.

Given the outrage expressed within the art world at the nasty things said by conservatives, it may seem contradictory for the same art world to support Wojnarowicz's words. But these words must be placed within the context of existing power relations. No matter how strident his voice might be, Wojnarowicz, as an artist, as a gay man, and as a person with AIDS, has very little power. A distinction must be made, as many in the legal profession would argue, between the words of the powerful and those of the powerless. The demagoguery of someone like Senator Helms, a public figure and a powerful politician, is simply not the same as the demagoguery of a relatively powerless artist making a statement in the context of an art exhibition. Unlike Helms, Wojnarowicz's words may be his *only* weapons. Additionally, Wojnarowicz's remarks do exist in a literary context. He depicts himself in the essay as someone suffering from the side effects of the AIDS drug AZT, as someone suffering from "an intense claustrophobic feeling of fucking doom." Hallucinations and pained descriptions of his surroundings are interrupted by expressions of anger at those public figures who have attacked the homosexual community. The essay does indeed criticize public figures in a strident manner, but it roots this critique honestly in the realities of the artist's life.

But even if the rhetorical strategies in Wojnarowicz's work are justifiable, a general question still exists: Have the strategies of opposition adopted by political artists been used appropriately? To communicate successfully in the manipulated environment of public discourse, contemporary political artists have often chosen to turn up the volume of their work, becoming more strident as social control deepens. The NEA debate, and the ensuing discussions of many polemical works of art, raised the uncomfortable possibility that polemical strategies are not the most effective way to create meaningful social change. Such strategies, formed in reaction to the conservative agenda, may not be able to escape the reductive logic of that agenda. It is conceivable that political artists, beginning with an oversimplified view of power, and arguing this view polemically, have themselves created a distorted picture of social experience. While challenging one set of stereotypes, political artists may at times project another false view of identity, a view that reinforces conditions of inequality.

Take, for instance, the work of performance artist Karen Finley. Finley, along with several other performance artists, moved into the center of the controversy when the NEA denied her a grant that had been awarded by a review panel. This panel reflected the consensus within the art world that Finley is an important artist who is deserving of government support. Her work offers a moving and persuasive condemnation of violence against women. Speaking with a rage that makes her words all the more convincing, she offers an explicit and even relentless critique of power. Yet Finley's work also provided for some critics an example of the limitations of much oppositional art lionized during the NEA debate. Finley's representation of the powerless, of "real people" and their victimization, was particularly troubling to many. Various works placed laborers, children, people with AIDS, and performance artists at the mercy of patriarchy; across these works, all suffering began to seem equal, including the suffering of the artist. The artist even appeared to offer herself as a Christ-like stand-in for all oppressed people, a gesture that seemed false and patronizing. This projection of the universality of suffering effaced to a considerable degree the historical and social particulars surrounding the exercise of power and the experience of powerlessness. Although she meant to represent the struggles of these people as she saw them, some critics felt that Finley had drawn false stereotypes of people who had little public opportunity to contest her viewpoint.

Critic Margaret Spillane was one who raised this point:

> All the controversy [surrounding Finley's work] seemed to promise a bare-knuckled assault on those barriers separating the privileged from the powerless. But...the individual victims she promised to evoke...turned out to be carelessly assembled amalgams of bourgeois Americans' cultural shorthand for those they believe exist beneath them.
> ("The Culture of Narcissism," p. 300)

To Spillane, this indicated "the art-making population's troublingly restricted notion of who its audience needs to be, and its equally troubling lack of alarm at who is being entirely left out." Indeed, the presumptions of Finley's performances are more disturbing when one considers her privileged audience. When critical art is tailored to a privileged, liberal audience, there is the risk that the art experience will become nothing more than a ritual release of guilt. When oppositional art becomes a part of the art-world status quo, certified by cultural institutions that manage the avant-garde, it may in this way assume a new role, perpetuating the very authority it seeks to challenge.

It may seem counterproductive, even wrongheaded, to raise the issue of political art's absorption into the mainstream, given the extent to which such art has been attacked during the NEA controversy. After all, when everything is said and done, Karen Finley and other like-minded artists are still on the margins, and their works are still a challenge to the status quo. They may gain notoriety briefly, but this is not the same as fame. Yet questions about the effectiveness and purpose of political art were raised again and again by artists and critics over the course of the debate.

To offer another example: Artist Holly Hughes, when the NEA refused her a grant for works addressing the subject of lesbianism, rightfully protested the homophobia that was evident in Congress and at the NEA. In a piece written with Richard Elovich, she pointed out that "because we gay artists, particularly lesbian artists, are so invisible, our problems are invisible as well. So we must demand visibility, or the issue will be lost" ("Homophobia at the NEA," p. 254). But the reality of this homophobia did not prevent critic Sarah Schulman from drawing attention to the compromises many lesbian artists must confront when they receive NEA funding. She was troubled by the tokenism at work in the funding structure, and warned that the few lesbian artists who become successful should not presume that this success gives them the right to speak for their community:

> Before funding, [lesbian] work was supported by the audience and determined by the lives, needs and experiences of the community. Now, through the new tokenism, a few political and apolitical sensibilities are permitted to be contained within the dominant culture. Individuals are even easier than political movements to contain. As a result, a single style is declared to be representative of a

hugely diverse community that it cannot represent. ("Is the NEA Good for Gay Art?" p. 257)

In her essay, Schulman also argued more broadly about the art world's failure to address social reality. She worried that the art world's priorities had gone astray, and she describes the response of many artists to the controversy over government funding as "fetishized egomania." "We are living in a city of 90,000 homeless people [New York]. No one is getting the services and funding that they need. I wish that these artists could see themselves in relation to their own society and place the NEA event in a broader political context."

As these arguments suggest, in spite of strategies that are immediate and powerful, political art hasn't had a clear effect on society; worse, artists seem bound by the insularity of their field. This insularity was apparent in the ways the art world chose to defend itself during the NEA controversy. Artists and art institutions were attacked for challenging conservative beliefs, for supporting artwork that offered a more complicated picture of American identity than conservatives could tolerate. In particular, conservatives were worried about artworks that manifested gay and lesbian desire. Such art could "promote" homosexuality, it was argued. Now, it is not at all clear that art, or images generally, have such a direct correlation to behavior. But it makes sense that gay and lesbian artists want to celebrate their sexualities just as heterosexual artists do; art that manifests gay and lesbian desire will help to legitimize these sexualities. When attacked for supporting such art, though, the art world unfortunately did not defend it explicitly. Instead, many behaved as if content *didn't* matter, emphasizing the right to free speech rather than the right to sexuality. As a result, many arguments deliberately sidestepped what was really on people's minds, reinforcing the perception of an art world that was insulated and aloof. (Note, for example, the defense of Mapplethorpe's work during the Cincinnati obscenity trial: art experts testified to the aesthetic merits of his photographs, describing their "symmetry" and so on, rather than openly discussing the history of the representation of gay desire.) Many in the art world seemed reluctant to engage the larger public, wanting instead to be left alone to pursue business as usual.

The argument over the NEA could have been expanded to call attention to many censorious silences that exist in American society. Instead, it became a battle for power between two sectors of the intelligentsia: the cultural elite and the religious conservative elite. Both sides spoke *for* the larger public, but neither side seemed to have much connection to this public. While the Right cloaked its arguments in the guise of "outraged populism," the Left invented a supportive public that instinctively understood both freedom of speech and the rights of artists.

Consequently, artists left the debate as disconnected from society as they were in the beginning. Art, like political argument, remained a luxury available only to the members of one elite or the other. Artists at times acted as if people had no right to be provoked by provocative art — a response that revealed the core of the art world's own problems. In the end, many artists and institutions chose to defend a conventional, institutionalized avant-gardism, one that proposes a separation between art and everyday life. In this view of art production, artists are visionary and privileged members of a vanguard, speaking primarily to other members of the vanguard, and only incidentally to a wider audience. This model of the art world stands in contrast to the real conditions of art practice revealed by the culture war. There are in fact many different art worlds, each with a different relationship to the larger culture, each with a different agenda, a different manner of speaking, and a different audience. The exact relationship of any of these groups to the general public — and to each other, for that matter — is unknown, and will remain so, until artists can overcome many of the existing limitations upon public speech, not the least of which are the many assumptions upon which art practice is currently based.

In the end, conservatives and liberals both seemed to agree that contemporary art has much potential as an agent of social change. For many progressives, the defense of the NEA was also an attempt to sustain this potential, to defend a cultural arena where change and difference could be proposed. Once this small public space has been defended, it needs to be expanded; simply *securing* the art world cannot be a sufficient measure of success. Cultural institutions could more deliberately promote a renewal of public life; a shared public culture might be created that encourages larger numbers of people to examine society in detail. If artists protect themselves, but cannot circumvent the marginalization of their practice — if artists cannot link themselves with larger social practices and struggles — then the free speech of artists will fall on deaf ears.

The NEA could encourage this work. Rather than backing away from risky art, it could provide funding for new educational approaches to controversial subjects. It could encourage art organizations to strengthen their relationships to communities, and it could encourage work that addresses the changing conditions of our society. Such approaches will of course be controversial, for as I have argued, the NEA debates were not really about funding, but about how the public realm should be constituted. Conservative politicians will no doubt continue, through legislation and demonology, to silence the arts as part of a larger effort to create conformity. But democracy will move forward only if difference is tolerated and respected. A healthy democratic practice does not create universal agreement or identity but gives voice to competing agendas, and creates opportunities for negotiation among agendas.

Censorship is not only the repression of an utterance; it is an attempt to impose order by limiting social experience. Political theorists Ernesto Laclau and Chantal Mouffe have written that the political logic of totalitarianism is one in which

> the state raises itself to the status of the sole possessor of the truth of the social order, whether in the name of the proletariat or of the nation, and seeks to control all the networks of sociability. In the face of the radical indeterminacy which democracy opens up, this involves an attempt to reimpose an absolute center, and to re-establish the closure which will thus restore unity.[25]

This accurately describes the logic behind the attack on NEA. In the end, censorship of the arts reveals the failure of democratic institutions to articulate and defend the complexity and diversity of the American public. The NEA debate contained many lessons about art's relationship to society, but it also raised many questions about the future of American democracy.

1. Often an anthology opens with a neutral introduction in which the editor disguises his or her point of view. As the reader will discover, I have not taken this approach. I have endeavored to criticize both the right and the left, but it will soon be apparent that my sympathies are progressive ones. Consequently, I encourage the reader to consider this introduction as but one more selection among the many included in this book. Taken together, the selections in this volume give all viewpoints sufficient representation. My thanks to those individuals who do not share my perspective, but who gave me permission to reprint their work.

   This introduction is based on two previously published articles of mine: "The Cultural Contradictions of Conservatism," *New Art Examiner* 17:10 (June 1990), pp. 24–29, and "What Is To Be Undone: Rethinking Political Art," *New Art Examiner* 18:10 (Summer 1991), pp. 25–28.

2. This quote and previous quotes in paragraph from James Cooper, "After the NEA Firestorm, What Happens Then?", *New York City Tribune*, June 27, 1989.

3. This quote and previous quote in the paragraph are from James Cooper, "We Must Recapture the Culture," *New York City Tribune*, April 1990.

4. *Congressional Record*, Senate, Sept. 28, 1989, p. S 12115.

5. Wildmon is also the director of a coalition called Christian Leaders for Responsible Television (CLeaR-TV). For more comprehensive information on Wildmon, see Christopher Finan, "Rev. Wildmon's Censorship Crusade," *Newsletter on Intellectual Freedom* (Nov. 1989), pp. 213; Amy Virshup, "The Missionary's Position," *Manhattan, Inc.* (July 1989), pp. 84–91; and Connaught Marshner, "How Don Wildmon Is Beating the Princes of Porn," *Conservative Digest* (March 1988), pp. 75–82.

6. Marshner, "How Don Wildmon," p. 80.

7. Donald Wildmon, "A Time for Decision," speech to the National Religious Broadcasters, Feb. 10, 1982.

8. Donald Wildmon, fundraising letter of the National Federation of Decency, beginning "Dear Fellow Christian," undated.

9. "Interview with the Rev. Donald Wildmon," *Southern Partisan* (second quarter, 1989), p. 38.

10. Donald Wildmon, "Are Media Biased? Well, Is Water Wet?", *USA Today* (May 11, 1984).

11. Donald Wildmon, "This Controversy Goes to the Heart of Religion," *USA Today* (July 25, 1988).

12. Fred Clarkson, "Culture Buster," *Village Voice* (October 10, 1989).

13. Interview with Samuel Lipman, *Vantage Point* 8 (1986).

14. Samuel Lipman, "The NEA: Looking Back, and Looking Ahead," *New Criterion* 7 (Sept. 1988), pp. 7–8.

15. *Ibid*, p. 13.

16. Samuel Lipman, "Leadership in Democratic Culture: The Case of Nancy Hanks," *New Criterion* 7 (Nov. 1988), p.1.

17. Charles Heatherly, ed., *Mandate for Leadership: Policy Management in a Conservative Administration* (Washington, D.C.: Heritage Foundation, 1981), pp. 1051–56.

18. Quoted in Walter Karp, "Liberty under Siege: The Reagan Administration's Taste for Autocracy," *Harper's* (Nov. 1986), pp. 53–67.

19. For a detailed account, see Walter Karp, *Liberty under Siege: American Politics, 1976–1988* (New York: Henry Holt, 1988), and Kevin Boyle, ed., *Article 19 World*

Report 1988: Information, Freedom and Censorship (New York: Times Books, 1988), pp. 118–26.

20. 111 *Congressional Record* 4594 (1965); quoted in "Authorizing Legislation and Legislative History Regarding Non-interference in the Content of Projects," National Endowment for the Arts internal study, unpublished.

21. Senate Committee on Labor and Public Welfare, S. Rep. No. 103, 90th Congress, 2d Session 3–4 (1968).

22. *Congressional Record* (July 31, 1985), p. 21902.

23. House Committee on Education and Labor, markup of H.R. 3248 (Sept. 11, 1985), p. 69. Quoted in "Authorizing Legislation and Legislative History."

24. Heatherly, ed., *Mandate for Leadership*, p. 1055.

25. Ernesto Laclau and Chantal Mouffe, *Hegemony and Socialist Strategy: Towards a Radical Democratic Politics* (London: Verso, 1985), p. 188

■ Rev. Donald Wildmon, letter concerning Serrano's *Piss Christ*, April 5, 1989

Rev. Donald Wildmon, one of the leading religious activists in the NEA debate, is the executive director of the American Family Association.

Dear ——:

We should have known it would come to this. In a recent art exhibition displayed in several museums throughout the country, one "work of art" was a very large, vivid photograph of a crucifix submerged in urine. The work, by Andres Serrano, was titled "Piss Christ." When asked, since he had worked with urine, what could be expected next, Mr. Serrano said, "Semen." And, of course, defecation will follow that.

The bias and bigotry against Christians, which has dominated television and movies for the past decade or more, has now moved over to the art museums.

We Christians must, in my opinion, accept part of the responsibility that such has come to pass. For various and sundry reasons, most of us have refused to publicly respond to the anti-Christian bias and bigotry found in various parts of our society, especially the media.

"The Last Temptation of Christ" presented Jesus as a tormented, deranged, human-only sinner; Madonna represented Christ having sex with a priest in her new video "Like a Prayer"; and now a crucifix submerged in urine and titled "Piss Christ."

As a young child growing up, I would never, ever have dreamed that I would live to see such demeaning disrespect and desecration of Christ in our country that is present today. Maybe, before the physical persecution of Christians begins, we will gain the courage to stand against such bigotry. I hope so.

Sincerely,

Donald E. Wildmon

Executive Director

■ Debate in Senate over the NEA, statements by Sen. Alfonse D'Amato and Sen. Jesse Helms, with letter of protest to NEA's Hugh Southern, May 18, 1989

Alfonse D'Amato is a Republican senator representing the state of New York. Jesse Helms is a Republican senator representing the state of North Carolina. He was the leader of the anti-NEA campaign in the U.S. Senate.

The PRESIDING OFFICER. The Senator from New York.

Mr. D'AMATO. Thank you, Mr. President.

Mr. President, several weeks ago, I began to receive a number of letters, phone calls, and postcards from constituents throughout the State concerning art work by Andres Serrano. They express a feeling of shock, of outrage, and anger.

They said, "How dare you spend our taxpayers' money on this trash." They all objected to taxpayers' money being used for a piece of so-called art work which, to be quite candid, I am somewhat reluctant to utter its title. This so-called piece of art is a deplorable, despicable display of vulgarity. The art work in question is a photograph of the crucifix submerged in the artist's urine.

This artist received $15,000 for his work from the National Endowment for the Arts, through the Southeastern Center for Contemporary Art.

Well, if this is what contemporary art has sunk to, this level, this outrage, this indignity — some may want to sanction that, and that is fine. But not with the use of taxpayers' money. This is not a question of free speech. This is a question of abuse of taxpayers' money. If we allow this group of so-called art experts to get away with this, to defame us and to use our money, well, then we do not deserve to be in office.

That is why, Mr. President, I am proud of the Members, who in literally a matter of minutes — over 20, about 25 — joined me in signing a strong letter of protest to the Endowment. Here is a picture, and the title is "Piss Christ." Incredible.

To add insult to injury, after this group of so-called art experts picked this artist for this $15,000 prize — of taxpayers' money; we paid for this, our taxpayers — I do not blame people for being outraged and angered, and they should be angered at us, unless we do something to change this. If this continues and if this goes unrectified, where will it end? They will say, "This is free speech." Well, if you want free speech, you want to draw dirty pictures, you want to do anything you want, that is your business, but not with taxpayers' money. This is an outrage, and our people's tax dollars should not support this trash, and we should not be giving it the dignity. And after this piece of trash and this artist received this award, to make matters worse, the Awards in Visual Arts, this wonderful publication was put together; and who was it financed by, partially? By none other than the National Endowment for the Arts. What a disgrace.

They not only see this garbage, they can say we did not know he engaged in this kind of filth, but then they see fit to distribute it through the Nation and brag about it and allow their names to be used, instead of calling and saying, you get our name out of that.

Mr. President, we better see to it that —

The PRESIDING OFFICER. The Senator's time has expired.

Mr. D'AMATO. Mr. President, I ask unanimous consent that I might be permitted 2 more minutes.

The PRESIDING OFFICER. Without objection, it is so ordered.

Mr. D'AMATO. The purpose for which the Endowment was established, and I quote, "to support the survival of the best of all forms that reflect the American heritage in its full range of cultural and ethnic diversity and to provide national leadership on behalf of the arts."

Mr. President, I submit this is a distortion of those purposes. It does not reflect on the full range of cultural and ethnic diversity; rather, it is a perversion of those principles. If people want to be perverse, in terms of what they recognize as art or culture, so be it, but not with my money, not with the taxpayers' dollars, and certainly not under the mantle of this great Nation. This is a disgrace.

Mr. President, I ask unanimous consent that the letter to the National Endowment for the Arts be printed in the RECORD.

There being no objection, the letter was ordered to be printed in the RECORD, as follows:

U.S. Senate, Washington, DC, May 18, 1989

Mr. Hugh Southern, Acting Chairman, National Endowment for the Arts, Washington, DC.

Dear Mr. Southern: We recently learned of the Endowment's support for a so-called "work of art" by Andres Serrano entitled "Piss Christ." We write to express our outrage and to suggest in the strongest terms that the procedures used by the Endowment to award and support artists be reformed.

The piece in question is a large and vivid photograph of Christ on a crucifix submerged in the artist's urine. This work is shocking, abhorrent and completely undeserving of any recognition whatsoever. Millions of taxpayers' are rightfully incensed that their hard-earned dollars were used to honor and support Serrano's work.

There is a clear flaw in the procedures used to select art and artists deserving of taxpayers' support. That fact is evidenced by the Serrano work itself. More-over, after the artist was selected and honored for his "contributions" to the field of art, his work was exhibited at government expense and with the imprimatur of the Endowment.

This matter does not involve freedom of artistic expression—it does involve the question whether American taxpayers should be forced to support such trash.

And finally, simply because the Endowment and the Southeastern Center for Contemporary Art (SECCA) did not have a direct hand in choosing Serrano's work, does not absolve either of responsibility. The fact that both the Endowment and the SECCA with taxpayer dollars promoted this work as part of the Awards in Visual Arts exhibition, is reason enough to be outraged.

We urged the Endowment to comprehensively review its procedures and determine what steps will be taken to prevent such abuses from recurring in the future.

We await your response.

Sincerely,

Alfonse D'Amato, Bob Kerrey, Warren R. Rudman, Rudy Boschwitz, Dennis DeConcini, Pete Wilson, Bob Dole, Chuck Grassley, James A. McClure, John Heinz, Wendell Ford, Howell Heflin, Harry Reid, Richard Shelby, John W. Warner, Larry Pressler, Conrad Burns, Tom Harkin, Trent Lott, Jesse Helms, John McCain, Arlen Specter, Steve Symms.

Mr. HELMS. Mr. President, the Senator from New York is absolutely correct in his indignation and in his description of the blasphemy of the so-called artwork. I do not know Mr. Andres Serrano, and I hope I never meet him. Because he is not an artist, he is a jerk.

Let us examine exactly what this bird did to get $15,000 of the taxpayers' money through the so-called National Endowment for the Arts. If they have no more judgment than that, it ought to be abolished and all funds returned to the taxpayer.

What this Serrano fellow did, he filled a bottle with his own urine and then stuck a crucifix down there — Jesus Christ on a cross. He set it up on a table and took a picture of it.

For that, the National Endowment for the Arts gave him $15,000, to honor him as an artist.

I say again, Mr. President, he is not an artist. He is a jerk. And he is taunting the American people, just as others are, in terms of Christianity. And I resent it. And I do not hesitate to say so.

I am not going to call the name that he applied to this work of art.

In naming it, he was taunting the American people. He was seeking to create indignation. That is all right for him to be a jerk but let him be a jerk on his own time and with his own resources. Do not dishonor our Lord. I resent it and I think the vast majority of the American people do. And I also resent the National Endowment for the Arts spending the taxpayers' money to honor this guy.

This program, supported by the National Endowment, is administered by the Southeastern Center for Contemporary Art. They call it SECCA. I am sorry to say it is in my home State.

After Mr. Serrano's selection, this photograph and some of his other works were exhibited in several cities around the country with the approval and the support of the National Endowment.

Horsefeathers. If we have sunk so low in this country as to tolerate and condone this sort of thing, then we become a part of it.

The question is obvious. On what conceivable basis does anybody who would engage in such blasphemy and insensitivity toward the religious community deserve to be honored? The answer to that is: he does not. He deserved to be rebuked and ignored because he is not an artist. Anybody who would do such a despicable thing — and get $15,000 in tax money for it — well, it tells you something about the state of this Government and the way it spends the money taken from the taxpayer.

So no wonder all of the people calling my office are indignant. The Constitution may prevent the Government from prohibiting this Serrano fellow's — laughably, I will describe it — "artistic expression." It certainly does not require the American taxpayers or the Federal Government to fund, promote, honor, approve, or condone it. None of the above.

Mr. President, the National Endowment's procedures for selecting artists and works of art deserving of taxpayer support are badly, badly flawed if this is an example of the kind of programs they fund with taxpayers' money.

I have sent word to the Endowment that I want them to review their funding criteria to ensure abuses such as this never happen again. The preliminary report we got from one person with whom we talked was sort of "Down, boy, we know what we are doing."

Well, they do not know what they are doing. They are insulting the very fundamental basis of this country. I say again I resent it.

■Patrick Buchanan, Losing the War for America's Culture?, *Washington Times*, May 22, 1989

Patrick Buchanan is a nationally syndicated columnist and television commentator. He was a Republican candidate for President during 1991-92.

As altarpiece of his exhibit, Andres Serrano has a photograph of a crucifix, a replica of Christ dying on the cross. The unusual feature of Mr. Serrano's exhibit, however, is that his crucifix is submerged in a vat of urine, his own. Lest one miss the point, it is titled "Piss Christ"; others are "Piss God" and "Piss Pope."

Mr. Serrano's pièce de résistance apparently captivated judges of The Awards in the Visual Arts program of the Southeastern Center for Contemporary Art of Winston-Salem, N.C., who chose it for display and tour.

According to James Cooper, art critic of The New York City Tribune, AVA is funded by the National Endowment for the Arts, which, in 1985, gave Mr. Serrano its own grant of $15,000 for "creating art works composed from human body parts and decapitated heads of animals exhibited in glass vats." Your tax dollars at work.

The downhill slide of American culture gathers momentum. In a year, we have seen Martin Scorsese's "The Last Temptation of Christ" — portraying Jesus as an adulterous wimp — nominated for an Academy Award, and a modern art exhibit in Chicago where patrons were invited to walk on an American flag.

Rising above New York's West Side Highway, for a late summer unveiling, is a 75-foot-high mural celebrating Marx, Lenin, Trotsky, Mao, Castro and Che, a six-story shrine to communism, a Marxist Mount Rushmore in Greenwich Village. Funding for the "Pathfinder Mural" comes in part from Managua's Ministry of Culture.

"[F]or those who create the popular culture... patriotism is no longer in style," President Ronald Reagan warned in his farewell address. It was a dramatic understatement; America's art and culture are, more and more, openly anti-Christian, anti-American, nihilistic.

About last year's "Committed to Print" exhibit at the New York Museum of Modern Art, Mr. Cooper writes: "The visitor is bombarded with picture after picture, gallery after gallery, of supposed crimes that the United States has inflicted.... President Reagan is portrayed... as a bloodthirsty vampire urging a rabid fanged dog to kill innocent Latin American peasants. Another picture portrays an ocean of skulls filling the mall in front of the United States Capital.... Pictures of Lt. William Calley, blackened skulls, dead babies, all serve to inculcate in the mind of the viewer one continuous unending image of America's past and present 'sins.' Nowhere is there any evidence of the achievements of American capitalism or democracy. Instead, posters of heroic Red Chinese soldiers... and Malcolm X are offered to remind us of the glorious political alternatives available by embracing socialism, communism, or worse."

While the right has been busy winning primaries and elections, cutting taxes and funding anti-communist guerrillas abroad, the left has been quietly seizing all the commanding heights of American art and culture. Mr. Cooper, who edits the excellent little magazine American Arts Quarterly, is direct in his blame, scathing in his commentary:

"Conservatives have not even made the attempt of creating their own culture program during the last 100 years. Nor has the religious community, despite a tradition of glorious art that has produced Gothic cathedrals, the Sistine Chapel, the music of Johann Sebastian Bach and the art of Raphael, Durer and Rembrandt.

"American churches, business corporations, and government and educational institutions have... meekly embraced without protest a nihilist, existential, relativist, secular humanist culture they profess to abhor. Later, they wonder why films are made that are as sacrilegious as 'The Last Temptation of Christ'... or why art shows that are blatantly pro-communist can... be seen at such locations as the Museum of Modern Art.

"The reason for all of this is simple. Those who believe in absolute values such as God and beauty do nothing, and those who believe in existential humanism have captured the culture. Businessmen, political leaders and bankers have failed to recognize the importance of culture as a force for good and a force for evil....

"Political leaders in Washington believe that the battle against communism is being fought in the jungles of Asia and Central America, while failing to realize the war is also raging on the battlefield of the arts within our own borders.

"The United States spends $5 billion a year on the arts, but no one questions the nihilist values this art disseminates to the American public. The conservatives simply bury their heads in the sand and do nothing."

Is he wrong? So, what is to be done?

"Conservatives and the religious community that comprise the vast middle-American population should actively support those artists that advocate the same values and ideas as they do. They should also choose to withdraw support and funding from the modernist culture they profess to despise. In short, they should do what the liberals did long ago — 'capture the culture'."

Surely the place to begin is with the National Endowment of the Arts, whose new chairman is to be selected, soon, by president George Bush.

A nation absorbs its values through its art. A corrupt culture will produce a corrupt people, and vice versa; between rotten art, films, plays and books — and rotten behavior — the correlation is absolute. The hour is late; America needs a cultural revolution in the '90s as sweeping as its political revolution in the '80s.

End of sermon. Amen.

■ Sen. Slade Gorton, On the Official Funding of Religious Bigotry, statement to the Senate, May 31, 1989 (excerpt)

Slade Gordon is a Republican senator representing the state of Washington.

M r. President, I do not claim to fathom the rationalizations for much contemporary visual art. Given that one of the most generously reviewed exhibitions of recent times was the artist Judy Chicago's mixed media depictions of female genitalia arranged on dinner plates and that one of the masterpieces of conceptual art was minted as the artist himself was thrown out of a window into a tremendous pile of horse manure, am I supposed to? I believe I speak for the common man and the uncommon intellectual when I confess my indifference, at best, to these heroics.

They originate not only in nihilism but in the more innocent misconception that the great philosopher of aesthetics Benedetto Croce called the intellectualist error. A lesser philosopher put it this way, "If you've got a message, send a telegram." Croce, however, was more thorough. "Confusions between the methods of art and those of the philosophic sciences," he stated, "have been frequent. Thus it has often been held to the task of art to expand concepts, to unite the intelligible with the sensible, to represent ideas of universals: putting art in the place of science." But this, what he called "the theory of art as supporting theses," he rejected, for he believed that "Aesthetic consideration...

pays attention always and only to the adequateness of expression, that is to say, to beauty."

The intellectualist error leads almost without fail to abuse. If artists are to be pedagogues, they will want to wake up their sleepy and foolish students; that is, everyone in the world, and, on occasion, to shock and to offend them. Croce writes of an artist who "may try to conceal his internal emptiness in a flood of words... in painting that dazzles the eye, or by heaping together great architectural masses which arrest and astonish us."

This practice is no longer aberrant, it is a way of life, and sometimes one can hardly determine if a contemporary artist is contributing to the development of art or to the history of publicity. George Bernard Shaw wore a shiny green suit to the theater, to attract attention to the fact that he wrote plays. The stratagem was so potent that it has worked its way through our century down to this day, and the suit's the thing now; you don't have to bother about the plays.

Mr. Serrano, no doubt, wants publicity, and he is getting it. Indeed, I am giving it to him. His trick is to make his opponents, in their attempt to drown him, pour so much water into the lock that they raise up his boat. And then he tells them what he's doing, mainly for the thrill of it, but also because it is certain to open the sluice for more. To quote Mr. Serrano:

"I feel when people attack a work of art to such a great extent, they imbue it with a far greater power than when they ignore it and, in that, I'm flattered that they think it deserves such attention."

This declaration is obviously calculated to do to his critics what banderillas do to a bull — irate them, weaken them, drive them wild.

I cannot think of a better response to this calculated provocation than to quote the consummate artist, William Shakespeare, whose Hamlet expresses indignation at something very similar.

"Why, look you now, how unworthy a thing you make of me!" Hamlet says.

"You would play upon me, you would seem to know my stops, you would pluck out the heart of my mystery, you would sound me from the lowest note to the top of my compass... do you think I am easier to be played on than a pipe? Call me what instrument you will, though you can fret me, you cannot play upon me."

Now, you know my opinion of the tradition Mr. Serrano exploits, and you know I believe that absent didacticism, gimmickry, shock, and mockery, works such as his have a tendency to disappear. But this is not a bullfight and he is not a matador. I know that the heart of his strategy depends on the overreaction of those who would by instinct and passion suppress his sacrilege as readily as they would defend their own children, for, indeed, he has assaulted that which they hold most holy, sacred, and dear.

But, no, I refuse to enter that trap, and will not allow him or his partisans to cloud his abuse by diverting the issue to that of freedom of expression. He has the right to display his picture. There is no question that he has that right. It is almost absolute. I would sell my grandmother, shoot my dog, what have you, before I would fail to defend that right. On February 22 of this year, in my remarks concerning the Rushdie affair, I made clear that I hold to his position and that I do so in service of what I believe is a vital and fundamental principle.

And in the case of Mr. Serrano as is in the case of Mr. Rushdie, neither the transparency of his intentions nor the quality of his work can prejudice it.

Let us even assume, for the sake of argument, hypothetically, as a fiction, a conjecture, a speculation, a purely academic exercise, that his picture is a great work of art. Great works of art can be sacrilegious: not only in theory, but in fact. For example, Michelangelo's statue of Moses is fitted with a pair of horns. Generations, and generations of Jews have been stung by that, but the statue, without a doubt, is great art. So let us assume, for the sake of argument, that Mr. Serrano's picture which is deeply offensive to Christians, is of the same caliber as Michelangelo's Moses, which is deeply offensive to Jews. What is the role of the state in these matters? Does it dare subsidize sacrilege? Does it dare not subsidize Michelangelo?

The answer touches upon the question of the limits of government, which is right and proper both for the Chamber and for our time, and the answer is clear. *The state must confine itself to its own interests, and art must be free. Neither subsidy nor censure are appropriate, for the state, with its unrivalled power, must not take sides in purely symbolic disputes.* This judgment has honorable origins, a long history, a basis in reason, and several illustrative parallels.

It would be relatively easy to preclude SECCA from receiving Government funds on other, more practical grounds. In this matter the layers of unaccountability are much like those of shell corporations established on islands that vanish at high tide. Passing from the constituent to the Treasury, to the NEA, to SECCA, through the panel of judges, to laureate, the money flows freely, with neither obstruction nor delay, from citizen to Serrano. But what of traffic in the other direction? Does any kind of accountability run the other way? No. At every step, as in the famous Thomas Nast cartoon of the Tweed ring, someone is pointing a finger at someone else and saying, "We can't possibly interfere with the artistic choices made by our grantees." To cite part of a letter I received from the NEA: "This limitation reflects concern that Federal funding for the arts would result in government intervention in the substance of artistic projects."

I ask you, is a $15,000 fellowship, a travelling exhibition, and the imprimatur of and association with the National Endowment for the Arts something that is neutral? Is it of no effect? If it is, what is its purpose? And if it is, as anyone can see, the promotion and advancement of one artist as opposed to another, of his work and of his philosophy, of his style and approach, how can providing support be less an "intervention in the substance of artistic projects" than would be withdrawing support?

The Government and its compensated agents choose. They must choose; they have no other means of accomplishing the distribution. And to make the choice, they must have criteria and they must exercise their judgment. How can it be that if the people who provide funds for this program — the taxpayers — are spurred to exercise their judgment and proffer their criteria, it is to be criticized as intervention, whereas if the judges and the panels do the same, it is not? We are told that if the citizenry has predilections, leanings, principles, convictions, an aesthetic, they must be held in abeyance for fear of intervention.

But if the judges have predilections, leanings, principles, convictions, an aesthetic, they may be exercised, for that is freedom of expression.

The scheme I have outlined, or, rather, uncovered, is one manifestation of the principle that the bureaucracy wields more power than those who have empowered it. It depends upon an inequality in the flow of funding and accountability, an inequality sustained by bureaucratic faith in contradictions and inconsistencies that are so obvious as to be surreal.

Where is the consensus for "Piss Christ"? Is there anyone in this body who will stand to declare that Americans should subsidize religious bigotry? Is there anyone who will declare that this is not religious bigotry? What will the NEA pay for next? A mockery of the Holocaust? A parody of slave ships? A comedy on the decimation of the American Indian? A satire of the massacre in the Katyn Forest?

To those who might say that for the Government to remain disengaged from things like "Piss Christ" is to limit freedom of expression, I say that to assert this is merely to transform high principles into stepping stones that lead to the public trough. The ill-considered reasoning behind such an argument is that if the Government does not nurture people like Mr. Serrano it is therefore oppressing them. This view, I submit, is a self-serving belief in a political principle that does not exist; namely, that the state owes all things to all people and has neither the discretion nor the moral right to abstain from any facet of activity or to reject any petitioning for funds.

To the contrary, government requires, above all, and almost always, discretion. The least of the examples I can think of is that Mr. Serrano was competing with 500 other artists. The Government chose 10 and rejected 490. So much for the myth that it cannot bring its discretion to bear.

My view is founded on the conviction that good government is a matter as much of restraint as of action. By the kind of encouragement the NEA offered to the creator of "Piss Christ," the state usurps its citizens' independence and self-sufficiency and therefore the power and effectiveness of the Government itself, which derives in turn from these very qualities.

And in offering this species of encouragement, the Government takes sides — in esthetics, in philosophy, in politics, and, in this case, in a theological dispute, for no matter how poor and distasteful Mr. Serrano's argument, it is nonetheless, at least symbolically, a religious argument, and the Government of the United States should not take sides in religious arguments. Here, by subsidizing one of the parties, it has done so, and that is wrong.

We have in the Constitution a direct prohibition of established religion. By immediate inference, this means that we cannot diminish one religion, lest another, the one unburdened, rise out of proportion.

If art and religion are to be free of state influence, then they must indeed be free of state influence. If they are to be free of censure, they cannot depend on subsidy. As for the religious bigotry here in question, sacrilege exists; it will always exist; and it is not the business of the Government of the United States to root it out. But neither is it the business of the United States to support it. Though Mr. Serrano and SECCA may enjoy near perfect liberty from constraint, they cannot expect the privilege of requiring the support of those from whom they desire non-interference, for that is tyranny. I propose that the Government of the United States withdraw from the question entirely, that it separate itself, its influence, its resources, its finances, from SECCA and Mr. Serrano, allowing them the near perfect liberty to reflect upon what they have done, liberty unimpeded by further U.S. Government support.

Mr. President, I propose that the NEA deprive SECCA of Federal funding for a period of say 5 years, and until such times as it is obvious that SECCA is administered responsibly. Moreover, if the NEA finds itself unable to take such a momentous step, this Congress should expressly prohibit NEA from providing such support.

■Joshua P. Smith, Why the Corcoran Made a Big Mistake, *Washington Post,* June 18, 1989

Joshua P. Smith is a curator, historian, and art collector.

Last Monday, the Corcoran Gallery of Art stunned the community and the art world by announcing the sudden cancellation of its exhibition of photographs: "Robert Mapplethorpe: The Perfect Moment," scheduled to open July 1. Included in this large retrospective organized by the University of Pennsylvania's Institute of Contemporary Art (ICA) is much sexually explicit work and a number of homoerotic images, as well as nudes of children. It had already appeared in Philadelphia and Chicago without incident and is scheduled to appear in several other American venues, none of which has expressed concern about participating in the tour. The Whitney Museum of Art in New York City has organized another major retrospective of Mapplethorpe's work that also has been exhibited without incident. Mapplethorpe, who died of AIDS in March, is widely regarded as one of the major photographers of the past two decades. A work of his is currently on display in the National Gallery of Art's highly selective and important photography exhibition: "On the Art of Fixing a Shadow."

It is still not clear exactly why the Corcoran cancelled the exhibition. Officials there have expressed the concern that the show would drag the museum into the already raging battle over the National Endowment for the Arts (NEA) funding of artistic work that is alleged to be offensive. (The ICA received a $30,000 NEA grant for the show; the Corcoran did not receive NEA funds for this exhibition but receives NEA and other federal monies for other projects.) The NEA is currently under attack by many members of Congress, led by Sens. Jesse Helms (R-N.C.) and Alfonse D'Amato (R-N.Y.), for funding a fellowship program in North Carolina that in turn supported an artist who made a photograph they find blasphemous. Fear has been expressed by some arts advocates that having the Mapplethorpe show in Washington at this time could harm the NEA during the congressional appropriations process, or during its impending reauthorization hearings.

The Corcoran's capitulation to outside pressures resulting in its cancellation of this show is likely to have many significant adverse consequences. The cancellation of an imminent and funded traveling show is extremely rare within the museum community. The recent cancellation, five days before its opening, by the Scottish National Gallery of an exhibition of Austrian artists developed with national museums of Austria, Switzerland and West Germany has caused an uproar in the European museum community.

The Corcoran's withdrawal from the Mapplethorpe exhibition may very well harm the museum in a fundamental way. In a single action, whether self-inflicted or coerced, the Corcoran may lose its credibility. Any serious museum will hesitate before working with it in the future. Artists and lenders may refuse works for Corcoran exhibitions in a show of displeasure with the gallery's action. The Corcoran may experience difficulty in attracting and keeping talented staff. Viewers may not be able to trust exhibitions and scholars may not be able to rely on publications of the Corcoran for fear they have been censored or influenced by outside pressures. In sum, the Corcoran Gallery of Art may no longer be considered a significant venue for contemporary art.

Washington's growing reputation as a major center for the exhibition of contemporary art also will be damaged. The Corcoran, ironically, has striven to be a leader in this area by establishing a position of curator of contemporary art and an ongoing series of contemporary exhibitions. Other Washington museums have recently become quite active and proficient in exhibiting contemporary art, but this dramatic cancellation will open Washington to charges that it is at best lacking in sophistication and at worst timid or even philistine.

The Corcoran's decision is also bad for artists, who rely on museum exhibitions to develop their careers and to perpetuate their work and reputations. The message the cancellation sends artists is that they must conform to "acceptable" norms as dictated by outside interest groups in order to have museum shows. The Corcoran argued unconvincingly that the cancellation of the photography show was taking the side of and protecting the artist.

The Corcoran also stated that its decision was not censorship. Yet the cancellation could deny its public the ability to see the works of a photographic master who has two major retrospectives exhibited all over the country. Moreover, Mapplethorpe has been shown previously in Washington in exhibitions at the Corcoran itself and at the Middendorf and old Lunn galleries several times, with the work at Lunn including much of the objectionable material. The work of this artist has not changed; only the times have become more cautious and, perhaps, intolerant.

Even without getting into questions of constitutionality, there is no doubt that what we may view has been limited. Any time our opportunity to see artwork is proscribed, that is censorship. I do not mean to sound too alarmist, but the logical extension of creating a category of state-approved art leads to state-condemned degenerate art, a tradition we normally associate with totalitarian regimes.

Censorship of art will result in boring, lifeless art. This art will offend no one and challenge and inspire no one. Creativity and the human spirit require exploration and risk, as does life. Artists in a free and open society have been looked to as leaders in dealing with strong, provocative, controversial and avant-garde issues. To restrain artists is to infringe on free expression in an open and vital society.

It is noteworthy that the Mapplethorpe incident and the other controversy involving NEA funding concern photographs. That second situation involves a photograph, attacked as blasphemous, by Andres Serrano, an established and talented artist who is included in an exhibition now on view that I curated at the National Museum of American Art.

The photograph as a medium presents the viewer with a certain undeniable reality. It implies that the scene or incident in the photograph took place, whether it was staged or candid. If the same image were painted it would not be as "real" or as provocative to the viewer. Also, because we are most familiar with photographs through family snapshots, newspapers, magazines and traditional documentary-style scenes and portraits, seeing allegedly obscene, homoerotic, or blasphemous subjects in photographs makes them especially threatening.

There is, in fact, a danger that what is the actual target of political and religious interest groups is not the work of art but the lifestyle portrayed. What may be the real issue is the veiled hostility toward homosexuals or the mistaken belief of actual, not esthetic, blasphemy by the artist. Somehow, because a photograph is seen by people as a literal as well as esthetic representation, it makes the abnormal or deviant normal, and it becomes more than just a work of art. This is why emotions about it are so strong. In addition, the fact that Mapplethorpe was openly homosexual and Serrano is Hispanic makes them easier targets.

The cancellation of the Mapplethorpe show, done by the Corcoran ostensibly for political reasons, was a political mistake. This regrettable action can only give forces that protest against certain art or that would withhold or withdraw funds sure and certain encouragement to continue to apply pressure. Every show becomes the potential target of outside political, religious, or financial pressures. It not only makes shows that are scheduled cancellable but, ultimately, will dictate what is scheduled in the first place.

All this will lead to even more intrusive government, as well as corporate, attempts to control exhibitions through funding and intimidation. The worst effect will be self-censorship by museums for fear of controversy. If this is permitted to happen we shall lack the free expression necessary to protect our other freedoms and to give our society vision and inspiration for the next century.

■ Mapplethorpe Agonistes, *Washington Times,* June 20, 1989

Last week the Corcoran Gallery of Art decided to cancel a photographic exhibit of the late Robert Mapplethorpe, whose aesthetic imagination seems to have been limited largely to close-ups of penises and what are demurely called "homoerotic" encounters captured in the bars of downtown Manhattan. The Oscar Wilde Fan Club may be piqued, but the Corcoran's action was probably the best thing to happen to American arts since Philip Roth lost the manuscript of a novel in a New York men's room.

According to the local aesthetes, the wowsers and the philistines have us in their grip. "I'm appalled," says Jock Reynolds, director of the Washington Project for the Arts, "I'm amazed that people are this fearful of the power of art, and it's appalling that an institution dedicated to art — and that's what the inscription says on the Corcoran building — should be so fearful of supporting individual artists' work in a situation like this." "When one thinks of the terrors Washington generates and sends out into the world," says New York art dealer Robert Miller, "the thought that depiction of the naked human body might be disturbing to Washington seems ludicrous."

In their compulsion to feel persecuted, many artists suspect that the cancellation was the work of the National Endowment for the Arts, which provides federal funding for the creative arts and is subject to congressional control. Some glimpse of the standards to which the NEA subscribes was obtained recently in its financial support for artist Andres Serrano's depiction of a crucified Christ submerged in a bottle of Mr. Serrano's own urine.

Actually, both the NEA and the Corcoran deny there was any political pressure. The Mapplethorpe exhibit at the Corcoran received no NEA funding, though the NEA did fund the same exhibit in Pennsylvania. NEA acting chairman Hugh Southern says his agency did not request cancellation, and a spokeswoman for the Corcoran also denies the gallery's decision was politically motivated. "Our mission," she said, "is providing education, not potential political platforms."

The growling about "censorship" is therefore without basis, but even if the NEA or Congress had intervened, it still would be irrelevant. If artists are going to pig out at the public trough, they have to expect that taxpayers who pick up the tab for their swill might want to keep an eye on what the artists give in return. If it's as offensive as what Mr. Mapplethorpe and Mr. Serrano excreted, the taxpayers might well decide that $600 toilet seats in the Pentagon are a better investment.

Finally, there's the question of whether art extends to the infliction on the public of exotic sexual preoccupations or gratuitous insults to religious sensibilities. Maybe it does, but when a society's arbiters of taste and beauty are so alienated from the cultural mainstream that they can think of nothing more creative than calculated ugliness and virulence, people who appreciate real beauty are entitled to flush the products of their imaginations down the nearest drainpipe.

■ Samuel Lipman, Say No to Trash, *New York Times,* June 23, 1989

Samuel Lipman is a music critic and the publisher of The New Criterion. *He served as a member of the NEA's National Council on the Arts from 1982 to 1988.*

In canceling the Robert Mapplethorpe exhibition last week, Washington's Corcoran Gallery did more than refuse to show a few raunchy photographs of what the press, unable to print them, primly called "explicit homoerotic and violent images." Because the exhibition was supported in part by public funds from the Congressionally embattled National Endowment for the Arts, the Corcoran doubtless considered financial self-interest in arriving at its decision. One hopes those responsible are aware that in saying no to Mapplethorpe, they were exercising the right to say no to an entire theory of art.

This theory assumes, to quote an official of the neighboring Hirshhorn Museum, that art "often deals with extremities of the human condition. It is not to be expected that, when it does that, everyone is going to be pleased or happy with it." The criterion of art thus becomes its ability to outrage, to (in the Hirshhorn official's words) "really touch raw nerves."

Despite its occasional usefulness, this theory ignores the vast corpus of great art that elevates, enlightens, consoles and encourages our lives. The shock appeal of art is questionable when it encompasses only such fripperies as displaying inane texts on electronic signboards in the fashion of Jenny Holzer; it becomes vastly more deleterious when it advances, as Mapplethorpe does, gross images of sexual profligacy, sadomasochism and the bestial treatment of human beings.

In a free society, it is neither possible nor desirable to go very far in prohibiting the private activities that inspire this outré art. People have always had their private pleasures, and as long as these pleasures remain private, confined to consenting adults, and not immediately injurious, the public weal remains undisturbed. But now we are told that what has been private must be made public. We are told that it is the true function of art to accommodate us to feelings and actions that we — and societies and nations before us — have found objectionable and even appalling.

In evaluating art, the viewer's role is thus only to approve. We are told that whatever the content of art, its very status as art entitles it to immunity from restraint. There are certainly those who will claim that the Mapplethorpe photographs are art, and therefore to be criticized, if at all, solely on aesthetic, never on moral, grounds. Are we to believe that the moral neutrality with which we are urged to view this art is shared by its proponents? Can it, rather, be possible that it is the very content so many find objectionable that recommends the art to its highly vocal backers?

Further, there are those who would have us believe that because we are not compelled to witness what we as individuals find morally unacceptable, we cannot refuse to make it available for others. Taking this position not only ignores our responsibility for others; it ignores the dreadful changes made in our own lives, and the lives of our children, by the availability of this decadence everywhere, from high art to popular culture.

It is undeniable that there is a large market for the hitherto forbidden. Upscale magazines trumpet the most shocking manifestations of what passes for new art. A rampant media culture profits hugely from the pleasing, and the lowering, of every taste.

Just as it is neither possible nor desirable to do much about regulating private sexual behavior, little can be done legally about the moral outrages of culture, either high or popular. But we can say no, and not only to our own participation as individuals in this trash. We can decline to make it available to the public through the use of our private facilities and funds; this, the Corcoran, acting as a private institution, has now done.

There is still more to be done. Acting on our behalf as citizens, our Government agencies — in particular the National Endowment for the Arts — can redirect their energies away from being the validators of the latest fancies to hit the art market. Instead, public art support might more fully concentrate on what it does so well: the championing of the great art of the past, its regeneration in the present and its transmission to the future. This would mean saying yes to civilization. It is a policy change that deserves our prompt attention. One hopes that the Corcoran, by saying no to Robert Mapplethorpe, has begun the process.

■ Robert Brustein, Don't Punish the Arts, *New York Times,* June 23, 1989

Robert Brustein is the artistic director of the American Repertory Theater in Cambridge, Mass.

The decision of the Corcoran Gallery to cancel a retrospective of the works of photographer Robert Mapplethorpe has caused a firestorm. The action was not based on a curator's objection to the material, which might have been a tiny bit more defensible (one photo showed a black man urinating into a white man's mouth.) It was a pre-emptive maneuver, amid growing Government intervention in the arts, to protect the museum's $292,000 in Federal funding from Congressional retaliation.

The threat is real. In another flap, a photo displayed in North Carolina of a crucifix dipped in urine prompted the estimable Representative Sidney R. Yates, usually a friend of the arts, to propose limiting the freedom of the National Endowment for the Arts to award grants to independent arts groups, who might sponsor works that Congress finds objectionable. The same photograph inspired Senator Alfonse D'Amato and 26 Senators to sign a letter assailing the Endowment for funding "anti-Christian bigotry" — even while acknowledging that the Endowment had no direct hand in sponsoring the event.

Apparently freedom of expression remains a Federal guarantee — unless supported by Federal subsidy. A staff member to Senator D'Amato said that the Senator was "absolutely opposed to censorship, but we are talking about taxpayers' dollars." (Half dollars would be more accurate: the Endowment's funding has been frozen at $170 million for eight straight years.) But Senator D'Amato's concern is touching in one so deeply implicated in the burgeoning Federal housing scandal.

It is typical of our new age of ethical purity that the accusers are often more tarnished than the accused. Still, the issue of artistic freedom and Federal subsidy is knotty. Senator Slade Gorton of Washington has said that "if art and religion are to be free of state influence... they cannot depend on subsidy." His colleagues are proving him right. Certainly the history of arts funding — beginning with the scuttled Federal Theater in the 30's — is clouded by coercion and suppression masquerading as concern for our moral and political well-being.

But Federal subsidy of the arts in our country accounts for only about 5 percent of the total budgets of established arts institutions, as compared to between 60 and 100 percent in more civilized nations. (West Germany gives $6 *billion* to theater alone.) Still, in the mean-spirited climate bequeathed us by the Reagan legacy, in which the arts are impoverished along with the poor, in which philanthropy is discouraged by the new tax laws and in which corporate and foundation giving usually goes to special projects designated by the donor, the Endowment's unrestricted 5 percent contribution remains indispensable.

The Endowment is designed by charter as a buffer between art and government, to prevent politicians from voting directly on artists or projects. Grants are made on the advice of professional panels, which are rarely, if ever, overruled.

During the Carter Administration, this policy was undermined from the left by considerations of race, sex, ethnicity and geography. This social agenda still influences funding — consider the recent decision in Michigan to withhold grants from the Detroit Symphony until it hired a black musician. But today these liberal pressures have been joined by pressures from the right, with artists being subjected to standards of religious piety.

Granted, some artists like to flout prevailing codes. But to cut off the sponsoring agencies in retaliation is to impose punitive moral constraints on independent aesthetic activity. It is on the basis of quality, not morality, that posterity judges art. While awaiting that verdict, arts organizations must not cave in to political intimidation for fear of losing grants.

Many taxpayers unwillingly contribute to a lot more unpleasant projects than the arts; people offended by provocative photos, unlike those who live near nuclear installations, can comfortably stay home. Once subsidized artistic activity becomes subject to Government manipulation, we resemble the official culture of Stalinist Russia. Once we allow lawmakers to become art critics, we take the first step into the world of Ayatollah Khomeini, whose murderous review of *The Satanic Verses* still chills the heart of everyone committed to free expression.

■ Richard Grenier, A Burning Issue Lights Artistic Ire, *Washington Times,* June 28, 1989

Richard Grenier is a columnist for the Washington Times.

Egged on by the Supreme Court, would I burn Robert Mapplethorpe?

The guy's dead already, remember. I'm no murderer. That great voice is silenced, that great eye blinded, that great catamite taken from us by AIDS. When will we get another Corcoran-class photographer to take divinely aesthetic pictures of a "black man urinating into a white man's mouth" (as sympathetically reported by U.S. family newspapers), or of the photographer himself in full posterior nudity being penetrated anally by a bullwhip (likewise)?

Mr. Mapplethorpe's untimely departure leaves our civilization poorer, I'm telling you. I'm lucky I saw his full show in cosmopolitan, sophisticated Philadelphia before the yahoos of Washington started imposing on great art the aesthetic tastes of Peoria.

I wouldn't dig him up. I'm no grave robber, either. But inspired by the Supreme Court's ruling allowing the burning of the American flag as free expression, I'm just imagining Mr. Mapplethorpe's dead body lying around someplace, and me seized with a desire to express myself.

Greg Johnson cried: *"Red, white, and blue, I spit on you,"* and I could yell, *"Mapplethorpe, you're a dork,"* but that's pretty thin gruel. So I think I'd sprinkle him with kerosene and burn him up.

Now there are emotional people in this country who attach a sacred character to a dead person's remains. (You noticed how often those who condemned flag-burning were called "emotional.") But the American Civil Liberties Union will explain to you that burial, as a religion-derived custom, has no legitimacy, as church and state are separate in this country. And preserving dead bodies is clearly ethnocentric. Hindus burn their dead. Parsees expose them to be eaten by vultures. Are our customs superior?

So, peacefully, harming nobody, expressing myself freely in the constitutional way that makes us so different from Hitler's Germany, Stalin's Russia, Ayatollah Ruhollah Khomeini's Iran, and Deng Xiaoping's China (all invoked in sanctifying both Robert Mapplethorpe and the right to burn the flag), I'd burn the guy up. I think I'd beat the rap, too. Or it would be interesting to find out.

And I have a secret weapon: *Art.* If I wanted to do more than win over the Supreme Court, and craved the support of the entire intellectual community, I'd set fire to this Mapplethorpe, and not just as self-expression, but as *performance art,* a kind of performance that even the NEA hasn't heard of yet. I'd invite all the curators and art critics, announcing that this isn't recommended for children, and burn him up, creating a new art form.

And I'd do my darnedest to get a $15,000 grant from the National Endowment for the Arts, like Andres Serrano, who did the renowned Christ in Urine. (It amazes me that Greg Johnson didn't have a grant to burn the flag in Dallas.)

Then let those polyester-suited, philistine yokels try to stop me. Ho, ho! Every freedom-loving artist worthy of the name would rush to my support! I'd really shame the bumpkins then.

Because the artistic community has its own 11th commandment: *Thou shalt grant federal funds to art that's too intellectual for you to understand, you rube.* This keeps high-class art out of the hands of the rabble, who are too coarse to appreciate it and can't tell Marcel Duchamp from a marcel wave.

But would I actually get my $15,000 grant to burn Robert Mapplethorpe? Because there's a flaw in my argument, and I'm man enough to admit it.

As in Chicago, I could get official sponsorship for an American flag displayed on the floor with an invitation to walk on it. I could get official support for art demeaning almost any of this country's institutions: sexual, political or religious. But could I demean gays? Women? Minorities?

Because this whole controversy has taken place as if those favoring the Mapplethorpe Show (and the right to burn the flag), those shuddering at "censorship," were supporting absolute freedom and the total separation of art from content. But the most ruthless content censorship takes place before art even comes close to reaching the public. Is every novel written published? Every play produced? Every painting exhibited? Above all in museums? The moral pieties of the culture barons just happen to be different from those of ordinary Americans. They censor, in darkness, every day.

Public money goes into any amount of junk-art gleefully and maniacally denigrating everything that ordinary people hold sacred — which seems to be the point. And all I want to do, in a spirit of moral uplift is burn Robert Mapplethorpe's corpse if I find it lying around someplace. But will the NEA fund me? Bitter laughter.

Mr. Mapplethorpe himself admitted to drawing inspiration from the pornography shops of Manhattan's 42nd Street: "Basically I'm selfish. I did them [his 'sex pictures'] for myself — because I wanted to. I wasn't trying to educate anyone. I was experimenting with my sensibilities."

A credo of such egocentricity I'm provisionally willing to adopt as my own, conveniently reversing myself, since it spares me the need to even express anything. In burning Robert Mapplethorpe all I have to do is experiment with my sensibilities.

Actually I don't care if I have to buy the kerosene myself. If I find this guy's body lying around someplace, I'm going to burn it.

■Freeborn G. Jewett Jr. and David Lloyd Kreeger, The Corcoran: We Did the Right Thing, *Washington Post,* June 29, 1989

Freeborn G. Jewett Jr. is the former president and David Lloyd Kreeger was the former chairman of the board of trustees of the Corcoran Gallery of Art.

The decision of the director and board of trustees of the Corcoran Gallery of Art to withdraw from the tour of the Robert Mapplethorpe photography exhibition created a sharp reaction by the press and the museum community, some condemning and some supporting the decision. Because of the scope and intensity of the criticism, the Corcoran management and the board of trustees have reviewed our action in depth. The conclusion reached is that the decision to withdraw was prudent and sound.

Opinions may differ about the propriety of items in contemporary art exhibitions. Under universally respected principles of artistic freedom of expression, a museum would not censor controversial items within a generally meritorious artistic presentation. In certain circumstances, however, a public exhibition of controversial items may be so inflammatory and provocative as to invite consequences that negate its educational and aesthetic value. In the opinion of the director, supported by the board of trustees of the Corcoran, the Mapplethorpe exhibition was precisely such a case.

The exhibition was to be held in Washington, the seat of the federal government. In another photographic exhibition shown earlier this year at museums in Los Angeles, Pittsburgh and Richmond, one photograph was considered to have transcended the limits of bad taste. Approximately 106 members of Congress contacted the National Endowment for the Arts to question the $15,000 grant made to the artist, while 36 senators expressed outrage, calling for reform of the NEA's grant-awarding process.

We deplore any attempt by government, directly or indirectly, to censor the artistic judgment of artists and museums, and indeed the NEA is forbidden by law from interfering with the content of the exhibitions it supports. Nevertheless, the basic freedom of the agency to award grants according to the best judgment of its experts and the size of its annual appropriation are being severely examined in both houses of Congress to determine whether restraints on the operations of the agency or budget cuts should be imposed.

The Mapplethorpe exhibition contains a number of photographs that some may deem shocking and past the bounds of artistic license. Others may consider them acceptable within the context of the exhibition and in the light of the artist's traditional freedom to express himself. It is not our function to mediate such an issue nor to delineate the boundary between artistic freedom and institutional responsibility.

But in the circumstances of a particular situation, it is very much our responsibility to exercise our best judgment as to the best interests of our institution, however difficult the choices may be. It is indeed our function to ensure that the Corcoran does not damage itself or the NEA and the greater arts community. Weighing these considerations, and being fully aware of the public controversy about the propriety of our action, the director and the board of trustees on June 26 reaffirmed the Corcoran's withdrawal from the tour of the Mapplethorpe exhibition as the prudent and wise course of action at this time.

■ Nicols Fox, NEA Under Siege, *New Art Examiner,* Summer 1989 (excerpt)

Nicols Fox is a contributing editor to the New Art Examiner, *and is a former editor of* The Northeast, *the newspaper of the Episcopal Diocese of Maine.*

Public funding for the arts has never had an easy time of it before Congress, but when the endowment was set up more than 20 years ago, defending Abstract Expressionism or Conceptualism before a skeptical Congress demanded no more than establishing a position of aesthetic superiority. It would be fair to say that most members of Congress feel themselves at a disadvantage and ill-equipped to make professional and credible aesthetic judgments, but they are, on the contrary, fully prepared to substitute moral indignation when it serves a political purpose. A large percentage of the population can be guaranteed to support a protest against art funded by tax dollars (by however a circuitous path) which might be considered immoral, anti-Christian, or blasphemous. Indignation, especially moral indignation, is a sure crowd pleaser.

Despite a 20-year commitment to federal funding for the arts, which endows it with a certain cultural value, our society has unofficially labeled its production and exhibition "peripheral." Thus, in an age of tight budgets, art is an easy target. In addition, when it offends or threatens or questions some prevailing wisdom, it becomes a sitting duck for the self-righteous outrage of those who have consistently opposed funding cultural activity. When President Reagan, early in his first term, expressed a desire to drastically cut funding for the arts, he was simply articulating the conservative agenda, which historically views any funding activity of the federal government beyond defense with considerable suspicion. A high-level assistant in the Office of Management and Budget summed up the philosophy when he asked this reporter at a cocktail party, "Do you believe in government funding for public television?" An affirmative answer prompted an obvious conclusion: "Then you're a Liberal."

Contributing to the present environment of challenge is the fact that the activities of art traditionally have not been conducted in full view of the public, as television conducts its affairs, but within the intellectual confines of the art cognoscenti. The relative inaccessibility of much art since Modernism provided artists with a certain freedom — out of the public view artists might undertake

47

what they wished, with little fear of condemnation. But it also incurred the alienation of those who had been left out of the picture, so to speak.

For 20 or more years now an attempt has been made to reverse the isolation of art. Government funding for the arts has never been copious, but the meager resources of the endowment have been directed, in part not only to supporting artistic production but to increasing public accessibility to art through education and the support of exhibitions — to, in effect, democratize art. At the same time, we have attempted to neutralize it. A middle-class society that is expected to bring art into its homes will eventually ask that it behave according to middle-class standards. It will demand that art maintain a certain *politesse* — that it not pee on the carpet.

From the beginning, the National Endowment has understood that danger: It foresaw the scrutiny its funding would receive from Congress and the pressures that would be brought to bear. Those who established the procedures for distributing funds devised elaborate systems specifically designed to relieve government officials of the task of decision-making and to turn those responsibilities over to acknowledged and respected experts in the field — with the obvious benefit of being able to point the finger elsewhere when the plan backfired. But even as the endowment understood that art funding is dangerous — that art is potentially dangerous — it also acknowledged that to censor or in any way impose the standards of the government upon what was being sponsored would render the entire enterprise pointless. Government art — art officially sanctioned and inoffensive, totally apolitical, and capable of pleasing all those voters who make a practice of writing their representatives — is virtually guaranteed to be art that history quickly forgets. The endowment knew that by attempting the essentially dangerous undertaking of supporting and encouraging the best the arts had to offer, it was courting trouble and trouble came...

Serrano is a well-established artist, widely exhibited, who has previously won an artist fellowship grant from the NEA in 1986. His work is, in his own words, "an ongoing investigation(s) of such bodily fluids as milk, blood, and urine." Marcia Tucker, director of the New Museum of Contemporary Art, who nominated Serrano for the AVA, has been quoted as saying that his use of bodily fluids is discomforting because it "indicates the extent to which we're unable to deal with our humanity. That is, no doubt, part of the power of Andres's work, to render the sacred secular and vice versa."

Ted Potter of SECCA said, "According to Serrano, the photograph is a protest against the profiteering of sacred imagery. And the plastic cross is a classic symbol for the religion-for-profit industry that panders its message on television and radio. As a disturbing and challenging artistic statement, Serrano's work explores how spiritual belief has been exploited and spiritual values debased."

Howard Risatti, associate professor of art history at Virginia Commonwealth University, pointed out that "Serrano's work deplores the way Christian symbols have been drained of spiritual meaning and replaced by blind dogma — something analogous to what Khomeini did in Iran."

Paul Perrot, who is director of the Virginia Museum, where the work was last seen publicly, said the photograph "cruelly juxtaposes the sacred and the profane to shock the viewer into a reconsideration of the image and its true meaning." Says [critic Donald] Kuspit, "What they are afraid of, is that it may not be what it seems. The plastic Christ was already found in society — society made it. What Serrano is doing by means of irony is revealing that they are the ones who have violated the spirit of Christ."

From a purely theological perspective, the case has fascinating implications. Fundamentalist Christians have no love for the crucifix image — it is shunned by most Protestant sects as being macabre, overemotional and, to some, a symbol of icon worship. In rushing to the defense of the apparent debasement of this symbol, the Protestant Methodist Wildmon joins Roman Catholics who have also protested the photograph. Thus, Serrano has managed to do what the ecumenical movement has not — brought the Roman Catholic and Protestant faiths together on an issue other than abortion.

Irony abounds in this affair. In the current supermarket atmosphere that characterizes Christianity, an extraordinary diversity of beliefs is not only tolerated but supported by those who call themselves Christians. Those who rise in outrage against the *Piss Christ* photograph raised not a whimper of protest against the long-running Praise the Lord Club (PTL) heresy. Jim and Tammy Bakker were allowed to preach and practice, in the name of Christianity, a doctrine of pure materialism, a gospel of goods and getting and an eternal life in the hot tub — the antitheses, to be precise, of Christ's Sermon on the Mount.

Those who protest the iconoclastic nature of Serrano's work seem afflicted with a historical amnesia that fails to recall the foundations of the Christian faith — a series of acts that were undoubtedly considered blasphemous or even heretical in their time. One would not have to stretch the imagination too far to see the parallel in Serrano's protest against the profiteering of sacred imagery and Christ's confrontational actions in throwing the money changers out of the temple. Indeed, throughout the history of art the various interpretations of the image of Christ have provoked controversy. The Renaissance itself departed drastically from the rigidity of the Orthodox Tradition of religious representation — a departure to which the Orthodox have never become reconciled — and Holman Hunt's portrayal of Christ as a humble carpenter in his workshop brought cries of foul from those who saw the painting as insulting, degrading, and, indeed, blasphemous.

Nor should it be forgotten that the Protestant Church was founded on what the Christian Church of the time saw as heresy. The chief reformers of the day, such as Luther, were dismayed by abuses similar to those that Serrano's work is said to challenge.

This is not to propose canonization for Serrano. In explaining *Piss Christ*, he says, "Complex and unresolved feelings about my own Catholic upbringing inform this work which helps me to redefine and personalize my relationship with God. For me, art is a moral and spiritual obligation that cuts across all manner of pretense and speaks directly to the soul. Although I am no longer a member of the Catholic Church, I consider myself a Christian and I practice my faith through my work." But the history of art is filled with examples of those who have profited from the shock value of their work; only Serrano can say if his motives were pure.

There is a long history of those who profess to support the church reacting in an anti-Christian manner to what they perceive to be anti-Christian, ignoring the call in the Gospel of Luke (6:27–28): "But I say unto you which hear, Love your enemies, do good to them which hate you. Bless them that curse you and pray for them which despitefully use you." Wars have been fought and thumb-screws applied in the name of all that is good and holy, and even today a battle rages in Northern Ireland between two forces, each of whom claims to have God on its side.

The point is that Christianity has managed somehow to rise above the perpetual abuses of its most basic tenets, and will undoubtedly continue to do so. Jesus Christ is perfectly capable of defending himself in this matter — if it is indeed required...

Art can be strong stuff. In any totalitarian regime it is one of the first things suppressed. In our condition of moral superiority as a democratic society we have prodded the Soviet Union for years to loosen its hold on its writers and painters. Now it is doing so at precisely the same moment that our own tolerance for dissent would appear to be weakening. The current wave of hypersensitivity is an acknowledgement of the incipient power of art to shape the culture. And it may be an overture to another shift in political thinking from that which has dominated for the past eight years. Christianity is being used as a cover for conservative paranoia. Kuspit says, "The effort to label Modernist art 'degenerate' was already made in 1937 by the Nazis. This effort to censor and control the arts, which are an expression of the creative and free human spirit, amounts to authoritarianism and in effect is the beginning of the end of all that we have meant by our civilization since its Judeo-Hellenic beginnings."

If, as [James] Cooper says and [Patrick] Buchanan quotes, the right has relinquished control of the culture to the left, it may well be because conserva-tives have chosen to dominate another forum. The right has its culture — as expressed by television and films and music — all supported by the funding source considered most appropriate by conservatives: free enterprise. As always, serious art — that produced with the intention of expanding aesthetic frontiers or challenging the conventional wisdom — must struggle. It is out of respect for those things which do not fare well in the marketplace — at least not in their own time — that we have chosen to lend the support of government to the arts. But if this support is to produce anything of value, that art must be free to pursue whatever it chooses.

■ Hilton Kramer, Is Art Above the Laws of Decency?, *New York Times,* July 2, 1989

Hilton Kramer is the editor of The New Criterion, *and the art critic of* The New York Observer.

The fierce controversy now raging over the decision of the Corcoran Gallery of Art in Washington to cancel an exhibition of photographs by the late Robert Mapplethorpe was an event waiting to happen. If it hadn't happened at this time and at this institution, sooner or later it would surely have erupted elsewhere. The wonder is that it didn't occur earlier, for it involves an issue that has haunted our arts institutions, their supporters and their public for as long as Government money — taxpayers' money — has come to play the major role it now does in financing the arts.

The issue may be briefly and in the most general terms stated as follows: Should public standards of decency and civility be observed in determining which works of art or art events are to be selected for the Government's support? Or, to state the issue another way, is everything and anything to be permitted in the name of art? Or, to state the issue in still another way, is art now to be considered such an absolute value that no other standard — no standard of taste, no social or moral standard — is to be allowed to play any role in determining what sort of art it is appropriate for the Government to support?

The Corcoran Gallery's decision was prompted by the special character of Mapplethorpe's sexual imagery and a quite reasonable fear on the part of the museum's leadership that a showing of such pictures in Washington right now — especially in an exhibition partly financed by the National Endowment for the Arts — would result in grave damage both to the Corcoran itself and to the whole program of Government support for the arts.

Yet it may help to put this controversy in perspective to be reminded that it isn't only in relation to the exhibition of provocative sexual images that this issue has lately arisen. In the storm caused by Richard Serra's now legendary sculpture, "Tilted Arc," which came into existence as a United States Government commission, the question of sexual imagery played no part. "Tilted Arc" consisted of an immense and completely abstract steel wall, and thus belonged to the genre of overscale Minimalist sculpture in which representational imagery of any kind is entirely absent.

What proved to be so bitterly offensive to the community that "Tilted Arc" was commissioned to serve was its total lack of amenity — indeed, its stated goal of provoking the most negative and disruptive response to the site the sculpture dominated with an arrogant disregard for the mental well-being and physical convenience of the people who were obliged to come into contact with the work in the course of their daily employment.

When the General Services Administration, the Federal agency that had commissioned "Tilted Arc" through its Art-in-Architecture program, conducted a public hearing over the fate of this work, a number of art-world eminences claimed, predictably, that the removal of the offending sculpture from its site on the plaza of the Javits Federal Building in lower Manhattan would constitute an act of cultural barbarism no different in spirit from the campaigns waged against artistic freedom in Hitler's Germany and Stalin's Russia. My own view of the matter, if I may paraphrase a famous observation by George Orwell, is that you would have to be an art-world intellectual to believe a thing like that. At the very least, such a belief betrays a woeful lack of understanding of the categorical differences — political and moral differences — that distinguish acts of violently enforced totalitarian repression from the inevitable disagreements of taste and value that are a legitimate and indispensable feature of democratic societies.

In the case of Richard Serra, moreover, it was certainly possible to admire him as a sculptor while thoroughly approving the decision to remove "Tilted Arc" from its site. This was, in fact, my own position. As a member of the prize jury for the 1985 Carnegie International Exhibition in Pittsburgh, I did not hesitate to award the top prize that year to the sculpture that Mr. Serra created for the plaza of the Carnegie Museum of Art. While I found "Tilted Arc" to be repulsive in every respect, I found the Carnegie's sculpture to be a very beautiful work of art. Which proves what? Only that we are not obliged to accept, either as critics or as citizens, every judgment rendered by the art-world establishment as inviolable or irreversible writ, especially where the public has an urgent and legitimate claim to a grievance. To suggest that such grievances and the need to address them are in any way comparable to acts of totalitarian repression contributes nothing but an element of demagoguery and intimidation to what ought to be a serious debate about what standards are to be observed in spending the taxpayers' money on public financing of the arts.

Getting the Issue Exactly Wrong

In the case of the Mapplethorpe exhibition, which the Corcoran Gallery found it prudent on June 13 to cancel prior to its opening, even in the face of what everyone knew would be the inevitable uproar, we are once again being asked to accept the judgment of the art-world establishment as absolute and incontestable. (The fact that the Washington Project for the Arts immediately appropriated the right to show the exhibition in Washington only serves to underscore this point.) We are being told, in other words, that no one outside the professional art establishment has a right to question or oppose the exhibition of Mapplethorpe's work even when it is being shown at the Government's expense. In this instance, to be sure, the Government did not cause the photographs in question to be created. Mercifully, they were not commissioned by a Government agency. But such an agency did contribute funds to support their public exhibition, and by so doing it gave the public and its elected representatives the right to have a voice in assessing the probable consequence of such an exhibition — a task that the art establishment has lately shown itself to be utterly incapable of performing in any disinterested way.

Here again, to suggest that the public's legitimate interest in this matter amounts to political repression is to get the whole issue exactly wrong. The public's right to have an interest in the fate of this exhibition began on the day that tax dollars were allocated for its public display. There was no public outcry, after all, though there was a certain amount of private outrage, when Mapplethorpe's pictures were exhibited in commercial galleries. Some of the people who went to the galleries to see the photographs, unaware of what it was they would be seeing, had plenty of reason to be shocked at what they saw depicted in the work. This was especially the case, as I myself witnessed on one occasion, with parents who are in the habit of making the rounds of the art galleries in the company of their young children.

Public Money for Pornography?

What is it, then, about some of these photographs — the ones that are the cause of the trouble — that makes them so offensive? It isn't simply that they depict male nudity. There are male nudes in the Minor White retrospective now on view at the Museum of Modern Art that no one, as far as I know, has made any fuss about. In today's cultural climate, in which it has become commonplace for schoolchildren to be instructed in the use of condoms, it takes a lot more than a museum exhibition of pictures showing the male genitals to cause an uproar.

What one finds in many Mapplethorpe photographs is something else — so absolute and extreme a concentration on male sexual endowments that every other attribute of the human subject is reduced to insignificance. In these photographs, men are rendered as nothing but sexual — which is to say, homosexual — objects. Or, as the poet Richard Howard wrote in a tribute to Mapplethorpe, "The male genitals are often presented... as surrogates for the face."

Even so, these homoerotic idealizations of male sexuality are not the most extreme of Mapplethorpe's pictures. That dubious honor belongs to the pictures that celebrate in graphic and grisly detail what Richard Marshall, the curator who organized a Mapplethorpe retrospective at the Whitney Museum last summer — not the same exhibition as the one in dispute at the Corcoran, by the way — identified as the "sadomasochistic theme." In this case, it is a theme enacted by male homosexual partners whom we may presume to be consenting adults — consenting not only to the sexual practices depicted but to Mapplethorpe's role in photographing them.

The Issue Is Not Esthetics

I cannot bring myself to describe these pictures in all their gruesome particularities, and it is doubtful that this newspaper would agree to publish such a description even if I could bring myself to write one. (There can be no question either, of course, of illustrating such pictures on this page, which raises an interesting and not irrelevant question: Should public funds be used to exhibit pictures which the press even in our liberated era still finds too explicit or repulsive to publish?) Suffice it to say that Mr. Marshall, who presumably knows what he is talking about in this matter, assured us in the Whitney catalogue that

Mapplethorpe made these pictures "not as a voyeur but as an advocate" and "sympathetic participant."

Even in a social environment as emancipated from conventional sexual attitudes are ours is today, to exhibit photographic images of this sort, which are designed to aggrandize and abet erotic rituals involving coercion, degradation, bloodshed and the infliction of pain, cannot be regarded as anything but a violation of public decency. Such pictures have long circulated in private, of course. They belonged, and were seen to belong, to the realm of specialized erotica. In that realm, it was clearly understood that the primary function of such images was to promote sexual practices commonly regarded as unruly and perverse, or to aid in fantasizing about such practices. The appeal of such images for those who were drawn to them lay precisely in the fact that they were forbidden. They belonged, in other words, to the world of pornography.

It may be asked whether the disputed Mapplethorpe pictures really differ from earlier works of art that, owing to their violation of conventional taste, caused the public to denounce them, only to embrace them later as treasured classics. The example that comes to mind is Manet, whose two most famous paintings, "Déjeuner sur l'Herbe" and "Olympia" (both 1863), were attacked as indecent when they were first exhibited in Paris.

For a true counterpart to Mapplethorpe in 19th-century art, however, it isn't in a master like Manet but in graphic artists who specialized in pornographic images that we will find an appropriate parallel, and we still don't see much of that art on public exhibition in our museums even today.

What has turned these Mapplethorpe photographs into a public controversy is not that they exist. We may not approve of their existence, and we may certainly regard both the creation and the consumption of them as a form of social pathology. But so long as they remained a private taste, they could not, I believe, be seen to be a threat to public decency. What has made them a public issue is the demand that is now being made to accord these hitherto forbidden images the status of perfectly respectable works of art, to exhibit them without restriction in public institutions, and to require our Government to provide funds for their public exhibition.

Ostensibly, these are demands that are being made in the name of art. That isn't the whole story, of course — it never is where art is made to serve extra-artistic purposes — but before looking into the extra-artistic aspects of this matter, a prior question must be addressed. Are these disputed pictures works of art? My own answer to this question, as far as the Mapplethorpe pictures are concerned, is: Alas, I suppose they are. But so, I believe, was Richard Serra's "Tilted Arc" a work of art. This is not to say that either "Tilted Arc" or the Mapplethorpe pictures belong to the highest levels of art — in my opinion, they do not — but I know of no way to exclude them from the realm of art itself. Failed art, even pernicious art, still remains art in some sense.

Writing some years ago about the Marquis de Sade, to cite a relevant example, Edmund Wilson observed that "the Marquis constitutes, unquestionably, one of the hardest cases to handle in the whole history of literature." Yet Wilson felt obliged, however reluctantly, to include Sade in the history of literature, and for similar reasons I believe we must accord Mapplethorpe a

54

place — though not the exalted place being claimed for him — in the annals of art photography. It doesn't solve any of the problems raised by the Mapplethorpe pictures to say they aren't art. It is only a way of running away from the difficult issue, which doesn't lie in the realm of esthetics.

What has to be acknowledged in this debate is a fact of cultural life that the art-world establishment has never been willing to deal with — namely, that not all forms of art are socially benign in either their intentions or their effects. Everybody knows — certainly every intelligent parent knows — that certain forms of popular culture have a devastating effect on the moral sensibilities of the young. Well, it is not less true that certain forms of high culture are capable of having something other than a socially desirable impact on the sensibilities of young and old alike. How we, as adult citizens, wish to deal in our own lives with this antisocial element in the arts should not, I think, be a matter for the Government to determine, for systematic programs of censorship are likely to have consequences that are detrimental to our liberties. (The question of protecting children is another matter entirely.) It is when our Government intervenes in this process by supporting the kind of art that is seen to be antisocial that we as citizens have a right to be heard — not, I hasten to add, in order to deny the artist his freedom of expression, but to have a voice in determining what our representatives in the Government are going to support and thus validate in our name.

A Dedication to Pernicious Ideas

Unfortunately, professional opinion in the art world can no longer be depended upon to make wise decisions in these matters. (If it could, there never would have been a "Tilted Arc" controversy or the current uproar over the Mapplethorpe pictures.) There is in the professional art world a sentimental attachment to the idea that art is at its best when it is most extreme and disruptive. This is the point of view that prompted an art student in Chicago to think he was creating a valid work of art by spreading out an American flag on the floor and inviting the public to walk on it, and then recording their responses to what was at the time a proscribed practice (now that the Supreme Court has ruled in its favor, I suspect that this particular idea will lose some of its appeal to "advanced" taste). It was this notion of equating artistic originality with sheer provocation that also led the Southeastern Center for Contemporary Art to give a grant of the Government's money to Andres Serrano, now famous for the work that consists of a photograph of Christ on the Cross submerged in the artist's urine. This is the kind of thing people mean when they talk about the so-called "cutting edge." Basically, it is a sentimentalization as well as a commercialization of the old idea of the avant-garde, which everyone knows no longer exists — except, possibly, in the realm of fashion design and advertising. The phenomenon of the avant-garde in art died a long time ago, and now lies buried under the millions of dollars that have been spent on the art that bears its name.

In lieu of an authentic avant-garde in art, we now have something else — that famous "cutting edge" that looks more and more to an extra-artistic content for its fundamental raison d'être. In the case of "Tilted Arc," the "cutting edge" element consisted of the sculptor's wish to deconstruct and otherwise render uninhabitable the public site the sculpture was designed to occupy. In the case of the disputed Mapplethorpe pictures, it consists of the attempt to force upon the public the acceptance of the values of a sexual sub-culture that the public at large finds loathsome — and here I do not mean homosexuality as such but the particular practices depicted in the most extreme of these pictures. In both cases, we are being asked to accept the unacceptable in the name of art, but this is sheer hypocrisy, and all the parties concerned know it is hypocrisy. What we are being asked to support and embrace in the name of art is an attitude toward life, which nowadays is where the real cutting edge (no quotation marks required) is to be found.

If our agencies of Government are incapable of making this distinction between art and life, the public will have more and more reason to be concerned with the way tax dollars are being spent in the name of art. The problem won't go away, and it can't be argued away by cries of repression or censorship. Much of what the Government spends on the arts still goes — and ought to go — to supporting the highest achievements of our civilization, and it would be a tragedy for our country and our culture if that support were to be lost because of a few obtuse decisions and a dedication in some quarters to outmoded and even pernicious ideas. But if the arts community is not prepared to correct the outrages committed in its name, there will be no shortage of other elements in our society ready and eager to impose drastic remedies. This is a problem that the art world has brought upon itself.

■Judith Reisman, Promoting Child Abuse as Art, *Washington Times,* July 7, 1989

Judith Reisman is the associate director of research for the American Family Association.

In our democracy, most Americans would take it as given that artists should not be hamstrung and controlled by politicians. With this in mind, the Washington Project for the Arts plans to exhibit the contested Robert Mapplethorpe's photos from July 21 through Aug. 13.

But the "censorship at the Corcoran" debate has censored some critical public-policy issues.

There are values and rights close to the hearts of most artists and other citizens which have been ignored in the Mapplethorpe conflict. For example, how do today's art juries treat traditional religious art and art which trivializes racism, or AIDS or the abuse of young children?

With this in mind, the art and general community are probably unaware that Mr. Mapplethorpe's photos of "nude children" could qualify as child-pornography "pandering." When art experts censor these facts from their public remarks,

56

they taint the entire artistic community with their own ignorance, indifference or preference for the criminal sexual victimization of children.

In the midst of pandemic reports of child sexual abuse, the art community needs to ask itself why "artistic" child pornography (e.g., Angelo Cozzi, David Hamilton) has too often been accepted.

One-directional spokespersons for the art community are historically worrisome. In "Art in the Third Reich" (1979) Berthold Hinz notes that under Hitler's National Socialism the art establishment (roughly 20,000 artists) had a shared vision, eagerly condemning religion and propagandizing fascism through their paintings, sculptures, illustrations and photos.

On this note, rumor to the contrary, while homosexuality was formally condemned, much fascist art remained "homoerotic" in content. Deceptively condemning other art as "degenerate," fascist artists glamorized dominance, (recall Mr. Mapplethorpe's photo of master and slave), "supermen," sadism and "child nudes."

How did Mr. Mapplethorpe present "child nudes"? Note "Honey, 1976." "Honey" is roughly 6 years old, dirty and unkempt, her stringy hair hanging limply about her thin little face as she crouches on the cold steps of an old building. A worn, sleeveless dress skims her tiny form. Mr. Mapplethorpe's eye, and camera, peep under the child's skirt to expose her hairless genitalia provocatively to the world — just as thousands of other child molesters/pornographers before and after him. The violation beings to mind Susan Sontag in "On Photography" (1977):

"Like sexual voyeurism, [photography] is a way of at least tacitly, often explicitly, encouraging whatever is going on to keep on happening... to be in complicity with whatever makes a subject interesting, worth photographing — including, when that is the interest, another person's pain or misfortune."

Are we in complicity, encouraging this child's pain and misfortune? Looking closely one cannot miss "Honey"'s large, sad eyes. But unlike viewing a Dorothea Lange, Bourke-White or Ansel Adams photo, one does not focus on her eyes — *for they are not Mr. Mapplethorpe's focus.* In keeping with his candid sexual interest in adult males and their genitals, Mr. Mapplethorpe's camera reveals his sexual interest in children and their genitals.

Susan Sontag's warning is from one who respects the power of photography. She implies that unless one protests such photos one is an accessory, permitting "whatever is going on to keep on happening." In this case it could be argued that Mr. Mapplethorpe enlists us in the child's photographic molestation. In fact, the photo advertises the availability of this vulnerable child (and, by extension, all children) for photographic assault and rape. It would be purchased by child sex abusers as child pornography, which is what it is.

Moreover, contrast "Honey" with Mr. Mapplethorpe's domineering "Self-Portrait, 1983." Mr. Mapplethorpe stands before the black metal outline of a pseudosatanic "star." He wears a costly black leather coat and his hands, covered by black leather gloves, grasp a black (circa 1920) tommy gun pressed aggressively across his chest. A white silk scarf (a "richly textured fabric") is glamorously tossed about his neck as he stares out at the viewer.

Another, masochistic Mr. Mapplethorpe is revealed in Dominick Dunne's review of a "self-portrait" in which he allowed a photo of his rectum "with a bull whip up it" to be hung in a museum.

It is important to ask, "What then was Mr. Mapplethorpe's self- or national vision?" Was is that of "a child-molesting-rectum with a bull-whip implant, at the ready with his tommy gun"?

Would his own death from AIDS, (commonly an "anal recipient" disease) not preclude (in a national museum) "encouraging" the sadistic acts which, on the evidence, facilitate AIDS? How would Mr. Mapplethorpe's public self-portrait (fully protected head-to-toe by tommy gun and leather) compare with his public portrait of "Honey" (vulnerably unprotected and genitally available)?

And, would our artists really justify the racism inherent in Mr. Mapplethorpe's view of a black-man-as-the-sum-of-his-phallus? The white man (Mr. Mapplethorpe) dresses the black man (no name), in a well-tailored, three-piece suit. He then photographically lynches him, decapitating head and knees, leaving only an unzipped fly from which, says Dunne, hangs an "elephantine-size black penis."

In 1934, back in Washington, D.C., when Germany was preparing to conquer the world, retired Navy Adm. Hugh L. Rodman demanded that a federally funded painting of drunken sailors ("The Fleet's In") be removed from the Corcoran's exhibit, saying it "gave the public the wrong idea about sailors." "Right artistic... but not true of the Navy." Others asked, should government "subsidize libels on the national defense?"

Art instructs viscerally, not necessarily truthfully. And, as noted, artists have not infrequently been propagandists.

In 1934, Adm. Rodman held, not without merit, that portraying American sailors as drunks was libel, hazardous to a nation on the brink of World War II.

Pandemic child sexual abuse, AIDS and racism suggest ours is no less a perilous era. With this in mind, it may be prudent for WPA to rethink Mr. Mapplethorpe and the AIDS fund-raiser scheduled in his name.

What photographer would instruct in the joy of AIDS-efficient anal-sadism, pontificate on the bliss of disembodied sex, racism and adult sexual access to small children without — à la Sontag — "encouraging" it to "keep on happening."

■Grace Glueck, Art on the Firing Line, *New York Times,* July 9, 1989 (excerpt)

Grace Glueck is an art critic for the New York Times.

When, at the prospect of Congressional disfavor, the Corcoran Gallery of Art in Washington canceled a touring show of photographs by the late Robert Mapplethorpe, financed in part by the National Endowment for the Arts, the action raised issues about artistic freedom and censorship that bear directly on public support for the arts in this country.

Should such support include the right to sanitize art? Should a museum be subject to political pressures, or should its role as a protector of art entitle it to immunity from them? Should the public be kept from seeing a show it has helped pay for? What does a museum owe an artist to whose work it has committed itself? And who should decide how taxpayers' dollars are used — legislators, panels of esthetic experts or the "public," whoever that constitutes?

The Mapplethorpe show is a retrospective of the artist's work that contains images depicting homosexual and heterosexual erotic acts and explicit sadomasochistic practices in which black and white, naked or leather-clad men and women assume erotic poses. Along with these photographs are fashionable portraits of the rich and trendy, elegant floral arrangements and naked children — images that might not necessarily be considered indecent if viewed singly but that in this context seem provocative. (Signs accompanying the show on its tour suggested that it might be unsuitable for children.)

Opposition to the exhibition by members of Congress, among them, Senator Jesse Helms, Republican of North Carolina, Senator Alfonse M. D'Amato, Republican of New York, and Representative Dick Armey, Republican of Texas, has focused on the question of whether Government money should be used to support art that can be considered by some to be blasphemous or pornographic.

"I clearly know offensive art when I see it," said Representative Armey in a recent statement. "And there ought to be a way for the endowment to establish procedures where they can clearly deny funding for art like that. The arts do serve a role of probing the frontiers, but I would say let that be funded from the private sector."

In the simplest terms, the Mapplethorpe case could be called a tug of war between two hallowed elements — the First Amendment guarantee of free speech and the community perception of what is pornographic or indecent. Yet to put it that way ignores the symbolic role of artists and museums in our culture. Artists are important to us, among other reasons, because of their ability to express what is deep or hidden in our consciousness, what we cannot or will not express ourselves. And museums are traditionally the neutral sanctuaries — entered voluntarily by the public — for this expression. What we see there may not always be esthetic, uplifting, or even civil, but that is the necessary license we grant to art.

A New Furor and a New Initiative

Cancellation of the Mapplethorpe show last month — coming after recent incidents involving artists criticized by elected officials and citizens' groups for works in which a flag was provocatively spread on a floor and a crucifix was submerged in urine — has not only created a new furor but has now prompted a specific legislative initiative that would make the National Endowment for the Arts more accountable for the nature of what it finances.

Recently, Representative Sidney R. Yates, the Illinois Democrat who heads the House subcommittee that authorizes the annual budget for the arts endowment, has proposed that the endowment itself be in charge of all of its grants, with subcontracting organizations no longer allowed to make grants in their own right. But Representative Yates remains a firm believer that the endowment, not legislators, should be the judge of its grantees.

To some people, the Corcoran's cancellation of the show was censorship, despite the protestations of Dr. Christina Orr-Cahall, the museum's director. "After all," she said in an interview last week, "the institution has a right to make a choice, too, right up until the exhibition goes on the wall. Canceling it is certainly preferable to the censorship of taking things out."

In the Corcoran case, the public was prevented from seeing a scheduled exhibition because the museum anticipated that certain Congressmen would judge its content as unsuitable and, in Dr. Orr-Cahall's opinion, penalize the National Endowment.

"The very notion that Government pressure has resulted in the inability of people to see an art exhibition is distressing and threatening," said Floyd Abrams, a lawyer specializing in First Amendment cases....

"A Dangerous Precedent"

In the opinion of Dr. Jacob Neusner, University Professor at Brown University and a Reagan-appointed member of the National Council on the Arts — an advisory body to the endowment — the Corcoran's decision "set a dangerous precedent in cancelling an artist's show because it was controversial."

"It was pusillanimous and dishonest in the extreme," Dr. Neusner continued. "There was absolutely no pressure on them from the endowment, and to say they were defending us is ridiculous. It is our job to take the heat, and our process knows how to deal with controversy. But they betrayed the process by acting as censors. In doing so, they raised the stakes. Had they not, the whole thing would've gone away. A Congressman or two might have visited the show and complained, and that would have been the end of it. Now it will never go away."

The decision to cancel, Dr. Orr-Cahall said, occurred against a background of Congressional dismay over National Endowment financing for an earlier exhibition in North Carolina. The show included a photograph by Andres Serrano, an artist, of a plastic crucifix submerged in his urine. The decision to cancel was also influenced by newspaper stories reporting that the endowment planned to review its grant processes, presumably because of the Serrano and Mapplethorpe issues.

"We were just in the wrong place at the wrong time," Dr. Orr-Cahall said. The Mapplethorpe show "was scheduled for July 1, to run during a month when the endowment's budget would be under consideration at various levels of Congress. We had the institutional responsibility to decide if this was the right environment in which to present the show.

"There would have been a lot of folderol about it, with attention directed away from substantive issues, such as the effort in Congress to emasculate the endowment. It would be a three-ring circus in which Mapplethorpe's work would never be looked at in its own right. We knew that certain Congressmen were just waiting for us to open the show, and we felt we shouldn't bow to that pressure. It was a no-win situation. We decided we wouldn't be anyone's political platform...."

"We never questioned the importance of the show," Dr. Orr-Cahall said. "Our decision wasn't about the esthetics of the work, but about the circumstances in which it was to be shown. It was a matter of time and place." She also confirmed reports that the Corcoran's lawyers had raised the issue of child pornography in connection with the show, pointing out that some of the images might be in violation of local laws. "But we certainly didn't use that as an excuse not to mount it," she said.

In the wake of the Corcoran's decision, the Washington Project for the Arts, an artists' group that also receives Federal financing, has undertaken to bring the Mapplethorpe show to Washington from July 21 through Aug. 13.

On Reflection After the Vote

But although a majority of the Corcoran's board voted to support the decision, there was a feeling among some board members that it was wrong for the museum to disavow the artistic judgment it exercised — under a previous director, to be sure — in committing itself to the show in the first place, that it would have been more exemplary to go ahead with it and let the chips fall where they may.

"I'm disappointed that external pressures, political or otherwise, have caused the Corcoran to second-guess its artistic judgment and in the process relinquish our responsibility to be, as is carved in stone over the entrance, 'Dedicated to Art,'" said Robert Lehrman, a Corcoran board member who has also served on the board of the Washington Project for the Arts.

"I'm deeply concerned," he said, "that this signals a willingness to be bullied and pressured by outside factions whose interests are not those of the Corcoran."

According to Tom Armstrong, director of the Whitney Museum of American Art, "When an art museum reverses a decision based on professional judgment because of outside pressure, the integrity of the museum is severely impaired." The Whitney mounted a separate Mapplethorpe exhibition of photographs last summer. However, it contained fewer of the most provocative Mapplethorpe images than the show scheduled for the Corcoran.

Except for a few letters, no public or legislative protest attended the Mapplethorpe show at two prior stops on its scheduled six-museum tour, the Institute of Contemporary Art in Philadelphia and the Museum of Contemporary Art in Chicago. Both institutions receive financing from their state arts councils. The Mapplethorpe show organized by the Whitney came and went also without incident.

Homosexuality is a subject that has deep emotional resonance for many people. For some, the show was certainly distasteful. The fact that it was photography rather than painting, with identifiable subjects, made the erotic confrontations more uncomfortable. Yet would anyone argue that the hideous, even depraved imagery of Goya's "black" paintings — the most famous of which shows an act of cannibalism — not be exhibited in a museum? Or that the public should be "saved" from viewing Picasso's late paintings and etchings with their graphic, highly charged erotic themes (heterosexual, to be sure)?

Whatever one thinks of Mapplethorpe as an artist — and there are critics on both sides — his images are intended as art, presented as such and are judged to be art by those qualified in such matters. They have been chosen for exhibition by well-established art institutions....

The Public Role and Tax Dollars

To pre-empt the public's chance to make its own judgments — ironically the very public whose tax dollars helped finance the show is, in the opinion of Jock Reynolds, an artist and director of the Washington Project for the Arts, "an insult to that public's intelligence."

If the Corcoran acted in bad faith toward the public, it did so toward the artist as well, according to Mr. Reynolds. "The Corcoran made a commitment to Mapplethorpe," Mr. Reynolds said. "When an institution says it wants to work with an artist, it creates a bond both with the artist and with the larger artists' community. By breaking the bond in the Mapplethorpe case they broke their commitment to the artistic community as a whole. Their action would give other artists real pause as to how they might deal with other kinds of work."

At the height of the controversy last month, J. Carter Brown, director of the National Gallery of Art in Washington, was asked at a National Press Club luncheon to comment on the question of artistic expression versus community standards raised by the Mapplethorpe matter.

"There's a principle involved here, which is at the heart of what it means to be an American, and that is freedom," Mr. Brown said. "All of us in this country emigrated here, and a great number for a reason, which was to achieve the kind of freedom denied under other systems. And as we watch the other systems and historically look at them in the degenerate art show that Hitler had, or what the Soviets did to suppress their artists, and what is happening in capitals in the Far East, we have to recognize how fragile our freedoms are and how important it is to defend the process and to keep a sense of our First Amendment."

Although some Congressmen have argued that taxpayers' money should not be used to support exhibitions containing material that many might find offensive, what some consider offensive is not regarded as such by all. Taxpayers include arts professionals and many others who would favor the freedom of cultural expression that would allow a Mapplethorpe show.

The money given to the arts by the Federal Government through the endowment — about $170 million in 1988 and not substantially increased for many years — is certainly a token sum compared with government arts expenditures in other countries and, say, the vastness of Federal subsidies to such applicants as, for example, the savings and loan industry.

Yet it is highly important money, not merely because it confers prestige but because it provides support for unpopular or controversial projects that other fiscal sources shun. Most of the grants given by the endowment, except for

62

individual fellowships, have to be matched locally, and thus such projects have the additional weight of community support.

The review processes of the endowment are carried out by professional peer panels in which esthetic judgements are made by those with expertise in their fields. They may not be perfect. The essential question raised by the Mapplethorpe and Serrano disputes, however, is whether that approach will endure and whether the endowment, which in its nearly 25 years of existence has remained remarkably free from political interference, will continue to be so.

■ National Association of Artists' Organizations (NAAO), statement regarding censorship, July 16, 1989

NAAO is the major professional association for alternative, artist-run organizations.

We believe in the inalienable right of artists to freedom of expression. The freedom to create art is a form of free speech protected by the First Amendment. Artists must be accorded this freedom without threat of censorship. Those who receive public funds deserve the freedom to create and support art regardless of its possible interpretation by some as disagreeable or offensive. The American public has the right of access to these creations. American tax dollars must support the constitutional right to free speech.

■ Helen Frankenthaler, Did We Spawn an Arts Monster?, *New York Times,* July 17, 1989

Helen Frankenthaler is an artist and a member of the NEA's National Council on the Arts.

When I was appointed to the advisory council of the National Endowment for the Arts, I understood that the council received its charter from the Federal government. It functions as an autonomous body devoted to the pursuit and support of quality in the art and culture of America — past, present, future.

Now, two incendiary issues (involving the exhibition of photographs by Andres Serrano and Robert Mapplethorpe) have brought an avalanche of reaction, including a punitive reduction in the Endowment's budget.

I, for one, would not want to support the two artists mentioned, but once supported, we must allow them to be shown. With all the fuss, I think a number of crucial points have to be made.

Granted, we are "fed" by Government permit and budgets, but censorship and Government interference in the directions and standards of art are dangerous and not part of the democratic process. A country depends on its culture and cultural freedom; it is lost without it.

If that healthy atmosphere is censored or dictated, the life of every citizen is at stake. Witness throughout history the results in Germany, the Soviet Union, China, etc. We must not smother the expression of art anymore than we should suppress or annihilate protests and parades, all part of our unique and precious democracy.

These facts are what continue to make our country as great as it is. It's our insurance — fragile, to be cherished. We must be proud of it and defend it.

But there are other issues in these particular cases. It is heartbreaking both, as an artist *and* as a taxpayer(!), for me to make these remarks, and as a painter on the council I find myself in a bind: Congress in a censoring uproar on one hand and, alas, a mediocre art enterprise on the other! Sad, indeed.

By "mediocre art enterprise" I mean: Has the council run its course in terms of doing a necessary quality job? Should it change its course from within? Is it possible? I myself find the council — the recommendations of the panels and the grants given — of increasingly dubious quality. Is the council, once a helping hand, now beginning to spawn an art monster? Do we lose art along the way, in the guise of endorsing experimentation?

I think the council is in trouble, in my eyes as well as in the eyes of much of the public. But this should be handled as an in-house — small "h" — matter.

As conceived, the peer panel system is ideal, but frequently it no longer functions for the council board in its job of "quality sifting." Despite the deserved grants, I see more and more non-deserving recipients. I feel there was a time when I experienced loftier minds, relatively unloaded with politics, fashion and chic. They encouraged the endurance of a great tradition and protected important development in the arts. I recall spirited, productive discussions and arguments.

Naturally, it is assumed that many of us often feel aghast at some of the awards, but I feel that way more and more, and I am not alone. Have we "had it" — like many now defunct, once productive, agencies?

I hope not. There are too many benefits to individuals and institutions and to the cultural life of the entire nation. Realizing that we are a Government agency, can we now get at our problems and make quality changes? Can we?

Last week, the Endowment received, as one Congressman called it, a "slap on the wrist" from the House Appropriations Committee. In terms of money, it is a small amount, but it's a foreboding gesture. Quality control is the issue: raise the level. We need more connoisseurs of culture.

■ Richard Goldstein, The Critic and the Commissar: Hilton Kramer's New Criterion, *Village Voice,* July 18, 1989

Richard Goldstein is a regular contributor to the **Village Voice.**

C ensorship is a game of contradiction. Its "unintended consequences" — to use a phrase neocons adore — are always worse than the intended ones. And in the end, the censor is transformed into the creature he or she abhors.

Hilton Kramer's remarks on the Robert Mapplethorpe controversy in the July 2 *New York Times* fit this scenario to a T. They begin —as pleas for censorship often do — with a brave defense of cherished values, and end in a demand for sweeping regulations to impose those values by decree.

For that bastion of croissant-journalism, the Sunday Arts & Leisure section, to publish Kramer on the controversy swirling around Mapplethorpe and the National Endowment for the Arts was a bit like asking Lyndon LaRouche to cover Queen Elizabeth's jubilee, so the *Times* countered a week later with an urgent rebuttal by Grace Glueck. But it was Kramer's diatribe that shook the art world, which, after years of fending off the fiscal long knives of the Reaganites, finds itself Bushwacked by the current hysteria over cross and flag.

Kramer has much to gain from this national moral panic. As a voluble cultural conservative and the editor of *The New Criterion*, a journal funded by prominent right-wing foundations, he has been at the forefront of demands to change the liberal ideology of arts funding. The current assault on the NEA gives Kramer a new opening to attack the decentralized structure of that agency and many of the institutions it supports. In the past, Kramer has argued that this system favors the enemies of democracy — by which he means the Left. How much more resonant these days to rail against subsidized indecency.

"Should public standards of decency and civility be observed in determining which works of art or art events are to be selected for the Government's support?" Kramer asks, then answers this rhetorical question with a resounding "aye." In much the manner of Tipper Gore, he warns: "If the arts community is not prepared to correct the outrages committed in its name, there will be no shortage of other elements in our society ready and eager to impose drastic remedies." As in Tipper's attack on offensive lyrics and music videos, the real target here is the "industry" that allows such outrages to occur. "This is a problem," Kramer fumes, "that the art world has brought upon itself."

As it turns out, the by-now notorious exhibition of Mapplethorpe's photographs, canceled by the Corcoran Gallery of Art in Washington, D.C., will soon open at the aptly named WPA (Washington Project for the Arts). But the Mapplethorpe furor has led to proposed legislation that would require the NEA to oversee individual grants by any arts institution that is federally funded. This demand for an oversight process — which could dramatically tighten the reins on arts funding — did not begin with the Mapplethorpe show, but with works by an artist named Andres Serrano, whose photograph of a crucifix soaked in urine raised the wrath of fundamentalists and their factota in Congress. But Mapplethorpe's art is better suited to the terms of Kramer's argument. The neocon sensibility (with its roots in minority faiths) still has a modicum of respect for the separation of church and state, and it must occur to some of the *Commentary/New Criterion* crowd that any religious test for government subsidy of the arts means stepping ever so gingerly on the Ayatollah's magic carpet. But no such compunctions exist for these folks where sex is concerned — especially homosex.

"I cannot bring myself to describe these pictures in all their gruesome particularity," Kramer writes, "and it is doubtful that this newspaper would agree to publish such a description even if I could bring myself to write one." With these words, Kramer springs perhaps the most dangerous trap he will encounter on the tortuous route from distinguished critic to demagogic censor. Raising what he calls an "interesting and not irrelevant question," he asks: "Should public funds be used to exhibit pictures which the press even in our liberated era still finds too explicit or repulsive to publish?" Never mind the injury such a standard would inflict on the freedom we grant artists to transgress upon the boundaries of mass media, or the distinction it obliterates between what people expect to find in a gallery and a newspaper. Kramer's criterion for acceptable art would exclude a considerable body of words and images — from many centuries — that could not appear in a newspaper that advertises its adherence to what is "fit to print."

Kramer cannot really believe that the Brooklyn Museum should be deprived of public funds because it chose last year to exhibit two erotic paintings by Gustave Courbet. These paintings could not be published in the *Times*. But, though some feminists objected to this show on many of the same grounds that Kramer applies to Mapplethorpe, the powers that be were unmoved. This suggests that it is not the explicitness of Mapplethorpe's imagery that has stirred up such a storm, but its context — specifically its homoerotic context. To a heterosexual male eye, Courbet's closeup of a hairy and voluptuous vagina may not seem offensive, but that same viewer might turn cartwheels when confronted by Mapplethorpe's image of a black man's penis jutting from the fly of a business suit. "In these photographs, men are rendered as nothing but sexual — which is to say, homosexual," Kramer snips. It is not a point he has ever made about the women in Courbet, perhaps because it is conventional in Western art for women to be rendered as nothing but sexual.

The past decade has seen a profusion of dissident erotic art by women and gays — some of it publicly funded, to the consternation of social conservatives. This tolerance is a fragile flower; to Kramer, no doubt, a *fleur du mal*. But he denies that his objections to Mapplethorpe are based on the artist's sexuality. "I do not mean homosexuality as such," Kramer insists, only the "attempt to force... acceptance of the values of a sexual subculture that the public at large finds loathsome." He is referring to the sadomasochistic content of some of Mapplethorpe's work — an undercurrent that is complex, compelling, and disturbing. Kramer calls this work "pernicious," but surely some feminists would apply the same term to Courbet's art, and regard his rendering of the female body as emblems of dominance and submission. Though these two artists can hardly be said to share a common sensibility, both struggled to decode the signs of sexuality around them; both sought to redefine the human ideal in terms all-too-beholden to the actual texture of desire. Sexism does not originate in art, and neither does the allure of s&m. Yet Kramer would blame the artist for meeting Ezra Pound's criterion: being "the antennae of the race."

One would think the entire argument over Mapplethorpe could be resolved in a single question: Are these images art? "Alas, I suppose they are," Kramer writes, but that does not prevent him from labeling them pornography. So much for the time-honored distinction between the two. So much for the capacities of the adult ego to distinguish between image and reality, or the much-vaunted power of art to transform even the basest human experience. For Kramer, "images of this sort, which are designed to aggrandize and abet erotic rituals involving coercion, degradation, bloodshed and the infliction of pain, cannot be regarded as anything but a violation of public decency." This is a standard Women Against Pornography would welcome, but one not even the current Supreme Court is willing to apply.

We may never agree on what constitutes pernicious art, though we might agree that it exists. (For instance, the ranks of anti-Semitic poets include T.S. Eliot, founder of *The Criterion*, the magazine for which Kramer's journal is named.) Such questions are properly reserved for the debate that surrounds controversial culture. Hold seminars about the Mapplethorpe show; boycott it, if you wish; restrict it to adults (or Democrats), if you must. But when you force the NEA to examine every grant it issues according to the ever-wavering standards of political probity, you open the door to suppression of all art that does not bolster the consensus — and not just about sex.

This is Hilton Kramer's real project; an artist's fascination with sadomasochism is, for him, the tip of a large and very chilling iceberg. For years, he has been hectoring the NEA over its funding of artists — and even other critics — whose politics he regards as onerous. Writing in *The New Criterion* about NEA subsidies of art critics in 1983, Kramer rued the fact that "a great many [grants] went as a matter of course to people who were publicly opposed to just about every policy of the United States government except the one that put money in their own pockets." For Kramer, the very fact that power at this agency is shared by political appointees, peer panels, and a staff of arts professionals is an abdication of the government's duty to shape American culture. Perhaps the proudest achievement of arts funding in this nation (and this state) has been its relative insulation from the political process, despite an occasional tantrum from the vox populi.

Kramer and his publisher, Samuel Lipman (himself a dark-horse candidate for NEA chairman), have been waging an aggressive campaign against this hands-off policy. "Acting on our behalf as citizens," Lipman recently wrote in a *Times* jeremiad of his own, "our government agencies — particularly the NEA — can redirect their energies away from being the validators of the latest fancies to hit the art market. Instead, public art support might more fully concentrate on... the championing of great art of the past... This would mean saying yes to civilization." It would also mean leeching minority artists, as well as dissidents and deviants, from the ranks of the funded. The result would be as grand and bland as any Official Culture.

Why pick on this tiny agency? Because, over the past 20 years, the NEA has grown into a significant force in cultural production. Empowered by liberal Republicans during the Nixon years, the agency withstood the Reagan revolution and actually grew in influence. Through its suasion over corporate funders and its system of direct and indirect grants to artists, institutions, and state arts councils, the NEA today is at the center of an elaborate funding network. Most arts organizations that achieve nonprofit status are tied into this conduit; indeed, most artists of merit who cannot attract a mass audience will sooner or later be touched by its largesse.

So when Kramer ponders whether "public standards of decency and civility" ought to govern arts funding, he's not just talking about a singular honor reserved for the best and brightest. He's talking about the entire fabric of the fine arts in America. He's talking about a mechanism of control over playwrights and performance artists, composers and choreographers, producers and programmers (at public broadcasting stations). He's talking about setting a new criterion that could change the face of culture in our time.

"To subordinate art to politics — even... *our* politics — is not only to diminish its power to shape our civilization at its highest level of aspiration, but to condemn it to a role that amounts to little more than social engineering." So wrote Hilton Kramer in *The New Criterion* in 1983. Today, this champion of modernism is the purveyor of a policy that would rigidify and revise American art along precisely political lines. Such is the unintended consequence of censorship, and such is its capacity to turn an intellectual into the thing he most despises. Kramer the critic has become a commissar.

■ Michael Brenson, The Many Roles of Mapplethorpe, Acted Out in Ever-Shifting Images, *New York Times,* July 22, 1989

Michael Brenson is an art critic and historian.

The first photograph in "Robert Mapplethorpe: The Perfect Moment" (yes, *that* Mapplethorpe retrospective), which opens tonight at the Washington Project for the Arts, is a 1988 self-portrait. Floating like an apparition in the darkness at the upper right is the pale face of the artist, who had been ill for some time; he died of AIDS in March at the age of 42. His lips are pursed, his eyes fixed. His drawn face has begun to wither.

At the lower left, the artist's fist is wrapped around a cane with a skull knob. The fist, too, floats; because it is more sharply focused than the head, it pushes toward us. The cane and skull are phallic; a fist served as a sexual organ in one of Mapplethorpe's most notorious images. So if this self-portrait is vulnerable and timid, it is also defiantly unrepentant. The last laugh may appear to be on him, but if you look long enough the face begins to smile.

Much of this difficult, uneven and important artist is in this work. While deadly serious, Mapplethorpe often had a twinkle in his eye. His photography is not so much shameless as beyond shame. Formally and psychologically, he was fascinated by the relationship between light and dark, black and white. Like Andy Warhol, whom he admired, he was raised a Roman Catholic and he continued to depend upon Catholic iconography and ritual: in this self-portrait, he presents himself as bishop or priest.

Mapplethorpe had the imagination to find the edge between lucidity and pathology, seductiveness and cruelty, submission and domination. And he had the gift to make photographs in which the expression and even the condition of a face seem to be in the process of change. One of Mapplethorpe's most remarkable works is a 1980 self-portrait with naked torso and made-up face in which there is a sense of actually watching a woman trying to get out of a man's body.

This exhibition should be seen. It is extremely unfortunate that the Corcoran Gallery of Art canceled it last month in the hope of averting a political outcry. It is a blessing for Washington, a city still struggling to remove the stigma of provincialism, that the Washington Project for the Arts — a contemporary arts organization founded in 1975 and partly run by artists — jumped in.

The storm over the exhibition involved the $30,000 that the National Endowment for the Arts gave the Institute of Contemporary Art in Philadelphia, the organizing institution. The question for some politicians was whether an artist who produced X-rated work that seemed to spit in the face of middle-class mores and values should receive Government funds. The endowment should be applauded for contributing to this show.

As much as he has been made out to be a renegade and outlaw, Mapplethorpe is an utterly mainstream artist. He loved freshness and glamour and was obsessed with the moment, which his photographs always reflect. In his restricted spaces and his feeling for abstraction and attentiveness to every shape, edge and texture, Mapplethorpe is a child of the Formalism of the 1960's. In his commitment to images that could deal directly with his life, he shared the hunger for subject matter and narrative that helped shape the art of the 1970's. In his insistence upon total control, his photographs reflect the austerity of some of the most widely discussed art of the past few years.

Mapplethorpe is also part of his time in his hope — expressed in the catalogue interview with Janet Kardon, who put the show together — that his work would "be seen more in the context of all mediums of art and not just photography." He fought all forms of isolation. He was determined to blur boundaries between genres, genders and races. The effectiveness with which he captures the sexual, racial and social instability of the 1980's is one reason his work is so valuable and threatening.

It also helps explain why we are not close to understanding him fully. Mapplethorpe was always moving in different directions. He was attracted to flowers that were both male and female. He liked to see breasts as buttocks and arms as legs. He did a book with Lisa Lyons, a bodybuilder who changed identities from picture to picture. He photographed himself as dandy, thug and diva. On the stage of his photography, he could play any role he wanted.

The power of the Mapplethorpe esthetic has a great deal to do with sex and death. Mapplethorpe was most interested in the moment just before full flowering. He wanted the human body before it bore a trace of decay. His images of figures moving toward ripeness are a rejection of death, of which there is no sign.

But to capture that moment, Mapplethorpe had to freeze it. Everything, down to the tiniest detail, is controlled. Nothing is left to chance. Mastery is total. Figures and flowers turn into statues in a space without air. They are, in a sense, dead. Mapplethorpe's art is at the same time a bitter struggle against death and a wholehearted embrace of it.

The exhibition includes more than 150 works spanning 20 years, from the early appropriation of religious and pornographic images; to the recurring photographs of the singer Patti Smith; to the self-portraits and portraits of celebrities; to the tiresome flowers and seminal nudes for which Mapplethorpe may be best known.

The exhibition ends with the "X, Y and Z Portfolios." The 1978 "X Portfolio" documents a lust for domination and submission that ends in sexual humiliation and mutilation. Even in the most objectionable image, Mapplethorpe sees clearly, suggesting that the fear of sexual amputation and the need for sexual power go hand in hand. There is nothing else in the show even remotely as extreme as the images here.

The 1978 "Y Portfolio" is only flowers, tenuous and sexual. In the 1981 "Z Portfolio," Mapplethorpe places on a pedestal the sexuality of black men. Each of the three portfolios has 13 photographs that measure a little more than a foot square. The portfolios were meant to be seen together.

They were not included in the Mapplethorpe retrospective last year at the Whitney Museum of American Art in New York City. They need to be here. Mapplethorpe fought against sexual secrets. He saw sexuality as the root of everything, and seems, at least at one point, to have held the widespread assumption that it is only by realizing all sexual fantasies and liberating all sexual energy that full freedom and ecstasy are possible. In the "X Portfolio" the obsession with sexuality and death is pushed almost to the end.

Mapplethorpe is not a marginal figure. On television, desire is turned loose in a hundred different directions and there is hardly a product that is not sold by arousing a wish for sexual possession and power. American culture swings back and forth between domination and submission — rushing to put people on pedestals and then rushing just as hard to prove they are indeed no different and perhaps worse than you and I. Mapplethorpe found an edge that cuts deep, and it is not going to be blunted for a while.

■American Family Association, press release on the NEA, July 25, 1989

Under its director, Rev. Donald Wildmon, the American Family Association — a Christian organization — helped lead the campaign against the NEA.

In the past few weeks Americans have discovered that their tax dollars are being used to sponsor photographic exhibits that are extremely offensive, demeaning and pornographic. First we discovered that our tax dollars went to support Andres Serrano, who was given a $15,000 prize for photographing a crucifix of Christ submerged in a vase filled with Serrano's urine and named "Piss Christ."

Now we learn that the homosexual photographs of Robert Mapplethorpe have been funded at taxpayers expense through the National Endowment for the Arts, an agency of the federal government. One of Mapplethorpe's government funded photos, entitled "Honey," is that of a little girl about four years old. She has a sad face and looks scared, but the focus of the camera is on the child's genitals below her uplifted dress. The government helped fund the violation of this innocent little girl and the exposing of her private area to the public.

The exhibit of photos by Mapplethorpe, a homosexual who died of AIDS earlier this year, contains homoerotic photos that are nothing less than taxpayer funded homosexual pornography. Mr. Mapplethorpe's taxpayer funded work includes a photograph of a man crouched over, his penis on a block, named "Mr. 10½." For pedophile homosexuals, there a shot of a nude little boy, about eight, proudly displaying his penis.

Another of Mapplethorpe's tax funded photographs is that of a man dressed in a three piece suit entitled "Man in Polyester Suit." The photograph focuses on the exposed sexual organ of the man. Still another of Mapplethorpe's tax funded photographs is that of a man standing nude with an erection.

The response by the National Endowment for the Arts to the public outcry against these "works of art" has been that "artists" such as Mapplethorpe and Serrano are an elite group of people, superior in talent to the working masses, who deserve to be supported by the NEA with $171 million tax dollars imposed on the working people of America.

The American taxpayer is being *forced* to help fund such pornography through the NEA. Carpenters are artists also, but the government doesn't give them $171 million to support their art. Truck drivers, factory workers, carpenters, and sales clerks are all artists, but the government doesn't force taxpayers to give them $171 million a year to support their art.

The NEA does not consider the carpenter, truck driver, factory worker, or sales clerk equal to those artists who take a photograph of Christ submerged in urine and call it "Piss Christ," or who take a photograph of an innocent little girl's vagina and name it "Honey," or of a man's penis and name it "Mr. 10½."

The NEA feels that their artists are an elite group who should not have to put their art to the test every other American must face in a capitalistic society.

The NEA has even placed this elite group above accountability. Hugh Southern, acting chairman of NEA, said that "In order to assure that the government neither promotes nor suppresses particular points of view, the Endowment and its staff are forbidden by its authorizing legislation and substantial legislative history from interfering with the content of the work it supports." The NEA receives $171 million in tax money and tells Congress and the taxpayers to get lost.

We ask that the Senate stop all funding to the National Endowment for the Arts, or provide equal funding for all other groups of artists — carpenters, brick masons, truck drivers, sales clerks, etc. It is inconceivable that a Senator would vote to give $171 million for projects such as those of Serrano or Mapplethorpe. AFA is trying to secure enough copies of the book depicting Mapplethorpe's "art" to provide every Senator a copy. However, because of pressure from the NEA, we have been unable to secure even a single copy of the book. The single copy we have came from a third party.

We ask that other Americans, working artists who are not supported by tax dollars, join us in contacting their Senators and ask that the government end their $171 million support for pornography and anti-Christian bigotry. We hope that taxpaying voters will hold accountable Senators who vote to fund such "art." Let the NEA and the artists they support meet the same test as other artists in our society — the demand of the marketplace. The NEA will still receive their millions from private grants, and if the "works of art" have merit they will succeed in the marketplace.

Artists such as Serrano and Mapplethorpe will still be free to produce their "art," but not with the tax dollars of truck drivers, brick masons, carpenters, and factory workers who must compete in the marketplace.

The First Amendment guarantees freedom of speech, not funding for speech. The American taxpayer should no longer be forced to support artists such as Mapplethorpe and Serrano.

■ Debate in Senate over Helms amendment, including
statements by Senators Jesse Helms, Howard
Metzenbaum, John Chafee, Dan Coates, Edward
Kennedy, Timothy Wirth, James Jeffords, Claiborn Pell,
Daniel Patrick Moynihan, John Heinz, and text of Helms
amendment, July 26, 1989 (excerpts)

Jesse Helms is a Republican senator representing the state of North Caro-
lina; Howard Metzenbaum is a Democratic senator representing the state of
Ohio; John Chafee is a Republican senator representing the state of Rhode
Island; Dan Coates is a Republican senator representing the state of Indi-
ana; Edward Kennedy is a Democratic senator representing the state of
Massachusettes; Timothy Wirth is a Democratic senator representing the
state of Colorado; James Jeffords is a Republican senator representing the
state of Vermont; Claiborn Pell is a Democratic senator representing the
state of Rhode Island; Daniel Patrick Moynihan is a Democratic senator
representing the state of New York; John Heinz is a Republican senator rep-
resenting the state of Pennsylvania.

A MENDMENT NO. 420

(Purpose: To prohibit the use of appropriated funds for the dissemination,
promotion, or production of obscene or indecent materials or materials denigrating a particular religion)

MR. HELMS. Mr. President, I send an amendment to the desk and ask for
its immediate consideration.

The PRESIDING OFFICER. The clerk will report.

The legislative clerk read as follows:

The Senator from North Carolina [Mr. Helms] proposes an amendment
numbered 420.

Mr. HELMS. Mr. President, I ask unanimous consent that reading of the
amendment be dispensed with.

The PRESIDING OFFICER. Without objection, it is so ordered.

The amendment is as follows:

On page 94, line 16, strike the period and insert the following: ", provided
that this section will become effective one day after the date of enactment.

Sec. limitations.

None of the funds authorized to be appropriated pursuant to this Act may
be used to promote, disseminate, or produce —

(1) obscene or indecent materials, including but not limited to depictions of
    sadomasochism, homo-eroticism, the exploitation of children, or individ-
    uals engaged in sex acts; or

73

(2) material which denigrates the objects or beliefs of the adherents of a particular religion or non-religion; or

(3) material which denigrates, debases, or reviles a person, group or class of citizens on the basis of race, creed, sex, handicap, age, or national origin.

Mr. HELMS. Mr. President, this amendment has been agreed to on both sides, I believe. I very much appreciate it.

Mr. President, I believe we are all aware of the controversy surrounding the use of Federal funds, via the National Endowment for the Arts [NEA], to support so-called works of art by Andres Serrano and Robert Mapplethorpe. My amendment would prevent the NEA from funding such immoral trash in the future. Specifically, my amendment prohibits the use of the NEA's funds to support obscene or indecent materials, or materials which denigrate the objects or beliefs of a particular religion.

I applaud the efforts of my distinguished colleagues from West Virginia, Mr. BYRD, and from Idaho, Mr. McCLURE, to address this issue in both the Appropriations Subcommittee on the Interior, and the full Appropriations Committee. Cutting off funding to the Southeastern Center for Contemporary Art [SECCA] in Winston-Salem and the Institute for Contemporary Art in Philadelphia will certainly prevent them from misusing Federal funds for the next 5 years. However, as much as I agree with the measures, the committee's efforts do not go far enough because they will not prevent such blasphemous or immoral behavior by other institutions or artists with Government funds. That is why I have offered my amendment.

Frankly, Mr. President, I have fundamental questions about why the Federal Government is involved in supporting artists the taxpayers have refused to support in the marketplace. My concern in this regard is heightened when I hear the arts community and the media saying that any restriction at all on Federal funding would amount to censorship. What they seem to be saying is that we in Congress must choose between: First, absolutely no Federal presence in the arts; or second, granting artists the absolute freedom to use tax dollars as they wish, regardless of how vulgar, blasphemous, or despicable their works may be.

If we indeed must make this choice, then the Federal Government should get out of the arts. However, I do not believe we are limited to those two choices and my amendment attempts to make a compromise between them. It simply provides for some common sense restrictions on what is and is not an appropriate use of Federal funding for the arts. It does not prevent the production or creation of vulgar works, it merely prevents the use of Federal funds to support them.

Mr. President, I remind my colleagues that the distinguished Senator from New York and I called attention to Mr. Serrano's so-called work of art, which portrays Jesus Christ submerged in a bottle of the artist's urine, on May 18. We pointed out that the National Endowment for the Arts had not only supported a $15,000 award honoring Mr. Serrano for it, but they also helped promote and exhibit the work as well.

Over 25 Senators — Democrats and Republicans — expressed their outrage that day by cosigning a letter to Hugh Southern, the Endowment's acting chairman, asking him to review their procedures and to determine what steps are needed to prevent such abuses from recurring in the future. Mr. Southern replied on June 6 that he too was personally offended by Mr. Serrano's so-called art, but that — as I have heard time after time on this issue — the Endowment is prevented by its authorizing language from promoting or suppressing particular points of view.

Mr. Southern's letter goes on to endorse the Endowment's panel review system as a means of ensuring competence and integrity in grant decisions, and he states that the Endowment will review their processes to be sure they are effective and maintain the highest artistic integrity and quality.

However, Mr. President, shortly after receiving Mr. Southern's response, I became aware of yet another example of the competence, integrity and quality of the Endowment's panel review system. It is a federally supported exhibit entitled: "Robert Mapplethorpe: The Perfect Moment." The Corcoran Gallery of Art had planned to open the show here in Washington on July 1, but abruptly canceled it citing the danger the exhibit poses to future Federal funding for the arts. The Washington Project for the Arts subsequently agreed to make their facilities available and opened the show last Friday, July 21.

Mr. President, the National Endowment, the Corcoran, and others in the arts community felt the Mapplethorpe exhibit endangered Federal funding for the arts because the patently offensive collection of homo-erotic pornography and sexually explicit nudes of children was put together with the help of a $30,000 grant from the Endowment. The exhibit was assembled by the University of Pennsylvania's Institute for Contemporary Art as a retrospective look at Mr. Mapplethorpe's work after his recent death from AIDS. It has already appeared in Philadelphia and Chicago with the Endowment's official endorsement.

I have a catalog of the show and Senators need to see it to believe it. However, the catalog is only a survey, not a complete inventory, of what was in the Endowment's show. If Senators are interested, I have a list and description of the photographs appearing in the show but not the catalog because even the catalog's publishers knew they were too vulgar to be included — as sick as that book is.

Vanity Fair magazine ran an article on another collection of Mapplethorpe's works which appears at the Whitney Museum of Modern Art in New York. This collection included many of the photographs currently in the NEA funded exhibit. There are unspeakable portrayals which I cannot described on the floor of the Senate.

Mr. President, this pornography is sick. But Mapplethorpe's sick art does not seem to be an isolated incident. Yet another artist exhibited some of this sickening obscenity in my own State. The Duke Museum of Art at Duke University had a show deceptively titled "Morality Tales: History Painting in the 1980's." One painting, entitled "First Sex," depicts a nude woman on her back, legs open, knees up, and a little boy leaning against her leg looking into her face while two sexually aroused older boys wait in the background. Another work shows a man urinating on a boy lying in a gutter. Other, more despicable, works were included as well.

I could go on and on, Mr. President, about the sick art that has been displayed around the country. These shows are outrageous. And, like Serrano's blasphemy, the most outrageous thing is that some of the shows, like Mapplethorpe's are financed with our tax dollars. Again, I invite Senators to see what taxpayers got for $30,000 dollars.

Mr. President, how did the Endowment's vaunted panel review system approve a grant for this pornography? It was approved because the panel only received a description, provided by the Endowment's staff, which read as follows:

To support a mid-career summary of the work of photographer Robert Mapplethorpe. Although all aspects of the artist's work — the still-lifes, nudes, and portraits — will be included, the exhibition will focus on Mapplethorpe's unique pieces where photographic images interact with richly textured fabrics within carefully design frames.

Mr. President, what a useless and misleading description. No legitimate panel of experts would know from this description that the collection included explicit homo-erotic pornography and child obscenity. Yet none of the descriptions for other projects funded by the Endowment at the time were any better. Indeed, Mr. President, Mr. Jack Neusner — who sat on the panel approving the Mapplethorpe exhibit — was mystified as to how he had approved a show of this character. He knows now that he was misled.

Mr. President, I was hopeful Washington would be spared this exhibit when the Corcoran canceled it. I only wish the Corcoran had canceled the show out of a sense of public decency and not as part of a calculated attempt to shield themselves and the Endowment from criticism in Congress.

Some accuse us of censorship because we threaten to cut off Federal funding, yet they are the ones who refuse to share the contents of their exhibits with the taxpayers' elected representatives. For example, the Southeastern Center for Contemporary Art in Winston-Salem refused to send me copies of requested works despite their earlier promises to the contrary. If what such institutions promote and exhibit is legitimate art, then why are they afraid for the taxpayers and Congress to see what they do?

Mr. President, there is a fundamental difference between Government censorship — the preemption of publication or production — and governmental refusal to pay for such publication and production. Artists have a right, it is said, to express their feelings as they wish: only a philistine would suggest otherwise. Fair enough, but no artist has a preemptive claim on the tax dollars of the American people; time for them, as President Reagan used to say, "to go out and test the magic of the marketplace."

Congress attaches strings to Federal funds all the time. Churches must follow strict Federal guidelines in order to participate in Federal programs for the poor and needy — even when those guidelines violate their religious tenets. For example, a U.S. District Court in Alabama recently held that a practicing witch employed by the Salvation Army in a women's shelter could not be fired because the shelter was federally funded.

Mr. President, there have been instances where public outrage has forced artists to remove works from public display. For instance, shortly after Mayor

76

Harold Washington's death, a work portraying him as a transvestite was forcibly removed from a show in Chicago. Another work on display at Richmond's airport was voluntarily removed after the night crew complained about a racial epithet which had been inscribed on it. There was little real protest from the arts community in these instances.

Mr. President, at a minimum, we need to prohibit the Endowment from using Federal dollars to fund filth like Mr. Serrano's and Mr. Mapplethorpe's. If it does not violate criminal statutes and the private sector is willing to pay for it, fine! However, if Federal funds are used, then Congress needs to ensure the sensitivities of all groups — regardless of race, creed, sex, national origin, handicap, or age — are respected.

Federal funding for sadomasochism, homoeroticism, and child pornography is an insult to taxpayers. Americans for the most part are moral, decent people and they have a right not to be denigrated, offended, or mocked with their own tax dollars. My amendment would protect that right.

Mr. President, if Senators want the Federal Government funding pornography, sadomasochism, or art for pedophiles, they should vote against my amendment. However, if they think most voters and taxpayers are offended by Federal support for such art, they should vote for my amendment.

Mr. BYRD addressed the Chair.

The PRESIDING OFFICER. The Senator from West Virginia.

Mr. BYRD. Mr. President, the Senator has discussed this amendment with me. I am ready to accept it and take it to conference.

Mr. McCLURE addressed the Chair.

The PRESIDING OFFICER. The Senator from Idaho.

Mr. McCLURE. Mr. President, I think the Senator addresses the question that has caught the attention of many people. The exact formulation of the response is very difficult to debate. But we have looked at this amendment. We are willing to accept it and, as the Senator from West Virginia says, take it to the conference to see what we can work out in the conference.

Mr. HELMS. I thank the Senator. I thank both managers of the bill.

Mr. METZENBAUM addressed the Chair,

The PRESIDING OFFICER. The Senator from Ohio.

Mr. METZENBAUM. Mr. President, I rise not to oppose this amendment, and I certainly do not rise to support it, but I want to rise to indicate my concern about an amendment that in essence reads well. Nobody thinks you ought to be using funds to promote, disseminate, or produce the various items as mentioned in this amendment. But I have a concern, and I feel I should express it, about the U.S. Congress deciding what is and what is not art. In all fairness to the Senator from North Carolina, he does not do that directly in this amendment. When you read his amendment, it is very hard to say this part is objectionable or that part is objectionable. I do not rise for that purpose.

I rise to say that the Senator has a concern about whether politicians, people who run for public office, ought to be determining the basis of whether you like or do not like it — probably it is easier to dislike some of the art that has been in the public eye more recently — and whether or not we ought to be making a determination of art standards for this country.

Certainly, I wonder whether or not we ought to be doing it on the floor of the U.S. Senate on an amendment that has just come to the attention I think of probably most of us. I am not certain whether the manager of the bill knew about the amendment before. Certainly, I had not seen the amendment before. And I am not going to oppose it because it is hard to oppose an amendment of this kind. It sounds so right.

Yet, I feel there is a strong concern that I have that we are gradually encroaching more and more in the whole area of the Congress telling the art world what is art, what is not art, what funds can be used, spent for, and what they cannot be spent for. I do not think it will be adding to the fulfillment of the culture of this Nation if we do that.

It is for that reason that I rise to say a word of concern about the amendment. As previously indicated, I am not going to oppose it. But I think it is the kind of precedent that does not speak well for the Congress of the United States.

Mr. HELMS addressed the Chair.

The PRESIDING OFFICER. The Senator from North Carolina.

Mr. HELMS. Mr. President, I offer my amendment precisely because the so-called art community fails to understand — or deliberately refuses to understand — that a difference exists between an artist's right to free expression, and his right to have the Government, that is to say the taxpayers, pay him for his work.

I cannot go into detail about the crudeness and depravity of the art in question. I will not even acknowledge that it is art. I do not even acknowledge that the fellow who did it was an artist. I think he was a jerk and I said so back in May.

But in any case, I reiterate that there is a fundamental difference between government censorship, the preemption of publication or production, and government's refusal to pay for such publication and production. That is the point of my amendment.

If Senators want to talk about censorship, then we should talk about the real censorship going on in America. Every day the national media censor religious and conservative viewpoints while the avant garde in the art world mock art that is beautiful and uplifting — even as they extol so-called art which is shocking and depraved....

Mr. COATS. Mr. President, I have no interest in engaging in subtle aesthetic debate. The definition of art is an issue for the Academy, not the Legislature.

The Senate has no role as art critic. And it certainly has no role as censor.

But its primary and defining role is to determine if public funds are spent in the public interest.

I come to this debate with only one question: Do we in Congress have the right to take money from citizens, on penalty of imprisonment, and then use it to offend their most deeply held religious and moral beliefs?

There is no question that those beliefs have been purposely and maliciously assaulted. Over the last few months we have been exposed to publicly funded images that were intended to provoke outrage — erotic photography of children, pictures of one man urinating into the mouth of another, presentations of homoerotic sadomasochism.

They remind a balanced mind of nothing so much as snapshots of a tourist in hell.

Religious images have also seen desecration at the public expense — including a crucifix suspended in urine. Albert Camus once talked of people who "climb on the cross to be seen from afar, trampling on him who has hung there so long." This is the spirit that animates these unspeakable works of a deformed and calloused conscience.

The question before us is not a determination of artistic merit. It is not a debate over the imposition of State censorship. It is an argument over the use of public funds.

And here the issue is unmistakably clear. There is no possible justification, even in the most exalted dreams and pronouncements of the artistic establishment, to appropriate taxpayer's money for these ends. It is a formula for everdeepening social resentment, with large numbers of citizens viewing their own Government as an enemy of the cherished beliefs by which they order their lives. And it adds insult to their pain by forcing them to pay for it.

Mr. President, I add my enthusiastic support to Senator HELM's bill. And I can muster little patience with those who imagine that artistic freedom is identical to feeding at the public trough.

Mr. KENNEDY. Mr. President, I share the reservations expressed about this amendment, and I hope that the conferees will give careful consideration to whether the Congress should pursue this course in funding the arts.

In 1965, when the National Endowment for the Arts and Humanities was created, Congress agreed "that the encouragement and support of national progress and scholarship in the humanities and the arts, while primarily a matter of private and local initiative is also an appropriate matter of concern to the Federal Government."

We have had a quarter century to monitor the Arts and Humanities Endowments. I am pleased with the growth and development of these small but effective agencies. Many important cultural and scholarly works have been funded. Quality programming and outreach to new audiences have been a hallmark of these activities.

Much of the success of the Endowments can be attributed to the peer panel review system. When Congress instituted the Endowments, it wisely assigned the review and assessment of program grants to professionals in the arts community, who can most accurately weigh the relative merits of individual applicants.

It was a conscious effort at that time to separate the review process from political interference. Nothing has occurred in the intervening quarter century which diminishes the wisdom of that decision or that suggests a long-term benefit in undermining the peer system.

We have heard a great deal in recent months about several controversial grants awarded in the past year by the Arts Endowment. Without the peer system, there would have been persistent and chronic controversies of grant awards throughout the last 24 years.

A responsible discussion of funding for the Endowment should recognize that controversial grants are aberrations, and not commonplace occurrences, in the grant-making process.

No grant-making process is foolproof, but the peer system comes as close to that goal as possible.

The grants in question, totaling $45,000, have subsidized work that is provocative and that is distasteful and offensive to large numbers of Americans.

But it is also disturbing to me that the response of Congress threatens the peer system of review and overall funding for the already underfunded Arts Endowment.

It is foolish for Congress because of the questionable awards to jeopardize a well-respected program with a 24-year track record.

A more responsible approach would be to enact stricter accountability in the grant-making process, especially when funds are channeled through intermediary agencies. The ultimate responsibility and accountability for all grants rests with the National Council on the Arts. Congress intended that result, and steps should be taken to insure that the Council carries out its mandate as effectively and judiciously as possible. A tightening of restrictions on sub-grants would go a long way toward preventing future congressional second-guessing in situations such as the present.

A new chairman of the Arts Endowment will be coming on board in the fall and he, too, can be involved in the search for more effective ways to continue the Endowment on a long-term path of growth and excellence — which has been its path for the last 24 years under both Republican and Democratic chairman.

The Federal Government has a role and responsibility to support the arts and create an environment in our country which encourages a lively cultural community. Congress must not put itself in the position of serving as a board of censors for the arts....

Mr. WIRTH. Mr. President, I rise today to speak about funding in the fiscal 1990 Interior appropriations legislation for the National Endowment for the Arts [NEA]. Recently, the NEA has come under severe criticism for its support of programs which provided granted for exhibits of two artists noted for their controversial topics.

In reaction to their support of the work of Andres Serrano and Robert Mapplethorpe, the Senate Interior Appropriations Subcommittee chose to include language prohibiting the National Endowment for the Arts from issuing a direct grant award for 5 years to either the Southeastern Center for Contemporary Art [SECCA] in North Carolina or the Institute of Contemporary Art [ICA] at the University of Pennsylvania.

Mr. President, I believe that this provision is an overreaction and unwarranted. Both these organizations applied for and accurately completed a rigorous review process by both their peers and by members of the Presidentially appointed National Council on the Arts to receive NEA grants. The organizations, in an effort to ensure that the projects were within the scope of public taste, also raised matching dollar-for-dollar funds from individuals, State, and local art agencies, foundations, and corporations.

It is wrong to punish these individual organizations simply for their involvement in projects that created some controversy when, in fact, the organizations were in complete compliance with the established review system and the grants were approved by the National Council on the Arts. In this case, the Senate is inappropriately micromanaging by singling out SECCA and ICA.

I am also deeply concerned that this provision sets a very dangerous precedent of legislating a moral code on the value of particular works of art. This action could effectively censor all artists and museums for years to come. Museums will restrain or suppress their creativity in providing quality exhibits to the public, fearing the loss of Federal funds. This will assuredly lead to the loss of private, local funding as well. Will Congress next end Federal funding for public radio and television if a controversial story or documentary were aired? This action comes perilously close to the kind of censorship that has not been tolerated in our Nation since its inception.

The formulation of policy from heated reaction to public controversy is a sure way to make bad decisions. A 5-year prohibition of NEA grant awards to SECCA and ICA is not fair to the affected agencies and bodes ill for the continued public support of art organizations in Colorado and the rest of the Nation. I hope my colleagues carefully consider the ramifications of this action when legislation is reviewed in conference.

Mr. President, I yield the floor....

Mr. JEFFORDS. I am extremely disturbed by the restrictions placed upon arts funding by the committee. I think that in cutting off funds for two very fine institutions, the Institute of Contemporary Art in Philadelphia, and the Southeastern Center for Contemporary Art in North Carolina, we are edging dangerously close to censorship. The arguments used in defense of what amounts to punishment of these two organizations sounds dangerously close to those used by those who wish to banish certain books from our public schools. Worse yet, by cutting off future support for the organizations in question, we are censoring artists and works which we have not even seen, and which, because of this legislation, many people may not get to see.

Mr. President I do not wish to begin a debate here over the merits of the art in question. That we could have devoted more time here in the Congress to such a great debate, a very eloquent debate, I think would have been beneficial and indeed educational. I am delighted that that kind of debate is taking place in the press, in classrooms, in art galleries and on the streets. Perhaps the greater good that is to come of all this controversy is that people are taking notice of the incredible power that is inherent in art. A power, and this has been said before, that cuts to the raw nerve of the individual and the life blood of individual freedom.

Artistic expression is perhaps one of the most individual of all freedoms we have in society, and one which the National Endowment for the Arts has sought to promote, and which I hope the members of this body will agree to protect.

That this discussion has been sullied into a debate over what kind of punishment should fit a perceived crime against offended individuals is an insult to those who are involved in creative endeavors everywhere. It is ironic that after having witnessed the millions of Chinese students in Tiananmen Square, many of them the children of those who were punished severely for so-called offenses during the Chinese cultural revolution, that we are face forward on the precipice of our own dangerous cultural revolution. Censorship in the arts, as imposed by this bill, to censor those organizations in question in this legislation that we are protecting many taxpayers. Not just taxpayers who find the works in question morally offensive, but those who may have a completely different interpretation of them. Taxpayers who may actually like them. I am worried about setting this dangerous precedent, whereby only those organizations who promote works deemed acceptable on one, will find the reward of public funds awaiting them.

The arts in this country have taken a drubbing for too long. They have suffered from a lack of promotion on a large public scale. Some might even say a lack of understanding. Are we promoting better appreciation of the arts by cutting funds during a debate that attempts to make an excuse for direct censorship? We are threatening to cut off two organizations that have incredible potential to bring many kinds of art to many people. We are not surrounded, as Europeans are, by generations and generations of art that so permeates society that it almost numbs the senses. We have to create it for ourselves. What we create should be a reflection of ourselves. It will be diverse. It may at times be provocative. I hope it will always remain uncensored.

If I may quote someone who has said this better than I, J. Carter Brown, director of the National Gallery of Art:

> "There is a principle involved here, which is at the heart of what it means to be an American, and that is freedom. All of us in this country emigrated here, and a great number for a reason, which was to achieve the kind of freedom denied under other systems. And as we watch the other systems and historically look at them in the degenerate art show that Hitler had, or what the Soviets did to suppress their artists, and what is happening in capitals in the Far East, we have to recognize how fragile our freedoms are, how important it is to defend the process and to keep a sense of our First Amendment."

Mr. President, I yield the floor.

Mr. PELL. Mr. President, as one member of this body who was deeply involved in helping establish the National Endowment for the Arts 25 years ago, I want to convey to my colleagues some of my views of the current controversy regarding grant review procedures.

The National Endowment for the Arts is a remarkable agency that was set up after careful and lengthy debate as to just what role the Government can and should play in the support of culture in the United States. The landmark public law of 1965 states that:

"It is necessary and appropriate for the Federal Government to help create and sustain not only a climate encouraging freedom of thought, imagination and inquiry but also the material conditions facilitating the release of this creative talent."

The success of this unique agency has, in fact, exceeded all my expectations. The leadership of the Endowment in cultural support has helped bring arts programs into the far corners of every State in the country. It has led to the tremendous expansion in the fields of opera, dance, theater and symphony orchestras and it has helped nurture the creative talents of our writers, composers, and artists. A relatively modest investment of Federal funds has done so much to enrich the lives of the American people.

In regard to the current controversy over a few works of art, I can understand the depth of feeling of many of my colleagues. I find the works in question fully as offensive, objectionable and obscene as they do. In my mind, serious errors in judgment were made when such works were recommended for funding by their respective review panels.

But it is precisely this system of review by peer panels that has been responsible for the broad-based effectiveness of the National Endowment for the Arts over the long run. The Endowment has made over 85,000 grants to projects and individuals in the United States with an amazing degree of impartiality and good judgment. Of this number, only a handful have aroused any kind of controversy at all. The Endowment's record for fairness in funding quality and diversity is hard to equal anywhere else in the Federal Government.

When we structured the Endowment, we were careful to put the artistic decisionmaking in the hands of outside experts and away from the influence of government where it would be almost impossible to agree on standards. These peers reviewers, with very few exceptions, have served us well in making objective and balanced judgements.

No such system can be infallible, however, and for this reason, I have repeatedly sought ways to improve upon peer panel and review in my role as chairman of the Subcommittee on Education, Arts, and Humanities. To this day no one has come up with a fairer and more intelligent method of disbursing Federal funds to the arts. But I am always willing to hear any proposals. The 1990 reauthorization of the Endowment will provide a forum for further debate in this regard.

In light of the current controversy, I have asked the Acting Chairman of the Endowment to set aside time for an in-depth discussion of agency review procedures at the upcoming meeting of the National Council on the Arts. Council members are Presidentially appointed individuals who are charged with advising the Chairman as to policies, programs, and procedures. Any recommendations they may have to strengthen these procedures will be carefully considered in the reauthorization process.

I have reservations about the provision in the Senate bill that would deny Endowment funds to the Institute of Contemporary Art at the University of Pennsylvania and the Southeastern Center for Contemporary Art in North Carolina. These are fine institutions which serve as important cultural resources in their communities. I believe such action is unnecessarily punitive. It imposes the views of a branch of government on a process that was intended to be free of such involvement. My colleagues should know that this action may well have a dire chilling effect on our national cultural community and weaken the Endowment.

I fully understand the sentiment which gave rise to this provision. But to my mind, we should not take precipitous action in the heat of a controversy. Rather, we should look at this situation in the place where it belongs, namely, the reauthorization of the Arts Endowment, a process that will begin later this year.

I believe we should strike this provision, but I know where the votes are on this matter and that such an effort would not be successful. The amendment proposed by Senator HELMS troubles me as well. It moves us ever closer to government censorship which is odious to our basic American values. It also restricts the ability of the Endowment to use impartial experts to judge excellence in the arts. I have faith in the peer review system and its ability to decide what art is worthy of our Nation's support....

Mr. MOYNIHAN. Mr. President, I rise in opposition. For the first time in the near quarter-century life of the National Endowment for the Arts, we have before us an appropriations bill which prohibits the grant of funds to two named institutions. Specifically it is provided:

> "That until October 1, 1994, none of the funds provided to the National Endowment for the Arts may be used for a direct grant to the Southeastern Center of Contemporary Art (SECCA) in Winston-Salem, North Carolina or for the Institute of Contemporary Art at the University of Pennsylvania."

This prohibition arises in consequence of a grant made to one photographer, and the exhibit of the work of another photographer.

The Senate report of June 8, 1985, which accompanied the legislation establishing the foundation clearly foresaw that such efforts such as this might be made in the years to come, and just as clearly recorded the view of the Congress that they should be resisted in the most adamant and absolute degree:

> "The committee affirms that the intent of this act should be the encouragement of free inquiry and expression. The committee wishes to make clear that conformity for its own sake is not to be encouraged, and that no undue preference should be given to any particular style or school of thought or expression."

I have no wish to escalate the issues involved here. We are not dealing with censorship, per se. Nothing in the bill before us in any way inhibits the first amendment right of these artists to exhibit their work, and it would be nothing new in our experience if the present controversies brought their work to a wider audience than might otherwise be the case. For generations the fondest hope of many a writer was that his or her work might be "banned in Boston" in the expectation that sales elsewhere might thereby be considerably improved. Nor yet need we be over-apprehensive of the effect of this action on the artistic community which is not unfamiliar with controversy, nor yet especially averse to it. It is after all just half a century since the painter John Sloan wrote:

> "It would be good to have a Ministry of Fine Art. Then we would know where the enemy is."

I would accordingly suggest to the Senate that the issue is not "them" but us. Do we really want it to be recorded that the Senate of the United States, in the 101st Congress of this Republic, is so insensible to the traditions of liberty in our land, so fearful of what is different and new and intentionally disturbing, so anxious to record our timidity that we would sanction institutions for acting precisely as they are meant to act? Which is to say, art institutions supporting artists and exhibiting their work?

More. Are we so little mindful of the diversity of our Nation, and the centrality of censorship and persecution in the experience of not just a few but I would almost say every religious and ethnic inheritance in this land? I think of the hymn sung at Catholic masses when I was a child:

Faith of our fathers! living still
> In spite of dungeon, fire and sword
Oh how our hearts be high with joy,
> Whene'er we hear the glorious word.
Faith of our fathers, Holy faith!
We will be true to thee till death.

Is there a congregation in the land today that does not or could not pronounce the same sentiments with the same conviction that what once was is no more, certainly no more in these United States?

And most poignant of all, are we so insensible to the shining witness to the all-important value of freedom of expression which we see displayed in nations across Europe and Asia which so recently seemed lost in totalitarian darkness?

This too will pass. I wish to record that I am fully aware of the disinclination of the principal manager of the bill to see these provisions become law. I fully expect that good sense and good humor prevail.

Still, the event needs to be protested.

Milton's was not the first voice raised in this abiding struggle, but surely the greatest. Wordsworth invoked his name in a subsequent age.

"Milton! thou shouldst be living at this hour: England hath need of thee;" Nor is ours a land bereft of sages. Milton, yes. But Mencken more!

Mr. President, I will vote "no."

Mr. HEINZ. Mr. President, I would like to briefly share with the distinguished managers of the fiscal year 1990 Interior Appropriations Bill my strong opposition to the section of this measure — title II — relating to the specific treatment of funding for the National Endowment for the Arts [NEA].

According to language in H.R. 2788, Mr. President, two art exhibitors and NEA grantees, one located in Philadelphia, the Institute of Contemporary Art at the University of Pennsylvania, would be unable to receive direct NEA grants until late 1994. I am strongly opposed to unjustly targeting and essentially singling out these two art facilities, and urge Members during the conference committee to eliminate this provision.

Mr. President, I am extremely concerned with the dangerous precedent Congress is setting and the unfortunate message we are sending to artists, art organizations, patrons, and those with an appreciation for experiencing the variety of American and international art. With this action, we are not only in essence serving as a censor of art to be displayed throughout our Nation's public galleries, but being punitive and even downright mean.

Let's face it, this provision puts Congress on record as penalizing two non-Federal and private institutions who organized and/or supported the controversial works of photographers Robert Mapplethorpe and Andres Serrano.

To my knowledge, the University of Pennsylvania — Institute of Contemporary Art followed proper NEA procedures in securing NEA grant money. Now, the institute is being penalized for its desire to present a variety of artistic expressions to its patrons. If there is fault, it lies not with the institute, but the NEA for lax or inappropriate guidelines.

Imposing a 5-year ban on NEA grants to the Institute of Contemporary Art at the University of Pennsylvania and the Southern Center for Contemporary Art in North Carolina is both artistically and fiscally devastating to these fine institutions and their patrons. There is no obligation for Congress to use taxpayers' money to support art the public finds offensive. But let us understand that it is not the artist nor the private patron that we should call to account. To do so sets an unprecedented and chilling parameter we would be well advised to avoid.

■ Patrick Buchanan, Pursued by Baying Yahoos, *Washington Times,* August 2, 1989

Patrick Buchanan is a nationally syndicated columnist and television commentator. He was a Republican candidate for President during 1991-92.

The "Senate's most persistent yahoo," bellowed Tom Wicker; "as wily and contemptible a character as one could hope to meet," bayed Jonathan Yardley in *The Washington Post.*

What's got the boys bananas is an amendment by Sen. Jesse Helms, North Carolina Republican, to ban federal funding, through the National Endowment for the Arts, for "obscene or indecent materials, including... depictions of sadomasochism, homoeroticism, the exploitation of children, or individuals engaged in sex acts." Whistled through without dissent, the amendment will become law, if a conference committee does not peel it off the $10.9 billion Interior bill.

Propulsion for Mr. Helms' amendment comes from the now-famous photographic exhibit by the late Robert Mapplethorpe, tossed out of the Corcoran Gallery, which features a little girl with her dress up, one man about the urinate in the mouth of another, an elephantine penis hanging out of a pair of pants, and the "artist's" nude photo of himself, with a bullwhip sticking out of his rectum.

"[T]he artistry is transparent," coos Hank Burchard of *The Post.* "His eye for the human figure, male and female, is superb, but what is most compelling about his nude studies is the lack of any suggestion that the models are being manipulated."

(Query: If Mapplethorpe's photos are that good, why doesn't *The Post* publish them?)

Jeffrey Tucker of the Ludwig Von Mises Institute, however, was revolted, especially by "Tie Rack"... an icon of the Virgin Mary, desecrated and constructed to hold neckties. Mary's hands were pierced with pins and strung between them was a crucifix. Her mouth was bleeding from both sides. And her halo was changed so that it stabbed her on the side of her bleeding neck.

The photos would "be great stuff for any Bible-belt yahoo to wave in front of the folks back home," mocks Mr. Burchard. But Swift's *Gulliver's Travels*, where the squalid creatures first appear, reveals yahoos to be moral twins of the dead pervert with the bullwhip whose work so enthralled Hank Burchard.

Excuse me, but God bless Jesse Helms!

His retabling of this issue, after the House thought it sidetracked it, with a tiny nick in the NEA budget, is a deliverance.

For the Mapplethorpe exhibit, along with the NEA-underwritten "Piss Christ" (Andres Serrano's self-titled photo of a crucifix in a vat of his own urine), and the paralysis that has gripped the "arts" crowd, as decent folks demand they condemn such filth, is raising America's consciousness to the moral squalor of so much modern art, and the amorality and cowardice of art "critics" whose duty it presumably was to maintain some standards.

This episode is going to do for the "arts community" what the cave-in to the Filthy Speech Movement and student riots did for the academic community in the '60s; i.e., strip them of respect and make them objects of ridicule.

"Art is the signature of man," said G.K. Chesterton. Sculptor and art historian H. Reed Armstrong adds: "Whether it be the religious fervor of the Middle Ages, the humanism of the Renaissance, or the romanticism of the 19th century, the visual artist is the medium who most faithfully reflects the spirit of the age.

"The 'Art' of the twentieth century is a fearful indictment of our culture. It is the fruitless art of 'liberated man,' disunited from the cause of his being... the 'artist' of today 'fulfills himself' as does the cancerous cell, in total disregard of the life of the organism which feeds and nourishes it."

T.S. Eliot saw it coming. Culture, he wrote, 50 years ago, is the "incarnation... of the religion of a people."

"If Christianity goes, the whole of our culture goes. Then you must start painfully again, and you cannot put on a new culture ready made. You must wait for the grass to grow to feed the sheep to give the wool out of which your new coat will be made. You must pass through many centuries of barbarism... But we can at least try to save something of those goods of which we are the common trustees: the legacy of Greece, Rome and Israel, and the legacy of Europe throughout the last 2,000 years. In a world which has seen such material devastation as ours, these spiritual possessions are in imminent peril."

Barbarism! The precise word, as we observe journalistic yahoos hail poor, pathetic Robert Mapplethorpe for having photographed, for their amusement, the degraded acts by which he killed himself.

What's to be done?

We can defund the poisoners of culture, the polluters of art; we can sweep up the debris that passes for modern art outside so many public buildings; we can discredit self-anointed critics who have forfeited our trust. America is not yet Weimar.

"A whole paradigm shift to New Age paganism has taken over the arts," Reed Armstrong wrote me recently. "Conservatives had best become interested in art if they wish to see civilization survive into the 21st century."

This is all-important: Not simply to cut out the rot, but to seek out, to find, to celebrate the good, the true, the beautiful. But, first, tell Jesse to hold the fort; help is on the way.

■ George Will, The Helms Bludgeon, *Washington Post,* August 3, 1989

George Will is a nationally syndicated columnist.

Sen. Pat Moynihan (D-N.Y.) sent a two-sentence note attached to his statement opposing the legislation that would forbid the National Endowment for the Arts from supporting art that is "obscene or indecent" or is hostile to almost any individual or group for almost any reason. Moynihan's note said: "The '20s are coming on fast? I *knew* we would regret the end of Cold War."

Perhaps that is it. Detente has relieved us from seriousness. We have returned to "normalcy" and do not remember how to act sensibly.

The legislation moved by Sen. Jesse Helms (R-N.C.) is a foolish reaction to two photographic exhibits supported by institutions receiving NEA funds, exhibits that included photos of sadomasochistic practices and a crucifix in a jar of urine. The amendment is a recipe for timidity, paralysis and, of course, litigation. But many of the arguments — or the hysteria and arrogance serving as arguments — against the amendment are intellectually incoherent, indeed anti-intellectual.

Opponents of the amendment say government is obligated to support art and equally obligated not to think about what art is or is good for. They argue that government support for the arts serves the public interest, but that government cannot express an interest in the kind of art that is supported.

The argument for subsidizing the arts must be communitarian, not severely individualistic. It must be that it serves some social good, not just that it gives pleasure to individuals (artists, certainly, and perhaps viewers). Were that the argument, there would be as strong an argument — stronger on strictly democratic grounds — for subsidizing bowling or poker.

Artists who say art has a public purpose say that purpose can include discomforting the comfortable. Shocking the bourgeoisie is fun and, arguably, good for one and all, but it is cheeky of artists to say the bourgeoisie is obligated to subsidize the shocking. America's bourgeoisie has a remarkable record of generously subsidizing the ridiculing, despising and subversion of itself. If you doubt that, examine a public university's liberal-arts curriculum.

Another problem for the NEA is art that eschews all purpose, art that is not shocking but baffling to the common viewer. What of the post-minimalist artist who exhibited a pig in a cage? The artist who draped a curtain across the Colorado valley? The "environmental artist" whose "kinetic sculpture" was a bucket of fireworks atop the Brooklyn Bridge? The police called that a bomb.

A milestone in the liberation of art from the law was the 1928 court ruling that Brancusi's "Bird in Space" — a graceful shaft symbolizing flight, but not resembling a bird — was sculpture and therefore not subject to import duties. Customs agents would not be defining art.

But artists welcomed government into their world in the form of NEA subsidies. Subsidies require reasoning about public purposes. Yet some artists deny that art has any such purpose.

Abstract art and its degenerate progeny were once celebrated as "democratic" because purged of "academicism" and immediately "accessible" to "understanding" by everyone. But this was the egalitarianism of nihilism, art equally understood by everyone because it had no meaning. Having no content, it was immune to the charge of elitism. But the people don't like it, preferring art depicting the human condition and passions about it.

The artist Robert Rauschenberg, wanting no restrictions on his entitlements and no critical standards to inhibit his fun, says: "It is extremely important that art be unjustifiable." But government expenditures must be justified. Some years ago someone asked the NEA to support this work of art. He would dribble ink from Haley, Idaho, to Cody, Wyoming, birthplaces of Ezra Pound and Jackson Pollock respectively. The NEA refused. It must have had a reason.

If art has no improving power or purpose, it has no claim on the interest of government. So advocates of government support for the arts must say that art serves society.

There is a long American tradition of support on the grounds that the arts elevate the public mind by bringing it into contact with beauty and even ameliorate social pathologies. But if the power of art is profound, it need not be benign. And the policy of public subsidies must distinguish between art that serves an elevating purpose and that that does not.

The Helms amendment should be quietly killed. However, alarmists relishing the fun of faking great fear about the impending end of civilization say the ruckus over the amendment will have a "chilling effect" on the NEA. If that means the NEA may think more often about the public interest in the visual arts, then, good.

If, as some artists say, no one can say what art is (or, hence, what the adjective "fine" means as a modifier), then art becomes a classification that does not classify. Then the NEA should be the NEE — National Endowment for Everything. It will need a bigger budget.

■ Robert Hughes, A Loony Parody of Cultural Democracy, *Time*, August 14, 1989

Robert Hughes is the art critic for Time *magazine.*

Senator Jesse Helms, that noted paleo-conservative, has taken up the cudgels against the most distinguished and useful vehicle of patronage in American cultural life, the National Endowment for the Arts. Neoconservatives want to keep the NEA because they would like to run it. Paleos like Helms don't greatly care whether it exists or not; if attacking it can serve a larger agenda, fine.

Last year NEA money totaling $45,000 was used by the Corcoran museum for an exhibition by the photographer Robert Mapplethorpe and by an institution that gave an award to the artist Andres Serrano. One of Serrano's pieces was a photo of a plastic crucifix immersed in the artist's urine — a fairly conventional piece of postsurrealist blasphemy, which, though likely to have less effect on established religion than a horsefly on a tank, was bound to irk some people. Mapplethorpe's show was to contain some icy, polished and (to most straights and one surmises, at least a few Republican gays) deeply repulsive photos of S and M queens doing this and that to one another.

As soon as the dewlaps of Senator Helms' patriarchal wrath started shaking at its door, the Corcoran caved in and canceled Mapplethorpe's show. Unappeased, the ayatullah of North Carolina proposed a measure that would forbid the NEA to give money to "promote, disseminate or produce" anything "obscene or indecent" or derogatory of "the objects or beliefs of the adherents of a particular religion or non-religion" — which, taken literally, comprises any image or belief of any kind, religious or secular.

In effect, this would make the NEA hostage to every crank, ideologue and God botherer in America. A grant for an exhibition of Gothic ivories could be pulled on the grounds that the material was offensive to Jews (much medieval art is anti-Semitic), to Muslims (what about those scenes of false prophets in hell with Muhammad?) or, for that matter, to atheists offended by the intrusion of religious propaganda into a museum. A radical feminist could plausibly argue that her "nonreligious" beliefs were offended by the sexism of Rubens' nudes or Picasso's *Vollard Suite*. Doubtless a fire worshiper would claim that the presence of extinguishers in a theater was repugnant to his god.

In short, what the amendment proposes is a loony parody of cultural democracy in which everyone becomes his or her own Cato the Censor. Clearly, Jesse Helms has no doubt that the NEA must be punished if it strays from what he fancies to be the center line of American ethical belief. The truth is, of course, that no such line exists — not in a society as vast, various and eclectic as the real America. Helms' amendment might have played in Papua, where a Government spokesman defended the banning of Martin Scorsese's *The Last Temptation of Christ* on the grounds that "our people traditionally set much store on dreams and hallucinations." But in the U.S., no.

The problem is compounded by the fact that the NEA is not a ministry of culture. It does not commission large works to reflect glory on the state, or set firm policy for other institutions. Its $169 million budget is tiny — less than one-third the projected price of one Stealth bomber, or, to put it another way, only ten times the recent cost of a single painting by Jasper Johns. The French government spends three times the NEA's budget each year on music, theater and dance alone ($560 million in 1989). German government spending on culture runs at around $4.5 billion, repeat, billion a year.

The extreme conservative view is that support of the contemporary arts is not the business of government. Never mind that quite a few people who were not exactly radicals, from Rameses II to Louis XIV and Pope Urban VIII, thought otherwise and thus endowed the world with parts of the Egypt, the Paris and the Rome we have today. New culture is optional — slippery stuff, ambiguous in its meanings, uncertain in its returns. Away with it! Let the corporations underwrite it!

The fetish of supply-side culture was one of the worst legacies of the Reagan years. Though the Great Communicator was frustrated in his attempt to abolish the Endowment in 1981, he made sure that more Government money went to military bands than to the entire budget of the NEA. Oom-pah-pah culture to fit a time of oom-pah-pah politics. After all, who could say that the arts needed support outside the marketplace at a time when star orchestra conductors were treated like sacred elephants and the art market was turning into a freakish potlatch for new money?

Conversely, why bother to support what market Darwinism seems to condemn to obscurity? "I have fundamental questions," Helms grated, "about why the Federal Government is supporting artists the taxpayers have refused to support in the marketplace." But this was exactly what the NEA was created, in 1965, to do — and it was the wisest of decisions. Lots of admirable art does badly at first; its rewards to the patron are not immediate and may never come. Hence the need for the NEA. It is there to help the self-realization of culture that is not immediately successful.

Corporate underwriting has produced some magnificent results for American libraries, museums, ballets, theaters and orchestras — for institutional culture, across the board. But today it is shrinking badly, and it requires a delicate balance with Government funding to work well. Corporations' underwriting money comes out of their promotion budgets and — not unreasonably, since their goal is to make money — they want to be associated with popular, prestigious events. It's no trick to get Universal Widget to underwrite a Renoir show, or one of those PBS nature series (six hours of granola TV, with bugs copulating to Mozart). But try them with newer, more controversial, or more demanding work and watch the faces in the boardroom drop. Corporate is nervous money; it needs the NEA for reassurance as a Good Housekeeping Seal of Approval. Our problem, despite conservative rant, is too little Government support for the arts, not too much. Even if we had a ministry of culture to parade the roosters, we would still need the NEA to look after the eggs.

91

■ Allen Ginsberg, letter concerning NEA, August 14, 1989

Allen Ginsberg is a well-known poet, a member of the Executive Board of the American P.E.N. Center, and a distinguished professor of English at Brooklyn College.

D ear ——

Re: Sen. Jesse Helms Arts-Control Amendment to Fiscal 1990 Interior Agency Appropriation Bill:

This arts censorship rot gut originated in the beer-soaked bucks of Joseph Coors, was moonshined in Heritage Foundation think-tanks, and is peddled nationwide by notorious tobacco-cult Senator Jesse Helms.

These alcohol-nicotine kingpins have the insolence to appoint themselves arbiters of Public Morality.

Legal narcotics pushers wrapped in the flag, they threaten to give the needle to any politician opposing their takeover of culturally free turf in America.

After thirty years' broadcast liberty, my poem "Howl" was bumped off the air in public 1988 by a Heritage Foundation-Sen. Helms-FCC 24 hour-a-day ban on mystific. "Indecency."

These hypocrite scoundrels have muscled their way into museums already, and plan to extend their own control-addiction to arts councils, humanities programs, universities. How long will Congress, the Public & Arts be held hostage to this cultural Mafia?

> Allan Ginsberg, Poet
> Member, American Institute of Arts & Letters
> Executive Board, American P.E.N. Center; Member,
> Freedom to Write Committee
> Distinguished Professor of English, Brooklyn College

■ Down with the Senate Art Police!, *Revolutionary Worker,* August 14, 1989 (excerpt)

Revolutionary Worker is the newspaper of the Revolutionary Communist Party (RCP) in the United States.

I t is a heavy sign of the extremism of the times when the U.S. government decides at the national level to openly let down the banner of "pluralism" in the arts — if only for state-funded works. Even though the oppressed people know from their life experience that they do not have "freedom of expression" in this country, this is a big calling card for the U.S. internationally. So the decision to come out with open government censorship in the arts is a dangerous move by the ruling class.

The Helms amendment represents a leap in a campaign of censorship in the arts that has been developing steadily for some time now. A deadly game is being played where it is said that the clampdowns are demanded by the "outraged citizenry" and "taxpayers" who are finally putting their foot down. But what's actually behind these moves is a desperate attempt by the powers-that-be to keep their empire together in the face of a very unpredictable world situation. A culture which brings back and enforces belief in the patriarchal family, god, and country is a necessary part of their program.

In a country fattened off the backs of the oppressed people of the world, there is an audience for this reactionary agenda, and these social forces are being marshalled. But this campaign is being directed by more sinister and powerful forces — the U.S. ruling class. And this ruling class does not represent the interests of the majority of people in this country.

And to anyone who knows anything about history, this whole art censorship thing has a definite fascistic tone to it — a gestapo morality and method is being promoted by men who hold high office in this land.

Patrick Buchanan, former Reagan speechwriter, recently called works like Serrano's and Mapplethorpe's "degenerate art." This term "degenerate art" was actually the *official* term used by Nazi Germany to designate modern art and any art which did not show "genetically healthy family life and landscapes of the fatherland"! Even a journalist was prompted to ask Buchanan if he was *consciously* using those words....

The Helms amendment targets directly a very broad section of artists and intellectuals, bringing even some of the most officially respected and relatively privileged into contradiction with the powers-that-be. Even if this amendment does not make it totally intact through the Congress this fall, it is aimed at sending a chill through the entire arts arena. The government is hoping that many institutions will not want to risk Helms-style Inquisitions and possible funding cuts. As the director of a museum in Los Angeles commented: "The panels, the staff, everybody is going to be gun-shy. Even if the conference committee does the sane thing... the chill is going to continue."

The implications are far-reaching. As artist Leon Golub said to the *RW*: "By using what he thinks are the most extreme examples, by making a kind of mass movement out of it, Helms is trying to scare the artists away from taking too many chances. And the struggle over this could spill over into other areas, even education. Certainly self-censorship will happen among some artists. This is a given."

And most importantly, the new Helms code is designed to shut up progressive artists in order to outlaw art that challenges the poisonous social relations and political system — a point well appreciated by protesters who arrived at a recent anti-NEA-censorship demonstration bound and gagged in American flags....

The bourgeoisie takes very seriously the impact of art on society — the ability of art to concentrate ideas in powerful ways, provoking people into challenging the way things are or, on the other hand, freezing people in their old prejudices. Even the most "innocent cultural undertakings" are considered dangerous in these days when the needs of the system for social control dictate turning back the clock and reversing verdicts from the 1960s on every significant question from the role of women to racism to "my country right or wrong." As Joey Johnson has said, "This is a sick and dying empire, clutching at its symbols."

This cultural war is very sharp right now because it concentrates big questions that are up in society as a whole. And NOW IS NOT THE TIME FOR REBEL ARTISTS TO BE ON THE DEFENSIVE. NOW IS THE TIME TO TAKE THE POLITICAL OFFENSIVE, going up in the face of the powers-that-be with genuinely liberating works of art that take on *all* the oppressive relations, and supporting the artists who defy the censors.

■ Robert Samuelson, Highbrow Pork Barrel, *Washington Post*, August 16, 1989

Robert Samuelson is a columnist.

I once suggested that Congress consider creating a National Endowment for Rodeo. The proposal's point was to show that rodeo subsidies are as worthy as "art" subsidies. Going beyond the irony, I urged abolishing the National Endowment for the Arts (NEA). This prompted the usual fan mail. One reader speculated that my cultural tastes ran to watching women's mud wrestling. Suppose they did. Should government then subsidize what I consider art?

The recent furor over allegedly obscene art financed by the NEA has only confirmed the wisdom of my view. Genuine art is about self-expression. It flows from individual imagination, ingenuity, joy and rage. By definition, it is undefinable. Standards are always subjective. In a democratic society there is a permanent conflict between artistic freedom and political accountability for "art" supported by public money.

Sen. Jesse Helms, Republican of North Carolina, is correct when he says taxpayers shouldn't have to pay for art that most Americans find offensive or indecent. (The current cause célèbre: a picture of a crucifix floating in urine, funded by an NEA grant.) But Helms' critics are also correct when they decry censorship and warn against government imposing standards of conformity and respectability. There's an easy escape from this impasse. Get government out of the arts. Then artists could create without fear, and congressmen would have no cause for complaint.

Now I was not born yesterday. I know that the chances of Congress erasing the NEA are about one in 25,000. But we can at least see it for what it is — highbrow pork barrel. By this, I mean that the NEA spends public monies to pay for what are basically private pleasures and pursuits. I do not mean that no good comes from these grants. But the good goes primarily to the individual

94

artists and art groups that receive the grants and to their relatively small audiences. Public benefits are meager.

There's a serious issue here, as political scientist Edward Banfield has argued. What are the legitimate uses of national government? Our federal government is the mechanism by which we tax ourselves to meet collective national needs. Subsidizing "art" fails this elementary test. It does not meet an important national need. Neither do subsidies for "good" television or the "humanities": the missions of the Corporation for Public Broadcasting and the National Endowment for the Humanities.

Suppose someone actually proposed a National Endowment for Rodeo with a $169 million budget, which is the 1989 budget for the NEA. Grants would go to individual rodeo riders ("to foster bull-riding skills") and to rodeo shows ("to make rodeos more available to the public"). Questions would arise. Why do rodeo riders and fans merit special treatment? Do they create some public benefit?

It's considered uncouth to ask similar questions of public support for opera, sculpture, painting or television. But, of course, the same questions apply. Grants from the NEA go mainly to individual artists or arts organizations. In 1988 the New York Philharmonic received $286,000; the San Francisco Opera Association got $330,000; the Denver Center for Performing Arts got $75,000. There were grants of about $10,000 each to 55 small literary magazines, and 89 sculptors got grants of about $5,000 apiece.

What justifies the subsidies? The idea that our artistic future depends on federal handouts to free artists from commercial pressures falters on two counts. It overlooks the complexity of creative motivation and ignores the corrupting influences of government grantsmanship. Herman Melville did not need an NEA grant to write; Winslow Homer did not need an NEA grant to paint. Art consumers benefit from the NEA, because their ticket prices are indirectly subsidized. But these are mainly higher-income people who deserve no subsidy. In 1987 only a quarter of the public attended opera or musical theater, reports pollster Louis Harris. But half of those with incomes exceeding $50,000 attended. Museum and theater attendance reflect similar income patterns.

Public-television subsidies are also highbrow pork barrel. On average, public TV draws about 4 percent of prime-time viewers. The "MacNeil/Lehrer News-Hour" receives the largest grant from the Corporation for Public Broadcasting (CPB), $4.3 million in 1989. It's a superb program, but what public purpose does it serve? Can anyone claim there isn't enough news? My guess is that its audience consists heavily of news junkies, who read newspapers and magazines, and watch CNN. The program doesn't inform the uninformed but better informs the well-informed.

No great (or even minor) national harm would occur if Congress axed these cultural agencies. Museums wouldn't vanish; the NEA provides a tiny share of their funds. Neither would public television stations; they rely on the CPB for only about 11 percent of their money. The CPB's children's programs with distinct instructional value could be moved to the Department of Education. In any case, "Sesame Street" would survive. Oscar the Grouch and his pals are a tiny industry appearing on toys and clothes.

Some arts groups would retrench, and others would die. Many would find new funding sources; in 1987 private giving for cultural activities totaled $6.4 billion. The great undercurrents of American art would continue undisturbed, because they're driven by forces — the search to understand self and society, the passion of individual artists — far more powerful than the U.S. Treasury. And the $550 million spent by the three main cultural agencies could be used for more legitimate public needs: for example, reducing the budget deficit or improving Medicaid.

As I said, this won't happen. The obscenity tempest probably won't even provoke a serious examination of government and the arts. Arts and public-broadcasting advocates cast any questioning of federal financing as an assault on the Temples of Culture by the Huns. Like all groups feeding at the federal trough, they've created a rhetoric equating their self-interest with the national interest.

Most congressmen accept these fictitious claims because Congress enjoys the power and, on occasion, finds the agencies useful whipping boys. It's a marriage of convenience that, however, dishonest, seems fated to endure.

■ Arthur Danto, Art and Taxpayers, *The Nation*, August 21/28, 1989

Arthur Danto is a philosopher, and the art critic of The Nation.

The Corcoran Gallery's pre-emptive decision in June to cancel a planned exhibition of Robert Mapplethorpe's photographs in order to forestall Congressional indignation at their content brought far greater notoriety to the now-famous images than showing them would have. Many of the same photographs of men who engage in the sexual domination of other willing men were presented at the Whitney Museum in New York City last year to no greater stir than some isolated tongue-clucking and wonderment as to what the museum thought it was doing. Indeed, *The Nation* was nearly alone in drawing attention to the homoerotic content of those explicit images in a show whose works conveyed a homoerotic sensibility whatever the subject, even when flowers or faces [see Danto, "Art," September 26, 1988]. The issue that had to be raised was how to respond to such charged representations in works of the highest photographic beauty. Mapplethorpe was still alive, although his sickness with AIDS was common knowledge in the art world, and that gave a certain solemn urgency to the showing of those sexually unsettling pictures. It was Mapplethorpe's wish that they be shown, as if he regarded them as an artistic testament.

The position of many neoconservatives is that this is not the kind of art taxpayers want to support. Hilton Kramer advanced this view in *The New York Times* recently. And this is now the position of the United States Senate — as a result of the July 26 passage of Jesse Helms' amendment banning Federal support for "obscene or indecent" art. But the issue could not be more obscurely framed. It is imperative to distinguish taxpayers from individuals who pay taxes, as we distinguish the uniform from the individual who wears it. As individuals, we have divergent aesthetic preferences. Kramer has little interest in supporting art that others find of great interest. But aesthetic preference does not enter into the concept of the taxpayer, which is a civic category. What does enter into it is freedom. It is very much in the interest of every taxpayer that freedom be supported, even — or especially — in its most extreme expressions. However divided individuals are on matters of taste, freedom is in the interest of every citizen. The taxpayer does not support one form of art and withhold support from another as a taxpayer, except in the special case of public art. The taxpayer supports the freedom to make and show art, even when it is art of a kind this or that *individual* finds repugnant.

Mapplethorpe did not make these photographs to test his freedoms. They are disturbing images for many, exciting images for some, but were not intended to strike a blow for artistic liberty (though perhaps for sexual liberty). They very much belong to an intersection of the art world and a certain erotic underground, and they have never been easy to view. The Whitney demonstrated that they could be shown to a wide audience without inducing riots.

Although there may never come a time when one can look at their subjects as commonplace, like female nudes or landscapes or still lifes, these works contrast completely with the now-also-notorious photograph by Andres Serrano of a plastic Jesus in a pool of pee. They contrast as well with the recent gesture, by a senior at the School of the Art Institute of Chicago, of laying a U.S. flag on the floor in a student exhibition so that visitors found it necessary to walk on it. Both works were intended to offend, and did offend. People responded indignantly and directly, by confrontations, demonstrations, protest. It would have been absurd to argue that they ought not to have done this on the ground that the objects were art. Art has the privileges of freedom only because it is a form of expression. And to be seriously interested in making an expression is to be seriously prepared to endure the consequences of making it. It is also not an offense to counter outrage with outrage. On the contrary, it is taking art seriously to do so. One cannot distance the flag and think of it as an arresting composition of stars and bars. One cannot distance one of the powerful religious symbols of the West and view a derogatory photograph of it merely as a formal composition.

It is healthy for art to vacate the position of pure aestheticism in which conservative critics seek to imprison it, and to try to affect the way viewers respond to the most meaningful matters of their lives. It is healthy for the museum to play a role in the life of its time rather than to stand outside as a cloister for aesthetic delectations. Art has been primarily aesthetic only throughout a very brief interval of its history of political, moral and religious engagement. As taxpayers our interest is solely in everyone's freedom to participate in the thought of the age.

Whatever grave reservations regarding Congress may have motivated the directors of the Corcoran, they weakened the entire social fabric by yielding their freedom. Their decision should have been to show the work, whose merit they must have believed in to have scheduled the exhibition. Since then individual members of Congress have revealed themselves as enemies of freedom by letting their aesthetic attitudes corrupt their political integrity as custodians of the deepest values of a democratic society.

■ Frederick Hart, Contemporary Art Is Perverted Art, *Washington Post*, August 22, 1989

Frederick Hart is a sculptor whose works include the Vietnam Veterans Memorial statue. He is a member of the Commission of Fine Arts in Washington D.C.

The air is becoming suffocatingly pungent with the incense of pious indignation from the art world concerning Congress' reaction to the way the National Endowment for the Arts is spending taxpayers' money.

What is taking place is yet another perverse manipulation of the public by the contemporary art establishment. The public, through its instrument, Congress, has reacted to the baiting and taunting of its sense of decency by the art world through its instrument, the NEA. Underneath its outrage, the art world can barely contain its secret delight at this publicity bonanza featuring a heroic scenario of free spirits versus troglodytes.

What eludes the public is the current philosophy and practice of art, which not only delights in but thrives on a belief system of deliberate contempt for the public. In order to understand this, you have to understand the values of art today and how contemporary art is intellectually packaged for the marketplace. To grasp this is also to grasp the sorry moral condition of art today and how this is shriveling art, making it less and less a meaningful endeavor.

Since the beginnings of bohemianism in art in the late 19th century, rejection by the public has become the traditional hallmark of what comes to be regarded as great art. An offended public is a critical necessity for the attainment of credentials by any artist. The idea that art and artist must be initially misunderstood and rejected has become doctrine in the mythology of great art, and consequently it has become one of the primary criteria in evaluating the historical importance of a given artist. The art world embraced this fable in the late 19th century and has been running hard with it ever since.

There is, however, a critical difference between then and now. Life in the late 19th century was heavily regimented by strict societal mores: the public expression of emotion and sexuality was severely repressed. When art and literature broke through those layers of repression, people were offended, outraged and ill at ease about the truths they discovered about themselves. But we live in a different world. Today, "repression" is a bad word. Nothing is ever, ever repressed. Everything is discussed, analyzed and ventilated by people ranging from Phil Donahue in the morning to Larry King at night, day in and day out. It's gotten damned hard if not almost impossible to offend anyone anymore.

But art persists. Every artist worth his salt yearns to create works of art that are (mistakenly perceived, of course) so offensive, so insulting to the public as to earn him a clear judgment of genius for his success at being misunderstood.

It has become the intense pastime of contemporary art to pursue controversy, the bigger the better, as a form of art. But the artist has had to reach farther and deeper to find some new twist with which to offend. A simple-minded little sophomoric gimmick of making people walk on the flag to make a cute point arouses vast passion and national controversy — for which artist and art world pat each other on the back.

What is really going on is the cynical aggrandizement of art and artist at the expense of sacred public sentiments — profound sentiments embodied by symbols, such as the flag or the crucifix, which the public has a right and a duty to treasure and protect.

When one looks back at the majestic sweep of art in history and its awesome and magnificent accomplishments, how nasty and midget like are so many of the products and so much of the philosophy of contemporary art by comparison. Once, art served society rather than biting at its heels while demanding unequivocal financial support. Once, under the banner of beauty and order, art was a rich and meaningful embellishment of life, embracing — not desecrating — its ideals, its aspirations and its values.

Not so today.

Look about you. The artlessness of contemporary life has come about because of a breakdown in the fundamental philosophy of art and who it is created for. The flaw is not with a public that refuses to nourish the arts. Rather it is with a practice of art that refuses to nourish the public. The public has been so bullied intellectually by the proponents of contemporary art that it has wearily resigned itself to just about any idiocy that is put before it and calls itself art. But the common man has his limits, and they are reached when some of these things emerge from the sanctuary of the padded cells of galleries and museums and are put in public places, where the public is forced to live with them and pay for them.

If one visited a town or a city in Renaissance Italy, the motive of art and its resulting products would come off entirely differently. Art was not then thought of as an end in itself but as another form of service. When the Italian peasant looked about, he saw an array of dedicated embellishments from his church to his public buildings, fountains and plazas. The artwork, which was exquisitely created, embraced his values, his religious beliefs, his history, his aspirations and his ideals. It was meant to give enrichment through its artistry but, more important, to give purpose through its meaning. It was, as Dante called sculpture, "visible speech." It was not created for art's sake but for his sake.

The measure of achievement in art was determined by the degree to which that art was considered ennobling. Art and society had achieved a wonderful responsibility for each other. Art summarized, with masterful visual eloquence born of a sense of beauty, the striving of civilization to find order and purpose in the universe. This service to truth was more important than the endeavor of art itself. And it was this dedication to service that gave art its moral authority.

This moral authority is the critical element by which a society regards art either as an essential and meaningful part of life, as in Renaissance Italy or, as today, a superfluous bit of fluff, mainly indulged in by a small snobbish minority. Art is regarded by contemporary society much the same way architects now regard art — not as an essence, but as a high-rent amenity.

The most touching and noble impulse toward "visible speech" in recent times was the short-lived creation of the Statue of Democracy in Tiananmen Square. Naively executed, it was nonetheless a wonderful display of the unique ability of art to embody and enhance concisely and movingly a deeply felt public yearning for an ideal of a just society. The profound meaning the statue had for tens of millions of people gives the art a value and moral authority of profound significance.

In ancient Greece, which generated 2,500 years of Western art, there existed no distinction between aesthetics and ethics in the judgment of a work of art. Works of art achieved greatness by embodying great ideas, as well as by sheer mastery of the medium. The inspiration and the motivation for that mastery were in the nobility of the ideas pursued.

It is the contemporary renunciation of the moral responsibility of art that is the source of the recent hostilities between art and public. The cutback of funds by Congress is a graphic display of the public's declining conviction of the importance of art, caused by a self-absorbed art that has lost all sense of obligation to the public good and the betterment of man. It is possible to live without art, and if the nourishment provided by art continues to be so nauseating, life without art will become, for some, desirable.

If art is to flourish in the 21st century, it must renew its moral authority by philosophically and fundamentally rededicating itself to life rather than art. Art must again touch our lives, our fears and cares. It must evoke our dreams and give hope to the darkness.

■ Sen. Jesse Helms, It's the Job of Congress to Define What's Art, *USA Today*, September 8, 1989

Jesse Helms is a Republican senator representing the state of North Carolina. He was the leader of the anti-NEA campaign in the U.S. Senate.

WASHINGTON — Three questions often raised about my amendment, and my responses, are:

Should federal funding of the arts be tied to content?

My answer: Of course. Congress has the clear responsibility to oversee the expenditure of all federal funds — including the arts. The American people in the vast majority are aghast to learn that their tax money has been used to reward artists (e.g., the Mapplethorpe exhibit) who choose to depict sadomasochism, perverted homoerotic sex acts and even sexual exploitation of children.

I do not propose that Congress "censor" artists. I do propose that Congress put an end to the use of federal funds to support outrageous "art" that is clearly designed to poison our culture. Those who insist on producing such garbage should be required to do it on their own time and with their own money. The taxpayers should not be required to pay for it.

Who should decide what art is suitable?

My answer: The real question is whether freedom is to be equated with decadence. I say, absolutely not. The National Endowment for the Arts has, all along, had the responsibility to decide what "art" is suitable for federal funding. The NEA has defaulted upon that responsibility. Congress should henceforth require that the NEA's funding decisions be opened to the public. Sunlight is the best disinfectant.

What are the implications for the freedom of artistic expression?

My answer: None. Artists who seek to shock and offend the public can still do so — but at their own expense. I reiterate for the purpose of emphasis that *censorship* is not involved when the government refuses to subsidize such "artists." People who want to scrawl dirty words on the men's room wall should furnish their own walls and their own crayons. It is tyranny, as Thomas Jefferson said in another context, to force taxpayers to support private activities which are by intent abhorrent and repulsive.

The tremendous response we've received from throughout the country indicates that the vast majority of Americans support my amendment.

There have been a few suggestions that the language of my amendment is "too vague" and thus it would not be enforceable. That is nonsense.

There's nothing vague about it — and the Federal Communications Commission apparently is having no problem making the determination that various broadcasts are indecent and/or obscene.

If the FCC can handle its responsibility, certainly the National Endowment for the Arts should be able to do likewise.

▪ Hon. Dana Rohrabacher, statement to the House of Representatives, September 13, 1989 (excerpt)

Dana Rohrabacher is a Republican member of the House of Representatives, representing the state of Carolina. He was the leader of the anti-NEA campaign in the House.

M r. Speaker, American taxpayers are furious that their hard-earned money can be spent on so-called art that is obscene, indecent, blasphemous and racist. If we pass the gentleman from Ohio's motion to instruct without my amendment, we will be abrogating our responsibility, our sacred trust, to see that the dollars taxed away from our hard-working citizens are spent effectively and for ends consistent with their moral standards.

Mr. Speaker, a few weeks ago, I stood before the House and offered a simple amendment to the Interior appropriations bill. My amendment would have struck all Government funding of the National Endowment for the Arts.

Those who truly oppose Government control of the arts should oppose Government funding of the arts. Money for the arts should be left with the people, rather than taxed away, so they can make their own free determination as to what art they will or will not support, rather than giving that power to the state. But if the Government does tax away our people's hard-earned money in the name of supporting the arts, at the very least, standards should be set so that those funds are not used to subsidize obscenity or indecency, or used to denigrate someone's religion, or race, or sex.

Opponents of my amendment suggest that establishing standards for the use of taxpayers' money is a form of censorship. What kind of cockamamie logic is that? The question is sponsorship, not censorship. At a time of high deficit spending, when it is difficult to provide funds for the health needs of our elderly and for prenatal care, spending the taxpayers' dollars on art is itself questionable. Spending it on obscene or indecent art, or art that insults one's religion, is outrageous.

There has been a great deal of posturing on this issue. One wonders how many of those who are aggressively opposing the setting of these standards would be doing so, if it had been a photo of Martin Luther King or a symbol of the Jewish faith that had been submerged in a bottle of urine at taxpayers' expense.

Now we hear that the Helms language, which passed by the Senate without opposition, is too broad, unclear, a threat to legitimate art and freedom of expression. This strawman argument is being used to oppose the setting of any standards. The language of this amendment is direct, clear and understandable....

If there are some in this hall who have trouble understanding this clear and direct language, I am certain there are voters around this country who are willing to explain it to them in the next election. Americans believe in freedom of speech, but let there be no doubt, the American people do not want their tax dollars spent on obscenity and indecency or for denigrating Christianity or any other religion....

Yes, the NEA could still sponsor submerging photos of myself or Senator Helms or any other politician, but they could not use our tax dollars to put a crucifix of Jesus Christ in a bottle of urine, or denigrate any other religion; and do not tell the American people that they are bigoted, or tyrannical for insisting that standards be set so their hard earned tax dollars are not used for such trash and mean spirited invective against race, religion, sex or handicap.

Time magazine said that had Federal authorities chosen to do so, they could have prosecuted Robert Mapplethorpe for child pornography. Other projects sponsored by the NEA have included drawings of homosexual orgies, bestiality, and a Statue of Liberty turned into a transvestite, complete with male sex organs.

Why in the world are we permitting Federal tax dollars to be used to finance such trash? How in the name of representative government can anyone oppose the setting of standards to prevent this obscene misuse of tax dollars?

✓The censorship argument is without merit. Artists can do whatever they want on their own time and with their own dime. We, on the other hand, have a responsibility to see that tax dollars are spent for the betterment of our country.

■ Urine the Money, *Washington Times,* September 14, 1989

North Carolina's Sen. Jesse Helms may not look much like Jesus Christ, but some of America's artists have done him the honor of putting him in the same place they put the Man from Galilee. This summer in Phoenix, an "alternative" art center called the MARS Artspace displayed as an exhibit a photograph of Mr. Helms immersed in a Mason jar of the urine of an artist known only as "Cactus Jack." The MARS Artspace, it turns out, is funded by the National Endowment for the Arts — in other words, by you and your tax dollars.

Of course, Cactus Jack, whoever he is, didn't mean to honor Mr. Helms. His creation was a spinoff of artist Andres Serrano's "Piss Christ," a photograph of a crucifix submerged in Mr. Serrano's own liquid offal. That creation too was funded by $15,000 from the NEA, and Mr. Helms' response to what he considered a blasphemous use of the taxpayers' money and a waste of human waste was to sponsor legislation cutting off public funds for obscene and indecent artworks.

MARS art director Jason Sikes says his "immediate reaction" to Cactus Jack's inspiration "on a personal level was that it was hilarious.... My second reaction was that if we put it up, it could cause us problems." Even "alternative" artists have to eat and pay the rent, you see, and even as he was chuckling over how clever Cactus Jack's piece de resistance was, Mr. Sikes was beginning to worry whether the yokels might get fed up with him and his whole stupid center.

In the event, Mr. Sikes proceeded with the display and kept it on exhibit until Aug. 17, despite protest from philistines who just don't appreciate genius and clearly have no sense of humor. "We decided," proclaims Mr. Sikes valiantly, "an artist's freedom of expression was more important." But the belly laugh Mr. Sikes and his friends may have gotten from their calculated insult to Mr. Helms may cost them. Rep. Sidney Yates, chairman of the subcommittee that reviews NEA funding, says he doesn't think it's funny when artists make sport with members of Congress. "I don't think any member of Congress should be treated like that," says Mr. Yates of Cactus Jack's masterpiece.

Actually, a good many members of Congress probably deserve treatment far worse than even Cactus Jack's morbid imagination could conceive. It's ironic that at the same time many members of America's freeloading artistic establishment are furious because taxpayers are getting bored with picking up the check for the insulting, obscene and blasphemous junk that artists create, many members of Congress also are furious that Americans are growing tired of congressional pomposity, hypocrisy and outright corruption. It seems to be fine with Mr. Yates if wacked-out aesthetes smear their bodily fluids over mainstream American beliefs and values, but they better not even think about poking fun at congressmen.

The Senate was right to pass Mr. Helms' amendment. Cactus Jack's micturitions ought to be carried to the nearest sewer. The Mason jar can serve to hold Mr. Sike's income after Congress transfers his gallery to the free marketplace of ideas. And American taxpayers ought to put Mr. Helms' picture on their mantels for his courage in pushing an arrogant gang of parasites off the public dole.

■ Sen. John Danforth, statement to the Senate, September 29, 1989

John Danforth is a Republican senator representing the state of Missouri.

Mr. President, I have unfortunately had the opportunity to look very briefly at the exhibits that the Senator from North Carolina has brought to the floor and everything that has been said about them is true. These are gross. These are terrible. These are totally indefensible. I do not think they are art.

Mr. President, however I do not believe that the issue before us tonight is whether we like or do not like these pictures. I do not like them and my guess is that not a single resident of my State would like them. They would not like the idea of the Government paying for them. I am sorry Government did pay for them.

That is not the issue before us. The issue is very simple: The Senator from Texas used the expression, and I think it was very well chosen, the question is: What is suitable art? And the issue before the Senate is very simple, and it is whether we in the U.S. Senate should attempt to make definitions of what we consider to be suitable art.

Maybe there should not be any National Endowment for the Arts. Maybe the Government should never be in the business of making judgments of taste, because that is what the NEA does. I think that is an arguable position. But the question is not whether the NEA should do it or not do it. We have already decided that the NEA is in that business.

The question is whether we in the Congress of the United States should try to establish some criteria by which we define what is or is not suitable art. That is what the Senator from North Carolina does by his amendment. His amendment does not say that the Mapplethorpe exhibition is pornography and it should not be funded. He does not say that. He goes much more broadly than that. He does not say that Mr. Serrano should or should not be funded by the NEA.

He goes much more broadly than that in the terms of his amendment, and I want to read a couple paragraphs because we have been focusing on obscenity and I think everybody knows that obscenity has been a problem for the Supreme Court of the United States. But he also says in paragraph 2 that the amendment covers material which denigrates the object or beliefs of the adherents of a particular religion or nonreligion.

Mr. President, consider what that means: Material which denigrates the object or beliefs of the adherents of a particular religion or nonreligion.

Does it denigrate the object of a religion to portray Christ as a clown? Well, the musical "Godspell" did just that. It portrayed Christ as a clown. Could it be found by some administrator that the portrayal of Christ as a clown denigrates the object of somebody's religion? Of course it could.

"Godspell" probably would be covered by the breadth of this amendment.

How about a portrayal of Christ as a wild animal? Would that portrayal denigrate a person's religion? Well, C.S. Lewis did that in "The Lion, the Witch and the Wardrobe." It was a book about Christianity and the Christ figure was a lion and some administrator, some bureaucrat could have said that denigrates a person's religion. C.S. Lewis spent his academic and literary life describing his religious beliefs which were very, very profound beliefs.

How about in the world of music? Could it be said that the beliefs of the Quaker faith are denigrated by "Onward Christian Soldiers Marching as to War"?

And then how about the question of race. I remember from my own part of the country, "Tom Sawyer" and "Huckleberry Finn." There have been those throughout the last number of decades who have tried for one reason or another to get "Tom Sawyer" and "Huckleberry Finn" off of the shelves of our schools.

This amendment would say that "Tom Sawyer" would not have qualified for an NEA grant and "Huckleberry Finn" because it could be argued that they denigrated an individual, namely Nigger Jim, as he was called according to his race.

Or how about creed? Can we think of anything in the annals of literature that denigrates an individual because of his religion? How about the "Merchant of Venice"? How about William Shakespeare himself? Would that be covered by this amendment? I think it would be. This amendment is not just about Mapplethorpe. It is also about Shakespeare.

And in our own time in American literature Alice Walker's great little book, "The Color Purple," made into a movie, clearly denigrates men.

And this amendment says that material that denigrates or reviles a person on the basis of sex falls within the parameters. I take it that "The Color Purple" would not have qualified for an NEA grant.

How about age? I do not remember the name of the book, but I do remember that Bill Cosby, the famous comedian, wrote a book about kids. It is a spoof of children, and his television programs are always doing that. And I take it that those programs and that book denigrate people on the basis of age.

Then there is national origin which is also covered material that denigrates or reviles on the basis of national origin. Perhaps "The Godfather." The head of Paramount Theaters was visiting with me recently. I said, "What is the greatest movie you ever made?" He said, "The two Godfather movies taken together, absolutely the essence of American art" and it would be covered by this amendment.

I am not for Mapplethorpe. I am sick that a dollar of taxpayer money went to pay for this kind of junk. I am sick about it. I could just see the faces of the people of Sedalia, or Cabool, or Mountain Grove, MO, if they were told that they had to pay for this. It truly is outlandish. That is not the issue.

The issue is: How good are we at defining whether something is suitable art or not-suitable art and how do we draw those definitions? And should we really write definitions on the floor of the Senate which cover "Godspell," and "Tom Sawyer," and the "Merchant of Venice," and "The Color Purple," and "The Godfather?" Mr. President, I think the answer is no.

■ Carole S. Vance, The War on Culture, *Art in America,* September 1989

Carole S. Vance is an anthropologist at the Columbia University School of Public Health, and the editor of Pleasure and Danger: Exploring Female Sexuality.

The storm that had been brewing over the National Endowment for the Arts (NEA) funding broke on the Senate floor on May 18, as Senator Alfonse D'Amato rose to denounce Andres Serrano's photograph *Piss Christ* as "trash." "This so-called piece of art is a deplorable, despicable display of vulgarity," he said. Within minutes over 20 senators rushed to join him in sending a letter to Hugh Southern, acting chair of the NEA, demanding to know what steps the agency would take to change its grant procedures. "This work is shocking, abhorrent and completely undeserving of any recognition whatsoever," the senators wrote.[1] For emphasis, Senator D'Amato dramatically ripped up a copy of the exhibition catalogue containing Serrano's photograph.

Not to be outdone, Senator Jesse Helms joined in the denunciation: "The Senator from New York is absolutely correct in his indignation and in his description of the blasphemy of the so-called art work. I do not know Mr. Andres Serrano, and I hope I never meet him. Because he is not an artist, he is a jerk." He continued, "Let him be a jerk on his own time and with his own resources. Do not dishonor our Lord."[2]

The object of their wrath was a 60-by-40-inch Cibachrome print depicting a wood-and-plastic crucifix submerged in yellow liquid — the artist's urine. The photograph had been shown in an uneventful three-city exhibit organized by the Southeastern Center for Contemporary Art (SECCA), a recipient of NEA funds. A juried panel appointed by SECCA had selected Serrano and nine others from some 500 applicants to win $15,000 fellowships and appear in the show, "Awards in the Visual Arts 7." How the senators came to know and care about this regional show was not accidental.

Although the show had closed by the end of January 1989, throughout the spring the right-wing American Family Association, based in Tupelo, Mississippi, attacked the photo, the exhibition and its sponsors. The association and its executive director, United Methodist minister Rev. Donald Wildmon, were practiced in fomenting public opposition to allegedly "immoral, anti-Christian" images and had led protests against Martin Scorsese's film *The Last Temptation of Christ* the previous summer. The AFA newsletter, with an estimated circulation 380,000 including 178,000 churches, according to association spokesmen,[3] urged concerned citizens to protest the art work and demand that responsible NEA officials be fired, The newsletter provided the relevant names and addresses, and letters poured in to congressmen, senators and the NEA. A full-fledged moral panic had begun.

Swept up in the mounting hysteria was another photographic exhibit scheduled to open on July 1 at the Corcoran Gallery of Art in Washington, D.C. The 150-work retrospective, "Robert Mapplethorpe: The Perfect Moment," was organized by the University of Pennsylvania's Institute of Contemporary Art (ICA), which had received $30,000 for the show from the NEA. The show included the range of Mapplethorpe's images: formal portraiture, flowers, children and carefully posed erotic scenes — sexually explicit, gay and sadomasochistic. The show had been well received in Philadelphia and Chicago, but by June 8, Representative Dick Armey (R-Tex) sent Southern a letter signed by over 100 congressmen denouncing grants for Mapplethorpe as well as Serrano, and threatening to seek cuts in the agency's $170-million budget soon up for approval. Armey wanted the NEA to end its sponsorship of "morally reprehensible trash,"[4] and he wanted new grant guidelines that would "clearly pay respect to public standards of taste and decency."[5] Armey claimed he could "blow their budget out of the water"[6] by circulating the Mapplethorpe catalogue to fellow legislators prior to the House vote on the NEA appropriation. Before long, about 50 senators and 150 representatives had contacted the NEA about its funding.[7]

Amid these continuing attacks on the NEA, rumors circulated that the Corcoran would cancel the show. Director Christina Orr-Cahall staunchly rejected such rumors one week, saying, "This is the work of major American artist who's well known, so we're not doing anything out of the ordinary."[8] But by the next week she had caved in, saying, "We really felt this exhibit was at the wrong place at the wrong time."[9] The director attempted an ingenious argument in a statement issued though a museum spokesperson: far from being censorship, she claimed, the cancellation actually protected the artist's work. "We decided to err on the side of the artist, who had the right to have his work presented in a non-sensationalized, non-political environment, and who deserves not to be the hostage for larger issues of relevance to us all," Orr-Cahall stated. "If you think about this for a long time, as we did, this is not censorship; in fact, this is the full artistic freedom which we all support."[10] Astounded by the Corcoran decision, artists and arts groups mounted protests, lobbied and formed anti-censorship organizations, while a local alternative space, The Washington Project for the Arts (WPA), hastily arranged to show the Mapplethorpe exhibition.

The Corcoran cancellation scarcely put an end to the controversy, however. Instead, attacks on NEA funding intensified in the House and Senate, focusing on the 1990 budget appropriations and on new regulations that would limit or possibly end NEA subcontracts to arts organizations.[11] Angry representatives wanted to gut the budget, though they were beaten back in the House by more moderate amendments which indicated disapproval of the Serrano and Mapplethorpe grants by deducting their total cost ($45,000) from next year's allocation. By late July, Sen. Jesse Helms introduced a Senate amendment that would forbid the funding of "offensive," "indecent" and otherwise controversial art and transfer monies previously allocated for visual arts to support "folk art" and local projects. The furor is likely to continue throughout the fall, since the NEA will be up for its mandated, five-year reauthorization, and the right-wing campaign against images has apparently been heartened by its success. In Chicago, for example, protestors assailed an Eric Fischl painting of a fully clothed boy looking at a naked man swinging at a baseball on the grounds that it promotes "child molestation" and is, in any case, not "realistic," and therefore, bad art.[12]

The arts community was astounded by this chain of events — artists personally reviled, exhibitions withdrawn and under attack, the NEA budget threatened, all because of a few images. Ironically, those who specialize in producing and interpreting images were surprised that any images could have such power. But what was new to the art community is, in fact, a staple of contemporary right-wing politics.

In the past ten years, conservative and fundamentalist groups have deployed and perfected techniques of grass-roots and mass mobilization around social issues, usually centering on sexuality, gender and religion. In these campaigns, symbols figure prominently, both as highly condensed statements of moral concern and as powerful spurs to emotion and action. In moral campaigns, fundamentalists select a negative symbol which is highly arousing to their own constituency and which is difficult or problematic for their opponents to defend. The symbol, often taken literally, out of context and always denying the possibility of irony or multiple interpretations, is waved like a red flag before their constituents. The arousing stimulus could be an "un-Christian" passage from an evolution textbook, explicit information from a high school sex-education curriculum or "degrading" pornography said to be available in the local adult bookshop. In the antiabortion campaign, activists favor images of late-term fetuses or better yet, dead babies, displayed in jars. Primed with names and addresses of relevant elected and appointed officials, fundamentalist troops fire off volleys of letters, which cowed politicians take to be the expression of popular sentiment. Right-wing politicians opportunistically ride the ground swell of outrage, while centrists feel anxious and disempowered to stop it — now a familiar sight in the political landscape. But here, in the NEA controversy, there is something new.

Fundamentalists and conservatives are now directing mass-based symbolic mobilizations against "high culture." Previously, their efforts had focused on popular culture — the attack on rock music led by Tipper Gore, the protests against *The Last Temptation of Christ* and the Meese Commission's war against pornography.[13] Conservative and neoconservative intellectuals have also lamented the allegedly liberal bias of the university and the dilution of the classic literary canon by including "inferior" works by minority, female and gay authors, but these complaints have been made in books, journals and conferences, and have scarcely generated thousands of letters to Congress. Previous efforts to change the direction of the NEA had been made through institutional and bureaucratic channels — by appointing more conservative members to its governing body, the National Council on the Arts, by selecting a more conservative chair and in some cases by overturning grant decisions made by professional panels. Although antagonism to Eastern elites and upper-class culture has been a thread within fundamentalism, the NEA controversy marks the first time that this emotion has been tapped in mass political action.

Conservative columnist Patrick Buchanan sounded the alarm for this populist attack in a *Washington Times* column last June, calling for "a cultural revolution in the '90s as sweeping as the political revolution in the '80s."[14] Here may lie a clue to this new strategy: the Reagan political revolution has peaked, and with both legislatures under Democratic control, additional conservative gains on social issues through electoral channels seem unlikely. Under these conditions, the slower and more time-consuming — though perhaps more effective — method of changing public opinion and taste may be the best available option. For conservatives and fundamentalists, the arts community plays a significant role in setting standards and shaping public values: Buchanan writes, "The decade has seen an explosion of anti-American, anti-Christian, and nihilist 'art'.... [Many museums] now feature exhibits that can best be described as cultural trash,"[15] and "as in public television and public radio, a tiny clique, out of touch with America's traditional values, has wormed its way into control of the arts bureaucracy."[16] In an analogy chillingly reminiscent of Nazi cultural metaphors, Buchanan writes, "As with our rivers and lakes, we need to clean up our culture: for it is a well from which we must all drink. Just as a poisoned land will yield up poisonous fruits, so a polluted culture, left to fester and stink, can destroy a nation's soul."[17] Let the citizens be warned: "We should not subsidize decadence."[18] Amid such archaic language of moral pollution and degeneracy, it was not surprising that Mapplethorpe's gay and erotic images were at the center of controversy.

The second new element in the right's mass mobilization against the NEA and high culture has been its rhetorical disavowal of censorship per se and the cultivation of an artfully crafted distinction between absolute censorship and the denial of public funding. Senator D'Amato, for example, claimed, "This matter does not involve freedom of artistic expression — it does involve the question whether American taxpayers should be forced to support such trash."[19] In the battle for public opinion, "censorship" is a dirty word to mainstream audiences, and hard for conservatives to shake off because their recent battles to control school books, libraries and curricula have earned them reputations as ignorant book-burners. By using this hairsplitting rhetoric, conservatives can now happily disclaim any interest in censorship, and merely suggest that no public funds be used for "offensive" or "indecent" materials.[20] Conservatives had employed the "no public funds" argument before to deny federal funding for Medicaid abortions since 1976 and explicit safe-sex education for AIDS more recently. Fundamentalists have attempted to modernize their rhetoric in other social campaigns, too — antiabortionists borrow civil rights terms to speak about the "human rights" of the fetus, and antiporn zealots experiment with replacing their language of sin and lust with phrases about the "degradation of women" borrowed from antipornography feminism. In all cases, these incompatible languages have an uneasy coexistence. But modernized rhetoric cannot disguise the basic, censorious impulse which strikes out at NEA public funding precisely because it is a significant source of arts money, not a trivial one.

NEA funding permeates countless art institutions, schools and community groups, often making the difference between survival and going under; it also supports many individual artists. That NEA funds have in recent years been allocated according to formulas designed to achieve more democratic distribution — not limited to elite art centers or well-known artists — makes their impact all the more significant. A requirement that NEA-funded institutions and artists conform to a standard of "public taste," even in the face of available private funds, would have a profound impact. One obvious by-product would be installing the fiction of a singular public with a universally shared taste and the displacement of a diverse public composed of may constituencies with different tastes. In addition, the mingling of NEA and private funds, so typical in many institutions and exhibitions, would mean that NEA standards would spill over to the private sector, which is separate more in theory than in practice. Although NEA might fund only part of a project, its standards would prevail, since noncompliance would result in loss of funds.

No doubt the continuous contemplation of the standards of public taste that should obtain in publicly funded projects —continuous, since these can never be known with certainty — will itself increase self-censorship and caution across the board. There has always been considerable self-censorship in the art world when it comes to sexual images, and the evidence indicates that it is increasing: reports circulate about curators now examining their collections anew with an eye toward "disturbing" material that might arouse public ire, and increased hesitation to mount new exhibitions that contain unconventional material. In all these ways, artists have recognized the damage done by limiting the types of images that can be funded by public monies.

But more importantly, the very distinction between public and private is a false one, because the boundaries between these spheres are very permeable. Feminist scholarship has shown how the most seemingly personal and private decisions — having a baby, for example — are affected by a host of public laws and policies, ranging from available tax benefits to health services to day care. In the past century in America and England, major changes in family form, sexuality and gender arrangements have occurred in a complex web spanning public and private domains, which even historians are hard put to separate.[21] In struggles for social change, both reformers and traditionalists know that changes in personal life are intimately linked to changes in public domains — not only through legal regulation, but also through information, images and even access to physical space available in public arenas.

This is to say that what goes on in the public sphere is of vital importance for both the arts and for political culture. Because American traditions of publicly supported culture are limited by the innate conservatism of corporate sponsors and by the reduction of individual patronage following changes in the tax laws, relegating controversial images and art work to private philanthropy confines them to a frail and easily influenced source of support. Even given the NEA's history of bureaucratic interference, it is paradoxically public funding — insulated from the day-to-day interference of politicians and special-interest groups that the right wing would now impose — that permits the possibility of a heterodox culture. Though we might reject the overly literal connection conservatives like to make between images and action ("When teenagers read sex education, they go out and have sex"), we too know that diversity in images and expression in the public sector nurtures and sustains diversity in private life. When losses are suffered in public arenas, people for whom controversial or minority images are salient and affirming suffer a real defeat. Defending private rights — to behavior, to images, to information — is difficult without a publicly formed and visible community. People deprived of images become demoralized and isolated, and they become increasingly vulnerable to attacks on their private expression of nonconformity, which are inevitable once sources of public solidarity and resistance have been eliminated.

For these reasons, the desire to eliminate symbols, images and ideas they do not like from public space is basic to contemporary conservatives' and fundamentalists' politics about sexuality, gender and the family. On the one hand, this behavior may signal weakness, in that conservatives no longer have the power to directly control, for example, sexual behavior, and must content themselves with controlling a proxy, images of sexual behavior. The attack on Mapplethorpe's images, some of them gay, some sadomasochistic, can be understood in this light. Indeed, the savage critique of his photographs permitted a temporary revival of a vocabulary — "perverted, filth, trash" — that was customarily used against gays but has become unacceptable in mainstream political discourse, a result of sexual liberalization that conservatives hate. On the other hand, the attack on images, particularly "difficult" images in the public domain, may be the most effective point of cultural intervention now — particularly given the evident difficulty liberals have in mounting a strong and unambivalent response and given the way changes in public climate can be translated back to changes in legal rights — as, for example, in the erosion of support for abortion rights, where the image of the fetus has become central in the debate, erasing the image of the woman.

Because symbolic mobilizations and moral panics often leave in their wake residues of law and policy that remain in force long after the hysteria has subsided,[22] the fundamentalist attack on art and images requires a broad and vigorous response that goes beyond appeals to free speech. Free expression is a necessary principle in these debates, because of the steady protection it offers to all images, but it cannot be the only one. To be effective and not defensive, the art community needs to employ its interpretive skills to unmask the modernized rhetoric conservatives use to justify their traditional agenda, as well as to deconstruct the "difficult" images fundamentalists choose to set their campaigns in motion. Despite their uncanny intuition for culturally disturbing material, their focus on images also contains many sleights of hand (Do photographs of nude children necessarily equal child pornography?), and even displacement,[23] which we need to examine. Images we would allow to remain "disturbing" and unconsidered put us anxiously on the defensive and undermine our own response. In addition to defending free speech, it is essential to address why certain images are being attacked — Serrano's crucifix for mocking the excesses of religious exploitation[24] (a point evidently not lost on the televangelists and syndicated preachers who promptly assailed his "blasphemy") and Mapplethorpe's photographs for making minority sexual subcultures visible. If we are always afraid to offer a public defense of sexual images, then even in our rebuttal we have granted the right wing its most basic premise: sexuality is shameful and discrediting. It is not enough to defend the principle of free speech, while joining in denouncing the image, as some in the art world have done.[25]

The fundamentalist attack on images and the art world must be recognized not as an improbable and silly outburst of Yahoo-ism, but as a systematic part of a right-wing political program to restore traditional social arrangements and reduce diversity. The right wing is deeply committed to symbolic politics, both in using symbols to mobilize public sentiment and in understanding that, because images do stand in for and motivate social change, the arena of representation is a real ground for struggle. A vigorous defense of art and images begins from this insight.

1. Senator D'Amato's remarks and the text of the letter appear in the *Congressional Record*, vol. 135, no. 64, May 18, 1989, S 5594.
2. Senator Helms's remarks appear in the *Congressional Record*, vol. 135, no. 64, May 18, 1989, S 5595.
3. William H. Honan, "Congressional Anger Threatens Arts Endowment's Budget," *New York Times*, June 20, 1989, p. C20.
4. "People: Art, Trash and Funding," *International Herald Tribune*, June 15, 1989, p.20.
5. Ibid.
6. Honan, "Congressional Anger," p. C20.
7. Elizabeth Kastor, "Funding Art that Offends," *Washington Post*, June 7, 1989, p. C1.
8. Ibid., p. C3.
9. Elizabeth Kastor, "Corcoran Cancels Photo Exhibit," *Washington Post*, June 13, 1989, p. C1.
10. Elizabeth Kastor, "Corcoran Decision Provokes Outcry," *Washington Post*, June 14, 1989, p. B1.
11. Barbara Gamarekian, "Legislation Offered to Limit Grants by Arts Endowment," *New York Times*, June 21, 1989; Carla Hall, "For NEA, an Extra Step," *Washington Post*, June 22, 1989; Elizabeth Kastor, "Art and Accountability," *Washington Post*, June 30, 1989.
12. The Fischl painting *Boys at Bat*, 1979, was part of a traveling exhibition, "Diamonds Are Forever," on view at the Chicago Public Library Cultural Center. Ziff Fistrunk,

executive director of the Southside Chicago Sports Council, organized the protest. He objected that "I have trained players in Little League and semi-pro baseball, and at no time did I train them naked." *In These Times*, Aug. 1, 1989, p. 5. Thanks to Carole Tormollan for calling this incident to my attention.

13. Carole S. Vance, "The Meese Commission on the Road: Porn in the U.S.A.," *The Nation*, Aug. 29, 1986, pp. 65-82.

14. Patrick Buchanan, "How Can We Clean Up Our Art Act?" *Washington Post*, June 19, 1989.

15. Ibid.

16. Ibid.

17. Ibid.

18. Ibid.

19. *Congressional Record*, vol. 135, no. 64, May 18, 1989, S 5594.

20. Another ploy is to transmute the basic objection to Serrano's photograph, the unfortunately medieval-sounding "blasphemy," to more modern concerns with prejudice and civil rights. Donald Wildmon, for example, states, "Religious bigotry should not be supported by tax dollars." *Washington Times*, Apr. 26, 1989, p. A5.

    The slippage between these two frameworks, however, appears in a protest letter written to the *Richmond News-Leader* concerning Serrano's work: "The Virginia Museum should not be in the business of promoting and subsidizing hatred and intolerance. Would they pay the KKK to do work defaming blacks? Would they display a Jewish symbol under urine? Has Christianity become fair game in our society for any kind of blasphemy and slander?" (Mar. 18, 1989).

21. For 19th-century American history regarding sex and gender, see John D'Emilio and Estelle Freedman, *Intimate Matters*, New York, Harper and Row, 1988; for British history, see Jeffrey Weeks, *Sex, Politics and Society: The Regulation of Sexuality Since 1800*, New York, Longman, 1981.

22. The 19th-century Comstock Law, for example, passed during a frenzied concern about indecent literature, was used to suppress information about abortion and birth control in the United States well into the 20th century. For accounts of moral panics, see Weeks, *Sex, Politics and Society;* Judith Walkowitz, *Prostitution and Victorian Society: Women, Class, and the State*, Cambridge University Press, 1980; and Gayle Rubin, "Thinking Sex: Notes for a Radical Theory of the Politics of Sexuality," in Carole S. Vance, ed., *Pleasure and Danger: Exploring Female Sexuality*, Boston: Routledge & Kegan Paul, 1984, pp. 267-319.

23. Politically, the crusade against the NEA displaces scandal and charges of dishonesty from the attackers to those attacked. Senator Alfonse D'Amato took on the role of the chief NEA persecutor at a time when he himself is the subject of embarrassing questions, allegations and several inquiries about his role in the misuse of HUD low-income housing funds in his Long Island hometown.

    The crusade against "anti-Christian" images performs a similar function of diverting attention and memory from the recent fundamentalist religious scandals involving Jim and Tammy Bakker and Jimmy Swaggart, themselves implicated in numerous presumably "un-Christian" acts. Still unscathed fellow televangelist Pat Robertson called upon followers to join the attack on the NEA during a June 9 telecast on the Christian Broadcasting Network.

24. Andres Serrano described his photograph as "a protest against the commercialization of sacred imagery." See Honan, "Congressional Anger," p.C20.

25. For defenses of free speech that agree with or offer no rebuttal to conservative characterizations of the image, see the comments of Hugh Southern, acting chair of the NEA, who said, "I most certainly can understand that the work in question

has offended many people and appreciate the feelings of those who have protested it.... I personally found it offensive" (quoted in Kastor, "Funding Art That Offends," p.C3), and artist Helen Frankenthaler, who stated in her op-ed column, "I, for one, would not want to support the two artists mentioned, but once supported, we must allow them to be shown" ("Did We Spawn an Arts Monster?" *New York Times*, July 17, 1989, p. A17).

■John Stopford, Speakeasy, *New Art Examiner,* September 1989

John Stopford is an assistant professor of philosophy in the Department of Liberal Arts, School of the Art Institute of Chicago.

R ecent events involving controversial student exhibits at the School of the Art Institute of Chicago raise fundamental questions about the rights and responsibilities of artists, art educators, administrators, and audiences. While many have been offended by what they took to be the lampooning of a black mayor and the desecration of the American flag, it should be clear by now that offensiveness does not by itself justify suppressing an artist's freedom of expression. That right protects not only the expression of views that are attractive or popular, but also those that are distasteful and unpopular. Unless symbolic expression interferes with the legitimate interests and basic rights of others, society should not interfere through law or coercion with that freedom, whether in the interests of excellence, for the sake of the artist, or merely for reasons of dislike or preference.

In particular, an individual's acts of expression may be hurtful to others without attacking their constitutional rights. Little has been done to determine where an act of free speech ceases to be merely hurtful and becomes an interference with basic rights. But much that is perceived as harmful or threatening may not be so. Truth itself is often offensive at the first encounter. If offensiveness is made into a ground for suppressing the expression of a point of view, then those whose opinions are true may fear to express them lest they be judged offensive. And if their views are wrong or only partially correct, we deprive ourselves and others of that "clearer perception" of the truth of our own views which results from the clash of opinion.

Where the tendency of the modern world is to strengthen society and diminish the power of the individual, it is, in the words of John Stuart Mill, necessary to raise "a strong barrier of moral conviction" against the mischief of the imposition on the individual by society. When a viewpoint is highly unpopular, the basic liberty of freedom of expression should extend its maximum protection. And this is neither to endorse nor condemn the content of controversial, offensive, or unpopular views, but to protect the basic right to express them.

Many fair-minded people who agree that, no matter how offensive, the controversial exhibits should have been afforded the protection of the law may question the value of the works and the character of the institution from which they emerged. This is a reasonable concern. It is the nature of things that acts of iconoclasm directed against popular symbols and images will not meet with the approval of the majority. But many of those most readily offended by controversial works of art fail to reflect on the legitimacy of the questions that such works prompt, or on the good reasons for questioning the significance which we attach to many familiar images and the powerful effects they have on us.

Our understanding of the world is shaped by a barrage of images to which we are exposed in the interests, not of truth, but of persuasion and sometimes manipulation. This circumstance is so pervasive that it provokes no outcry even though the way the commercial and political image machines are deployed can be cynically indifferent to our persons, our humanity, and our well-being. Far too many people are happy to be wooed by images in a way that is flattering and pleasurable, without regard for their truthfulness or the intentions of those who present them.

Students of art who feel impelled to take popular images and manipulate them in such a way as to raise provocative questions deserve more sympathy. They are not guilty of trying to deceive us. They are not guilty of trying to sell us something we may not really need, or of pandering to our vanity. By openly dislocating our customary perceptions they risk our displeasure rather than flatter us. Having recognized the silent power of images, and the discrepancy between the images we hold up before ourselves and our actual behavior, they seek to provoke reflection on this discrepancy.

Those who lack a capacity for ironic self-reflection, those who are unable to scrutinize the meanings they attach to images, and many others may take offense. But if powerful images are to be allowed to play such an extensive role in shaping our perceptions and judgment, it must also be permissible to experiment with their influence. If we discourage such experiments, we merely leave the images to the control of those whose motives are manifestly not pure, who aim not to clarify but to sell, not to inform but to manipulate.

At a time when the acquisition of a sense of who we are is difficult, teachers have a special responsibility to encourage autonomy of judgment and their students' ability to develop a feeling for truth and the capacity to see "behind" or "through" appearances. Art seeks not to reinforce customary and utilitarian perceptions, but to compel us to explore the symbolic and perceptual constructions through which we habitually experience the world. Languages and other symbol systems characteristically invest more emotional force in signs and symbols than in the values which they represent. Where a powerful symbol is subjected to a profound manipulation, it is to be expected that the majority will interpret this as an attack on what that symbol stands for. But because of the inertia of our habitual perceptions, because of the need to freshen and revise them, and in the interests of a public which is concerned with truth itself and not merely with images of truth, such inquiry must not merely be tolerated, it must be encouraged.

Those who attach a higher value to a symbol than to what that symbol signifies have lost a sense of the relationship between language and what language represents. A sign which becomes an object of devotion without understanding is no more than a fetish. The meaning and significance of signs and symbols must always be open to public examination and discussion. Where the languages and signs through which we experience the world cannot be questioned through the public use of reason, there can be no freedom, but only mindless conformity or mindless rebellion.

Respect for a symbol, such as a flag, can only issue from an understanding of its role as a symbol and of the values which it symbolizes. Lawmakers who command a blind and unreflective attachment to symbols undermine the development of understanding and judgment among citizens. The desire to protect and privilege certain symbols may be well-motivated, but the interests of social unity will be served better by promoting thought about what these symbols stand for.

The prevailing defensiveness of art institutions regarding exhibits which they fear may be controversial is understandable, but it is a serious error. There are many considerations to take into account when displaying a work of art, and there is nothing pusillanimous or overly defensive in being concerned that public or official reaction to a controversial exhibit may undermine or disrupt the life of an institution. But those who are responsible for the physical and financial security of artistic establishments are also curators of freedom. They must see to it that in their anxiety to preserve their existence as institutions, they do not abandon their moral responsibilities. In striving to temper the ill consequences of popular displeasure, they have a duty to avoid surreptitiously or covertly imposing conditions which tend to subvert that freedom without which art is worthless.

There is a fine line between imposing prudentially motivated constraints on the time, place, and manner in which art is exhibited and censorship. Because it is so difficult to avoid making such constraints into vehicles of the restriction of free expression, the authorities must give absolute priority to the protection and encouragement of that freedom in their calculations. Those who do not understand the profound role freedom of expression plays in maintaining and enhancing the peaceful co-existence of a plurality of different viewpoints within a just society will swiftly sacrifice it for the sake of a quiet life. But in so doing they trade a limited benefit for a lasting value.

If we wish to maintain artistic institutions — schools, museums — which are fit for human beings to create and view art in, and not merely corporate mantlepieces, then we must be prepared to stand by unpopular works of art. The widespread distaste for the School of the Art Institute's decision to stand by the flag exhibit, and the nagging pressure to which it is still being subjected — from both near and far — for sticking to that decision, illustrate the kind of difficulties to which free institutions can expect to be subjected from time to time.

But what the school did was right. Had it capitulated in the face of the waves of popular emotion which ran against the exhibit, it would have avoided much pain and trouble. But it would also have betrayed the sincere aspirations of

116

thousands of present and future students whose chance of learning to think for themselves would have been placed under a dark and ominous shadow. Modern history shows that when individuals and minorities are exposed to the tyranny of public opinion, the only sensible thing to do is stand firm. It is to the credit of the School of the Art Institute that, forced into the minority role, it stood firm. May it continue to do so.

■ Steven Durland, Censorship, Multiculturalism, and Symbols, *High Performance,* Fall 1989 (excerpt)

Steven Durland is the editor of High Performance *magazine.*

Eventually you will have to ask: who is doing the art that's getting censored? Mapplethorpe was gay, Serrano is Hispanic. Scott Tyler is black. The San Diego billboard group is multicultural, promoting a black cause. While this censorship crisis may be a surprise to many, any multicultural, gay or feminist artist can give you a litany of examples. Were I to make the charge that these acts of censorship were motivated by racism, homophobia or sexism, I'm sure most of the perpetrators would argue vehemently that such was not the case. And I think they'd honestly believe it when they say it. So what gives?

What gives is that the voice of the dominant culture has never understood what it *actually* means when it so graciously legislate racial, sexual and gender equality. Subconsciously, they think they're giving everyone a chance to be just like them. A chance to live like white men. A chance to make art in the great Euro-Western tradition. They've failed to realize that few want to be like them. Rather, they want the freedom to be themselves, living their own religions, and their own histories, and their own cultures. Just like it says in the Constitution. And that is definitely a threat to a country that, in spite of its "Bill of Rights," imagines itself to be white, Christian, heterosexual and male.

There are some overriding art world ironies here. For years national, state and local funding agencies have made it a priority to assure that at least token funding go to representatives of these groups. You seldom hear of a peer panel review any more that doesn't make a point of noting sex and ethnicity in the distribution of money. What the people at the top have failed to realize, though, is that when you give a voice to people who've been denied for so long, what you're going to find out is that these people are really pissed (pun intended) off. No "Thank you, massa" here. They will immediately take the opportunity to point out racist governments and sexist religions and Christian hypocrisy. Sure it may be raw. But it's exercising the same right, used with a much greater sense of real "American" morality, that the dominant culture has used for so long to keep women in the home, blacks in their place, and gays on their death beds.

It's a fact that only ten percent of the families in the U.S. are representative of "male provider, woman in the home with the kids." Perhaps these men with their "women in the homes" have more time to write letters, and that's why this small population is dominating our cultural debate. I don't know. They've certainly managed a voice that vastly outnumbers their membership. Perhaps, in this particular instance, the art world is to blame for its own problems. Any elected official would recognize in an instant that no matter how much artists protest, when it's time to go to the polls, Wildmon's supporters are going to make their wives go out and vote, while the poorly networked and apolitical members of the art world are deconstructing sitcoms. A sad thought when you consider that the art world potentially has much more clout....

The final, overriding irony in all this, is that all parties involved — the artists, the conservative right, the Congress — are in the position of not being able to do anything about the things that are really upsetting them. To compensate, each group, in their own way, is attacking what is perceived to be a symbol of its antagonism. For the artists, those symbols may be the crucifixes of religious zealots, the flags of racist governments, or the sexual mores of oppressive cults. (Excuse me, but why *aren't* fanatic Christians who give lots of money to dubious minsters considered cultists? Where are the de-programmers when you need them?) For the conservative right, the art they attack is, for them, symbolic of a general breakdown in moral fiber. For Congress, this is their Grenada: a symbolic show of power directed toward a tiny, defenseless agency in a government over which they've lost control.

For the artists, working with symbols is the stock in trade. For the others, it's a cop out. The artists have done their job. They've called attention to some of our social, cultural and political failings. If Helms or Wildmon wants to "kill the messenger," they're just not doing their job.

To quote Hilton Kramer, "What we're being asked to support and embrace in the name of art is an attitude toward life." He's right. But unlike Mr. Kramer, I would see it as very positive to support an attitude — even a government supported policy — that champions freedom of expression. Especially when we're faced with the alternatives — the ones we generally associate with such names as Hitler, Stalin, Khomeini and Deng Xiaoping. Need we add Helms to that list?

■ Allan Sekula, "Gay-Bashing" as an Art Form, *Los Angeles Times*, October 21, 1989

Allan Sekula is a photographer and critic, and the director of the photography program at the California Institue of the Arts.

Conservatives have cooked up a grimly Malthusian policy for the arts, motivated partly by free-market economic dogma, party by an ideological (and public-relations) need to indulge in conspicuous displays of moral outrage. Press accounts have concentrated on the fulminations of Jesse Helms, giving scant attention to the real strategists of this cultural battle, the brave lieutenants of the intellectual right.

I'm thinking here of Hilton Kramer, former art critic for the *New York Times* and currently editor of the *New Criterion*, and Samuel Lipman, publisher of that journal of conservative cultural opinion. The cultural traditionalism they've been refining over the years is now having its day in the limelight, in the controversy over "obscene" art underwritten by tax dollars through the National Endowment for the Arts. The flash point was a scheduled exhibition, partly funded by the NEA, of the late Robert Mapplethorpe's work, photographs commonly described as "homoerotic" in content.

Kramer and Lipman have been seeking to restrict the funding of the arts endowment since the very beginning of the Reagan presidency. Ideologically, they are committed to a vision of late-modernist culture derived from the earlier modernism of T.S. Eliot. They seek to erect a stable, authoritative canon of great works of the past, and to defend practitioners of contemporary art who have an intelligent and polite dialogue with that canon. Artists with an impolite, aggressive or debunking attitude to the art of the past don't rank very high with Lipman and Kramer; for example, they don't like the Dadaists.

Lipman in particular would like to see the NEA become a ministry of dead art, funding only the historical endeavors of museums. This makes sense in conservative terms, since recent tax-law changes have removed incentives for private collectors to donate art to museums, and escalating art prices have made it difficult for museums to compete with these same private collectors. A real institutional crisis is brewing, precisely because of the speculative hypertrophy of the free market. You might say that Lipman favors a modest museum bail-out program based on shifting money from living art to dead art.

These people make a lot of noise about allowing contemporary art to succeed or fail in the marketplace. Kramer has no problem, he claims, with a *private* culture of homosexual eroticism. What bothers Kramer is the implied moral imprimatur of government funding for public art exhibitions.

Liberals are suffering from a failure of nerve in this regard, allowing the right wing to hold the moral and the economic high ground. We should be aggressive in exposing both the homophobia and the economic inconsistencies of the conservative argument.

Kramer is happy as long as homosexual culture remains in the closet, and he's even willing to accept a small homosexual aristocracy of taste within the art world. How generous.

What terrifies conservatives like him and Lipman is a truly popular, open homosexual culture, a culture capable of forging alliances and bonds with dissident and mainstream groups in this society. They worry about the sort of politicized gay and lesbian culture that has emerged since the Stonewall Rebellion of 1969 and is gathering strength now in response to the AIDS crisis.

Robert Mapplethorpe and gays in general are being stigmatized for taking seriously one of the utopian promises of the capitalist consumer economy: the promise of liberated desire. According to conservatives, gays and lesbians are suspect because they don't reproduce "normal" family life. They supposedly don't have children, and they often work in "frivolous" fields on the fringe of

119

the GNP. In other words, conservatives project their own fears of both unfettered desire and an impotent economy onto gay and lesbian people, who are easily scapegoated in a society obsessed with productivity.

Liberals in government are stigmatized for their willingness to support a "hedonistic" and "bohemian" culture. Lipman chastises the very modestly funded NEA for its "profligacy." Another conservative intellectual, Gertrude Himmelfarb, recently suggested a connection between the (supposed) spendthrift shortsightedness of Keynesian economics and John Maynard Keynes' personal life as a homosexual.

These are strange accusations that beg for both economic and psychological analysis. Sigmund Freud understood the phenomenon of the "reaction formation," the attempt to control a repressed wish. The parsimonious effort to control the orifices of government spending may well be a cover for the spendthrift impulses of conservatives themselves. Maybe conservatives are all closet Keynesians, secret believers in government deficit spending, notably of the military variety.

Samuel Lipman's *New Criterion* is handsomely funded by the ultra-conservative John M. Olin Foundation. Olin money comes not from some abstract patronage pool in the sky, but from the Olin Corp., a major chemical and munitions manufacturer. And where would Jesse Helms be without his two causes — tobacco subsidies and military aid to brutal Central American rightists? As threats to public health, Robert Mapplethorpe's deadpan late-1970s pictures of unwittingly unsafe sex between consenting adult men hardly compare.

It has been too easy for the "art world" — a label that suggests both cosmopolitanism and parochialism — to see itself as a unified body under attack by philistines. The art world is perfectly capable of dividing against itself under pressure from without. Some arts administrators have stated their willingness to "live with" a congressional funding compromise that stigmatizes "homoerotic" expression. This will create a zone of moral quarantine. Why should gay and lesbian artists have to live and work under this shadow? Why should any artist who wishes to speak about the complicated vicissitudes of sexuality have to endure the special scrutiny of the government? And why should any other artist accept this stigmatization of his or her colleagues?

A large and distinguished assemblage of artists is boycotting the Corcoran Gallery of Art, the Washington institution that volunteered to serve as the laboratory for conservative cultural policy by canceling a scheduled Mapplethorpe exhibition. The boycott is an appropriate and justified response, a kind of strike. The issue now is to develop common ground with other groups seeking to defend civil rights and liberties in an increasingly authoritarian society.

■ 101st Congress, Public Law 101-121, October 23, 1989 (excerpt)

This law included the final version of the Helms amendment agreed to by both the House and the Senate. The law singled out the ICA and SECCA, art spaces which had supported work by Mapplethrope or Serrano, and it set up an Independent Commission to review the NEA.

National Foundation On the Arts and the Humanities

National Endowment for the Arts Grants and Administration

For necessary expenses to carry out the National Foundation on the Arts and Humanities Act of 1965, as amended, $144,105,000 shall be available to the National Endowment for the Arts for the support of projects and productions in the arts through assistance to groups and individuals pursuant to section 5(c) of the Act, and for administering the functions of the Act: *Provided*, That not less than thirty days prior to the award of any direct grant to the Southeastern Center for Contemporary Art (SECCA) in Winston-Salem, North Carolina, or for the Institute of Contemporary Art at the University of Pennsylvania, the National Endowment for the Arts shall submit to the Committees on Appropriations of the House and Senate a notification of its intent to make such an award: *Provided further*, That said notification shall delineate the purposes of the award which is proposed to be made and the specific criteria used by the Endowment to justify selection of said award....

Sec. 304.

No part of any appropriation contained in this Act shall be available for any activity or the publication or distribution of literature that in any way tends to promote public support or opposition to any legislative proposal on which congressional action is not complete: *Provided*, That —

(a) None of the funds authorized to be appropriated for the National Endowment for the Arts or the National Endowment for the Humanities may be used to promote, disseminate, or produce materials which in the judgment of the National Endowment for the Arts or the National Endowment for the Humanities may be considered obscene, including but not limited to, depictions of sadomasochism, homoeroticism, the sexual exploitation of children, or individuals engaged in sex acts and which, when taken as a whole, do not have serious literary, artistic, political, or scientific value.

(b) It is the sense of the Congress:

(1) That under the present procedures employed for awarding National Endowment for the Arts grants, although the National Endowment for the Arts has had an excellent record over the years, it is possible for projects to be funded without adequate review of the artistic content or value of the work.

(2) That recently works have been funded which are without artistic value but which are criticized as pornographic and shocking by any standards.

(3) That censorship inhibits and stultifies the full expression of art.

(4) That free inquiry and expression is reaffirmed. Therefore, be it resolved:

    (A) That all artistic works do not have artistic or humanistic excellence and an application can include works that possess both nonexcellent and excellent portions.

    (B) That the Chairman of the National Endowment for the Arts has the responsibility to determine whether such an application should be funded.

    (C) That the National Endowment for the Arts must find a better method to seek out those works that have artistic excellence and to exclude those works which are without any redeeming literary, scholarly, cultural, or artistic value.

    (D) That a commission be established to review the National Endowment for the Arts grant making procedures, including those of its panel system, to determine whether there should be standards for grant making other than "substantial artistic and cultural significance, giving emphasis to American creativity and cultural diversity and the maintenance and encouragement of professional excellence" (20 U.S.C. 954(c)(1)) and if so, then what other standards. The criteria to be considered by the commission shall include but not be limited to possible standards where (a) applying contemporary community standards would find that the work taken as a whole appeals to a prurient interest; (b) the work depicts or describes in a patently offensive way, sexual conduct; and (c) the work, taken as a whole, lacks serious artistic and cultural value.

(c)(1) There is hereby established a temporary Independent Commission for the purpose of —

    (A) reviewing the National Endowment for the Arts grant making procedures, including those of its panel system; and

    (B) considering whether the standard for publicly funded art should be different than the standard for privately funded art.

(2) The Commission shall be composed of twelve members as follows:

    (A) four members appointed by the President;

    (B) four members appointed by the President upon the recommendation of the Speaker of the House of Representatives in consultation with the minority leader of the House of Representatives;

(C) four members appointed by the President upon the recommendation of the President pro tempore of the Senate in consultation with the minority leader of the Senate;

(D) the chairman shall be designated by vote of the Commission members; and

(E) a quorum for the purposes of conducting meetings shall be seven.

(3) Members of the Commission shall serve without pay. While away from their homes or regular places of business in the performance of services for the Commission, members of the Commission shall be allowed travel expenses, including per diem in lieu of subsistence, in the same manner as persons employed intermittently in Government service are allowed expenses under 5 U.S.C. 5703.

(4) The Commission may, for the purpose of carrying out its duties, hold such hearings, sit and act at such times and places, take such testimony, and receive such evidence, as the commission considers appropriate.

(5) The Commission shall issue a report to the Speaker of the House of Representatives and the President of the Senate no later than 180 days after the date of enactment of this Act.

(6) The Commission shall expire on September 30, 1990.

(7) Expenses of the Commission not to exceed $250,000, including administrative support, shall be furnished by the National Endowment for the Arts.

■ Rev. Pat Robertson, Christian Coalition direct mail, October 25, 1989 (excerpt)

Rev. Pat Robertson is the head of the Christian Broadcasting Network (CBN), a television evangelist, and the director of the Christian Coalition.

Dear ——

The enclosed red envelope contains graphic descriptions of homosexual erotic photographs that were funded by your tax dollars.

I'd never send you the photos, but I did want you to know about the vile contents of your tax funded material.

You'll be as outraged as I am when you open the envelope.

Your hard earned tax dollars paid for this trash.

And the ACLU and liberal Democrats in Washington are trying to tell us that we can't do anything about it.

Well, they're wrong.

Frankly, they're doing everything possible to keep this travesty quiet — they know that the voters back home would turn them out of office if they knew...

So they're calling anyone who attacks this garbage "censors" and they're hiding behind "free speech" and "freedom of expression" as a reason to continue funding this pornographic filth.

But I *won't* be silent. And I pray you won't either....

Last week I began a new organization to fight for our freedoms — The Christian Coalition. Once again I invite you to join me in making our voices heard.

As soon as I receive your membership form, I'll send you an official membership card and lapel pin.

You can begin wearing your lapel pin immediately to civic and political meetings as a way of identifying others who are concerned about the moral decadence that has invaded the heart of America.

We won't endorse any candidates or political parties — but we will speak out on issues — and we'll make sure candidates for office at every level know how we stand — and how we'll vote.

We'll organize chapters in every state, every Congressional District, and God willing, every precinct in America.

We'll register God-fearing Americans to vote and insist that candidates for every office tell us their views on religious freedom, abortion, prayers in schools, sex education, pornography, and other issues important to the moral fiber of our nation.

We'll sponsor rallies and debates and inform voters of positions held by those seeking office.

As an activist organization, The Christian Coalition will force America to face the moral issues that threaten to destroy us. . . .

Can I count on you?

Return your membership form today. Together we can begin to turn back the tide of pornography, filth and moral decay that is attacking every level of our society.

Sincerely,

Pat Robertson

[inside red envelope]

IMPORTANT — I encourage you to exercise your freedom immediately by destroying the vulgar information about the photographs.

TAX-PAYER FUNDED
Photographs Too Vulgar to Print

The following are descriptions of photographs funded by taxpayer dollars and displayed in galleries and art museums receiving Federal Funding. These photographs have been exhibited and available for children of any age when visiting these galleries.

1. A photo of a man with a bull-whip inserted in his rectum. This piece of "art" is listed as a self-portrait of the photographer.

2. A close-up of a man with his "pinkie" finger inserted in his penis.

3. A photo of a man urinating in another man's mouth.

4. A photo showing one man holding another man's genitals.

5. A photo of a man's arm (up to the forearm) in another man's rectum.

6. A photo of young pre-school girl with her genitals exposed.

7. A photo of naked children in bed with a naked man.

8. A photo of a man in a suit exposing himself.

9. A photo of a man with his genitals laying on a table.

■John Frohnmayer, letter to Susan Wyatt, November 3, 1989

John Frohnmayer is the former chairperson of the National Endowment for the Arts. Susan Wyatt was the executive director of Artists Space during the NEA controversy.

D ear Susan:

I very much appreciate that you brought the concerns raised by Artists Space's exhibition "Witness: Against Our Vanishing" to our attention. Pursuant to our conversations and the report of Andrew Oliver of my staff, who has reviewed the material to be exhibited and a draft of the catalogue, I understand that certain texts, photographs and other representations in the exhibition may offend the language of the FY 1990 Appropriation Act (P.L. 101-121).

The grant for this exhibition was made in FY 1989 and thus technically would not be subject to that provision of the FY 1990 Appropriation Act, which I enclose for your ready reference. I note that at the time the application for the exhibition was reviewed at the Endowment, in February of this year, no materials had been selected for inclusion, and our panel did not review any of the objects to be exhibited. Given our recent review, and the current political climate, I believe that the use of Endowment funds to exhibit or publish this work is in violation of the spirit of the Congressional directive.

Because of the recent criticism the Endowment has come under and the seriousness of Congress's directive, we must all work together to ensure that projects funded by the Endowment do not violate either the spirit or the letter of the law. The message has been clearly and strongly conveyed to us that Congress means business.

On this basis, I believe that the Endowment's funds may not be used to exhibit or publish this material. Therefore, Artists Space should relinquish the Endowment's grant for the exhibition. Additionally, please employ the following disclaimer in appropriate ways (e.g. as an addendum to press releases) to correct the misapprehension of our support for this exhibition:

"The National Endowment for the Arts has not supported this exhibition or its catalogue."

While I recognize the difficulties these actions may cause for Artists Space, I believe it is in our mutual best interest to follow these steps. We are anxious to work with you to assure that your commitment to artistic excellence is not abridged and the law is fully obeyed. The best way for that to happen is if we communicate frequently. Please call me directly at 202/682-5414 should you have questions.

Sincerely,

John E. Frohnmayer
Chairman

■ Susan Wyatt, response to John Frohnmayer, November 8, 1989

Dear Mr. Frohnmayer:

Pursuant to your letter of November 3, 1989 I am writing to inform you that our Board has met and voted unanimously not to relinquish the funds.

Sincerely,

Susan Wyatt
Executive Director

■ David Wojnarowicz, Postcards from America: X-rays from Hell, *Witnesses* exhibition catalog, November 1989 (excerpt)

David Wojnarowicz is an artist.

My friend across the table says, "There are no more people in their 30's. We're all dying out. One of my four best friends just went into the hospital yesterday and he underwent a blood transfusion and is now suddenly blind in one eye. The doctors don't know what it is..." My eyes are still scanning the table; I know a hug or a pat on the shoulder won't answer the question mark in his voice. And I have a low threshold for this information. The AZT is kicking in with one of its little side-effects: increased mental activity which in translation means I wake up these mornings with an intense claustrophobic feeling of fucking doom. It also means that one word too many can send me to the window kicking out panes of glass, or at least that's my impulse (the fact that winter is coming holds me in check). My eyes scan the surfaces of walls and tables to provide balance to the weight of words. A 35mm camera containing the unprocessed images of red and blue and green faces in close-up profile screaming, a large postcard of a stuffed gorilla pounding its dusty chest in a museum diorama, a small bottle of hydrocortisone to keep my face from turning into a mass of peeling red and yellow flaking skin, an airline ticket to Normal, Illinois to work on a print, a small plaster model of a generic Mexican pyramid looking like it was made in Aztec kindergarten, a tiny motor-car with a tiny Goofy driving at the wheel...

My friend across the table says, "The other three of my four best friends are dead and I'm afraid that I won't see this friend again." My eyes settle on a six-inch tall rubber model of Frankenstein from the Universal Pictures Tour gift shop, TM 1931; his hands are enormous and my head fills up with replaceable body parts; with seeing the guy in the hospital; seeing myself and my friend across the table in line for replaceable body parts; my wandering eyes aren't staving off the anxiety of his words; behind his words, so I say, "You know... he can still rally back... maybe... I mean people do come back from the edge of death..."

"Well," he says, "He lost thirty pounds in a few weeks..."

A boxed cassette of someone's interview with me in which I talk about diagnosis and how it simply underlined what I knew existed anyway. Not just the disease but the sense of death in the American landscape. How when I was out west this summer standing in the mountains of a small city in New Mexico I got a sudden and intense feeling of rage looking at those post card perfect slopes and clouds. For all I knew I was the only person for miles and all alone and I didn't trust that fucking mountain's serenity. I mean it was just bullshit. I couldn't buy the con of nature's beauty; all I could see was death. The rest of my life is being unwound and seen through a frame of death. My anger is more about this culture's refusal to deal with mortality. My rage is really about the fact that WHEN I WAS TOLD THAT I'D CONTRACTED THIS VIRUS IT DIDN'T TAKE ME LONG TO REALIZE THAT I'D CONTRACTED A DISEASED SOCIETY AS WELL.

On the table is today's newspaper with a picture of Cardinal O'Connor saying he'd like to take part in operation rescue's blocking of abortion clinics but his lawyers are advising against it. This fat cannibal from that house of walking swastikas up on fifth avenue should lose his church tax-exempt status and pay retroactive taxes from the last couple centuries. Shut down our clinics and we will shut down your 'church.' I believe in the death penalty for people in positions of power who commit crimes against humanity, i.e., fascism. This creep in black skirts has kept safer-sex information off the local television stations and mass transit advertising spaces for the last eight years of the AIDS epidemic thereby helping thousands and thousands to their unnecessary deaths....

My friend across the table says, "I don't know how much longer I can go on... Maybe I should just kill myself." I looked up from the Frankenstein doll, stopped trying to twist its yellow head off and looked at him. He was looking out the window at a sexy Puerto Rican guy standing on the street below. I asked him, "If tomorrow you could take a pill that would let you die quickly and quietly, would you do it?"

"No," he said, "Not yet."

"There's too much work to do," I said.

"That's right," he said.

"There's still a lot of work to do..."

I am a bundle of contradictions that shift constantly. This is a comfort to me because to contradict myself dismantles the mental/physical chains of the verbal code. I abstract this disease I have in the same way you abstract death. Sometimes I don't think about this disease for hours. This process lets me get work done, and work gives me life, or at least makes sense of living for short periods of time. But because I abstract this disease, it periodically knocks me on my ass with its relentlessness. With almost any other illness you take for granted that within a week or month the illness will end and the wonderful part of the human body called the mind will go about its job erasing evidence of the pain and discomfort previously experienced. But with AIDS or HIV infections one never gets that luxury and I find myself after a while responding to it for a fractured moment with my pre-AIDS thought processes: "Alright this is enough already; it should just go away." But each day's dose of medicine, or the intermittent aerosol pentamidine treatments, or the sexy stranger nodding to you on the street corner or across the room at a party, reminds you in a clearer than clear way that at this point in history the virus' activity is forever. Outside my windows there are thousands of people without homes who are trying to deal with having AIDS. If I think my life at times has a nightmare quality about it because of the society in which I live and that society's almost total inability to deal with this disease in anything other than a conservative agenda, think for a moment what it would be to be facing winter winds and shit menus at the limited shelters, and the rampant T.B. and the rapes, muggings, stabbings in those shelters, and the overwhelmed clinics and sometimes indifferent clinic doctors, and the fact that drug trials are not open to people of color or the poor unless they have a private physician who can monitor the experimental drugs they would need to take, and they don't have those kinds of doctors in clinics because doctors in clinics are constantly rotated and intravenous drug users have to be clean of drugs for two years before they'll be considered for drug trials, and yet there are nine-month waiting periods just to get assigned to a treatment program, so picture yourself with a couple of the 350 opportunistic infections and unable to respond to a few drugs released by the foot-dragging FDA and having to maintain a junk habit; or even having to try and kick that habit without any clinical help and also keep yourself alive two years to get a drug that you need immediately — thank you Ed Koch; thank you Stephen Josephs; thank you Frank Young; thank you AMA.

I scratch my head at the hysteria surrounding the actions of the repulsive senator from zombieland who has been trying to dismantle the NEA for supporting the work of Andres Serrano and Robert Mapplethorpe. Although the anger sparked within the art community is certainly justified and hopefully will grow stronger; the actions by Helms and D'Amato only follow standards that have been formed and implemented by the "arts" community itself. The major museums in New York, not to mention museums around the country, are just as guilty of this kind of selective cultural support and denial. It is a standard practice to make invisible any kind of sexual imaging other than white straight male erotic fantasies — sex in America long ago slid into a small set of generic symbols; mention the word sex and the general public seems to imagine a couple of heterosexual positions on a bed - there are actual laws in the South forbidding anything else even between consenting adults. So people have found it necessary to define their sexuality in images, in photographs and drawings and movies in order to not disappear. Collectors have for the most part failed to support work that defines a particular person's sexuality, except for a few examples such as Mapplethorpe, and thus have perpetuated the invisibility of the myriad possibilities of sexual activity. The collectors' influence on what the museum shows continues this process secretly with behind the scenes manipulations of curators and money. Jesse Helms is, at the very least, making his attacks on freedom public; the collectors and museums responsible for censorship do theirs at elegant private parties or from the confines of their self-created closets.

It doesn't just stop at images — recently a critic/novelist had his novel reviewed by the New York Times Book Review and the reviewer took outrage at the novelist's descriptions of promiscuity, saying: "In this age of AIDS, the writer should show more restraint..." Not only do we have to contend with bonehead newscasters and conservative members of the medical profession telling us to "just say no" to sexuality itself rather than talk about safer sex possibilities, but we have people from the thought police spilling out from the ranks with admonitions that we shouldn't think about anything other than monogamous or safer sex. I'm beginning to believe that one of the last frontiers left for radical gesture is the imagination. At least in my ungoverned imagination I can fuck somebody without a rubber or I can, in the privacy of my own skull, douse Helms with a bucket of gasoline and set his putrid ass on fire or throw rep. William Dannemeyer off the empire state building. These fantasies give me distance from my outrage for a few seconds. They give me momentary comfort. Sexuality defined in images gives me comfort in a hostile world. They give me strength. I have always loved my anonymity and therein lies a contradiction because I also find comfort in seeing representations of my private experiences in the public environment. They need not be representations of my experiences — they can be the experiences of and by others that merely come close to my own or else disrupt the generic representations that have come to be the norm in the various medias outside my door. I find that when I witness diverse representations of "Reality" on a gallery wall or in a book or a movie or in the spoken word or performance, that the more diverse the representations, the more I feel there is room in the environment for my existence; that not the entire environment is hostile.

To make the *private* into something *public* is an action that has terrific repercussions in the pre-invented world. The government has the job of maintaining the day to day illusion of the ONE TRIBE NATION. Each public disclosure of a private reality becomes something of a magnet that can attract others with a similar frame of reference; thus each public disclosure of a fragment of private reality serves as a dismantling tool against the illusion of ONE TRIBE NATION; it lifts the curtains for a brief peek and reveals the possible existence of literally millions of tribes, the term GENERAL PUBLIC disintegrates. If GENERAL PUBLIC disintegrates, what happens next is the possibility of an X-RAY OF CIVILIZATION, an examination of its foundations. To turn our private grief at the loss of friends, family, lovers and strangers into something public would serve as another powerful dismantling tool. It would dispel the notion that this virus has a sexual orientation or the notion that the government and medical community has done very much to ease the spread or advancement of this disease.

■ Rev. Timothy Healy, statement to the House Subcommittee on Postsecondary Education, November 15, 1989 (excerpt)

The debate that has divided Congress and a good part of the Nation over the past few weeks is a real one. We all relish an argument when one side is clearly wrong and one side clearly right. This debate is tougher because it faces us with a real contradiction of rights. On the one hand is the right of the artist under the Constitution to freedom of expression; on the other hand the right of the nation's citizens to determine through their representatives where their tax dollars will go.

It might be well to clarify one semantic difficulty. The debate is about censorship, and any effort to pretend that it is not is misleading. Given the prestige of the Federal Government, the accolade that any grant from either national endowment bestows, and the artistic integrity and impartiality of the juries who work for the endowments, any canons of content-based condemnation are simply a priori restraint. Against the argument that the artist is free to write, to paint or compose as he pleases without federal subsidy must urge that to deprive an artist of access to that subsidy because of the content of his work is a clear and strong kind of censorship. The counter-argument is really a dodge which does not take into account the realities of the artistic marketplace or indeed, the rights of the artist himself.

In what follows I am working on three premises. The first is that the one totally unacceptable conclusion would be that the Federal Government should, in order to simplify and avoid conflict, cut off all subsidy. Second, I acknowledge the legitimacy of the present conflict and acknowledge also that like conflicts have occurred in the past (although not many given the total number of awards) and will occur in the future. These conflicts will be particularly acute for legislators who are vulnerable to public scrutiny and public criticism far more than are the administrators involved. The third premise on which I am working is that any reasonable solution will try to remove politics as far as possible not only from the normal working of federal support of the arts but above all from the conflicts that are sure to arise.

The course of the debate shows a definite confusion between law and morality. The moral order covers the entire spectrum of human activity, public, private, external, internal. The law on the other hand can only concern itself with external activity, and particularly activity that is social or public. What a man or woman does in private is beyond the reach of the law, and very much more beyond the reach of the law are a man or woman's thoughts, reactions, ideas. Elizabeth of England's statement, "I will not open windows into men's souls" is a good point of departure for this discussion.

Once law and morality are confused it is easy to arrive at such statements as "whatever is good ought to be legislated." That premise is bad enough. Even worse is the premise that "what is legal is moral" which deprives the law of the moral consensus on which it can stand and from which it is to be judged. The confusion of public and private morality, in other words mixing up of the realm of law with the realm of morals, is deadly.

Every government that has ever existed has always claimed "police power." Government is always concerned with public morals, public health, public safety, public order and a reasonable level of comfort in the course of civic life. The question that arises about all police authority is when and how it should be exercised and how much. That is simply another way of asking what is the relationship between freedom and restraint in civil society.

The answer seems to be that freedom may very well be an absolute as a goal, but it is hardly ever absolute as an exercise. Restraints in a democracy are justified because they enhance freedom, but they always enhance that freedom in a sphere somewhat distant from the act of restraint. All of us put up with red lights, because we want to use our cars to get someplace and the red light guarantees us freedom from chaos. All of us pay taxes because we want to use the roads, police, fire departments, ambulances and other services provided by government. Males among us put up with the draft, because we understood it as the only way to keep the nation free from foreign attack. In like manner, all of us accept that professionals should be qualified, because that prevents us from being hurt by them. Even teachers have to be qualified, to grant us and our children a certain freedom from ignorance. We accept multiple restraints in order to procure clean air and clean water, which is really a way of saying we want us and our descendants to enjoy freedom from want. Large cities have rent control programs, that free at least some of their citizens from arbitrary eviction.

All of this seems clear enough until we remember that constraint in one domain in order to free us in another may well damage a third domain, and sometimes that effect is hard or impossible to predict. Those who fought strenuously during World War I for the imposition of prohibition had a good aim in mind and felt that to achieve that good aim a legitimate restraint could be placed upon all citizens. As a matter of hard fact prohibition eroded the authority of the law itself, destroyed respect for government, and in this third domain the results were disastrous. That may lead us to the sardonic conclusion that logic is a poor guide in such matters, and indeed it is. The serious logic that lay behind prohibition did a great deal of damage in an area its proponents seemed never to have expected.

Confusing law and morality is a serious problem that has bedeviled every democratic society. On the other hand, the United States has elaborated over the years one serious step towards the solution, and that is a presumption always in favor of freedom. By law, custom and by conviction all of us lay the burden of proof on those who would constrain us. On the other hand, we are perfectly willing to acknowledge that when freedom is irresponsibly used, a penalty must be paid. It is clear however that our penalities follow the facts. Once a freedom has been abused, law can reasonably punish the abuser.

That fact leads us to a serious conclusion; Censorship in the civil order must be a juridical process. That means its premises and objectives must be defined by the norms of jurisprudence: and its forms of procedures should actually be judicial. In addition both its structure and workings must have serious community support.

Law can tolerate evils that morality condemns. The law looks only to what St. Thomas Aquinas defines as "possibility." We have a good law if it will be obeyed, if it is enforceable, and if it is so prudently drafted that it avoids at least most of the harmful effects that could flow from it. If a law does none of these things it is a bad law, no matter what the logic or the moral intensity behind it.

■John Russell, Statements of Grief and Survival in Show That Confronts AIDS, *New York Times*, November 16, 1989

John Russell is an art historian, and an art critic for the **New** York **Times.**

"Witnesses: Against Our Vanishing" at Artists Space (223 West Broadway, at White Street) has had a sustained, noisy, contentious and in some respects unwelcome buildup. Now the object of nationwide attention, it began as a low-key cry of grief and outrage from a group of artists, resident mainly on the Lower East Side of Manhattan.

One and all of them had had to come to terms with the ever-increasing impact of AIDS upon their community as a whole, upon those closest to them and, in many cases, upon themselves. The show was also intended, according to Susan Wyatt, the executive director of Artists Space, as "a kind of testimony of survival, of keeping the faith, despite the insidious nature of the disease and the prejudice surrounding it."

As such, it could have taken an elegiac form, and sometimes it does. Jo Shane, for instance, shows two vanity tables that have been outfitted with photographs and personal belongings that turn them into portable shrines for remembrance.

If we yield to an almost universal instinct and pull open a drawer, a mirror hidden inside may reflect our own face back at us. Another drawer opens to reveal a group of glass vials whose function we can guess for ourselves. It may also be that one of the glass bottles on the table is filled not with perfume but with the blood of the dead victim. Even so, and despite the overtones just described, these are shrines that play by the rules.

It also happens once or twice that sheer beauty of an ironical kind irradiates what is in reality as unpleasant a situation as can be wished upon us. In Philip-Lorca DiCorcia's color photography, "Vittorio," an AIDS patient lies in a hospital. All around him are the marks of festivity. Colored balloons ride the ceiling. A vintage summer straw hat makes a cameo appearance. Focus is everywhere soft and sweet. For the time it takes to activate the camera, pain and despair and indignity are defeated.

It can also happen that an artist pulls back from the immediate and takes a longer, wryer view. In one of Allen Frame's two-part black and white photo-diptychs, we get a paradoxical glimpse of the boisterous outdoors. Next, he spells out what it means to grow a little older, in the United States, and yet to have much the same feelings about much the same people.

That is, comparatively, the fun part of the show. But most of it has a deeper, darker character. These are not people who go quietly and obediently. When they die, they die in rage. Foul in mouth and sometimes foul in body, they speak of hatred, and choking. Who are we to reproach them for "questionable taste"? The traditional rules of mourning nowhere apply. To have watched them die is, as one witness says, "like surgery without anesthetic." Notions of "taste" can play no part in it.

The little drawing called "What Happened to My Lungs?" by Vittorio Scarpati is relevant to this. Made at a time when Scarpati's lungs had collapsed from AIDS related pneumonia and when he was in great pain for months on end, it has a free-running sardonic humor that may be "in questionable taste." But it is as an instance of man's unconquerable mind that it stays in the memory.

Those who are dying of AIDS, and those who will die of it in the years to come, are entitled to wonder whether all that could be done about it is actually being done. Theirs is, in that respect and in no other, a privileged position. Whatever they want to say, we should listen to. And in text and image of this exhibition, they do say it. If what they have to say and to show is sometimes shot through with a corrosive and terrible invective, who can be surprised?

Yet in times of great and irreversible trouble, art can be on our side. So it is, at any rate, with the self-portraits in which Darrel Ellis starts from photographs of himself by Robert Mapplethorpe and Peter Hujar and readjusts them, subtly, in ink on paper. The truth of those photographs is self-evident, but the pen-and-ink drawings carry with them an emotional charge that is no less true.

Though doubtless disconcerting at times to visitors who would come in unaltered to the purpose of the show, the show is neither gratuitous nor merely sensational. Nor is it defeatist in its general tone. Clarence Elie-Rivera's photographs of daily life in the Lower East Side scenes have a tumultuous vitality. Stephen Tashjian's full-length portrait of a young man has a rakish style that in this context is all its own.

There is, too, something memorably calm and constructive about the long series of photographs in which Dorit Cypis had herself photographed, naked, by four women friends. So far from being prurient, the 28 images offer an affectionate but impartial account of what it means to live in one's whole body, instead of primarily in one's head.

It also emerges from the show that a key feature of the experience of AIDS is the immense loneliness that it leaves among the bereft. Shellburne Thurber's photo-portraits of empty motel rooms bring that out without a "story," so all-permeating is the emptiness before us.

"Witnesses" is not primarily an art exhibition. It is an attempt to bear witness in terms of art. If some of it is unpleasant and disturbing, it could not be otherwise. In mounting the show, Artists Space has remained true to its original ambition, which was to give artists a chance to show work that, as yet, no one had been willing to take on. And if, in the matter of AIDS, there are barriers between "us" and "them," it is for us to break them down, not to build them higher.

■ Eric Gibson, Art, Morals, and NEA Taken for Granted, *Washington Times,* November 21, 1981

Eric Gibson is the art critic for the Washington Times.

The recent contretemps between Artists Space and National Endowment for the Arts Chairman John E. Frohnmayer can now be judged on its own merits, since the Manhattan organization's controversial show "Witnesses: Against Our Vanish" has finally opened.

After all the noise, however, "Witnesses" proves to be unremarkable — which is to say that most of the work in it is average at best. Like any show whose main aim is to drive home a "point" — in this case the ravages of AIDS on the Lower East Side of New York — we are supposed to exempt it from aesthetic judgments simply because its subject is deemed a worthy one.

The brouhaha erupted on Nov. 8 when Mr. Frohnmayer, in a letter to Susan Wyatt, director of Artists Space, said that he was withdrawing a $10,000 grant awarded for an exhibition titled "Witnesses: Against Our Vanishing." He did so, he said, to conform with the new law barring funds from exhibitions containing art that is "obscene, including sado-masochism, homoeroticism, the sexual exploitation of children or individuals engaged in sex acts," or lacking "serious literary, artistic, political or scientific value."

The show, curated by Nan Goldin, consisted of art by and about victims of AIDS. Its catalog, featuring outspoken attacks on Sen. Jesse Helms and Rep. William Dannemeyer, among others, was what had caught Mr. Frohnmayer's eye. He determined the show had become too "political." Miss Wyatt, after consulting her board, actually refused to return the grant money to NEA. But on Thursday, after hearing the arts world condemn him for days and days, Mr. Frohnmayer reversed his decision.

Mr. Frohnmayer saw the show before changing his mind. And what he saw was an exhibition you had to know, going in, was all about AIDS, because the work itself says almost nothing coherent about the disease. Exhibit most of the pieces in a neutral setting, and the viewer would have no clue as to what they were about.

And, despite all the hype, there was remarkably little of the sort of work that the new law, not to mention public decency, proscribes. There were about three works that could be described as being pornographic but nothing on the order of Robert Mapplethorpe's work.

Given the relatively prosaic, even anti-climatic nature of the exhibition, should it have had its grant withdrawn?

If, as he says, Mr. Frohnmayer had been misled by Artists Space, and the NEA was funding an exhibition substantially different from the one described in the proposal, then he had every right to act as he did.

More important, there is the matter of the law itself, which has narrowed the amount of elbow room available to Mr. Frohnmayer and his staff. The presence of but one image in any exhibition that contravenes any of the prohibitions in the new law — by being pornographic, for example — compels the withholding or withdrawal of funding.

In this case, there was such work — a photograph of an erect penis. Mr. Frohnmayer, it turns out, was right the first time to cancel the grant. Even *without* the law Mr. Frohnmayer would have been right to deny Artists Space funding, since the taxpayers, need it be said again, should not in the name of art be forced to underwrite material —in this case, a photograph of an erect penis — that can by any reasonable standard be described as indecent.

But the question is much broader than that. "Witnesses" is another one of those "cutting edge" events, an exhibition from the contemporary vanguard in which the standard of quality is not aesthetic achievement, but the extent to which the public can be "challenged," that is to say, confronted with material it will find shocking.

The rationale for this attitude is the worn-out adage, drawn from the early days of modernism but based on a misunderstanding of that period, that the only new art that is any good is the kind capable of setting the viewer's teeth on edge.

To the extent that this is true, it is true *only* about aesthetically disconcerting work — not morally disconcerting work.

Now, this isn't the sort of thing the government should really be underwriting — not just because it may be offensive, but because it is material of as yet uncertain value that a government grant validates as though it were an indispensable part of our cultural heritage.

It may become indispensable — though I doubt it — but until it does, there is no reason for the government to intervene. Far better to devote those resources to parts of our cultural heritage that have stood the test of time, and that may be in danger of slipping away.

↟ Besides, this "cutting edge" material is now so firmly a part of our cultural life that it doesn't need government support in the way most people believe.

↟ Art, and particularly contemporary art, has become such big business in the private sector that there are any number of corporations, foundations and private individuals only too eager to support it for whatever reason.

Artists Space boasts an impressive list of such supporters, ranging from the Morgan Guaranty Trust Co. to The Andy Warhol Foundation, nor is it alone in this respect. (Interestingly, the Robert Mapplethorpe foundation contributed to the cost of this exhibition.) The NEA grant of $10,000 represented only a third of the exhibition's cost. Without that backing Artists Space certainly could have found the money elsewhere.

If there was nothing remarkable about the show, the same cannot be said of the controversy itself. The decision of Susan Wyatt and the Artists Space board of directors to refuse to return the grant money was a gesture of astonishing arrogance, even lawlessness.

It was all the more shocking since among its members are prominent individuals from the academic and museum worlds, the sort of professionals who should have known better.

Nonetheless, it was most revealing of the way the art community — or one part of it — views itself and its place in the matter of government funding. It showed that it believed the private sector was the proper judge of how public money should be spent; that it views a discretionary disbursement as an irrevocable entitlement; and that art is of such pre-eminent value that it places all who are associated with it above the law.

Equally amazing were the actions of the new NEA chairman, Mr. Frohnmayer. His flip-flopping on the issue shows that he is a man who knows his own mind hardly at all.

He seems to have been completely at sea over the meaning of the law it is his job to carry out, applying quite the wrong standard — a "political" one — to the exhibition. And he also is making the same mistake that Corcoran Gallery Director Christina Orr-Cahall made during the Mapplethorpe controversy — he tried to accommodate a constituency rather than do the job he was hired to do. Twice he did this — first in withholding the grant clearly to assuage the wrath of Jesse Helms, and then going back on his decision when it was clear he had lost severely within the arts community.

But then, what does one expect? Mr. Frohnmayer, a lawyer and former arts administrator in Oregon, is a bureaucrat at a time the NEA needs bold leadership capable of directing it away from the sort of grant-making policies that have given us the likes of Mapplethorpe, Serrano and "Witnesses."

The whole episode has been most revealing, however, providing a foretaste of what we can expect with the passage of the new law. The art community, far from responding with carefully chosen exhibitions designed to avoid run-ins with the NEA, on the contrary seems inclined to up the ante each time by including at least one work calculated to provoke the kind of publicity-rich controversy "Witnesses" has done.

And, far from resolving it, the NEA now seems destined to address the funding question in the same manner as it has to date, namely by simply trying to muddle through.

■ Patrick Buchanan, Where a Wall Is Needed, *Washington Times*, November 22, 1989

Patrick Buchanan is a nationally syndicated columnist and television commentator. He was a Republican candidate for President during 1991-92.

This June, in Tiananmen Square, students, who had rallied at an artist's crude replica of the Statue of Liberty, were run over by the tanks of Deng Xiaoping. In Prague, Czechoslovakia, inspired by the playwright Vaclav Havel, thousands defy the neo-Stalinist regime.

Around the world, men of art make history; here, they just make fools of themselves.

Last week, composer Leonard Bernstein refused the National Medal of Art from President Bush. Why this contrived and petty insult to the president and first lady? Lenny wanted to protest the denial of a $10,000 grant to a New York exhibit of decadent art, i.e., photos of dying and sometimes naked homosexuals, introduced by a catalog which assailed Republican Sen. Jesse Helms of North Carolina and Cardinal John O'Connor.

Larry McMurtry, president of PEN, the international writers organization, also decried the decision of John Frohnmayer of the National Endowment for the Arts to withdraw the grant. But here are sample excerpts from the catalog, written by AIDS victim David Wojnarowicz and costing $7,000, which Mr. McMurtry et al. would have us fund:

"On the table is today's newspaper with a picture of Cardinal O'Connor saying he'd like to take part in Operation Rescue's blocking of abortion clinics but his lawyers are advising against it. This fat cannibal from that house of walking swastikas up on Fifth Avenue (St. Patrick's Cathedral) should lose his church tax-exempt status and pay retroactive taxes from the last couple centuries. Shut down our clinics and we will shut down your 'church.' I believe in the death penalty for people in positions of power who commit crimes against humanity, i.e., fascism. This creep in black skirts, etc....."

"At least in my ungoverned imagination ... I can ... douse [Jesse] Helms with a bucket of gasoline and set his putrid [expletive] on fire or throw Rep. William Dannemeyer off the Empire State Building."

When right-wing extremists used such rhetoric about President John F. Kennedy, liberals said it created the "atmosphere of hatred" that brought on his assassination. Now, they insist we subsidize ever-cruder defamations of conservatives and the Catholic Church.

What hypocrites. They will piously condemn the Rev. Jesse Jackson for not "speaking out" against his friend, Louis Farrakhan, who called Judaism a "gutter religion," but not one of them will stand up to the militant homosexuals' rhetoric of hatred against Roman Catholicism.

Responding to the heat, Mr. Frohnmayer wilted and restored the $10,000 grant, saying "The last thing I want to do is be crosswise with a major part of the endowment constituency."

Apparently, he has no problem being "crosswise" with Congress, or with the country, as he has promised his "constituency" to work for repeal of the Helms prohibition against the funding of filthy art.

In the '60s, the children of the counterculture wanted to be free to curse "Amerika," and to use "filthy speech." Now, in middle age, they wish to be subsidized even as they do so. Truly, they have never grown up; and, surely, a showdown is coming.

In Manhattan, on one entire side of a seven-story building, a 6,000-square-foot "Pathfinder Mural" is about to be unveiled. Funded in part by the New York State Council on the Arts, the gigantic mural features portraits of Marx, Lenin, Trotsky, Che Guevara, and, coming soon, Tomas Borge, Stalinist chief of the Sandinista secret police.

Ironic, is it not? In East Europe, the victims of communism tear down images of Marx and Lenin; in the arts capital of America, their portraits go up. While Cuban poet Valladares speaks out for America and freedom in the forums of the world, the huge image of his former torturer, Fidel Castro, rises over the Westside Highway.

In this diverse country, few really care about stopping angry gays from photographing one another; but, Americans do rightly care about using tax dollars to celebrate perversion or to manifest hatred.

Like the gay rights community, the arts community seems increasingly alienated from American society. And both suffer from an infantile disorder.

The gays yearly die by the thousands of AIDS, crying out in rage for what they cannot have: respect for a lifestyle Americans simply do not respect; billions for medical research to save them from the consequences of their own suicidal self-indulgence. Truly, these are lost souls, fighting a war against the Author of human nature, a war that no man can win.

What does the "arts community" want? To provoke a Middle America too busy and distracted to be provoked; and to be honored and subsidized by a society they appear to loathe.

Like spoiled children, our artists rant and rail at us; then cry "repression" and "censorship" when we threaten their allowance.

"Art has literally become a new religion," the writer Tom Wolfe said the other day, after sale of one of Picasso's early paintings for $40 million. A "cult," to be exact. But, just as the First Amendment protects the free exercise of religion, it always prohibits taxpayer funding. Between the arts and gay communities on one hand, and the U.S. Treasury on the other, we need to erect a "high wall of separation."

■Dr. Christina Orr-Cahall, statement following resignation from the Corcoran, December 1989

Dr. Christina Orr-Cahall was the director of the Corcoran Gallery of Art, and is now the director of the Norton Gallery and School of the Arts in Palm Beach.

Previously, I offered my resignation to the Board of Trustees of the Corcoran Gallery of Art and it was not accepted.

Today, I have tendered my irrevocable resignation to the Board of Trustees, effective February 1, 1990, and that resignation has been accepted.

For the last seven months, I have been at the center of a national debate over artistic freedom and government responsibility. These have been extraordinarily difficult months for all of us at the Corcoran as we were caught up in issues which reached far beyond our institution and their importance to the American public.

I believe deeply in freedom of artistic expression. My professional career has been based on a reputation of steadfast support for artists and contemporary art. That will continue to be the core of my personal and professional philosophy.

I would also like to take this opportunity to state that I deplore political actions which discriminate against the gay community. AIDS is devastating so many, including my friends and colleagues, and represents a tragedy for the art world today.

The decision, made on June 12, to cancel the Mapplethorpe exhibition, which triggered the present debate, was based on the consideration of factors which put at odds my responsibilities as an executive with my personal feelings as a deeply committed supporter of contemporary art. The issues in June and today are complex issues that continue to involve a number of competing values and considerations.

As a highly visible public institution with a broad-based audience and children's educational programs, coupled with the climate in Congress, the Corcoran was, according to counsel, likely to become a target and test case for the law, to establish the legal relationship between art and pornography, particularly child pornography. Many people believed that forcing a legal decision was not in the best interest of artistic freedom.

By June 8th, over 100 members of Congress had heard from their constituents concerning the use of taxpayers' monies in the funding of the Mapplethorpe exhibition. These members of Congress, in turn, notified the National Endowment for the Arts (NEA) of their concerns. The public debate had thus begun and quickly threatened to become a major issue. My concern at this point was to avoid having the Corcoran caught in the middle of a debate which it could not control, although that has been the end result.

The Corcoran chose not to publicly discuss the legal advice which contributed to our decision at the time. We all felt it would be inappropriate to raise this matter during the already controversial National Endowment for the Arts appropriation process. We did not want to contribute to any possible erosion of support for the NEA itself, or for its funding, which has been critical to artists and museums throughout the United States. This might very well be the case in what we said could be construed as saying, in the opinion of eminent legal counsel, that the NEA might be interpreted as funding pornography.

My primary obligation as the Corcoran's Chief Executive Officer and Director was to serve the institution's constituency and the public generally. Ideally, this would mean giving the public the opportunity to decide for itself what is art or, if they wished to ask, what is pornography and the relationship between the two. But the legal quandary haunted us. There were no precise precedents to follow. Accordingly, decisions had to be made after weighing all the institutional, cultural, and legal factors.

What was painful about my recommendation was that I had to come down on the side that is contrary to my own personal feelings. As an executive with overarching responsibilities to my Board, however, the circumstances compelled me to recommend that the Board of Trustees consider the exhibition's cancellation.

This was a confrontation waiting to happen, somewhere, at some art institution, at some time. The combination of circumstances unhappily made the Corcoran, in Washington, D.C., one block from The White House, the battleground.

The controversies over art and censorship have just begun, and many other boards, museum directors and staffs will have many of the same difficult problems and will have to make hard decisions. This will always be the case as institutions strive to safeguard the national commitment for support to the arts through the NEA and to protect freedom of expression. Ours was not an isolated example of such questions.

I have valued my tenure at the Corcoran and wish to emphasize the many outstanding qualities of the institution in both the museum and the art school. As the Corcoran moves toward the twenty-first century, it has begun an appropriate and healthy re-examination of its role in the art community, as a flagship cultural institution in the nation's capital.

I have decided to resign now in the hope that my withdrawal will end or abate this controversy with its continuing corrosive consequences, for the Corcoran, for me as its symbol, and for our community. The larger debate should continue.

■ Eleanor Heartney, Social Responsibility and Censorship, *Sculpture*, January/February 1990

Eleanor Heartney is an art critic.

Breaking into what was otherwise promising to be a desultory season, the censorship uproar seems to have galvanized the art world in a way that has not been seen since the much-ballyhooed resurrection of painting in the early '80s. There are marches, panels, articles, editorials and scores of exhibitions devoted to obscene, sacrilegious or otherwise objectionable art. Having at long last found a cause around which to rally, the art world is enjoying a rare consensus about its own importance as a last bastion of free expression in an increasingly censorious society. Still, there is something troubling in all the self-congratulatory rhetoric floating about — there is too little curiosity about the underlying causes of this situation, too few questions being asked about the lack of widespread interest in the art world's fight for artistic freedom, too many business-as-usual attempts to use the current controversy as a career-building strategy.

I am certainly no supporter of Jesse Helms, and I think that few rights are more important than freedom of expression. I am also aware that there are deeply cynical motives behind Helms' attack on Mapplethorpe and Serrano, among them the advancement of his own career and the desire to junk the National Endowment for the Arts altogether. However, it is important to keep in mind that his attack has been so successful because he has aligned himself with forces already in motion, as demonstrated by the removal of *Tilted Arc* last year and the pair of censorship flaps (one involving Scott Tyler's flag assemblage, the other involving a student's show that included an image of the late mayor Harold Washington in women's underwear) at the School of the Art Institute of Chicago.

There is a reason why these attacks are coming now, and it is only partly because the far right has seized on culture as its new political battleground. The attacks also represent the explosion of tensions long existing between the art world and society at large, tensions which originate in the contradictions inherent in wanting to have it both ways — to be allowed total artistic freedom (which generally translates into contempt for the philistine public) while enjoying public support for the arts.

The recent attacks have brought out all the old clichés about the value of art as "an essential component of our civilization," the "conscience of society," etc. And yet any casual gallery or contemporary art museum survey reveals that the majority of work on display has less to do with the expression of eternal or difficult truths than it does with fitting into the categories of high-priced collectibles or light entertainment. For decades the art world proper has resolutely separated itself from any sense of responsibility toward the social world, which makes the humanistic terms with which it defends itself now more than a little suspect.

The *Tilted Arc* controversy, which in many ways served as a harbinger of recent events, illustrates the doublethink that has so long governed the art world. As a piece of sculpture, there is much to commend *Tilted Arc*. As a piece of public art, it was remarkably wrongheaded — the product of the artist's desire to treat the plaza as an abstract space regardless of its function and meaning within the urban fabric. When local residents and workers pressed for its removal, the art world lined up unanimously behind Richard Serra, condemning the know-nothings who would have preferred a fountain and benches to a 120-foot wall of steel. One of the most instructive aspects of this controversy is how little weight was given to the claims of the users of the plaza — untrammeled artistic freedom became the ultimate value before which all other social considerations must fall.

Hans Haacke, meanwhile, has made a career of pointing out the art world's larger social considerations, focusing on the willingness of major art institutions to assist in the whitewashing of corporations whose practices have questionable economic, social and political consequences. In case after case, he has documented how such issues as apartheid, cancer risk and toxic waste are conveniently overlooked when sponsoring institutions like Mobil, Philip Morris and Alcan are willing to put up money to sponsor art exhibitions and projects. The Serra controversy and Haacke's investigations both point to a convenient doublethink that pervades the art world, in which "the enhancement of life" translates into making a bleak plaza bleaker for already beleaguered urban workers and "the conscience of society" can be purchased for a few institutional grants.

In a poll of museum directors on the censorship issue recently published in the *New Art Examiner*, Lynn Warren of Chicago's Museum of Contemporary Art was the only one to acknowledge that the art world might bear any responsibility for its current predicament. She asked, "Did the art community really believe it could 'reach a broader audience' without having to stop and think maybe that the broader audience wouldn't really know how to decipher those often morally bankrupt, cynical, obscure, self-referential and downright self-indulgent products contemporary artists are spewing forth? Or does the community believe that because the jaded, safe, thrill-seeking (cf. 'safe sex') New York art world thinks Robert Mapplethorpe's sadomasochistic imagery is the cat's meow, the public-at-large should swallow it whole (pun intended)? Or that a conservative Christian will stop himself and say, 'Now, I won't judge Mr. Serrano's *Piss Christ* until I've understood it in context.' The arts community has often been accused of being morally lax and socially arrogant; it seems the chickens are finally coming home to roost."

Such voices are rare at the moment. More typical is the spectacle I witnessed this fall at a panel on censorship organized by the New Museum. After an informative series of statements by representatives of some of the organizations which have been on the front lines, the floor was opened for discussion. One after another, artists got up to use the forum for various private agendas — promotion of their own work (the ever tiresome — I did it before Mapplethorpe and Serrano), passionate statements about artists' right to subsidy, etc. Finally, a young woman got up and posed what should have been the real focus of the discussion: How, she asked, do you justify this kind of work to the non-art public — what kind of education or outreach could be employed?

But before the panel could begin to address her question, another artist grabbed the microphone and launched into a dissertation on the erotic pleasures of Mapplethorpe's work. I left soon after and ran into the young questioner in the hall, frustrated as I was at the frenzy of self-aggrandizement we had just witnessed.

If anything more is to come out of the current censorship flap than a warm feeling of moral superiority over the ever obtuse masses, we in the art world need to take stock of our position vis-à-vis the rest of society. Does, in fact, the majority of art being made today have any significance to anyone outside the tight circle of collectors, dealers, artists, curators and critics who make up the current art system? If it doesn't, how can we continue to maintain, as Robert Brustein did recently in *The New Republic*, that "every artist has a First Amendment right to subsidy"?

It is true that a certain veneer of social concern is highly fashionable in art at the moment. However, the most commercially and critically successful of such efforts tend to be couched in sufficiently sophisticated postmodern form as not to alienate those potential collectors who benefit from the social inequities which the art would expose. A pair of cases in point: Ron Jones's recent AIDS show, in which the shape of deformed or diseased body cells became the basis for elegant, Brancusiesque sculptures, and Ashley Bickerton's nod to the current fashionability of environmental concerns with the exhibition of a set of slick, high-tech "time capsules" containing materials from the rapidly disappearing natural world. In both cases, real issues became mere fodder for the creation of highly commercial art objects. The current brouhaha has unleashed a lot of rhetoric about risk taking and art on the edge, but we need to keep our perspective about just what that means. In the United States, risk taking means accepting the dangers of grant cut-offs or career damage. In countries like China or Iran, it means literally putting one's life and liberty on the line.

Having long absolved itself of any real moral or social responsibility, the art world is in a poor position to take the high ground now. The spectre of censorship and the authoritarian agenda of the far right are truly alarming. But if we want to convince society that freedom of artistic expression really matters, we are first going to have to start believing it ourselves.

Jeff McMahon, letter to the Senate Subcommittee on Education, February 1, 1990

Jeff McMahon is a performance artist, choreographer, and filmmaker.

Dear Mr. Frohnmayer,

Several months ago, I made myself a promise: If I receive another Fellowship from the NEA, I would find some way to address the crisis the agency itself is facing, and my relationship to that as an artist. I did not feel I could simply take the money and let it go at that; perhaps I have the need to bite the hand that feeds me, to make sure it is not an empty glove.

I have been very fortunate in my relationship with the Endowment, having received five Choreography Fellowships, an Inter-Arts grant, and a Dance Film/Video grant. The NEA has taken a chance with me, and has made a vital difference in my development as an artist and as a presence in my culture. The money has given me time, and the honor has given me an affirmation of myself and my work. The investment my culture is making in me has made me invest more in my culture. I originally came to art from a political perspective, and it has been an ongoing struggle to discover the power of creative work distinct from my conception of politics. Discovering the language of art, the deep need for creativity to express things that political language cannot, has been a revelation. Because of this long and difficult process of discovery, I am deeply disturbed by forces within politics insisting that art toe the line of political expediency, timidity, and reaction.

I am speaking specifically of the incorporation of Public Law 101-121 into the NEA guidelines for grant recipients. I am aware that you cannot be held liable for the passing of this law, but am concerned with your actions and statements regarding its implementation.

When you were appointed Chairman, I felt an immediate sympathy and hope. Your response to the Artists Space show shattered that. I observed in dismay as you failed to provide neither reasoned nor impassioned perspective on the issues created by the confrontation between this contemptible law and the potent work being shown. Your opening moves were distressing, leading me to wonder if you fully understood the terms of engagement. Complicity, masquerading as compromise, had yielded too much of the field, and a strong action was needed to regain the sovereignty of art over its own terrain. Before even seeing the show, you withdrew funding; an egregious act of prior restraint. There can be no compromising on these issues, for we have not moved far enough forward in this society, and its relationship to the arts, to give us room for bashful backstepping. We do not look to primeval slime molds for opinions on evolution; nor should politicians such as Jesse Helms be consulted about art. It has moved beyond the boomerang of his agenda. Art should provide us with a vision, not a pandering to politics. It is a language that encompasses politics, but must not be trapped within it. The air is too thin in that smokey room. Samuel Beckett, asked why he wrote, said: "I could not have gone through the awful wretched mess of life without having left a stain upon the silence."

Some of us leave stains and shocks, others sweet songs, and they spread throughout the culture in ways we cannot always forsee or control. This is how culture grows and changes. Events in Eastern Europe have shown that, no matter how a government tries to impose its will, its perspective of "perfection," the voices that cry and carry over the wall eventually knock it down, leaving government lurking under toppled statues and torn-up statutes. We are not the innocent and stupid children imagined by the Ceausescus or Helms. Strong people are not threatened by the unfamiliar, the strange, or even the offensive. If our sense of culture were as strong as the arsenal purporting to defend it, perhaps we could call ourselves truly civilized. As it is, we must trust those who have not betrayed us, and artists look much better in this light than those who seek to silence them. Senators gorged on pork and PACS should not be making this choice for us. The blows against the NEA are part of a larger agenda, denying money to programs which educate or empower people to their own choices, while urging them to consume a brand-name blitzkrieg of cookies and sitcoms. These are the leaders that stage window-dressing wars, that coyly refuse to utter the names of devastating diseases while mincing around the ballroom in the tarted-up drag of decaying empire. We need artists. We need to know that they are not pretending to tell us everything, trying to win our votes or our salvation, who let us know there is a vast terrain of the imagination out there that we can occasionally enter. Great civilizations have always realized there are some people; artists, priests, medicine men and women, "great speakers," who are in touch with mysteries, languages, and experiences that are not comprehensible or palatable to one and all. The speaker may be Moses, it may be Vaclav Havel or David Wojnarowicz. There are voices screaming from this floundering ship, and they are not coming from the captains. We should be learning to listen harder, open our eyes wider, speak with the tongues of men and angels, and the many patois between.

As is often the case in pseudo-populist demagoguery, much noise is made regarding the use of "taxpayers' money." Let us give credit where credit is due, and rearrange some of the furniture here. The NEA is, by its carefully considered charter, not charged with creating a "National Art." The decisions on who and what get funded are, for the most part, made by artists, not apparatchiks. I do not consider the money I have received from the NEA as money from "The Government," but an investment in me by my peers, my culture, and my country. This cultural force is not, and should not be, subject to the vagaries of those at the temporary helm of the partisan government. It is this very depth and consistency that has made the NEA so respected, so generally immune from the opportunism plaguing other government programs. Contrast the NEA with HUD, the EPA, the NRC, the S&L "regulators." Perhaps senators snuggling up to such constituents as the tobacco death merchants, the oil-slick salesmen, and the go-go boys of borrow and burn economics feel unease around such relative virtue. The refusal to pronounce a politicized agenda, the struggle to serve a diverse constituency, enrages the critics of the NEA. They desire an arts agency on the Soviet model, approving only that which serves the needs of the state, or its murky euphemism "the people." We do not owe the government, nor the politicians feeding on it, anything. We owe our culture, our country, honest work for the faith it has placed in us. "Ask not what your country can do for you, but what you can do for your country," the critical term here is "country" not "government." We cannot go on allowing artists to be perceived as a dangerous and isolated caste, speaking only to themselves and distanced by economics and its dividing terms: uptown/downtown/avant-garde, etc. The money spent by the NEA is research and development, fertilizing our cultural future while giving extra help to the difficult crops. If we do not have the guts to do this, perhaps we should just redeem our dollars in Hollywood, and let them make trailers for crazed market capitalism, its smug merchants and shiny consumables.

We need art that seduces and offends, that challenges the order of our thoughts while giving them room to breathe. We should not be denied the haunting photographs by Philip Lorca di Corcia of AIDS sufferers, the immediate and impassioned anger of David Wojnarowicz, or the threatening beauty of a Mapplethorpe photo. The teacher who denies you the opportunity to judge for yourself, who feeds you opinions while denying the individual experience and information, is protecting himself, not enlightening others. Ditto for the cultural reactionaries and their politicians. What do they want hidden from us? How cunning to tell us it is too rough, and cheer the atavistic urge while tripping the bringer of fire. Challengers, to individuals and institutions, must come from a basic understanding of the language being used. Cultural lies begin as truths accepted or promulgated by "experts"; the Nazi geneticist claiming one race's superiority over another, deciding one kind of art is degenerate, and another that of a perfect race. "When I hear the word culture, I reach for my pistol"; now they just reach for an appropriations bill. History has its revenge. Whose work do we see in the museums, the Nazi "perfection" or the "degenerate" Egon Scheile? Who do we revere, Roy Cohn or Langston Hughes?

Your initial claim that the Artists Space show was primarily about politics, not aesthetics, is indicative of the schizophrenia usually required of artists in totalitarian societies. Ours is not such a society, although we must remain ever vigilant. Is the work of Leon Golub more politics than art? And Barbara Kruger? Artists are wholistic, encompassing a great many forms of discourse within their work. Judgments such as yours indicate a support for the kind of bloodless formalism that should not be the dominant identity for art in our culture. Art seeks to escape definition, re-contextualizing and re-awakening our senses, our souls, and often our politics.

The art world's response to AIDS mirrored the culture; hesitant, disorganized, and slow to realization. Perhaps it was too close to us; many middle-class artists never had a war so close to home. The site of the battle was inside our bodies and those we love. Art, so often the grace making the banalities of life bearable, seemed unable to find its voice, the eyes in the back of the head. And who, where, was the enemy? It has been in addressing dreaded "politics" that the Art/AIDS impasse collapsed. Groups like ACT-UP and Gran Fury created some of the strongest graphics and imagery/iconography seen in a long time. Their creative seizing and rebirthing of direct culture/political action has been a revelation to artists and the body politic. Sometimes they are effective, sometimes only offensive; just as much as the art that has accompanied these actions. Rage does not stop at the crosswalk for reason; if your body is on fire, you run. The recipes for such grass-roots action were not tested in the lab to account for all variables. There was not time. The surfaces have not been burnished by the academy. There was not time. But the work is vital, and for the most part, honest. Humanity comes through, in all its sloppiness, passion, hope, and bolts of vision. There is brilliance, but its coat is rather shabby, and its language rather rough. That is the place we are living in now. These are not the treacly sounds oozing out of the shining city on the hill. This is an art beautiful and soothing, ugly and erupting. Sometimes the lava pouring down the mountain burns us. Do we put a cork in the crater and close our eyes, or wake up to the rumbling beneath the earth and within our souls? We evolve in the way we look at our bodies, the ways in which we exist within them. The work at a show such as Artists Space makes this clear. David Wojnarowicz' essay was incendiary; how could it be otherwise? The shock of something REAL pulsed through me as I read it. His very existence is political, and the proof of this pudding was in the response it received. Truth hurts. If Senator Helms et al. don't want to hear these moans and shouts, let them retreat to Boccaccio's estate, and keep their fictions to themselves. Artists are waking up to the politics within, and to deny this would be to deny our very bodies, our breath. To ask that we cease being political beings, or itemize our actions as "artistic" or "political" is absurd. Would you ask this of Vaclav Havel, or Mario Vargas Llosa?...

My hope is that you will reaffirm the mandate and integrity of the agency you administer, resisting the intrusions of those who have no experience or understanding of art's transforming process, who distrust its shifting terrain. The NEA can and should grow and change, but nurtured by those who understand and revere creativity in all its forms, nascent and full-blooming. Talk to us, show us the hand inside the glove is open and not closed.

Yours,

Jeff McMahon

■ Hon. Dana Rohrabacher, "Dear Colleague" letter, February 5, 1990

Dana Rohrabacher is a Republican member of the House of Representatives, representing the state of California. He was the leader of the anti-NEA campaign in the House.

"Usually I get paid a lot of money for this, but tonight it's government funded!"

— Annie Sprinkle: "Post Porn Modernist" and Tax Dollar Recipient, after experiencing orgasm on stage

THE NATIONAL ENDOWMENT FOR THE ARTS IS AT IT AGAIN!

Dear Colleague:

Does the following performance sound like an appropriate use of tax dollars to you?

Star of 150 explicit, XXX-rated videos, Annie Sprinkle takes to the stage and ...

- Masturbates with various "sex toys" until she experiences orgasm.
- Performs oral sex with rubber penises, inviting the audience to massage her breasts.
- To conclude her performance, she opens her vaginal canal with a gynecological tool known as a speculum and invites audience members to the stage to inspect her.

Okay, now, hold onto your hats... and your wallet. Annie Sprinkle's titillating masterpiece received your constituents' tax dollars, in the following manner:

The New York Council for the Arts receives $500,000 in unrestricted funds from the National Endowment for the Arts every year. In turn, the Council chose to spend $25,000 on a performance series at the Kitchen Theatre in New York.

"Annie Sprinkle: Post Porn Modernist" was performed twelve times during that series.

A "Post Porn Modernist Manifesto," printed in the show's program, is written by "artists" who "celebrate sex as the nourishing life giving force.... We embrace our genitals as part, not separate, from our spirits.... We utilize sexually explicit words, pictures and performances to communicate our ideas and emotions."

Unfortunately, they are also utilizing taxpayer dollars.

Once again, of course, NEA backers are calling opponents of the Annie Sprinkle Show "censors," because we don't believe that Annie has a First Amendment right to taxpayers' dollars.

The executive director of The Kitchen, Bobbi Tsumagari, defended the "artistic quality" of Sprinkle's performance, defining the show as "a critical look at Sprinkle's personal experiences dealing with some of the most important issues of our time ...."

Mr. John Frohnmayer, the Chairman of the NEA, defended the grant, saying "The point is we are not the moral arbiter of this country. We're not going to run around and respond just because something happened somewhere that someone didn't like."

Let's remind Mr. Frohnmayer he is dealing with taxpayer funds and is accountable for how they are spent, just like every other head of every other federal agency.

If the NEA can't hold itself responsible to the U.S. taxpayer, it's our job to make them responsible.

Sincerely,

Dana Rohrabacher
Member of Congress

■ Hon. Pat Williams, "Dear Colleague" letter, February 12, 1990

Pat Williams is a Democratic member of the House of Representatives, representing the state of Montana. He was the leader of those in the House who supported the NEA.

Dear Colleague:

Recently you received what may be the Congresses' first X-rated "Dear Colleague" letter. The letter depicted in graphic detail a pornographic performance in New York City which supposedly was funded by the taxpayers through the National Endowment for the Arts. Titillating, perhaps, but not true.

The truth is, that performance didn't receive one penny of funding from the National Endowment for the Arts, nor, for that matter, from the New York Council for the Arts. The Council specifically excluded the X-rated performance artist from a grant.

In fact, the first time a penny of taxpayers' money was spent on Annie Sprinkle's performance was upon the publication of the Dear Colleague letter detailing her X-rated antics.

Mr. John Frohnmayer, Chairman of the National Endowment for the Arts, has repeatedly stated that the facts were made known before the circulation of the Dear Colleague letter. But the facts were ignored in some parts, and distorted in others. Among other distortions, the Chairman of the Endowment is quoted as "defending the grant." The Chairman made no such defense; there was no "grant" to be defended.

Such "Dear Colleague" letters are part of an organized attack on the Arts Endowment. Certain individuals and groups have set out to destroy the Endowment, and they apparently don't let the facts get in their way. Recent advertisements in the *Washington Times* and *USA Today* named 262 Members of Congress as supporters of pornography by their vote on NEA appropriations last year. Their purpose is obvious: to make the American public believe that the Endowment has deliberately set out to fund works that are offensive to the average American, and that a vote by members of Congress to support funding for the Endowment is a vote to support pornography and obscenity.

The question of freedom of artistic expression and accountability for the use of taxpayers' funds are legitimate issues to be raised in the reauthorization of the National Endowment for the Arts, a process that is underway. The Subcommittee, which I chair, has dealt with this issue in four hearings. On April 4, we are holding a hearing to allow Members a chance to be heard.

The work of the Subcommittee — indeed consideration by the Congress — as it weighs these issues will be made exceedingly difficult in this atmosphere of demagoguery, untruths, and half truths. And an agency which has enriched the cultural lives of Americans in every state and territory of this nation may very well be in jeopardy because of it.

I personally resent the attempt to paint any position other than one's own as tantamount to endorsing pornography, blasphemy, and obscenity.

Sincerely,

Pat Williams

American Family Association, Is This How You Want Your Tax Dollars Spent?, fundraising advertisement, *Washington Times,* February 13, 1990

Under its director Rev. Donald Wildmon, the American Family Association — a Christian organization— helped lead the campaign against the NEA.

"Usually I get paid a lot of money for this, but tonight it's government-funded!"

— Porn star Annie Sprinkle, speaking of her government funded "art" exhibit

The National Endowment for the Arts (NEA) is a federal agency which provides taxpayer funded grants, many of which support pornographic, anti-Christian "works of art." The NEA makes the grants available to members of the "arts" community and they are free to spend the tax funds without accountability to anyone for how the money is spent.

The NEA has a current budget of $171,000,000, which comes from your tax dollars. The list below is a sampling of "art" projects which the NEA has supported with funding.

- The NEA honored Andres Serrano with $15,000 in tax dollars in competition sponsored by the NEA. Serrano's entry included a photo of Christ on a cross submerged in Serrano's urine. He named the "work of art" Piss Christ.
- The NEA spent $30,000 to fund the homosexual photographs of Robert Mapplethorpe. The exhibit included these photos: "Honey" — a girl about four years old with a sad, scared face, the focus of the camera is on the child's genitals below her uplifted dress; "Mr. 10½" — a man crouched over, his penis on a block; "Jesse McBride" — a shot of a nude boy, about eight, proudly displaying his penis; one man urinating into another man's mouth (homosexuals call it "golden showers"); and one man with his fist and forearm up another man's rectum (homosexuals call it "fisting").

Time magazine said that, had this not been supported by the NEA, the exhibitor could have been charged with distributing child pornography.

- In Phoenix, Arizona, the NEA gave MARS Artspace $20,000 to help fund an exhibit featuring Cactus Jack's "Piss Helms," a photo of Senator Jesse Helms in a large jar of urine.
- The NEA gave $40,000 to the Gay Sunshine Press to publish sexually explicit homosexual stories and $25,000 to the Panjandrum Press for the same purpose.
- In New York, NEA funds helped pay for an exhibit which included booklets depicting one lesbian inserting a dildo into another, a photo album of group sex, a collection of crude drawings including one titled "Jesus Sucks" in which a mammoth woman is breast-feeding an infant. Another photo is of a man asking, "Is it a sin to f—— a priest?"

- With NEA help, PADD (Political Art Documentation Distribution) and Carnival Knowledge co-sponsored entertainment including a number called "Tapping and Talking Dirty" in which two women casually chat about fellatio and swallowing sperm.
- The organizers of the annual San Francisco Lesbian and Gay Film Festival expect to be given $20,000 by the NEA for their 1990 showing. The NEA gave them $10,000 in 1989 and $6,300 in 1988. The film festival features films for and about homosexual lifestyles, sexual activities and practices.
- In Houston, the NEA helped fund the exhibit "At Home with Themselves: Gay and Lesbian Couples" at the Houston Center for Photography.
- The NEA helped fund the exhibit "Degenerate with a capital D" in New York. The exhibit included posters that depict Senator Jesse Helms nailed to a cross (Exhibitor Shawn Eichman even sent several of the posters to Helms' home); Dread Scott's "Proper Way to Display a U.S. Flag" which encouraged gallery-goers to walk on the flag.
- In January, 1990, the NEA Creative Writing Fellowships gave $20,000 to three lesbian writers to help fund their homoerotic writings.
- In New York, the NEA provided $10,000 to help pay for an art exhibit in which angry homosexuals denounced Catholic clergyman John Cardinal O'Connor, calling him a "fat cannibal" and a "creep in black skirts" while St. Patrick's Cathedral was called a "house of walking swastikas on Fifth Avenue."
- NEA helped fund an exhibition including a bust of Jesus in drag (appearing as a transvestite), with a crown of thorns on His head, make-up around the eyes and female breasts.
- One of the latest exhibits funded with $25,000 of tax funds was entitled "Annie Sprinkle: Post-Porn Modernist." Annie Sprinkle is a porn movie star who has appeared in more than 150 X-rated, pornographic movies.

The art exhibit included Annie Sprinkle's live performances at the Kitchen Theater in New York and consisted of, among other things, spreading her legs and inviting the audience to inspect her vagina and cervix with the aid of a flashlight. As part of her tax-funded art exhibit, Annie did the following:

Masturbated with various "sex toys" until she supposedly experienced orgasms.

Invoked the spirits of ancient, sacred temple prostitutes. "I like to evoke spirits," she told the crowd. "They love having sex."

Performed oral sex on rubber penises (dildoes), and invited the audience to massage her breasts and photograph her scantily clad body. At the beginning of her tax-dollar funded exhibit she did a skit, called "100 Blow Jobs."

Also during Sprinkle's performance — after inducing the first orgasm with her favorite "sex toys" — she smiles and says to the audience, "Usually I get paid a lot of money for this, but tonight it's government-funded!"

Annie's main writer and only actor in the tax-dollar funded exhibit was Annie Sprinkle. A "Post-Porn Modernist Manifesto," printed in the show's program and signed by more than 20 people, states, "We embrace our genitals as part, not separate, from our spirits. We utilize sexually explicit words, pictures and performances to communicate our ideas and emotions."

Last year, Senator Jesse Helms introduced an amendment in the Senate which would have prohibited the NEA from using your tax dollars to support such exhibits as those listed above. The Senate passed it overwhelmingly. However, when the amendment was brought up in the House of Representatives by Congressman Dana Rohrabacher (R-CA), Congressman Ralph Regula (R-OH) offered a motion which refused to allow the House to vote on the Rohrabacher amendment. By using a tactical parliamentary move, Rep. Regula refused to yield the floor to Rep. Rohrabacher and thus kept the amendment from being voted on. Rep. Regula's action succeeded in its intent, that of allowing the NEA to continue to receive their millions of tax dollars to fund such "works of art."

Listed below are 262 Congressmen who voted for Regula's motion, thus supporting the NEA in its abuse and misuse of your tax dollars. Their address is: House of Representatives, Washington, DC 20515.
[ed: list deleted]

■ National Endowment for the Arts, Fact Sheet on American Family Association Fundraising Advertisement, February 1990

This fact sheet was prepared by the NEA in response to the charges made in the AFA's February 13, 1990 fundraising advertisement.

- The National Endowment for the Arts did not "honor" Andres (sic) Serrano with $15,000. The Endowment gave $75,000 (matched two-to-one with private money) to the Southeastern Center for Contemporary Art. The Center selected a panel. The panel selected Andres Serrano. The Center gave Serrano $15,000 of Endowment money based on the quality of his work.
- The National Endowment for the Arts did not "fund the homosexual photographs of Robert Mapplethorpe." It gave $30,000 matching grant to the Institute of Contemporary Art at the University of Pennsylvania to support an exhibition of more than 120 works by Robert Mapplethorpe. This artist's work has been shown in such distinguished museums as the St. Louis Art Museum, the Seattle Art Museum and the Cleveland Museum of Art.
- TIME magazine did *not* say "that, had this not been supported by the NEA, the exhibitor could have been charged with distributing child pornography." The statement is untrue; furthermore, TIME did not say it.
- The Arts Endowment did not give MARS Alternative Artspace $20,000. In 1989, it gave this organization $8,000 for their seasons of exhibitions.

152

One show, titled "Installations," included a photograph of Jesse Helms in beer. The entire cost of the exhibition was $180.

- The Arts Endowment's last grants to Gay Sunshine Press and to Panjandrum Press were in 1984 for amounts of $15,000 and $10,000, respectively. No grant has gone to either press since 1984, six years ago.
- With regard to an exhibit in New York that included booklets, photo album and drawings, the Endowment has no record of funding an exhibit as described.
- The Arts Endowment did not fund PADD (Political Art Documentation/Distribution). A $20,000 Arts Endowment grant *six years ago* supported an organization that presented Carnival Knowledge as one of a large number of exhibitions/events over the course of a year; the grantee organization spent $350 on fees for Carnival Knowledge.
- The Arts Endowment has supported the San Francisco International Lesbian and Gay Film Festival. The 1990 grant is $9,000, not $20,000, as stated.
- In Fiscal 1989, the Arts Endowment made a $20,000 grant to the Houston Center for its year-long program of exhibitions, lectures, and publications. The exhibition referenced, "At Home with Themselves: Gay and Lesbian Couples," was not included in the Center's application materials as the exhibit had not been booked. After the grant was made, the exhibition was shown at the Center, as one of a range of activities funded by the Arts Endowment, state and local government sources, private foundations, and individual members and donors in the community.
- Artists Space, an Endowment grantee organization, gave $250 to an individual involved with the exhibit, "Degenerate with a capital D."
- The National Endowment gave $20,000 fellowships to 97 writers out of more than 2,000 applicants this year based on the quality of samples submitted. The Endowment does not make decisions on grants based on the lifestyles of applicants.
- The Arts Endowment did not fund the New York catalogue with the cited comments about John Cardinal O'Connor and St. Patrick's Cathedral. It gave a $10,000 Fiscal 1989 grant to Artists Space for the exhibition "Witnesses: Against Our Vanishing," a show examining the impact of AIDS on the work of contemporary artists.
- A separate Fiscal 1989 grant to Illinois State University in Normal, Illinois supported a retrospective exhibition and catalogue of the work of this artist.
- With a Fiscal Year 1989 grant, the Arts Endowment helped fund an exhibition in New York that included a bust of Jesus. The exhibition closed in January.
- Neither the Arts Endowment nor the New York State Council on the Arts supported the Annie Sprinkle presentation. An Endowment grant for seasonal support and New York State Arts Council funds are received by the Kitchen, a multidisciplinary contemporary art space which presented this performance.

■John Frohnmayer, statement to the House Subcommittee on Postsecondary Education, March 5, 1990 (excerpt)

John Frohnmayer is the former chairperson of the National Endowment for the Arts.

The Endowment as a catalyst

The $119 million given by the Endowment for grants in 1988 generated over $1.36 billion in private funds. Not only are those astounding numbers in response to a modest investment by the government, but they speak to the audience for the arts in this country and the willingness of people in the private sector to pay for those arts which we, through the judgment of experts who serve on our panels, have deemed to be artistically excellent. The Endowment has always performed the function of being both a catalyst for other dollars and as a "good housekeeping seal of approval" on the artistic quality of the effort. Time and again we are told by our grantees that fundraising is substantially easier because of an Endowment grant. It is an endorsement — a mark of quality and achievement.

But one additional important point needs to be made. The Endowment has funded projects which simply have not succeeded or in a few cases have offended. In education, a child must be allowed to fail in order to know when he has succeeded. In the arts, if creativity is to flourish, some risk of failure is inevitable. Some experiments won't work. Some flights of imagination will crash. The Endowment has never sought to fund anything but excellent art, and has certainly never intended to offend. But a certain amount of leeway is necessary — a certain amount of tolerance — if the citizen-panel system is to work. This was aptly stated by Senator Pell in 1975 during a floor debate on reauthorization:

"It is unfortunate that, as we discuss the extension of the Endowment's legislation, there is a climate abroad in the Congress which supports the idea that every Federal grant must be totally in keeping with our own preconceptions and beliefs.

"I am afraid that... this same type of thinking will be urged upon us, for it is easy to grab a headline by reading the syllabus for a Federal grant totally out of context with the grant itself. However, I do believe that for any program to be successful, it must take an occasional chance, it must be willing to fund projects or proposals which could well backfire...

"When we first enacted the legislation which established both endowments, there was concern voiced by those calling themselves political conservatives about the possibility of Federal control of the arts and humanities.... [T]hose same skeptics, when it suits their own views, are now seeking to have not only Federal control, but also Congressional control of all Federal grants."

What does National Endowment for the Arts support do?

The National Endowment for the Arts has been successful in promoting creativity because its support means more for the recipient that just money; our support acknowledges the success of the applicant. One of the two or three best chamber clarinetists in the United States told me that because of a Fellowship he received from the Endowment in 1983, his whole career changed. He was encouraged and reinforced to pursue his art where, without that Fellowship, his life might have been much different.

Endowment support empowers the artist. One recipient recently said, "The investment my culture is making in me has made me invest more in my culture" (Jeff McMahon, NYC, Feb. 1, 1990). The Endowment grant challenges the artist to produce, to demonstrate her or his excellence, to prove that the grant was wisely given. Not all rise to the occasion, but the vast majority do, and every applicant strives for excellence.

National Endowment for the Arts support gives some measure of continuity to those core institutions which, through their continued excellence, preserve and enhance our cultural heritage. Support from the Endowment allows the creation of programs and a platform from which to grow.

The Endowment's support also has dispersed the opportunity for artistic growth both geographically and culturally. The preservation of the Native American tribal traditions through Endowment grants has offered an opportunity for cultural pride. Providing art to rural localities through artmobiles, touring, and public television and radio has made images and performances, virtually unknown 25 years ago, a part of the lives of people in remote areas.

Congress, over the last quarter century, has made an *investment* in the future of this country. It is an investment in the training, the discipline, and the artistry of our dancers, our musicians, and our painters. It is an investment in our composers, our choreographers and our architects. It is a recognition that while our existence is painful at times, we must acknowledge it, memorialize it, and live through it. Thus, the Arts Endowment was instrumental in creating the design competition which allowed a young graduate student at Yale, Maya Lin, to win the competition for the design of the Vietnam War Memorial — a moving and beautiful statement to a painful and disruptive period in our history.

The Endowment's success has been in its process.

The Endowment has created and sustained a climate encouraging freedom of thought, imagination and inquiry by bringing citizens who are experts in the arts to judge the applications. The Endowment has not created an "Academy." It has not decreed a single acceptable aesthetic. Rather it has reflected the wide diversity of our society.

As the 1965 Senate report on our authorizing legislation emphatically points out, the intent in the creation of the Arts Endowment was to "encourage... free inquiry and expression... [T]hat conformity for its own sake is not to be encouraged, and that no undue preference should be given to any particular style or school of thought or expression." To achieve that end the Arts Endowment uses peer panels.

Each year over 800 citizens who are expert in some area of the arts come to Washington to serve on panels that last from one to six days. These citizens make no small sacrifice in doing the work of the government since they often must travel far from their homes, leave their jobs or professions, and lose valuable work or job opportunities to serve the arts.

These panels function much like a jury in our justice system. Panels are from five to 15 individuals of widely diverse cultural, geographic, ethnic and stylistic backgrounds. They argue, they debate, they confer, and in the end, they decide which applications are the most deserving, the criteria always being quality and merit. The Endowment looks forward to working with the Independent Commission created by Congress in our FY 90 appropriations bill which will examine ways of improving the panel review process.

The system is far from perfect. It is maddeningly slow, inefficient and sometimes frustrating. It often results in compromises and sometimes may even be wrong. But it is the best system that the English and American jurisprudential heritage has been able to devise. And it is affirmed at both the Federal and local levels. It is affirmed by the National Council on the Arts, a distinguished Presidentially-appointed body of 26 citizens comprised of internationally known artists, arts administrators, patrons and distinguished citizens who review and approve or reject the panel recommendations. The Chairman of the Endowment makes the final decision based upon the recommendation of the panel and the National Council, and all grants which are recommended (with the exception of fellowships) are matched on at least a 1:1 and often a 4:1 or 5:1 basis *in the localities in which they are to be received*. Thus, there is local affirmation of these grants by the matching dollars, in virtually every case.

■ Vaclav Havel, statement for Arts Advocacy Day, March 18, 1990

Vaclav Havel is the prime minister of Czechoslovakia, and a writer.

To our fellow artists:

We know first hand how essential is a fierce, independent, creative artistic spirit to the attainment of freedom. Through a long night of repression and control, the artistic community in our land helped keep alive the unquenchable flame of freedom. And artists played a central role in helping organize our final transformation to a new democratic state.

There are those around the world, indeed even in those democracies with the longest tradition of free speech and expression, who would attempt to limit the artist to what is acceptable, conventional, and comfortable. They are unwilling to take the risks that real creativity entails. But an artist must challenge, must controvert the established order. To limit that creative spirit in the name of public sensibility is to deny to society one of its most significant resources.

We send our warm greetings and support to American artists who are meeting on March 30th in Washington to reaffirm their commitment to free artistic expression.

Vaclav Havel

■John W. Vester, William J. Gerhardt, and Mark Snyder, Mapplethorpe in Cincinnati, *Cincinnati Enquirer,* March 24, 1990

John W. Vester, M.D. is the director of research at the Good Samaritan Hospital, Cincinnati; William J. Gerhardt, M.D. is the director of the Department of Pediatrics at the Christ Hospital, Cincinnati; and Mark Snyder, M.D. is an orthopedic surgeon and orthopedic consultant to the Cincinnati Ballet.

In April, Cincinnati's Contemporary Arts Center (CAC) plans to display "The Perfect Moment," a collection of photographs by Robert Mapplethorpe. CAC director Dennis Barrie booked the show last spring after he viewed it in New York and found the show to be "stunning."

In the summer of 1989, "The Perfect Moment" ran smack into controversy. The National Endowment for the Arts (NEA) underwrote the show's display at the Corcoran Gallery of Art in Washington. When a number of U.S. senators learned of the content of some of the pictures that were being federally funded, "The Perfect Moment" was criticized, and the Corcoran gallery canceled the show. Why? It was art, right? CAC has compared the photos to the works of Michelangelo's frescos in the Sistine Chapel. Chad Wick of Central Trust, former chairman of the CAC's board, thinks Cincinnati is mature enough for "The Perfect Moment." And why wouldn't it be?

Some different photos

While most of Mapplethorpe's works are still lifes, portraits and nudes, which few would find offensive, a number of pictures are decidedly different. The following photographs, which were part of the NEA-funded exhibit, have caused the controversy.

- A self-portrait of Mapplethorpe with a bullwhip protruding from his rectum.
- A man hanging upside down, nude, with the arms and legs chained while another man is fondling the nude man's genitals.
- One man holding his penis and urinating into another man's open mouth.

- A man sticking a large cylinder up his own rectum.
- A closeup of a man sticking a finger up his penis.
- A man's fist and arm (to the forearm) in another man's rectum.
- Pictures of prepubescent children focusing on or displaying their genitals.

At the New York exhibit there was also a sequential frame photograph of a man masturbating and a man apparently performing cunnilingus with his head between the legs of a woman who is nude except for high heels and hose. It's no wonder that CAC has felt it necessary to work for months promoting the show.

CAC curator Jack Sawyer, in *Cincinnati* magazine, said the pictures of nude children are not exploitive, and that one picture of a little girl with her dress pulled up so that her vagina is exposed alludes to the Greek myth of innocence in the world. Where has Sawyer been? Children are abused sexually at an alarming rate. Child molesters persuade children to engage in sex or to pose for them by showing the children explicit pictures of other children, which is meant to lower their inhibitions to do what was in the pictures. Children should never be made the focus of sexual attention or interest. Not for a moment; not as entertainment; not as art.

The picture of a man's hand and arm inside another man's rectum shows "fisting." This is a dangerous sex act which can lead to irreparable damage to the intestinal tract and occasionally to death. CAC curator Sawyer has stated that this and other "pictures document sexual practices that are passé because of AIDS." Sawyer's understanding of AIDS transmission is incorrect, and he represents himself as an authority on sexual practices that are not passé. CAC's display of such pictures implies that these practices are acceptable, which is hardly responsible.

What message is conveyed by the other photographs? Who was having "a perfect moment" in the picture of one man urinating into another's mouth, in the picture of a cylinder being inserted into a man's rectum, or in sadomasochistic photographs? What perception of life is advocated? Love and mutual respect are not portrayed. On the contrary, sex, which is meant to be an intimate private expression of life, has been cheapened and degraded. Human beings are treated as animals to be abused for a moment's fun. Nothing is noble or personal. Instead, we are invited to be voyeurs and call it art.

Civilized society cannot afford to remain neutral in the face of such an assault. Civilized society promotes love, fidelity, responsible sexual relationships, marriage, family and human dignity. Urinating on people, sticking whips and cylinders up rectums, and engaging in sadomasochistic sex are degrading activities that diminish us all, particularly when these acts are spread out in public view.

Condemnation deserved

CAC is afraid to admit that some of Mapplethorpe's "perfect moments" ought to be condemned. As Alexander Pope once said, "Of all the causes which conspire to blind a man's erring judgment... is pride, the never-ending voice of fools." CAC admits that had the controversy over "The Perfect Moment" erupted before it was booked, they would have thought twice about it. CAC is too fearful to back down now because they feel they will look like they are not progressive.

Most distressing is that CAC did not realize "The Perfect Moment" had some less than perfect aspects before booking it. Leo Tolstoi wrote that "art is a human activity having for its purpose the transmission to others of the highest and best feelings to which men have risen." Saul Bellow wrote that art seeks "what is fundamental, enduring, essential." John F. Kennedy said that "art establishes the basic human truths which must serve as the touchstone of our judgment."

CAC serves the Cincinnati community best when it follows these great men, but serves us worst when it forces upon us a bizarre sexual vision that it cannot even criticize or mollify for fear of being called a rube.

■ Garrison Keillor, statement to the Senate Subcommittee on Education, March 29, 1990

Garrison Keillor is a humorist and an author.

M r. Chairman and members of the subcommittee: It's a pleasure to come down to Washington to speak in support of the National Endowment for the Arts, one of the wisest and happiest pieces of legislation ever to come through Congress.

I'm grateful to those who have so ably attacked the Endowment over the past year or so for making it necessary to defend it. I enjoy controversy and I recognize the adversary, they are us. My ancestors were Puritans from England. They arrived here in 1648 in the hope of finding greater restrictions than were permissible under English law at the time. But over the years, we Puritans have learned something about repression, and it's as true today as when my people arrived: man's interest in the forbidden is sharp and constant. If Congress doesn't do something about obscene art, we'll have to build galleries twice as big to hold the people who want to see it. And if Congress does do something about obscene art, the galleries will need to be even bigger than that.

All governments have honored artists when they are old and saintly and successful and almost dead, but 25 years ago, Congress decided to boldly and blindly support the arts, support the act of creation itself, and to encourage artists who are young and dangerous and unknown and very much alive. This courageous legislation has changed American life.

Today, in every city and state, when Americans talk up their home town, when the Chamber of Commerce puts out a brochure, invariably they mention the arts — a local orchestra or theater or museum or all three. It didn't used to be this way. Forty years ago, if an American man or woman meant to have an artistic career, you got on the train to New York. Today, you can be a violinist in North Carolina, a writer in Iowa, a painter in Utah. This is a small and lovely revolution that the National Endowment has helped to bring about. The Endowment has fostered thousands and thousands of artistic works — many of which will outlive you and me — but even more important, the Endowment has changed how we think about the arts. Today, no American family can be secure against the danger that one of its children may decide to become an artist.

I grew up in a family that never attended concerts or museums, never bought books. I never imagined that a person could be a writer.

Twice in my life, at crucial times, grants from the Endowment made it possible for me to be a writer. The first, in 1969, arrived when I was young, broke, married, with a baby, living on very little cash and a big vegetable garden. I was writing for the New Yorker at the time but they weren't aware of it. I wrote every morning and every night. I often had fantasies of finding a patron — a beggar would appear at my door one day, I'd give him an egg salad sandwich, and suddenly he'd turn into a man in a pinstripe suit, Prince Bob from the Guggenheim Foundation. But instead of him, I got a letter offering me a job for one month in the Writers in the Schools program in Minneapolis, funded by the NEA, directed by Molly LaBerge, which sent young writers into the schools to read and teach. In 1969, there were three such programs, in New York, California, and Minnesota; today, there's at least one in every state.

In 1974, a grant from the NEA enabled me and my colleagues at Minnesota Public Radio to start "A Prairie Home Companion." The help of the Endowment was crucial because the show wasn't that great to begin with. For our first broadcast, we had a crowd of twelve persons, and then we made the mistake of having an intermission and we lost half of them. The show wasn't obscene, just slow, and it took us a few years to figure out how to do a live radio show with folk music and comedy and stories about my home town of Lake Wobegon. By the time the show became popular and Lake Wobegon became so well-known that people thought it was real, the Endowment had vanished from the credits, its job done.

When you're starting out, it seems like nobody wants to give you a dime, and then, when you have a big success and have everything you could ever want, people can't do enough for you. The Endowment is there at the beginning, and that's the beauty of it.

When I was a young writer, I looked down on best-sellers as trash, but gradually over the years they improved and then suddenly one of them was mine. First, Lake Wobegon Days and then Leaving Home, and my desk filled up with offers to speak, to write, to appear, to endorse, which I've thoroughly enjoyed, but I remember very well when nobody else but my mother and the National Endowment was interested, and I'm grateful for this chance to express my thanks.

When I graduated from college, the degrees were given out in reverse order of merit, so I got mine early and had a chance to watch the others, and I remember the last graduate, the summest cum laude, a tall shy boy who walked up the stairs to the platform and en route stepped on the hem of his own gown and walked right up the inside of it. Like him, the Endowment has succeeded in embarrassing itself from time to time — to the considerable entertainment of us all — and like him, the Endowment keeps on going. It has contributed mightily to the creative genius of America — to the art and music and literature and theater and dance which, to my wife and other foreigners, is the most gorgeous aspect of this country. Long may it wave.

■ Monty Lobb Jr., The Side of Virtue and Dignity, *Cincinnati Enquirer,* March 30, 1990

Monty Lobb, Jr. served as the president of Cincinnati Citizens for Community Values during the Mapplethorpe trial.

Cincinnati has exploded in controversy over the exhibit of Robert Mapplethorpe's photographs, scheduled to be shown during April and May by the Contemporary Arts Center (CAC). CAC Director Dennis Barrie has charged that pressure has mounted to "censor" or cancel "The Perfect Moment," which is the official title of the exhibition. Barrie asserts that the issue concerns CAC's right to display what it pleases.

CAC and its supporters have framed the issue exactly wrong. As a wise sage once said, "That fellow seems to me to possess but one idea, and that is the wrong one." If sexually explicit and bizarre pictures are not obscene or child pornography, CAC has every right to exhibit them. The board and members of Citizens for Community Values do not oppose CAC's legitimate legal rights.

Civic responsibility

But if those rights are not the issue, what is? The issue is CAC's judgment, stewardship, civic responsibility and ethics. There are many things we have a right to do, but that we should not do.

It is surprising that CAC fails to appreciate its civic duty when 10% of its operating budget comes from our taxes and another 54% is donated through private gifts from the Cincinnati community, including the Cincinnati Institute of Fine Arts. CAC apparently appreciates that the public trust reposed in it might be challenged because of its significant support from public and private donations. Accordingly, CAC claims that no such funds will "go directly toward supporting" Mapplethorpe. Ah, but isn't that a careful adverb — "directly"? What this means is that public and fine-arts money is only being used to support the program generally through payment of CAC's overhead, administrative costs, salaries and rent. This point is not altered by CAC's recent decision not to accept disbursal of general funds from this year's Fine Arts Fund drive; CAC is currently operating on sums from last year's drive. Simply put, without public tax dollars and private charitable donations from the Fine Arts Fund, CAC would not be able to show "The Perfect Moment." So why shouldn't the citizens of Cincinnati have say in what CAC does?

I and others have been accused of wanting to "censor" CAC. That is nonsense. I have no power to do that. All I have is the power of persuasion; no one acts as a censor by encouraging CAC not to display certain extreme sexual photos. It is still CAC's choice.

CAC sanctimoniously acts as if I and everyone else must silently accept their every artistic fling without public or private comment or criticism. What's more, they expect me to pay for it, or at least a part of it. With all the demagoguery about free speech, rights and "censorship," somewhere on the way to the art show CAC forgot my rights.

Strangely, others in the artistic community suffer from the same double standard. When the Corcoran Art Gallery in Washington, D.C. decided to cancel the exhibition of Mapplethorpe's work, the art community was livid. The Corcoran was castigated so much that it finally apologized and forced its director to resign. Many artists no longer support the Corcoran, refuse to show their art there and have called others to join in the boycott. Why is it fair game for the Corcoran to be criticized and boycotted for its artistic decisions, but not CAC?

Barrie asserts that there could be no "moral or ethical" grounds to delete pictures from the exhibition. It seems that he does not know the difference between virtue and vice. One is reminded of the man referred to by Samuel Johnson, who wrote: "If he does really think that there is no distinction between virtue and vice, why, sir, when he leaves our houses, let us count our spoons?" Barrie knows that there is a legitimate moral objection to some Mapplethorpe pictures. That's why CAC has made an unprecedented public-relations effort. That's why CAC won't let children unaccompanied by an adult in the program and why it has segregated the roughest photographs from the rest of the exhibition.

If Mapplethorpe had done to animals what he has done to some human beings, and then photographed them, CAC would not be showing the program. And if it did, the outrage from the community and the animal-rights movement would be deafening. Imagine a dog being hung upside down and chained for the sexual pleasure of a man who wants to feel the dog's genitals. Substitute that dog with a nude man and you have a Mapplethorpe photo. Or how about sticking a large cylinder in the anus of a cat, or a man's arm and fist up a lamb's rectum. Substitute the animals for humans and you have Mapplethorpe. Better yet, what about urinating into the mouth of a rabbit; substitute the rabbit for a man and we have a "perfect moment." Why is something so unconscionable and cruel when it comes to animals somehow art when it comes to humans?

Chance to reconsider

I implore CAC to reconsider. CAC can take a stand that few other artists or gallery operators have been willing to consider. No doubt CAC feels pressured to appear de rigueur and progressive. Much of the artistic world is coercing CAC to follow the crowd. As Joseph Addison said, "When vice prevails, and impious men bear sway, a port of honor is a private station." While I call CAC to a private station, it is also an honorable one.

CAC, in Cincinnati, you have an uncommon opportunity. You can unchain that poor man, free him from his captor, and return his dignity. You can take the cylinders, fists and whips out of the rectums and heal the wounds of the abused. You can stop the man from urinating on his brother and give them both back their humanity. You can take the exposed children and return their childhood. You can take the little girl, pull down her dress, and restore her modesty. Please, for the love of humanity, why not side with virtue and dignity?

■ Edward Martenson, Public Support: A Contract with the Arts, *Between Acts,* Winter 1989-90

Edward Martenson is the executive director of the Guthrie Theater in Minneapolis.

Taxpayer support for the arts is not a handout. It is recompense for public service.

In 1965, the government began to subsidize the arts modestly, in ways that were carefully designed to address some important public purposes. Specifically, these public purposes were:

(1) advancement of the arts, and elevation of American culture;

(2) de-centralization, or enhanced availability of indigenous art in all regions; and

(3) price moderation, so that the arts are affordable to all citizens.

These public purposes are consistent with, but not primary to, the priorities of the artists whose activities are subsidized. Understandably, their primary focus in on creativity and command of craft.

For artists, contributed support is simply a necessary source of funds. Good art may be commercial, but it is not necessarily so; most great art of the past was not. Because the marketplace alone never has supported all art of great merit, artists always have depended on subsidy.

This fact is of concern to the public as well as to artists and private philanthropists. While private philanthropy can ensure the availability of art to the private patrons, public support is our way of ensuring that the arts are not limited to wealthy persons in two or three urban centers. Government, therefore, has a distinct purpose within the framework of arts funding: in a democracy, the public interest demands that art must be available to the many, not to the privileged few.

While government is not obligated to support the arts, a free society is obligated to guarantee the freedom for expression that is art's lifeblood. Not less than in the field of journalism, an atmosphere of free expression is essential to the vigor with which artists perform their function in society. It is no more in the public interest to tame the arts than it would be to hamstring the press.

Because freedom of expression is inconsistent with an exercise of political approval over the content of artworks, the very concept of public arts support depends on political self-restraint. In effect, the public accepts the possibility of an art work that offends as a price to be paid for the greater good that stems from broad availability of the arts in general.

(That public support for the arts is a fragile concept, easily upset by lack of political restraint, is recognized most clearly by its opponents. If they can impose a narrow standard for acceptability of content, they know that artists themselves may come to repudiate public support.)

In general, it is most reasonable to regard public art support as a social contract between public and artists. The public desires cultural advancement, de-centralized availability of the arts and the absence of class-oriented price barriers; in exchange it agrees to respect the a priori requirement for an atmosphere of artistic freedom. The artists desire financial assistance, and in exchange they agree to produce and disseminate their work in ways that serve the public purposes described above.

Obviously, this fragile arrangement can be jeopardized when taxpayers are offended by artworks they have helped to finance. That they may be offended is both understandable and legitimate. Art sometimes reflects the extremes of social reality as well as its middle. Its subject matter is the human condition in all its forms, including aspects of our behavior that some might find more comfortable to deny.

The predictable desire to formulate public policy so as to avoid controversy is no more logical in arts support than it is in relation to government actions in defense, nuclear energy or highway planning. If the test for the appropriateness of government action were that it generated no strong opposition, there would have been no progress in civil rights, labor relations or the environment, nor would we ever succeed in identifying locations for prisons and nuclear waste.

(Recent events suggest that those who are patient with controversy over some government actions, but cannot abide it over arts grants, are precisely the people who don't think art is important enough to disagree about.)

The ability of the people to disagree among themselves is a source of strength for our democratic system. Not every disagreement is the government's business to resolve, most particularly if it arises from a matter of taste. Conservatives and liberals agree on this point, but a surprising number from both camps believe that financial participation creates an obligation on lawmakers to establish limits for the public taste.

The appropriate test for government arts support — the one applied to other government programs — is whether most of the people agree most of the time. Public arts support meets this test with bi-partisan flying colors, because the vast majority of it flows to artists and arts institutions that clearly benefit the public.

The arts have held up their end of the social contract, serving the public interest in ways both qualitative and demonstrably quantifiable. In the lifetime of the NEA, resident theater institutions have expanded from 25 to over 400;

they are organized not-for-profit, and so work for public, not private gain; they are located in every region, not just in New York; they have extensive educational programs; and admission can be gained to most of them for the price of a movie. These are aspects of a public-spiritedness that stems from public support.

But the "contract" between artists and the public can remain strong only so long as public officials restrain themselves from exercising approval over the art's content. Unfortunately, political self-restraint is now undergoing its greatest test in 25 years of public arts support.

The burden of restraint is great for public officials precisely because they are public officials. Even on occasions when an art-work is outside the norms of good taste, lawmakers and the public could reasonably see it as an isolated case that does not affect the overall usefulness of public arts support. On the other hand, a lapse of restraint on the part of public officials necessarily involves an imposition of greater political control (whether or not literal censorship is involved), and the result is diminished freedom of expression for all.

It is true that withholding of subsidy is not necessarily the same as censorship. But it also is true that withholding of subsidy on grounds of disagreeable content could not be lawfully selective. Such a practice would be a first amendment infringement. (For example, the government may not withhold price support payments from a farmer because he advertises his support of a particular political party or position.)

Those who approve of withholding subsidy on content grounds do not seem aware that guidelines regarding the public acceptability of political, sexual and religious themes would apply to all who apply for NEA support. For this reason, systematic review of content poses a threat to the creative independence of all artists and arts organizations, regardless of their place in the aesthetic spectrum. Even without official censorship, the effect could be the same.

Much misconception stems from the impression that the NEA paid the entire cost of the two photo exhibitions that stimulated the recent controversy, and that it therefore is solely responsible for their availability. In fact, this is not true. The NEA's authorizing statute generally requires at least a one-for-one match for its grant funds; an important implication is that federal money generally cannot flow into an arts project unless it also is validated by private gifts and audience interest. The NEA is far from alone in having seen merit in these projects, and it was a minority partner in financing them.

What damage would be caused by the breakdown of public arts support?

Some suppose that the "punishment" would be felt only by artists and arts institutions, and, of course, it is true that the financial shock to them would be significant. Artists — actors, orchestra musicians, ballet dancers and writers, as well as visual artists — would be hungrier than they already are.

But the greater effect would be measured by a decline in the quality, quantity and scope of cultural services offered to the public. In particular, the arts would be far less able to pay attention to those important purposes that justified the public support in the first place.

Instead of a noble effort to elevate our civilization, we would embrace a cultural outlook that values only the lowest common denominator. Instead of trying to make the arts available in all regions, once again they would find financial sustenance only in the wealth-concentrated urban centers. And instead of trying to make the arts affordable to all, we would return to a time when the arts were only for the rich.

■ Hon. Ted Weiss, statement to the House Subcommittee on Postsecondary Education, April 4, 1990 (excerpt)

Ted Weiss is a Democratic member of the House of Representatives, representing the state of New York.

Clearly, the current restrictions and their many deleterious repercussions have begun to "chill," or more accurately to "freeze," artistic development in America. Let's heed the warning. We cannot allow Congress to stifle freedom of expression, that is, if we really cherish Art's manifold contributions to society.

Artists are society's watchers, critics, and champions. They speak the unspeakable, even if it manifests itself in horrifying, untidy, or esoteric manners. The painter George Groz frequently called attention to the vulgarity of Nazi Germany in the 20's and 30's. He was forced to flee to America. Manet, in the *Olympia*, a painting of a highly paid prostitute, called attention to the indecent sexual exploitation of women in 19th century France. He was chided by his contemporaries. Art that challenges existing prejudices serves a most important function; it helps us grow and reach a higher state of humanity.

There are other nations around the world which have standards for acceptable and unacceptable artistic expression. We call them totalitarian. In these nations, writers or artists who challenge the boundaries of acceptable expression are imprisoned or worse. Witness the death sentence decreed by the Ayatollah Khomeini on the writer Salman Rushdie because of perceived offense to the prophet Mohammed. Clearly, the U.S. Government must continue to stay out of the business of defining boundaries for acceptable artistic expression.

During this entire debate, some have argued that artistic freedom is fine, but if federal funds are used for a project, it must not be offensive or objectional. But it is folly to argue that if federal funds are used for a project, that project must be acceptable to all taxpayers. Those who make this argument might be uncomfortable with its ramifications. For example, many found the design of the Vietnam Veterans Memorial in Washington, D.C. objectionable, but few would now argue that federal funds should not have been used to support its construction on account of those objections.

The NEA's current grantmaking procedures were carefully designed to limit Government control over or political intervention in the process of federal support for artistic expression. This was done for a reason.

The NEA is designed to be unfettered. Its mission statement says, in part:

We must exercise care to preserve and improve the environment in which the arts have flourished. We must not under any circumstances, impose a single aesthetic standard or attempt to direct artistic content.

Clearly, then, Congressional restrictions will come into direct conflict with a major part of the NEA's purpose and will prevent the NEA from effectively performing its task and from fulfilling its mission. We are heading in that direction. If we continue down this path, the decision we and the arts community ultimately will be confronted with is what price in freedom and creativity are we willing to pay to have the government continue to fund the arts.

■ Hon. Mel Hancock, statement to the House Subcommittee on Postsecondary Education, April 4, 1990 (excerpt)

Mel Hannock is a Republican member of the House of Representatives, representing the state of Missouri.

There are a great many projects funded by the NEA which may not be obscene in the traditional moral sense but which are, nonetheless, an obscene waste of the taxpayers' money.

We hear reports of these elite NEA panels of artists feathering each other's nests and neglecting traditional and legitimate art projects. That is obscene.

When you look at the bureaucracy which has been created by the NEA, you start to realize it is the bureaucrats themselves which benefit the most from continued NEA funding.

Does it really take 267 federal employees and 800 paid consultants to give away money to artists? Does the NEA really need $18.6 million to administer this giveaway program? Does it really take 63 management personnel to manage 204 other employees — one manager for every 3.2 employees?

The NEA is just another wasteful bureaucracy to me. An obscene waste of taxpayer dollars, if you will, that needs to be cut out of the budget in favor of greater priorities.

What is more, we are hearing about new scandals all the time. It certainly makes you wonder what we don't know yet.

Now, however, the National Endowment for the Arts is making as arrogant request as has been made by any federal agency. They are asking for no "content restrictions" in their reauthorization. Simply put, they want no accountability.

Even if the NEA and its defenders are right that the literally obscene art projects are only a few dozen exceptions to the rule, this demand that they be given a completely free hand to throw away the taxpayers' money on indecent or simply wasteful projects is unthinkable.

A few mistakes now and then is one thing. If we didn't reauthorize every agency which made a few mistakes we'd shut down the federal government —

not that I'd mind that terribly much, but I'm sure you'll agree that would be going too far.

But what is altogether different is for a government agency to refuse to admit its mistakes, to unashamedly defend its mistakes, and to demand the right to deliberately make such mistakes in the future. At that point, we are no longer talking about mistakes — we are talking about a deliberate defiance of Congress and the American taxpayer. If the NEA will not admit its mistakes, it cannot correct them.

That cannot be tolerated. It would not be tolerated by any other agency. It should not be tolerated by the NEA.

I have come to the conclusion that the only way to protect the interests of the taxpayers is to completely defund and shut down the National Endowment for the Arts.

The thought that, after the NEA has demonstrated such a blatant disregard for the taxpayers and the oversight authority of Congress, this committee is seriously considering giving a blank check, an unrestricted mandate, to the National Endowment for the Arts to continue its wastage of taxpayer dollars is truly unbelievable. With any appropriation of tax dollars, we should not allow total discretion for the grantee with absolutely no Congressional oversight.

At the very least, I implore you to include language in the reauthorization for the NEA similar or stronger than the Helms language used in the NEA's last appropriation bill. Don't let these folks have free rein to throw taxpayer funds away on any offensive, outrageous project they can dream up.

Frankly, given the NEA's track record, even those standards will end up being meaningless. They will be ignored and circumvented. That is why I ideally recommend to this committee and my colleagues in Congress to oppose reauthorization of the NEA altogether.

The taxpayers have had enough. The NEA is a waste of taxpayer dollars. It refuses to be accountable. It is time we shut it down once and for all.

This is our duty as trustees of our constituents' hard-earned dollars. This obscene waste must be stopped.

■ Don Gray, letter to the Senate Subcommittee on Education, April 5, 1990

Don Gray is an artist and a critic.

Dear Senator Pell:

I would like to share my thoughts with you concerning the depleted condition of contemporary art and the National Endowment for the Arts, based on my thirty years experience in the art world, much of it in New York City.

As an artist and critic, I find myself in a difficult position concerning questions of censorship and the quality of contemporary art raised by the recent controversy over Robert Mapplethorpe's photographs, Andres Serrano's "Piss Christ" and the grant process of the NEA.

Artists must be allowed to do what they will. However, just because they call themselves "artists" and what they do "art" does not guarantee that what they produce will be good or worthwhile. Chances are, it won't. The majority of artists of any era produce inconsequential work.

But, to protect creative freedom and basic human rights, which effects all citizens, artists must not be censored.

This doesn't mean, however, that we have to view their works, buy them or pay tax dollars to fund their production. We all have the right of choice. To deny money to mediocre artists, or anyone else who doesn't deserve it is not censorship. Serious artists will work whether funded or not.

There is a slowly increasing awareness in the art world (the general public has been aware of it much longer, though perhaps not able to express it in sophisticated terms) that artifice and nihilism have been the fashionably dominant characteristics of the art of the past thirty or more years, regardless of style.

The dictionary gives several shades of meaning to the word "nihilism," but the one I'm referring to is "the belief that there is no meaning or purpose in existence." With such a negative premise, borrowed from the Dadaist anti-art position beginning during World War I, is it any wonder that most contemporary art is itself meaningless and purposeless except to scoff at society and genuine art, and mimic the depleted views of its creators and adherents? (The dictionary definition of Dada: "a cult in painting... characterized by... often formless expression and by nihilistic satire").

Like other aspects of our society, such art is essentially diseased. It is eroded by pseudo-creativity, dehumanization, triviality, venality and sterility.

All great men and women (and most other people) love life and the world. They may hate the horror that mankind produces, and our inevitable mortality, but they do not hate mankind. To them, there is both "meaning and purpose" in existence. As a result, their art is life enhancing.

Many contemporary artists are telling us by the kind of art they produce that they not only hate art, they hate mankind, they hate life and they hate the world. And they impose these views upon us every time they are commissioned to construct a public sculpture, paint a public mural or teach in universities (their negative, meaningless, often smart-aleck "art" is their revenge on the world).

Sadly, too many contemporary artists, in their destructive impotence, have more in common with the men who vandalize great art (smashing Michelangelo's "Pieta," slashing Rembrandt's "Nightwatch"), than with the great artists themselves (no doubt out of jealousy and outraged despair over the great artists' effectiveness and accomplishment, in contrast to their own lack of creative significance).

After all, one of the icons of Dadaist art is Marcel Duchamp's 1919 act of drawing a moustache and goatee on — and symbolically vandalizing — a reproduction of the Mona Lisa. This is a very close parallel to "Piss Christ."

If such artists view the world as "piss," does it really help the situation to "create an art work" where a photo of a crucifix is submerged in a bottle of the "artist's" urine? Or does it only echo, and add to, the fecal mire of society's misdirected, death-oriented values that is up to our chins anyway? Such "art" fails to offer alternatives to the horror, hatred and despair. It blocks us from the deeper truths that sustain us.

I am not shocked or offended by these images per se. In many years in the art world, I have seen or heard just about everything that's been possible to do to dishonor the name and practice of art. "Piss Christ" is simply a continuation of such works of the past twenty-thirty years as an "artist" canning his feces, another having himself shot in the arm, another masturbating in an art gallery, and yet another "artist" cutting off his penis piece by piece... all in the name of "art" (this last "creative" act proved fatal. Interesting isn't it, how little the fundamental decadence of contemporary art has changed? "Artists" repeat the same nihilistic ideas and means, revealing their essential creative barrenness).

These are extremes, of course, but the generally accepted contemporary art formulas tend, at one pole, toward decorative — often abstract — emptiness, through frigid pseudo-intellectuality, to nihilistic perversity at the other.

What does offend me — deeply — is the corruption of the meaning and purposes of art, whose centuries-long function has been to explore and express the totality of human experience in relation to the fundamentally spiritual basis of our existence on a tiny planet orbiting a fiery, distant sun in an immense and lonely universe.

Genuine art expresses the everyday, close-up realities of life, our problems and aspirations, within the context of this vast and profound spiritual dimension. It expresses the present without losing its roots in the past (and it does so by means of superior aesthetics). If ethical art values are to survive in an era of evil and corruption, art must also transcend the present by refusing to partake of that evil.

Just because Nazis murder Jews in gas chambers, doesn't mean the rest of us should do the same. We must rise above the evil status quo. The same with art. We must rise above contemporary artifice and nihilism to create genuine art in touch with timeless art and life issues.

Since the general level of contemporary art is so low, the higher aesthetic, emotional, philosophical and spiritual elements of art so debased, drastic action is called for in an attempt to heal it.

I feel all government funding of the visual arts should be eliminated.

By saying this, I do not acknowledge the government's right, or anyone else's right, to intrude upon the creative freedom of artists to do whatever they must. But the government (the taxpayer) also has the right not to have to pay for it.

If we lived in a Utopia, and it was possible to have a fair-minded grant system supportive of the artist's quest, I can think of nothing better than private and governmental funding to ease the creative and financial crises artists are heir to. But this is the real world. The situation has so degenerated that it is better to have no governmental money for the visual arts than to feed the cancer that continues to eat the life out of art.

The funding process is corrupted by self-interest, fad and fashion mongering, and the desire of art bureaucrats to perpetuate the anti-art, anti-life dictatorship controlling the art world... and art education (art educational institutions, like college football for the NFL, are the farm system of the art world, turning out generally brain-washed clones of fashionable art world artifice and nihilism).

The National Endowment grant selection process represents the worst kind of censorship of free creative thought. Not so amazingly, this censorship comes from within the art community itself, which they would have us believe represents the very bastion of freedom. On the contrary, any serious, potentially healing, redemptive, or unfashionably original art is denied access to the process.

Thus the NEA's emphasis on fashionable artifice and nihilism is, and has been, much more damaging to art, for many more years, than any well-intentioned probings by Congress. And yet, the art world has the hypocrisy of hypocrisies to cry "censorship" when anyone questions or suggests limits on their excesses.

Just as drugs, the destruction of our environment, hypocritical religious leaders, and corporate and governmental deception and misuse of funds are symptoms of the deterioration of values in America, a denatured, polluted art similarly represents a descent into decadence.

If these issues, and their consequences, were not so potentially lethal to the human body and spirit, one might simply watch art and life go on as they will, without question, comment or action. But since each issue is a result of individual and societal decay, and the decay of the leadership strata of America — and as such, a threat to our civilization — it is in our best interest to attempt to heal ourselves and our institutions.

We might make a start with art.

Sincerely,

Don Gray

■Joseph Papp, letter to John Frohnmayer, April 9, 1990, and John Frohnmayer, reply April 13, 1990

Joseph Papp was the producer of the New York Shakespeare Festival, and John Frohnmayer is the former chairperson of the National Endowment for the Arts. This exchange of letters precluded Papp's refusal of an NEA grant for the Festival.

Dear Mr. Frohnmayer:

The fracas over the obscenity issue and N.E.A. grants sprang into sharp focus upon my receiving your letter of approval in response to a New York Shakespeare Festival application for $50,000 toward the cost of our annual Festival Latino.

Your letter pressed me to note that acceptance of this grant was predicated on my observance of the restrictions contained in a recently passed piece of legislation affecting obscenity and N.E.A. grant giving.

I am warned herewith that if any of the works covered by the $50,000 grant to Festival Latino contained some aspect of the enumerated prohibitions (primarily of a sexual nature) the Festival may find itself in violation of its agreement with the N.E.A., if not the law as well. Such violation, though not specifically stated, would produce some punitive action, the least of which being a demand for the return of the grant and possibly being denied any further support from the N.E.A.

As head of a major theatrical institution, I have always cherished my freedom, defending it whenever it was challenged. My privileged right to make my own judgment in choosing this over that and that over this regardless of great varieties of societal pressure have been matters of principle, taste and artistic standards. To be asked, after meeting the tests of 35 years, to yield to circumscription and legislative prohibitions in the most vulnerable and inexplicable area of the arts, its content, is unthinkable, if not downright subversive.

Even if I did submit to the signing of what amounts to a loyalty oath, how am I to decide what others consider obscene? My personal views of what constitutes art and morality, may, and probably do, widely differ from those of the legislators who conceived the obscenity measure. And must I play the censor too, subject all plays and films from Latin America to microscopic scrutiny for some clue to sexual "aberration"? Who knows where sex may be lurking and in what disguise? I have no way of invoking community standards as some would have it. With what yardstick am I to measure the community standards of Rio de Janeiro?

With some dismay I have learned that a number of my colleagues will accept N.E.A. grants despite the restrictive clause in their agreements. The rationale is completely understandable: it is difficult to stand on principle when the need is so great. Further, it seems they are confident that reauthorization of N.E.A. funding will pass, and, in all likelihood, minus the restrictions.

I wish I could share this optimism. Perhaps time will prove this assessment to be correct. At the moment, I have serious doubts that reauthorization can make it through without some accommodation to the foes of N.E.A. I hope I'm wrong.

Right now, we need the $50,000 for the Latin Festival. To obtain this money, I am being asked to be party to a design which, in my opinion, is an abuse of the fundamental ethic in artistic endeavor. I have no desire to grandstand on this delicate issue. I certainly have not the slightest desire to push you into a corner. I do not want to break the law. I do not wish to relinquish the $50,000 grant. I do not wish to go through the motions of "signing" our agreement with the knowledge that I am bound, at one point or other, to violate, unwittingly, the prohibition I promise to observe.

Is this a dilemma, or isn't it?

We need the $50,000 for the Latin Festival, but something in my mind, my throat or my heart tells me not to go along.

What to do, Mr. Chairman? Your comments are eagerly awaited.

Sincerely,

Joseph Papp

Dear Mr. Papp:

I have your letter of April 9, 1990, and must admit that it causes me great concern. As you know, the law which you are asked to acknowledge was not one of our asking nor one which I thought necessary. Obscenity was illegal prior to that law, and of course is still illegal after it. Our reason for including it in the grant materials was to assure that all of our grantees were aware of this new legislation affecting fiscal year 1990.

With your record of 35 years of extraordinary service to the field and productions which have received artistic acclaim from all corners of the world, I cannot imagine that you would run afoul of this law. I also cannot give you legal advice, however, and suggest that you contact legal counsel to discuss your concerns.

I deeply regret that this language causes such concern. I hope you will be able to accept the grant; it is richly deserved.

Sincerely,

John E. Frohnmayer

■Robert V. Voorhees, Why Go to See Mapplethorpe?, *Cincinnati Enquirer*, April 14, 1990

Robert V. Voorhees teaches English at Cincinnati Country Day School.

The other day two of my senior English students gave provocative speeches on the Mapplethorpe phenomenon, reminding me that interest in this topic is everywhere in Cincinnati and has, amazingly, caused some of us to table our incessant chatter about sports for a while and engage in what is partly a serious intellectual discussion.

More recently I was reading one of Stephen Jay Gould's essays on natural history and encountered this timely observation: "I have often been amused by our vulgar tendency to take complex issues and break them into dichotomies...

with no acknowledgment of subtleties and intermediate positions — and nearly always with moral opprobrium attached to opponents."

How true of so much of the recent discussion of this exhibit in our city. What we often discover, of course, if we attempt to plumb a complex issue open-mindedly, is that truth inheres in those gray areas where ambiguity, ambivalence and paradox reign.

Studying the paradoxes

To wit: Some personal observations about the paradoxes which seem to me inherent in the present hubbub.

For the Supreme Court as well as us ordinary citizens, it has been difficult to distinguish between erotic art and pornography and also to decide who should be able to view the latter. My personal view is that some of Mapplethorpe is degenerate and nihilistic obscenity and also that it should be viewed and studied by any adult who wishes to consider herself or himself a thinking human being. To refuse to do so is to be content to live in that blandly comfortable zone of those wonderfully ignorant golfing club women in *Roger and Me* who were not only oblivious to the realities of the plight of their middle class and poor sisters but positively contemptuous of them as human beings.

In our cultural history Jefferson was one of the first to stress the paradox that the freest press and media will of necessity also be the most licentious. That freedom, of course, is the bedrock of our hope of enlightenment and is inti-mately related to our ability to be moral in the fullest sense. As the psychologist B.F. Skinner phrases it, "Goodness, like other aspects of dignity or worth, waxes as visible control wanes, and so, of course, does freedom." The insights here are, to me, essential. The more I am unreasonably restrained, the fewer become my opportunities to be a moral individual.

And yet, to be honest is to admit that there is that in Mapplethorpe which is obscene and decadent. No rationalizing will do. As annoying to me as censorship is, the often smug and affected voice of the pseudo artist (the one who almost invariably capitalizes the word "art" and applies it indiscriminately) who rationalizes decadence if it is displayed in effective lighting, a quirky and unusual perspective, or in some novel form.

In a wonderful essay on pornography, *Harper's* editor Lewis Lapham asks, "How is it possible to construe the degradation of human beings as a right... embodied in the First Amendment?" He rightly terms the most extreme forms of pornography nihilism and believes that "the nihilistic impulse slouches backward in time toward barbarism, magic and death."

Indeed. The photography of a human being urinating in another's mouth evokes images of Auschwitz and Dachau every bit as much as Mapplethorpe's breathtakingly beautiful nudes remind us of Michelangelo. In its totality the exhibit also reminds us that Mapplethorpe was both a fine artist and huckster, superbly able to recognize and accent natural beauty — and also fully aware of why we Americans go in droves to see *The Texas Chainsaw Massacre* and its ilk.

We must see all of the photos for yet another reason. In sum, they remind us who we are. I sometimes think that surprisingly many people in this city are uncomfortable with reality. Stephen Birmingham has written that "Cincinnati's style is one of playing it safe." And the Kansas City journalist Richard Rhodes, in an essay on the mind-set of the Midwest, has termed this region "Cupcake Land," the Holy Grail of which is "pleasantness, well-scrubbed and bland... petit point, paisley, wicker and Laura Ashley," a place which overvalues blind loyalty and conformity and harbors "a deep insecurity about the consequences of individual expression."

Well, be that as it may. Suffice it to say that decorum and purity can become just as pathological as obscenity. The hanged witches of Salem are eloquent testimony to the uncontrolled impulse to censor and purify.

Recognizing ourselves

Like Conrad's Marlowe we stare at that in the human experience which is bizarre and unreal, and if we have the courage to stay awhile and to think, we ultimately recognize part of ourselves, what we latently are. Our only real alternative is the sensory deprivation of suburbia and its sometimes smug self-righteousness.

Perhaps the ultimate reason why we should see all of Mapplethorpe is that doing so might disabuse us of the notion that we are somehow morally superior to this artist's sad homosexuals — or at least, in some deeper sense, help us to accept their humanity and existence.

■ Floyd Abrams and Samuel Lipman, What's Obscene?, *MacNeil/Lehrer NewsHour,* April 16, 1990

Floyd Abrams is a constitutional lawyer, and was a member of the Independent Commission. Samuel Lipman is a music critic and the publisher of The New Criterion. *He served as a member of the NEA's National Council on the Arts from 1982 to 1988. Robert MacNeil and Jim Lehrer are the hosts of the MacNeil/ Lehrer NewsHour.*

ROBERT MACNEIL: So who should decide what is obscene? That's what we debate now with Floyd Abrams, an attorney who specializes in first amendment cases, and Samuel Lipman, publisher of "The New Criterion," a conservative cultural magazine.

Mr. Abrams, what do you consider the important issue in the Cincinnati case?
FLOYD ABRAMS: Well, I think you've stated it. I think it's who decides. I'd expand that a bit, who decides what to see, who decides what's art. I would have thought that we had long since ruled for ourselves in this country that it's up to all of us to decide what art we want to see, what museums we want to go to, what art should be in museums or the like. And the idea of policemen walking around in museums, grand juries prowling about in museums, indictments,

criminal charges, seems to me anathema to American history and to the First Amendment.

MACNEIL: Mr. Lipman, what do you see as the issue here?

SAMUEL LIPMAN: I think the problem, in other words, the issue, is what control do people have over the kind of lives they want to live. The problem is that people have to have the ability through the democratic process to create conditions of minimum decency under which they, their families, and especially their children can live. That's what's called civilization. Without that, without these simple possibilities, we can't even have art, let alone free speech.

MACNEIL: Mr. Abrams, it's true that the Supreme Court in an important decision gave communities the right to decide their standards, their contemporary standards. It didn't give them the right, but it upheld the notion that there should be contemporary community standards when it comes to obscenity.

ABRAMS: That's true. What the Supreme Court also said though was that even though a community may want to ban art or a book or whatever, even if a community thinks something is obscene, they can't do it, unless the work taken as a whole has no serious artistic value at all. That is a central precept, a first amendment law, and an obscenity law because of the first amendment, and the notion that this museum in Cincinnati is showing artistic works which have no artistic value at all, no serious value at all, seems to me really absurd.

MACNEIL: Mr. Lipman, do you quarrel with that, that while a community can set its standard in what is obscene and Cincinnati has done it in other matters than this show, that it also has to meet the test that Mr. Abrams has just put that in taken as a whole, that an exhibition or a work has no artistic value?

LIPMAN: Well, I'm very surprised that a lawyer of Mr. Abrams' stature treats the Supreme Court and the body of law that we have in the United States as a given. The fact is that from the beginning of the republic, everything in the United States that is part of the body of law is subject to political decisions, sometimes by majority decisions, sometimes by 2/3 vote, but the fact is that even the Constitution, even the Supreme Court is subject to change. Courts change. At the end of the 19th century in Plessey versus Ferguson, it was decided that segregation was legal. In the 1950s, because Dwight Eisenhower chose Earl Warren as a Supreme Court justice it was decided, properly in my opinion, that segregation was illegal. What we are looking at is a political process. We are not looking here at an artistic process because I don't think that Cincinnati is about art. We are looking at the entire political process by which even the citizens of Cincinnati with whatever artistic tastes they have, they're probably not mine, but whatever artistic tastes they have, their rights as citizens of the United States to participate in the political process are the same as mine one for one.

MACNEIL: Mr. Abrams.

ABRAMS: I think there are two problems with that. First, I've correctly stated what the law is. I'm glad to talk to you about what the law ought to be. In terms of what it ought to be, I would think that the minimum protection for books, for works of art, for the like, ought to involve some assessment of whether this is sort of sleaze for sleaze's sake or make some attempt at being serious art or a serious book. You cannot seriously maintain that the citizens of Cincinnati or New York or anywhere else could just forage through libraries, taking out books because they think they don't like them or because they think they're offensive to them. Any one of us has the right to keep all the rest of us from engaging in censorship. And what I've heard you advocate so far is nothing less than censorship as a matter of routine.

LIPMAN: Well, I think to be accurate, what I have advocated is a trust in the democratic process and what is so extraordinary to me about this discussion over Mapplethorpe, and related matters, Serrano, Artists Space, Annie Sprinkle, what is so remarkable, it seems to me, is a combination of factors. One is that we're dealing in material that cannot be described. No newspaper has to my knowledge yet printed illustrations of the Mapplethorpe photos in question. To my knowledge, it has been very rarely —

MACNEIL: I know of at least one campus newspaper which has —

LIPMAN: Well, wouldn't you say that's the exception that proves the rule?

MACNEIL: Perhaps it is.

LIPMAN: The fact is that it's even been rare for it to be described that two of the most difficult photographs in the exhibition are representations of one man urinating in another man's mouth and a man with a finger up his penis. Now I don't like to be talking about that on television but that's what we're talking about. Now the second thing is —

MACNEIL: And your argument would be that the fact that those things are depicted photographically means it can't be art?

LIPMAN: No. My argument is that if we are to have fair discussion with the American people as part of the political process, we ought to be able to talk about what the material is and so far the most extraordinary gentility has ruled all of the media, but on the other hand, the position that the media has taken is that everything is permitted. And the other point I wanted to make is that I'm not saying that artists don't have a right to their opinions about what is art or even that art lovers don't have a right to an opinion about that. What I'm saying is that the citizens of the United States have a right to be a part of the process, not only by which art is judged, but by which they make their own lives. People have the right to know that they can send their child to the corner store for a loaf of bread and that the child will come back without damage to his body, his mind or his soul. That is what the decision is about and they have to make that decision, not me.

ABRAMS: But the decision that they have to make is where to send their child. The decision that they cannot make is whether I can view a work of art. The decision they cannot make is whether a library ought to contain a book or not. And what you're advocating is a sort of continuing plebiscite by which the public decides whether or not I or you or any of us can see work which may be, we may be in a minority in liking. Why would you say that?

LIPMAN: But my dear Mr. Abrams, democracy is the continuing plebiscite. The people of these states decided that they didn't wish to be governed by an English king. That's a very large thing. The people bear this right and I, whether I would bear it, would decide it in the same way as they would is not really important except insofar as I would campaign as vigorously as I could for what I wanted.

ABRAMS: That's why we have the Bill of Rights, that is to protect us against the majority telling us what we can see and what we can think and what we can watch and what we can feel. That is not a majority vote.

LIPMAN: But that is also why we have local government in Cincinnati that is elected and decides how to enforce the laws. What I am saying —

MACNEIL: What —

LIPMAN: Yes, go ahead.

MACNEIL: I get that point. What happens if the court in Cincinnati, what happens in your view if the court in Cincinnati decides that the prosecution doesn't meet the three tests that the Supreme Court says that it should meet, that it is sexually explicit, offensive sexually explicit material, that it is not, does not have value as art, and that it doesn't meet the local community standards? Suppose the court says it doesn't meet all those tests and throws out the prosecution?

LIPMAN: Well, what happens, I assume —

MACNEIL: What would you like to have happen?

LIPMAN: Well, what happens, I assume, is that the prosecution would have to decide whether it was to appeal and if the prosecution appealed, I would hope that the case would continue in normal fashion to the Supreme Court. At the Supreme Court, I would hope that the Justices responsible would perhaps take into account Justice Jackson's decision in the Terminiello case, that the Bill of Rights is not a suicide pact, that there are some things which governments must do to survive and societies must do to protect themselves. I'm not clear as to the point at which this line should be drawn. I would feel that the line between what you have chosen to call censorship and perfect freedom of expression, the line is shifting all the time. We work this line out as culture changes, as society changes.

MACNEIL: And you're saying it's time the Supreme Court redefined it, is that —

LIPMAN: I personally think that the Supreme Court definition is so weak and so attempting to cover everything that it has no force. That is simply my opinion. I believe, just as the proponents of civil rights in race matters have always felt, that this is a matter of continuing discussion and I think it would have been ridiculous in the 1940s to have told the National Association for the Advancement of Colored People I'm only telling you what's the law.

ABRAMS: You are quite right in saying that the law changes and interpretations of the law change. Where you're wrong is where you want the law to go and it seems to me that where you want the law to go is to give every community the sort of local option to define what is proper for their citizens to read and watch and look at and believe in. And that is nothing but a prescription for an official party line as determined democratically. If Cincinnati wants people not to watch this painting, they can determine it. I don't think so.

MACNEIL: In other words, you're saying that even if a large majority of the citizens in Cincinnati don't like that exhibition, they should not be able to prevent citizens, perhaps the small number of citizens who do want to go and see it.

ABRAMS: Even if there were only one citizen who wanted to go to that museum, I think he has an absolute right to do so.

LIPMAN: Well, I think that when one talks about one citizen, one is clearly making a kind of reduction in the situation. The problem is that we have to decide whether we will allow the same normal formation of policy to take place in the area of art and its relation to the public as we allow in every other area of American life. Let us talk about it. Let us fight it out in the polling places.

ABRAMS: And vote?

LIPMAN: And vote.

ABRAMS: Vote on books?

LIPMAN: Well, I guess I can't imagine anything that's forbidden to the American people to vote on.

ABRAMS: I can. Anything that violates the Bill of Rights.

LIPMAN: But you see we are in a process, continuing process of redefinition, so we continue to redecide that. You know as well as I do that Justices are actually named to the Supreme Court even by liberal presidents for political reasons.

ABRAMS: Sure, but that doesn't mean there's no such thing as law or no such thing as core values in the Bill of Rights. Surely, if the first amendment means anything —

MACNEIL: I have to wind it up now, gentlemen. Can you finish your sentence?

ABRAMS: Sure. If it means anything, it means that it's for each of us to decide for ourselves what we want to see.

MACNEIL: And do you have another sentence?

LIPMAN: It means that it is for each of us to decide for ourselves and then to attempt to build the kind of democratic society that we wish to live in.

MA NEIL: Okay, Mr. Lipman, Mr. Abrams, thank you both.

ABRAMS: Thank you.

LIPMAN: Thank you.

MACNEIL: Jim. America.

JIM LEHRER: Still to come on the NewsHour tonight, an environmental story from the Soviet Union, the legacy of Greta Garbo, and a Roger Rosenblatt essay.

John Frohnmayer, television interview with Rev. Pat Robertson, *The 700 Club*, April 23, 1990 (excerpt)

John Frohnmayer is the former chairperson of the National Endowment for the Arts. Rev. Pat Robertson is the head of the Christian Broadcasting Network (CBN), a television evangelist, and the director of the Christian Coalition.

PAT ROBERTSON: Joining us today in our Washington studios to explain his side of this controversial issue is the National Endowment for the Arts Chairman John Frohnmayer. Mr. Frohnmayer was appointed to his position in September of last year. Mr. Frohnmayer, I appreciate your willingness to come on the "700 Club." Before that oversight committee, speaking with Congressman Pat Williams, you did say that things that were broadcast on the "700 Club" were false. Would you elaborate on that please?

JOHN FROHNMAYER: Well, certainly, Pat, and thanks very much for allowing me this opportunity to be on the "700 Club" because I do think that your viewers are entitled to know what the National Endowment for the Arts is really about. This is an agency that's been around for 24 years, and over that time, we have helped millions of children, school children, to learn about the empowerment that the arts give people. We've taught them how to appreciate the beauty of language, and of music, and of dance, and of drama. And those kinds of things are very similar, I believe, to the kinds of things that you and I believe as Christians. So, this agency is not a pornographer. This agency is not a blasphemer. This agency is an agency that has really made a significant inroad into helping the American people. Let me give you just one other example. When we started — that is, when the Endowment first started in 1965 — there were 162 local arts agencies around this country. And now there are over 3,000 of them that have been promoted by the Endowment to help festivals and communities to experience the arts, because I believe that the arts glorify God, and the arts are a way that we as humans can express what it is to be fully human. And that's why I left the job that I had in Portland to come and be the head of the National Endowment for the Arts, because I really believe that the arts have something significant to contribute to our society.

ROBERTSON: Well, I don't think any of us would disagree with that, but you said that what we said on this program was false, and you said it to a congressional committee. And what we did was talk about the Mapplethorpe exhibit, and we showed the picture of the Serrano with the Christ on the cross submerged in urine with the title underneath it, "Piss Christ." Now, was that false for us to show that?

FROHNMAYER: Let me tell you, specifically, what I was referring to because it was an ad that was funded by the American Family Association which you then took and described in the show, and I'm sure all of us remember the Ninth Commandment and don't want to bear false witness. That's why I'm here. In that ad, which essentially your show endorsed, it talked about Annie

Sprinkle, which has been definitively been proved to have not been funded by the Endowment. The last money that was drawn down for reimbursement to that organization in New York was in August of '89, and Annie Sprinkle happened in '90.

ROBERTSON: You had a congressman, Dana Rohrabacher, just on this program showing that Annie Sprinkle said that her money had come from the New York Endowment of the Arts, which was funded by $500,000 from Washington.

FROHNMAYER: Well, who are you going to believe? A lady who has made 150 pornographic films? Or Kitty Carlisle Hart, the very highly respected head of the New York State Arts Commission, who said none of their money was involved? I mean, it's simply a matter of your taking the word of a lady who you despise in terms of what she has done.

ROBERTSON: All right. Let's leave Annie Sprinkle aside. What about Mapplethorpe? What about Serrano? There's no question that we were telling the truth about them, or is there a question about it?

FROHNMAYER: The unfortunate thing about the way that was cast is that people have said, "This is what the National Endowment for the Arts does." Two points on that, please. First of all, none of that was done since I've been at the National Endowment for the Arts. None of that was done since George Bush has been President. And secondly, this Endowment has probably funded a million separate images over the last 24 years. And we're talking about maybe 20 of those. It's simply a question of trying to paint with a very broad brush and sully the reputation of an agency that I think has probably done more to enlarge the spirit of the American people than any other federal agency that I know of.

ROBERTSON: But when you were interviewed by *USA Today*, they asked you specifically, "What would you do with Serrano? What would you do with Mapplethorpe?" And you said, "I would put them through the review process *again*. And they would be subject to consideration again." And you said, and I'm quoting your interview now: "It accuses us of funding homosexuals, and I plead guilty because we do not consider sexual orientation as a criteria for judging grants." Now, you said, "Nor do we assume that because of a person's sexual orientation that person will automatically disobey the law." Well, Mapplethorpe has got child pornography among other things. I mean, if someone is a pedophile, would that disqualify him from getting a federal grant?

FROHNMAYER: Well, Pat, what I'm going to do as the head of this agency is, I think, the same thing that you would do, and that is, I'm going to pray for wisdom and courage to do the very best job I can in fulfilling the mandate of this agency: and that is to produce the very best art we have in this country.

ROBERTSON: Come on, now. Very best art? Ladies and gentlemen, I want to shock you. Please, forgive me. I'd rather not say this, but Mr. Frohnmayer, this is what was funded: a photograph of a hand and forehand of one person in the rectum of another; a picture of a man putting his little finger in the urine — well, I don't want you to interrupt me because this is what you funded: a photo showing one man urinating into the mouth of another man; a close-up of a cylindrical object being introduced into the rectum of another; a self-portrait of

Mapplethorpe with a bullwhip hanging from his rectum; a couple of nude pictures of little children.

FROHNMAYER: What I'm trying to tell you is, I'm not here to defend that. I didn't tell you once that I'm here to defend that. What I told you is, this is a new ball game, a new administration.... I mean, I don't want to talk about those things that happened on somebody else's watch. What I want to tell you is, that this agency can really provide a very valuable service to the American people. And I think you do us a real disservice by focusing on about 20 photographs. They are, I think, if you take them by themselves, obnoxious and obscene by anybody's standards. I'm not here to defend those. I'm here to defend the record of this agency overall.

ROBERTSON: What we want to do is not just that. I mean, your agency funded an organization that called Cardinal O'Connor "a fat cannibal." And do you believe that the United States taxpayers' money should go to attack the Roman Catholic Church? It also had a picture of a thing that said, "Piss Pope." Do you believe we should attack the Roman Catholic Church as a nation?

FROHNMAYER: I do not believe that this Endowment should be funding things that are swastikas on synagogues or are defiling other people's religions. That is not what I am about, and again, the examples that you talk about are all examples that pre-date anything that this administration has done. So, what's really happening here is that you're crying that the house is on fire; the fireman has arrived, and you're hurling bricks at the fireman....

ROBERTSON: Let me ask you, why don't you come out and say, "Mapplethorpe is wrong. Serrano was wrong." The attack on Jesse Helms with the "Piss Helms" thing that was funded just a few months ago, possibly under your administration —

FROHNMAYER: No, it was not.

ROBERTSON: "Tongues of Flame" was not under your administration, the $10,000?

FROHNMAYER: That's right. That's a 1989 grant, and I was wrongfully accused of doing that by the Rev. Wildmon. The funding on that went out in September of 1989, and I was sworn in on October 3, and so, you know, you talk about these kinds of things but really I would like — and I would hope in the spirit of good faith — that you would listen to what it is we've said. I have a four-page list of quotes, which is clearly not all of them that I have made, quotes about my absolute opposition to obscenity. I'm going to leave them here with you because I want you to have them. I want you to know what my position is on these issues. I think it is really unfair to the Endowment for the people to claim that it should be abolished. What the Endowment can do is to really enhance the spirit of this country, and I think that's what we're really all about.

ROBERTSON: Mr. Frohnmayer, I want to ask you one question: are you as the head of this going to stop funding lesbian and gay films, obscene art, and anti-religious art? Are you going to stop funding those through your Endowment or not? Yes or no?

FROHNMAYER: I have said repeatedly that obscenity will not be funded under my watch, and I mean that with every fiber of my body.

ROBERTSON: But you have said that you didn't think so-called homo-erotic art is obscene. And in 1990, my friend, during your watch, you gave $9,000 to the San Francisco International Lesbian and Gay Film Festival. Now that's still going on.

FROHNMAYER: What I have said is that I do not believe that a person's sexual orientation is relevant to whether or not that person's going to break the law. And, quite frankly, I think, if we were to take the position that we can't fund people who have a certain sexual orientation, we'd be in court tomorrow on that issue. What I am saying is, we are going to look at the quality of the art that's proposed, and I have further said that I do not believe — and I think that this is fair — I do not believe that a person of a particular sexual orientation is automatically going to obey the law any more than I believe that a person of another sexual orientation is automatically going to obey the law. So, it's simply a question of trying to treat human beings as human beings. I think that that, again, is consistent to what we believe as Christians.

ROBERTSON: Well, I totally agree with those things, but on the other hand, I want you to know that I think I speak for the taxpayers of America, we're fed up to here with using our money for homo-erotic art and for anti-Christian diatribes by way-out fringe artists. And I think that's going to have to be stopped, and I, frankly, agree that the government has no part in getting engaged in that. It's unconstitutional. But let me ask you one last question: the agency funded an anti-Christian art exhibit saying "Piss Christ"; would you fund one that said "Glorify Jesus Christ and worship and exalt him," or would that be unconstitutional?

FROHNMAYER: I have a list for you — another list, which I'm that glad you asked about because I will also leave this with you — it's a list of grants which are very definitely Christian grants.... it goes on and on and on. Here, I've got a three-page list of those grants. So, what I'm really seeking from your viewers is a fair shake, an opportunity to look straight at this Endowment and the 85,000 grants that it's given — only 20 or so of which you talk about — and to say this agency has really produced a service for the country, and under my leadership, it's going to continue to do that. Thanks so much. I really appreciated you giving me an opportunity to be here.

ROBERTSON: Thank you.

■ Charles Krauthammer, Thinking Through Mapplethorpe, *Washington Post*, April 25, 1990

Charles Krauthammer is a nationally syndicated columnist.

When Dan Rather reports on the banned-in-Cincinnati exhibit of Robert Mapplethorpe's photographs, he does not show the homoerotic, pedo-philic or sadomasochistic pictures — the ones that brought the police and the courts, the ACLU and Jesse Helms, the censors and libertarians into the game. Television will show you the exquisite flower pictures and the tamer portraits. It *tells* you about the nasty ones.

Similarly, this newspaper does not publish, say, Mapplethorpe's self-portrait in leather with bull whip inserted in his rectum. Why not? This quite obviously is censorship. Why is the ACLU not protesting?

Because everyone, ACLU included, favors censorship in principle. No one protests the banning of Mapplethorpe's nastier pictures from television and newspapers because there is a general consensus that some things are not to be shown on the mass media. But as the media become less mass — as you go, for example, from network to cable to videocassette — more and more is permitted, until we reach the point where just about anything is permitted for viewing in the privacy of one's own bedroom.

This arrangement, which might be called censorship by classification, enjoys wide support because it is a reasonable way for a pluralistic society to deal with the question of obscenity and public standards. The question with Mapplethorpe is how to classify his art. Should it be classified as so outrageous and degrading as to be reserved for the most private sanctum (the home)? Or is it serious enough to deserve placement in a public institution such as an art gallery?

Note that even the museum curators who exhibit Mapplethorpe are careful to place the most offensive pictures in special rooms under special cover. Even they accept the principles of segregation.

Why do we — liberal curators, included — segregate certain types of material that are offensive or obscene? For two reasons. First, not to segregate is to risk assaulting the unwitting. To show, say, on the "CBS Evening News," a picture of one man urinating into the mouth of another (also in the Mapplethorpe exhibit) would be to assault the sensibilities of millions who did not seek it out. That violates the classic liberal dictum that you can do what you want to yourself so long as you do not harm others.

The other reason is that even if people aren't harming others, society has an interest in what people do to themselves. Libertarians don't like this kind of paternalism, but most people in this democracy believe society has the right to prevent consenting adults from, say, drug-taking or self-mutilation (selling a kidney for money, for example). In short, society has the right — the duty, even — to protect people against themselves.

We know that drugs can injure. But can art? "What reason is there to think that anyone was ever corrupted by a book?" asks Irving Kristol. "This last question, oddly enough, is asked by the very same people who seem convinced that advertisements in magazines or displays of violence on television do indeed have the power to corrupt."

Of course, art can corrupt. "If you believe that no one was ever corrupted by a book," Kristol points out, "you have also to believe that no one was ever improved by a book (or a play or a movie). You have to believe, in other words, that all art is morally trivial.... No one, not even a university professor, really believes that."

It is precisely because words and images have the power to degrade that society tries to restrict certain kinds of material to the smallest possible audience. That is why strip joints and porno houses are segregated into combat zones. Some things may not be displayed on billboards. Some may not be shown on TV. Some may not be shown in public galleries.

What goes where? That is the issue. It is one not of principle but of classification. It is thus far less cosmic than Pat Buchanan and the ACLU would like us to think. Take away all the posturing, and the issue with Mapplethorpe is not, as the civil libertarians pretend, "Are you for or against censorship?" The issue is "Where on the spectrum do you place Mapplethorpe?"

For what it's worth, where do I? Having seen the catalogue, though not the exhibit, I find his work too melancholy to be offensive, too decadent to be pornographic. Given current cultural norms — the slasher/skin flicks one can see nightly on cable, for example — even his rougher stuff is, in my view, correctly placed in a public art gallery.

The people of Cincinnati may, however, have a different standard. If they believe that Mapplethorpe's rougher stuff ranks a rung lower, why should they not be permitted to decide that it is too degrading to warrant public exhibit? Let these pictures be accessible to Cincinnatians by mail-order catalogue for study behind closed doors. That is no more an attack on the First Amendment than keeping these pictures off television.

The sophisticates howl at this judgment. They sneer at the yahoos of Ohio for their small, censoring minds. Well, if the sophisticates and the civil libertarians are so outraged by censorship, are they prepared to defend my project to have the bullwhip-in-rectum study blown up and featured on a Times Square billboard?

■John Buchanan, statement to the Senate Subcommittee on Education, April 27, 1990 (excerpt)

John Buchanan is the president of People for the American Way, and a former member of Congress.

Theology or Blasphemy?

A great deal of the criticism of the National Endowment for the Arts has come from the Religious Right and their allies. As an ordained Baptist minister and graduate of Southern Baptist Theological Seminary, I would like to let the committee know that there are alternative views to these religious leaders' interpretations of NEA-funded art works that they deplore.

Humanity is portrayed in the Bible as the crown of God's creation, created in His image. We humans are the only creatures to whom God gave the gift of creativity — only we are capable of painting, composing a symphony, writing a poem, or designing a cathedral. In the act of creativity we most perfectly reveal that we are created in the image of God.

According to the Bible, God also created the miracle of the human body and created the joys of human love for our good. This love in all its manifestations is neither vulgar, obscene nor pornographic.

Nevertheless, wrong-headed churchmen through the centuries have found evil in that which God made for good. For example, one of the early popes wanted to do away with Michelangelo's depiction of the Last Judgment in the Sistine Chapel, because the figures were naked. A blouse was painted on Mary because she was shown breastfeeding the baby Jesus. Figures on the ceiling of the Sistine Chapel were covered because of their nakedness. One pope ordered statues of nude forms thrown into the Tiber River because their beauty might distract the faithful. This kind of zealousness has continued through the centuries. It is no more appropriate today than it was hundreds of years ago.

I once heard a Baptist preacher describe dancing in terms so lewd and vulgar that he turned it into something evil and ugly. And yet at the Southwest Churches' Good Friday services a few weeks ago we concluded our worship with a wonderful Shaker hymn portraying Jesus as lord of the dance.

What about the controversial artworks brought to our attention by the Religious Right? What about the picture of the crucifix immersed in urine? Recently I spoke to my Sunday school class in a Baptist church in Washington. I told them about the controversy and the crucifix immersed in urine. I said, "That's shocking, isn't it?" They said, "Yes." I said, "That's outrageous, isn't it?" They said, "Yes." I said, "That's offensive, isn't is?" They said, "Yes." I said, "Therefore, it is a true expression of the meaning of the crucifixion to serious Christians, because Isaiah said: 'He was wounded for our transgressions, he was bruised for our iniquities: the chastisement of our peace was upon him; and with his stripes we are healed.'"

To most, if not all, Christians, the Cross represents Christ taking upon Himself our sin. So in addition to the terrible physical agony of a crucifixion, there was a spiritual agony of what our sinfulness and rebellion had heaped upon Him. Therefore the shocking picture of the crucifix in urine can be interpreted as a faithful portrayal of the shocking, outrageous, offensive reality of our sinfulness heaped upon Him. What is blasphemy to certain Religious Right leaders was to the artist a vivid statement of spiritual reality.

What about the painting of Christ shooting dope in another controversial exhibit? It is equally shocking, outrageous and offensive. Yet in this society and in this city and in many other places in the world, year after year, innocent young people are induced to dependency upon drugs. The agony on the face of that painting represents their agony as human beings. And Jesus said, "Even as ye have done it unto the least of these, my brethren, ye have done it unto me." Shocking art? Yes. Good theology? For me, yes. Do I believe that everyone has to agree with this interpretation of the picture? Absolutely not! That is what freedom is all about. That's what art is all about — to try to tell the truth, to try to portray reality, or shock us or move us into thinking about it.

Volumes have been written about the meaning of works of literature, music, and the visual arts, just as there are whole libraries of books written on various interpretations of the Bible. Those who want to confine us to one simplistic interpretation or limit our ability to consider works of art in all of their interpretations do an injustice to the richness of artistic expression, and diminish our freedom.

■ Bruce Fein, statement to the Senate Subcommittee on Education, April 27, 1990 (excerpt)

Bruce Fein is a constitutional lawyer.

Why Congress Should Be Concerned with NEA Subsidized Messages

A nation lives by symbols. When the government funds works of art, it necessarily gives tacit approval to the grantee and the goals he promotes with taxpayer dollars. As Justice Louis D. Brandeis lectured in *Olmstead v. U.S.* (1928), "Our Government is the potent, the omnipresent teacher. For good or for ill, it teaches the whole people by its example."

The government, accordingly, must be scrupulously concerned with the messages it sends to the public by underwriting specific types of art. Bigotry, for instance, intended to arouse racial or religious prejudice should receive no government backing. Suppose David Duke, a former member of the Ku Klux Klan and current member of the Louisiana legislature, requested a grant from NEA to paint a picture glorifying post-Reconstruction lynching of "niggers." To make the grant would signify government approval or indifference to racial bigotry, and would inflame race relations throughout the country.

Suppose a neo-Nazi sought NEA funding of a mural applauding the Holocaust. To underwrite the applicant would foster anti-Semitism, and suggest the government would be phlegmatic about private persecution of Jews.

The government is vitally interested in suppressing, not promoting, bigotry because it threatens democracy. Freedom and liberty cannot thrive in communities steeped in racial, ethnic, or religious prejudice, as the German Third Reich verifies.

President Harry Truman explained in 1952 that "Mutual respect and tolerance for the beliefs of others is the secret of the strength of this blessed land." Truman was echoing the sentiments conveyed by President George Washington in writing to a Hebrew Congregation in 1790. He asserted that our Government "gives to bigotry no sanction, and to persecution no assistance."

Exploiting the human instinct toward racial or religious intolerance in times of hardship, personal despair, or low esteem was the evil genius of Adolf Hitler. Writing in *Mein Kampf*, Hitler observed that the art of successful propaganda requires directing speech "more and more toward feeling, and only to a certain extent to so-called reason." That understanding is why many colleges and universities have embraced rules of student conduct that discipline stigmatiza-

187

tion or vilification for reasons unrelated to individual merit. The University of Michigan, for example, adopted a policy against "any behavior, verbal or physical, that stigmatizes or victimizes an individual on the basis of race, ethnicity, religion, age, marital status, handicap or Vietnam veteran status," and creates a demeaning educational environment. (On September 7, 1989, a federal district judge enjoined enforcement of the policy because of vagueness.)

It is said that identifying a malignant intent of the author of racially or religiously bigoted speech is unworkable. But proof of intent is a legal commonplace; it is an element of most crimes, libel suits, litigation addressing claims of racial or religious discrimination, and free speech challenges to removal of books from public school libraries. Even a dog knows the difference between a kick and an unwitting bump from his master!

It is said that if racially or bigoted speech is squelched, there will be no stopping point to prevention of genuine free speech. Nonsense! The progress of civilization has been the progress of making refinements and differentiations in the law. As Justice Oliver Wendell Holmes observed, all law depends on matters of degrees "as soon as it is civilized."

To search for a mechanism of public funding of the arts that is devoid of tacit expressions of government approval for the ideas promoted by grantees is a futile quest. In the public mind, the underwriter cannot be separated from the author. The U.S. Supreme Court has acknowledged that psychological phenomenon in declaring that government funding of religious institutions, even if limited to their secular endeavors, nevertheless frequently creates a prohibited appearance of state sponsorship of religion. See *School District of City of Grand Rapids v. Ball*, 473 U.S. 373 (1985).

Artists or scholars who receive government monies can easily exploit the financial tie to boost their ideas. Suppose a grantee authors a work that trumpets the asserted virtues of polygamy. He could thereafter proselytize that his ideas were sponsored and approved by the United States government, and thereby enhance his credibility. Grant recipients who lionized homosexual sodomy or hallucinogenic drugs might similarly claim the government as a votary of their viewpoints to fortify their acceptance in the marketplace.

The purposes of the First Amendment are undisturbed by government scrutiny of the artistic or scholastic ideas it promotes through subventions. Justice Brandeis delineated those purposes as four-fold in *Whitney v. California*, 247 U.S. 357 (1927) (concurring): to foster the discovery and spread of political truths; to make individuals free to develop their mental faculties; to make them happy by tolerating their ruminations and expressions; and, to avoid the hate and violence precipitated by censorship of ideas.

Curbs on government funding of particular ideological messages does not impair the quest for political truths. They leave undisturbed the right of all artists or scholars to challenge whatever orthodoxies they wish through private means. Indeed, their credibility may be enhanced by an absence of government financial ties. Their ideas may receive more rather than less attention (but not necessarily more acceptance) if denied government subsidies because public curiosity may be aroused by reasons assembled for the decision. Thus, *The*

Satanic Verses achieved instant popularity when it ignited thundering opposition and death threats from the Government of Iran.

History proves that government subsidized ideas enjoy no special prowess in a free marketplace of ideas. Who believes the Communist Chinese prevarications regarding the Tiananmen massacre of Chinese student dissidents? Of course, government sponsorship does not necessarily taint credibility if a reputation for truth has been established, as with the BBC and the Voice of America.

The danger that government funded ideas will necessarily enjoy a competitive advantage over their unsubsidized rivals in the United States marketplace is virtually non-existent, especially because the subsidies are minuscule in proportion to the solely privately sourced propagation of ideas.

Neither do government restrictions on underwriting ideas constrict individuals from honing their mental faculties. They remain free to read, write, compose, and to deliberate without intrusion by government. Concededly, more hours might be devoted to these mental tasks and challenges if the government guaranteed a handsome stipend or funds to purchase newspapers, broadcast stations, or movie studios to all who desired to engage in cogitative or communicative endeavors. But the First Amendment has never been thought to require government to underwrite all who pine for greater personal celebration or success in spreading ideas.

The individual fulfillment and enjoyment that stems from uncurbed ponderings and expositions of ideas is unthreatened by an absence of government funding. And, that absence will not breed the hate and violence associated with censorship because of the sweeping free speech protection in the First Amendment for opposing unconventional viewpoints, including flag burning.

Politics and art inevitably intersect. Exemplary are Picasso's "Guernica" and "Peace Dove," Longfellow's "Paul Revere's Ride," Francis Scott Key's "Star Spangled Banner," Charles Dickens' *Oliver Twist* and *A Tale of Two Cities*, William Shakespeare's "Julius Caesar," Thomas Nast's political cartoons, and Pete Seeger's folk songs.

NEA thus should consider how proposed works of art might enrich and strengthen democratic norms and aspirations in awarding grants. That task is comparable to the school teacher who selects readings from Alexander Pope over *Hustler Magazine* in order to promote a mastery of the English language and a penetrating understanding of human nature.

■ Hon. Henry Hyde, The Culture War, *National Review,* April 30, 1990

Henry Hyde is a Republican member of the House of Representatives, representing the state of Illinois.

I'm not quite sure what it says about America that one of the most intense public controversies in the months between the Tiananmen Square massacre and the breaching of the Berlin Wall had to do with homoerotic photographs and a crucifix suspended in a vat of urine.

My formulation is deliberately provocative. While Central and Eastern Europe were giving birth, in joy and pain, to the Revolution of 1989, Americans were transfixed by an argument over, let me say it again, homoerotic photographs and a crucifix suspended in a vat of urine. One might have been tempted to think that Oswald Spengler was right, and Francis Fukuyama wrong: the West was indeed headed down the slippery slope to decadence and irrelevance; but the "end of history" wouldn't be so much boring as appalling.

Whatever else can be said for or against our national media, their attention span is short: and so public life moves on. But we shouldn't be quite so eager to leave the debate over Mapplethorpe and Serrano behind us. For the Great Arts Controversy demonstrated that America is, in truth, involved in a *Kulturkampf* — a culture war, a war between cultures and a war about the very meaning of "culture."

Many people would prefer to deny this. But the conscientious public servant and the thoughtful citizen cannot afford to miss the full truth of our situation, for politics is, at its deepest level, a function of culture. The American *Kulturkampf* may be understood, to paraphrase Clausewitz, as civil war by other means.

It is best to be precise about the terminology here. By "culture war," I don't mean arguments over the relative merits of Mozart and Beethoven, *Henry V* on stage and *Henry V* on screen, Eliot and Auden, Tom Wolfe and E.L. Doctorow, the Chicago Symphony Orchestra and the New York Philharmonic. Nor do I mean the tensions between highbrows and lowbrows, between sports fans and opera buffs, between people who think Bruce Springsteen is the greatest artist alive and people who wouldn't know Bruce Springsteen if he rang their doorbell and asked to use the telephone.

No, by "culture war" I mean the struggle between those who believe that the norms of "bourgeois morality" (which is drawn in the main from classic Jewish and Christian morality) should form the ethical basis of our common life, and those who are determined that those norms will be replaced with a radical and thoroughgoing moral relativism. That the "relativism" in question is as absolutist and as condescendingly self-righteous as any sixteenth-century inquisitor is a nice irony. But that is the division in our house.

Whose Money?

The public-policy issue is, to my mind, not all that difficult to resolve. Public funds, in a democracy, are to be spent for public purposes, not for the satisfaction of individuals' aesthetic impulses. And if the impulse in question produces a work which is palpably offensive to the sensibilities of a significant proportion of the public, then that work ought not to be supported by public funds.

Ideally, the funding agencies would understand this principle and abide by it. Legislatures and courts are ill suited to setting the boundaries in an area such as this, as we should have learned from the days of Anthony Comstock and the Boston Watch and Ward Society. But when the funding agencies do not set the boundaries in a way that maintains public confidence, then the legislature must act.

To do so is not an act of censorship, *pace* President Bush. In announcing his support for continued federal funding of the National Endowment for the Arts, the President stated he didn't "know of anybody in the government... that should be set up to censor what you write or what you paint or how you express yourself." However, the President went on to say: "I am deeply offended by some of the filth that I see into which federal money has gone, and some of the sacrilegious, blasphemous depictions that are portrayed as art."

Congressman Dana Rohrabacher (R., Calif.), while cheered by the fact that the President doesn't like pornography any better than he likes broccoli, points out that "We're talking about sponsorship, not censorship." If the NEA were prohibited from funding certain types of work, no artist's right to create his work and display it would have been infringed. Censorship and refusal to subsidize are two very different things. All that a legislature would be saying is that the public has no responsibility to pay for a work that would give deep offense to a significant proportion of that public. On would hope that the artist, out of self-respect if nothing else, would agree.

There are those who argue that these kinds of entanglements are unavoidable and that we should therefore extract the Federal Government from the business of funding the arts. It may, over time, come to that. But I would hope not. It would be bad (although certainly not fatal) for the arts. But it would also say something deeply saddening about America: it would tell us that we simply can't reach agreement on a reasonable approach to issues at the intersection of politics and culture. And that is not the situation of choice for the American experiment in ordered liberty.

Negotiating the *Kulturkampf*

HOW MIGHT we craft an approach to the American *Kulturkampf* that would at least begin a civilized conversation about our differences? How do we argue these issues within the bounds of democratic tolerance: not the false tolerance that glosses over differences, but the true tolerance that engages differences forthrightly but civilly? Here are some themes that may be worth exploring.

1. *On the freedom of the artist:* Artists should, of course, be free from political coercion in their work. Those of us who have celebrated the triumph of Vaclav

Havel have no desire to shackle the poet, the composer, the painter, the dramatist, or the photographer.

The key question for the cultural debate, however, is: Freedom *for what?* The artist's purpose is surely not fulfilled in mere self-expression; for if self-expression were all there is to art, then a puppy chasing kittens would be as much an artist as Raphael, Vermeer, or Bach. Rather, as Thomas Aquinas wrote in the *Summa,* "The test of the artist does not lie in the will with which he goes to work, but in the excellence of the work he produces."

So the purpose of the artist's freedom is to help him and us to a fuller apprehension of, and delight in, the three transcendentals — the good, the true, and the beautiful. Lord Acton got it quite right: "Freedom is not the power to do what you want, but rather the right to do what you ought." Art detached from the quest for truth and goodness is, to repeat, simply self-expression and ultimately self-absorption. It is narcissism, and, like Narcissus, it inevitably destroys itself.

I am aware that this understanding of the purpose of artistic freedom can be dismissed as hopelessly provincial. But "art for art's sake" presents a serious problem to legislators who are expected at least to explain, if not to justify, their expenditure of tax dollars. We are now told that "great art forces us to abandon our most cherished values," but most people aren't pleased to have their most cherished values challenged, much less to pay for the experience. Franklin W. Robinson, director of a museum attached to the Rhode Island School of Design, has been quoted as saying: "Among the many things that art does for us all is that it challenges us, it demands that we rethink our assumptions about every issue in life, from religion to politics, from love to sex to death and afterlife." Thus the twentieth-century artist has changed the object of art from the three transcendentals to challenge and revolution.

The congressional reaction to what Carol Iannone called "the insistent and progressive artistic exploration of the forbidden frontiers of human experience" was predictable, but at least has drawn attention to the "works of art" involved and to the difficult issues of artistic freedom and congressional accountability. Censorship, discrimination — these words have unpleasant connotations. But when a limited amount of money must be distributed among a large number of applicants, some form of discrimination is inevitable. I was interested in a case of curatorial discretion written up in the October 1989 *Arts Journal.* Mr. Ted Potter, the director of the Southeastern Center for Contemporary Art, is quoted as explaining why he refused to display a videotape that was "grossly racist" as to both the black and the Jewish populations. Mr. Potter said: "It was just a straightforward case of racial slurs and bigotry, and I'm not interested in that, so we didn't show it."

Justice Potter Stewart once said that he couldn't define pornography, but he knew it when he saw it. I suggest that where racism and bigotry are present, most people, even congressmen, are capable of exercising curatorial discretion.

Modern artists also demean the memory of their precedessors when they suggest that any boundary-setting by public authorities is a threat to art itself. Evelyn Waugh was indulging in characteristic exaggeration when he wrote in 1939 that "most of the greatest art has appeared under systems of political tyranny." But there is something there to think about. Great art may have been created because it enjoyed the financial favor of public authorities at the time (whether the public authority in question was a prince or a president); but it endures because it enables men and women to discern the true and the good in fuller proportion than before.

2. *On democratic civility:* Public opinion cannot be the final touchstone of artistic merit. That, too, should go without saying. While it certainly would not be accurate to suggest that virtually all great artists experienced public rejection before they enjoyed (sometimes posthumous) acceptance — Haydn, Bach, and Brahms, to choose from just one art, were quite comfortably secure in public esteem — it is also true that public opinion can be slow to recognize artistic genius, particularly when that genius is consciously striving to break new aesthetic ground.

But there is a converse truth that is rarely acknowledged. Gratuitous insults to the religious sensibilities of fellow citizens, by artists or by anyone else, are damaging to civil comity and democratic tolerance. Whatever the art world may think, Americans remain an incorrigibly religious people. Happily for the Republic, the growth of American religiosity has, over the past two generations, bred an even greater religious tolerance: the overwhelming majority of Americans believe it to be the will of God that we not kill each other over what constitutes the will of God. One wonders, though, if the democratic courtesy of tolerance is always reciprocated.

Let me take the obvious example. Whatever ex-post-facto rationalizations Andres Serrano may have constructed, I cannot believe that his *Piss Christ* was anything other than a deliberate attempt to provoke: in this case, to provoke Christians. Suppose Mr. Serrano's work had involved suspending a Torah scroll in a vat of urine; would any reasonable person have doubted that this was a gross act of anti-Semitism? Or, at an entirely different level, suppose that Mr. Serrano had suspended a peace symbol in a vat of urine and labeled it *Piss Peace*? Can you believe that this would have been defended as legitimate artistic endeavor by the same people who defended the funding of *Piss Christ*? Whatever else it was, *Piss Christ* was a vicious violation of democratic civility.

The artist may well have a gift of insight that transcends the capabilities of less aesthetically endowed citizens. But that insight confers no right to indulge oneself in thoughtless — or, worse, deliberate — trashing of others' deepest convictions.

3. *Provocative or evocative?* Some people, in fact some quite distinguished people, seem to think that any expression issuing from an artist is art. Robert McCormick Adams, secretary of the Smithsonian Institution, has even argued that graffiti are art. Would that include, I'm immediately tempted to ask, graffiti spray-painted onto the East Building of the National Gallery of Art in Washington, of which Mr. Adams is a trustee? After all, the East Building provides a much more inviting canvas for the graffiti-ist than a New York subway car, and ever so many more people would have the opportunity to see the "artist's" work if it weren't buried underground and whisked away from the viewer within a minute or so.

My argument is not against provocation per se. The first two crashing chords (indeed the entire first movement) of Beethoven's Third Symphony were a deliberate provocation: a challenge to the genteel limits which had characterized earlier uses of the symphonic form. But this was provocation in the service of a larger end. It was not provocation for its own sake.

I am no philosopher of aesthetics, but I would suggest that we ought to consider the possibility that good art is evocative rather than provocative, although the evocative quality can sometimes involve the artist in provocative expressions. Provocation, in short, should be at the service of evocation.

Which immediately raises the question, Evocative of what? Again, with the caution of a philosophical amateur, I would suggest: evocative of man's highest and noblest aspirations, our aspirations for the good, the true, and the beautiful. Put another way, art as evocation is neither art at the service of some political program nor art as an ideological instrument, but art as one means by which man gains a glimpse of the transcendent dimension of the human experience.

Beyond the Neural Itch

I suppose this returns me, in a roundabout way, to my first point: that art is not, and must not be, mere self-indulgent self-expression. If we can agree on that — if we can agree that discipline, craftsmanship, and a purpose transcending the mere satisfying of a neural itch are of the essence of the truly artistic act — then we have marked off the ground on which we can intelligibly debate questions of boundary-setting, funding, and all the rest of the public-policy arts agenda.

And that would be no small accomplishment.

■ Stephen F. Rohde, Art of the State: Congressional Censorship of the NEA, COMM/ENT, Spring 1990 (excerpt)

Stephen F. Rohde practices constitutional and entertainment law in Los Angeles. He is a member of the board of directors of California Lawyers for the Arts.

The New NEA Restrictions are Unconstitutionally Vague

A. Fundamental Principle of Due Process: the Vagueness Doctrine and the NEA Standards

Any "statute which either forbids or requires the doing of an act in terms so vague that men of common intelligence must necessarily guess at its meaning and differ as to its application, violates the first essential of due process of law."[1]

This is a fundamental principle that applies across the entire spectrum of legislation.

The vagueness doctrine requires that any standard imposed by legislation be susceptible of objective measurement.[2] But in matters touching on vital First Amendment freedoms, this principle requires heightened scrutiny. Our zealous solicitude toward freedom of expression requires that "precision of regulation must be the touchstone" for laws which purport to burden or regulate speech.[3] Such exacting precision is necessary when it comes to First Amendment rights because the "[t]hreat of sanctions may deter... almost as potently as the actual application of sanctions."[4]

Four policy reasons underlie this special concern over vagueness: First, clearly defined statutes provide government officials with objective standards against which to judge the speech under consideration;[5] second, and closely related to the first, vague statutes inevitably invite arbitrary discretionary decisions;[6] third, laws restricting speech must be narrowly drawn to guarantee that protected speech is not punished along with unprotected speech,[7] and fourth, the enforcement of vague statutes will have a chilling effect on protected speech since many will steer far wide of any conflict with the government to avoid the time and expense of defending themselves.[8]

There is a hint in the Conference Report that Congress may be attempting to enact a definition of obscenity which goes beyond the *Miller* test. In setting forth the criteria which the Independent Commission is to consider in lieu of previously content-neutral NEA standards, the Report reads as follows:

> The criteria to be considered by the commission shall include but not be limited to possible standards where (a) applying contemporary community standards would find that the work taken as a whole appeals to a prurient interest; (b) the work depicts or describes in a patently offensive way, sexual conduct; and (c) the work, taken as a whole, lacks serious artistic and cultural value.[9]

But the actual standards set forth in *Miller* read as follows:

> The basic guidelines for the trier of fact must be:

> (a) whether "the average person, applying contemporary community standards" would find that the work, taken as a whole, appeals to the prurient interest...; (b) whether the work depicts or describes, in a patently offensive way, sexual conduct specifically defined by the applicable state law; and (c) whether the work, taken as a whole, lacks serious literary, artistic, political or scientific value.[10]

Several differences are immediately apparent. First, the Report eliminates the "average person" standard. It is unclear whether this was intentional, and it is even more unclear whether this would expand or contract the scope of material for which funding is prohibited. Arguably, the "average person," whoever that is, may be more tolerant of sexually explicit material than the chairperson of the NEA — on the other hand, perhaps not. The point is that the Report does not parallel *Miller* in this respect and is open to constitutional challenge.

Second, *Miller* requires that the "sexual conduct" in question be "specifically defined by the applicable state law."[11] The report has eliminated this requirement, thereby introducing far greater uncertainty. Presumably, the qualifying language was eliminated because the NEA is a creature of federal, not state, law and it may have seemed anomalous to the drafters to include a reference to "the applicable state law" in a federal statute. Of course, that only papers over the dilemma. Are the NEA standards to be applied on a national basis or a state-by-state basis? Can a grant be awarded to an artist for exhibition in Las Vegas (a place most commentators use as a code word for sin and debauchery), while the same work would be rejected if proposed by an artist for exhibition in New Hampshire (where no sin or debauchery occurs)? The Report provides no guidance.

Finally, and perhaps of greatest concern, is the fact that Congress has suggested severely limiting the third prong of the *Miller* test. Instead of condemning a work only if it, "taken as a whole, lacks serious literary, artistic, political, or scientific value," the Report condemns a work if it, "taken as a whole, lacks serious artistic and cultural value." Essentially, Congress would eliminate "literary... political, or scientific value" from the savings clause. Under *Miller*, so long as a work, taken as a whole, had serious literary, artistic, political, or scientific value, it could not constitutionally be found obscene. But, under Congress' new approach, the presence of literary, political, or scientific value apparently would *not* save a work.

This analysis is not mere idle theorizing. When it came time for Chairperson Frohnmayer to apply the new law, he promptly withdrew NEA funding for the AIDS exhibit at Artists Space regardless of its literary, political, and scientific value. The show's catalogue, containing the thought-provoking and controversial essay on AIDS by photographer David Wojnarowicz, had serious literary value, whether Frohnmayer and others agreed with it or not. The catalogue and the show itself, which protested the insensitivity of public officials to AIDS, had serious political value, whether Senator Helms, Representative Dannemayer, and Archbishop O'Connor agreed with it or not. And by publicizing the gravity of the AIDS epidemic and the need for greater government support for medical research, the show had serious scientific value as well.

Given these facts, it is astounding that instead of upholding the NEA grant because of its political value, Frohnmayer withdrew the NEA grant because of its political content. "I believe that political discourse ought to be in the political arena and not in a show sponsored by the endowment." Acknowledging that "there are lots of great works of art that are political," such as Picasso's *Guernica* and the plays of Bertolt Brecht, Frohnmayer posed the question: "Should the endowment be funding art whose primary intent is political?" Frohnmayer temporarily answered "No," but later reversed himself. Obviously, the NEA would be serving the highest purposes of its original goals if it sponsored another *Guernica* or plays like those by Brecht. Indeed, a recent NEA endowment helped to support the original production of Larry Gelbart's *Mastergate*, a satire on the Iran-Contra affair, at the American Repertory Theater in Cambridge, Massachusetts.

It is critical that the Independent Commission reject Congress' cramped views and forthrightly reaffirm the original mandate of the NEA. In particular, the importance of supporting art which reflects serious literary, artistic, political, and scientific value, regardless of its explicit sexual nature, must be reinforced.

B. The Vague Difference Between Sex and Obscenity

The Supreme Court has long held that "sex and obscenity are not synonymous."[12] This explains why current constitutional law protects works of literature, once banned or sought to be banned, such as Dreiser's *An American Tragedy*, Lawrence's *Lady Chatterly's Lover*, Miller's *Tropic of Cancer* and *Tropic of Capricorn*, and Joyce's *Ulysses*.[13]

Obviously, depictions of "sadomasochism," "homo-eroticism" or "individuals engaged in sex acts" could easily fall on the protected side of the sex/obscenity dichotomy. Frankly, so could some depictions of "the sexual exploitation of children," particularly where the purpose of those depictions is to condemn such exploitation or to educate the public to the horrors of such exploitation. By penalizing protected works of art, the new legislation clearly violates the First Amendment.

If there is any doubt that the term "obscene" as used in the new NEA restrictions is unconstitutionally vague, the additional terms render the new law hopelessly vague. In addition to "obscene" works, the new restrictions disqualify from NEA funding "depictions of sadomasochism, homo-eroticism, the sexual exploitation of children, or individuals engaged in sex acts." No definition of these terms can be found in the new legislation. It is uncertain whether each of these four additional areas must also be "obscene" or whether art which may fall into these categories is disqualified even if it is not itself "obscene" under the *Miller* test.

As separate categories of condemned art, these four classifications defy any clear and objective definition. "Sadomasochism" could include a wide variety of artistic depictions in which men or women are portrayed as submissive or subservient. "Homo-eroticism" could include photographs of homosexuals kissing, embracing or simply holding hands. More graphically, it could include paintings, drawings or photographs of nude homosexuals touching or caressing each other in ways that would not be obscene under the *Miller* test, but which would be considered shocking or offensive to many members of Congress.

"The sexual exploitation of children" is not a self-defining phrase. Many might consider the publication of a photograph of a nude child, without more, to fall within that category. Many more might consider the publication of a photograph of two nude children to fall within that category. Nevertheless, such photographs are constitutionally protected.[14] Indeed, a wide body of opinion believes that taboos against childhood nudity contribute to repressed sexual attitudes and anti-social behavior.[15] Would a play in which a character verbally describes child molestation constitute the "depiction of... the sexual exploitation of children?" Would photographs portraying children in coy or sexually suggestive poses come within this category?

On April 18, 1990, the U.S. Supreme Court, in a 6 to 3 decision, reversed the conviction of Clyde Osborne, who had been charged with violating an Ohio child pornography law for privately possessing four photographs of a nude fourteen year old boy.[16] The statute purported to make it a crime to possess material "that shows a minor who is not the person's child or ward in a state of nudity..."[17] Recognizing that "depictions of nudity, without more, constitute protected expression," the court ordered a new trial to determine whether "such nudity constitutes a lewd exhibition or involves a graphic focus on the genitals."[18]

The remaining phrase in the NEA legislation, the "depiction of... individuals engaged in sex acts" is also hopelessly vague. Presumably this must mean something different than "obscene" because legislators are presumed not to include redundant verbiage in their legislation. But if "sex acts" are not confined to "obscene sex acts," they could well include depictions which are outside the *Miller* standard and therefore protected by the First Amendment. The words "sex acts" are far from self-defining, and particularly when applied to books, poems, plays, paintings, photographs, sculptures, dances and other art forms, the words simply defy any definition sufficient for First Amendment purposes.

The new restrictions use terms which are reminiscent of a 1984 Indianapolis ordinance, later struck down in court, which made "pornography" a form of discrimination against women, giving rise to a panoply of civil and administrative remedies. The statute defined pornography as "a systematic practice of exploitation and subordination based on sex which differentially harms women," and included "the graphic sexually explicit subordination of women, whether in pictures or in words," in which women are presented, among other things, "as sexual objects for domination, conquest, violation, exploitation, possession, or use, or through postures or positions of servility or submission or display."[20] The ordinance also applied to "men, children, or transsexuals."[21]

A coalition of groups led by the American Booksellers Association, the Association for American Publishers, Inc., and the Freedom to Read Foundation successfully enjoined the ordinance and obtained a declaration that it was unconstitutional.[22] The opinions of the district court and the court of appeals catalogue numerous constitutional defects in the ordinance. For present purposes, the district court's discussion of the vagueness doctrine is particularly apt.[23] The court observed that it was "struck by the vagueness problems inherent in the definition of pornography, itself, more specifically, the term 'subordination of women.'"[24] The court pointed out that the term is not specifically defined in the Ordinance, and "it is almost impossible to settle in ones [sic] own mind or experience upon a single meaning or understanding of that term."[25] Indianapolis conceded that the term "pornography" was not the same as "obscenity" and that the ordinance did not purport to comply with the *Miller* test.[26]

> Nothing in the Ordinance, for instance, suggests whether the forbidden 'subordination of women' relates to a physical, social, psychological, religious, or emotional subordination or some other form or combination of these. What constitutes subordination under this Ordinance is left finally to the censorship committee or to individual plaintiffs who choose to bring actions to enforce provisions (of the Ordinance), and under any due process standards, that is unfair in a fundamental and constitutional sense.[27]

The court found that the "enumerated categories of pornography set out in the Ordinance are also plagued with these same constitutional deficiencies relating to vagueness." Terms such as "degradation," "abasement," and "inferior," found in the Ordinance, are "subjective terms, reflective of the observer's state of mind" and "arguably have several different meanings."[28]

> How then are buyers or sellers of literature, *e.g., The Witches of Eastwick*, by John Updike, to know if their interpretation of the prohibitions in the Ordinance comports with that of the censorship committee or the individuals who seek to privately enforce the Ordinance? The Ordinance clearly threatens to "trap the innocent by not providing fair warning," which makes its provisions impermissibly vague in violation of the Due Process Clause of the Fifth Amendment.[29]

The court concluded that the other words and phrases challenged by the plaintiffs were "mystifying."[30] Given the broad sweep of the Ordinance,[31] the court held that it was unconstitutionally vague in that persons subjected to the Ordinance "cannot reasonably steer between lawful and unlawful conduct, with confidence that they know what its terms prohibit."

With equal force it can be said that the new restrictions imposed on the NEA are "mystifying." They are purely "subjective" and "reflective of the observer's state of mind." An artist of reasonable intelligence simply cannot tell if his work may, in the opinion of his peers, let alone the chairperson of the NEA or any particular member of Congress, run afoul of these elastic standards.

Clearly, in writing the new regulations Congress did not use the "touchstone" of "precision" or "objective measurement." The new regulations are hopelessly vague and therefore abridge cherished First Amendment rights.

---

1. Connally v. General Construction Co., 269 U.S. 385, 391 (1926).
2. Keyishian v. Board of Regents, 385 U.S. 589, 603-604 (1967).
3. Interstate Circuit Inc. v. City of Dallas, 390 U.S. 676, 682 (1968) (quoting NAACP v. Button, 371 U.S. 415, 438 (1963)).
4. NAACP v. Button, 371 U.S. 415, 433 (1963).
5. Grayned v. City of Rockford, 408 U.S. 104, 108-109 (1972).
6. *Id*. at 109.
7. Stromberg v. California, 283 U.S. 359, 369 (1931).
8. City Council v. Taxpayers for Vincent, 466 U.S. 789, 797 (1984).
9. H.R. 2788, 101st Cong., 1st Sess., 135 Cong. Rec. S12967 (daily ed. Oct. 7, 1989).
10. *Miller*, 413 U.S. at 24. Ironically, the new NEA standards for fiscal year 1990 use the *Miller* standards, i.e., works "when taken as a whole, do not have serious literary, artistic, political, or scientific value."
11. 413 U.S. at 24.
12. Roth v. United States, 354 U.S. 476, 487 (1957).
13. FW/PBS, Inc. v. City of Dallas, 110 S. Ct. 596, 618 (1990) (Scalia, J., concurring in part and dissenting in part).
14. Sunshine Book Co. v. Summerfield, 355 U.S. 372 (1958); New York v. Ferber, 458 U.S. 747, 775 (1982).
15. "Whatever sex, whatever age, all children should feel that their bodies are not innately guilty of some shameful, unspeakable crime against decency." D.C. Smith & W. Sparks, Growing Up Without Shame (1986).

16. Osborne v. Ohio, No. 88-5986 (U.S. Apr. 18, 1990) (Lexis, Genfed library, US file). The majority opinion by Justice White found no constitutional defect in the criminalization of mere possession of child pornography, notwithstanding the holding in *Stanley v. Georgia* that private possession of obscene material was constitutionally protected by the right of privacy. "Given the importance of the State's interest in protecting the victims of child pornography, we cannot fault Ohio for attempting to stamp out this vice at all levels in the distribution chain." *Id.*

17. Ohio Rev. Code Ann. § 2907.323(a)(3) (Anderson 1986 & Supp. 1989). In addition to exemptions for parents and guardians, the statute excludes material "sold, disseminated, displayed, possessed, controlled, brought or caused to be brought into this state, or presented for a bona fide artistic, medical, scientific, educational, religious, governmental, judicial, or other proper purpose, by or to a physical, psychologist, sociologist, scientist, teacher, person pursuing bona fide studies or research, librarian, clergyman, prosecutor, judge, or other person having a proper interest in the material or performance." *Id.* The Ohio statute is one of the laws under which Cincinnati's Contemporary Art Center has been charged for exhibiting seven Mapplethorpe photographs.

18. In dissent, Justice Brennan, Marshall and Stevens warned that the "lewd exhibition" and "graphic focus" tests "not only fail to cure the overbreadth of the statute, but they also create a new problem of vagueness." *Osborne*, No. 88-5986 (U.S. Apr. 18, 1990) (Lexis, Genfed library, US file). The dissenters predicted that "[p]ictures of topless bathers at a Mediterranean beach, of teenagers in revealing dresses, and even of toddlers romping unclothed, all might be prohibited." *Id.*

19. General Ordinance No. 35 Indianapolis, Ind., Code of Indianapolis and Marion County, Ind., § 16 (1985).

20. *Id.* at § 16(3)(q)(V, t6) (1984).

21. *Id.* at § 16-3(q).

22. American Booksellers Ass'n, Inc. v. Hudnut, 598 F. Supp. 1316 (S.D. Indiana 1984), *aff'd*, 771 F.2d 323 (7th Cir. 1985). The ACLU's Feminist Anti-Censorship Task Force filed an amicus brief, written by the ACLU's Nan Hunter and New York University law professor Sylvia Law, arguing that the Indianapolis ordinance actually harmed women's rights by perpetuating sexual stereotypes.

23. 598 F. Supp. at 1337-39.

24. *Id.* at 1338.

25. *Id.* at 1338.

26. *Id.* at 1331.

27. *Id.* at 1338.

28. *Id.* at 1338–39.

29. *Id.* at 1339.

30. *Id.*

31. Examples of non-obscene films that plaintiffs claim will fall within the meaning of 'pornography' are: 'Dressed to Kill,' 'Ten,' 'Star 80,' 'Body Heat,' 'Swept Away,' and 'Last Tango In Paris.' Plaintiffs also contend that the following books would come within the Amendment: *The Witches of Eastwick*, by John Updike, *The Delta of Venus*, by Anais Nin, *The Other Side of Midnight*, by Sidney Shelton [sic], *Scruples*, by Judith Kratz, various James Bond novels by Ian Flemming, *The Carpetbaggers* by Harold Robbins." 598 F. Supp. at 1339 n.6.

■ Lucy Lippard, Andres Serrano: The Spirit and the Letter, *Art in America*, April 1990 (excerpt)

Lucy Lippard is an art critic, author, and activist. Her most recent book is Mixed Blessings: New Art in a Multicultural America.

Since 1984, Andres Serrano has developed a complex iconography that simultaneously exorcises the artist's experiences of Catholicism, criticizes the commercialization of sacred imagery and pays idiosyncratic homage to ideas that Christ originally stood for. Although his work is engendered by personal concerns, his sensuous surfaces, moodily glowing colors, monumental scale and harsh content are precise expressions of 1980s ambivalence. For all their iconoclasm, Serrano's jolting tableaux have ironically become icons of freedom in themselves, thanks to the esthetic vigilance of the American Family Association (AFA), which in April 1989 spied blasphemy in his photograph *Piss Christ* (as well as obscenity in the work of Robert Mapplethorpe), raised the alarm and brought down the wrath of Jesse Helms, the Moonies and other righteous souls on the arts establishment.[1]

Like the AFA, Serrano is obsessed with the flesh and bone of belief, but unlike them he deconstructs and destroys his own faith. Organized religion gives him a lot of trouble, though he remains a believer. He left the church at age 13 — "There must be some conflict between Catholicism and puberty"[2] — but like many lapsed Catholics, Serrano finds childhood experiences and conditioning hard to exorcise. He says his work is informed by "unresolved feelings about my own Catholic upbringing which help me redefine and personalized my relationship with God. For me, art is a moral and spiritual obligation that cuts across all manner of pretense and speaks directly to the soul."[3]

Serrano produces objects of great and seductive beauty which address some of the weightiest subject matter available to Western artists. He does so in the oblique — abstract and conceptual — terms of current art practice, while maintaining a uniquely high emotional temperature. *Piss Christ* — the object of censorial furor — is a darkly beautiful photographic image which would have raised no hackles had the title not given away the process of its making. The small wood-and-plastic crucifix becomes virtually monumental as it floats, photographically enlarged, in a deep golden, rosy glow that is both ominous and glorious. The bubbles wafting across the surface suggest a nebula. Yet the work's title, which is crucial to the enterprise, transforms this easily digestible cultural icon into a sign of rebellion or an object of disgust simply by changing the context in which it is seen.

Serrano is very much in the postmodernist mainstream when he talks about disrupting the pleasure of a spiritual comforting image. This strategy reflects his personal distrust of religion as much as it represents his understanding of current debates about photography's role in representation. If mainstream postmodernist artists (and critics) often seem to promulgate the same values as the culture they claim to oppose, then perhaps only those artists who have been forced to remain outside can instigate real change. In North America, artists of color, like Serrano, are forced to acquire a profound knowledge of both the dominant culture and of their own often perplexingly mixed cultures, even as they live precariously between the two — or among the many. Serrano's work is part of the "polyphonous discourse" many Third World scholars have been calling for; he challenges the boundaries formed by class and race, and between abstraction and representation, photography and painting, belief and disbelief.

Religious subject matter has been relatively fashionable during the 1980s, but religious belief is anathema to the at-best-skeptical and at-worst-cynical postmodernist enterprise. It is found primarily in art by people of color, for whom it represents not only a survival tactic but also defiance of spiritual vacuity in a society that perceives both religious and political belief as naive on the one hand and as dangerously manipulable on the other. Few artists have had the courage to tackle the complexities of religion from a position of belief. Not surprisingly, the subversive nature of Serrano's religious content was fully recognized only by the fundamentalists, who keep their eyes peeled for meaning — a secondary consideration for most mainstream art audiences.

Serrano's own way of defusing his iconography and fending off censorship is to insist that his images are intuitive and instinctual, multifaceted and open-ended, and that he himself is unable to pin them down. His 40-by-60 inch Cibachromes cannot be read on just one level; they are never merely socially antagonistic. Simultaneously representational and abstract, Serrano's works are visually bilingual in a world where the regressive xenophobia of "English Only" gains ground daily. They are culturally uneasy in a time of simplistic patriotism. Serrano has said that he hopes to "take a formal tradition and subvert it by inverting the images, abstracting that which we take for granted, in an attempt to question not only photography, but my own experience and social reality."[4]...

Since late 1986 Serrano's art has literally been made from body fluids — "life's vital fluids" — which he sees as "visually and symbolically charged with meaning."[5] Many of his recent works are entirely abstract, but in different "styles" — minimalist, geometric, monochromatic or "expressionist." The looming *Blood Cross* (blood in a cross-shaped Plexiglas container, made on Good Friday to symbolize "what the crucifixion and Christianity are all about — sacrifice") also mixes references to the healing power of the Red Cross and to the brutal history of Catholicism in this hemisphere. Its companion, *Milk Cross*, refers to the beneficent, maternal side of the Church or to the contained and lily-white "purity" of Western religious institutions. *Two Hearts* (1986) — large calves' hearts in a Plexiglas tank half filled with blood — was a transitional work in which the liquid tides began to rise.

Milk, Blood (1986), the first wholly abstract work, was influenced as much by "art symbolism" (Mondrian, Malevich) as by religious symbolism. It first appears to be a painting divided equally into red and white rectangles. It is in fact, as indicated by the title, a photo of two Plexiglas tanks holding red and white fluids. There is a perceptible tension between the "hard" flatness of the photographic object and the "soft" liquid presence of the subjects. This work was followed in 1987 by two monochromes — *Blood* and *Milk* — and the geometric *Circle of Blood*.

In 1988, Serrano decided that he needed a new color in his palette. "Piss was the natural choice." It offered a peculiarly dense luminosity, and being less "acceptable" than blood and milk, raised the ante on content. Blood poured into a tankful of urine (the "Piss and Blood" series of 1988) produced gorgeous sunsetlike veils. Other pouring experiments produced apocalyptic "landscapes" and even shadowy figures. *Winged Victory* (1988) represents an accidental and transient shape produced not by the classical sculpture but by a broken crucifix minus head and torso. The pouring of milk into blood, blood into milk, and juxtaposition of blood against milk, blend ideas of nourishment and pain in a single image.

Scale is Serrano's particular genius. The forms in his photographs exist in a vast, ambiguous space. Backlighting is judiciously used to enlarge them, pushing the objects photographed to the front of the picture plane. He minimizes quantity while emphasizing quality of detail, bypasses the anecdotal element inherent in his subject and achieves a monumental simplicity. The power of his photographs has several sources: formal clarity, an aura of understated but nightmarish unfamiliarity, a subdued but important connection to his multiracial, multicultural background and always the ambivalence about Catholicism as a symbol of authority which is (literally) the crux of the matter....

Although sexuality is only a subtext in Serrano's art, his work has triggered basic, and hypocritical, American reflexes: puritanism, and its alter ego, prurience. Serrano's and Mapplethorpe's images have both inspired deep official confusion: Jesse Helms told a reporter he was "embarrassed" to talk to his wife about them.[6] (Apparently the news that obscenity is usually in the eye of the beholder has not reached the bastions of the Born Again.)

At the same time, the controversy around Serrano and Mapplethorpe points up the ongoing alienation of art from the general public. While these works suffered drastically from being torn out of context by Helms and friends, a lot of current art would raise the hackles of the general public even in context. Serrano sees *Piss Christ* as an integral development in his work, and within the art context such a move can be taken for granted. It is naive, however (although not arrogantly naive, as in certain other recent artist-versus-public battles) to ignore the possibility of conflict when work emerges from the studio and gallery into the view of a broader public, especially in the rural South. Serrano is an urban artist of considerable political sophistication. Yet his genuine surprise and distress at the events of the past few months signals yet again the isolation of even the best-intentioned artists from their audiences. A decade after Donald Newman's "Nigger Drawings" show,[7] the relation of art to volatile real-life issues is still problematic; such issues are still generally avoided in the high-art "discourse," where the word "moral" is usually considered either laughable, rhetorical and/or the property of the Right....

Art with both spiritual depth and social meaning is for the most part homeless in this society, often separated by class and intention from art-world models, which is why the Right has been able to claim the territory. Serrano's art goes to the heart of an alienation whose complexities within cultural, racial and class contexts are just beginning to be perceived within the "multicultural" enthusiasm suddenly sweeping art institutions. As Serrano says, "Religion relies heavily on symbols and my job as an artist is to pursue the manipulation of that symbolism and explore its possibilities."[8] In this he has been politically astute; the extreme Right has also spent the 1980s discovering the power of symbolism, from the flag to the cock to the crucifix. There is, then, a certain justice in the fact that Serrano was singled out when the Right discovered art, that he has been dragged into one of the grand battles of the decade over symbolism in art and politics, that from an art world rich in "offensive" images, his work was recruited to carry the standard for freedom of expression.

Serrano adamantly denies making art to freak out the likes of the American Family Association, Jesse Helms or New York's Senator Al D'Amato, who histrionically ripped up a catalogue containing a reproduction of *Piss Christ* on the floor of the Senate. Yet he understands that there are certain factions that will always try to ensure that audiences don't think for themselves. "These special-interest groups are very small," he remarks, "but they manage to wield a lot of power by intimidating those people who are in charge. There's a billion-dollar Christ-for-Profit industry out there — what I want to know is, who monitors *them?* While these groups are busy weeding out what is to them morally objectionable on the airwaves and in our museums, who decides what is morally offensive in the religion industry?"[9]

Aside from its basic beauty as a series of objects, Serrano's work intentionally raises more questions than it answers. The context within which it demands to be viewed parallels rather than confirms the way art is conventionally perceived. A new respect for difference exposes contradictions that cannot and should not be resolved. Moreover, Serrano's work shows that the conventional notion of good taste with which we are raised and educated is based on an illusion of social order that is no longer possible (nor desirable) to believe in. We now look at art in the context of incoherence and disorder — a far more difficult task than following the prevailing rules.

---

1. Among the first to pick up on the AFA's alarm, in May 1989, were publications of the Reverend Sun Yung Moon's Unification Church: the *New York Tribune*, the *Washington Times* and *Insight* magazine. The best articles on the NEA/censorship issue I have read are Carole Vance, "The War on Culture," *Art in America* (Sept. 1989), and Nichols Fox, "NEA Under Siege," *New Art Examiner* (Summer 1989). I had my say at length in *Zeta* (Oct. 1989). In October, Congress approved restrictions on federal aid for "obscene" art or art lacking "serious literary, artistic, political, or scientific value," provoking further confrontations with the art community in the fall of 1989.

2. All quotations from the artist not otherwise cited are from an interview with the author, Oct. 18, 1989.

3. Serrano, unpublished statement, 1989.

4. *Ibid.*

5. Blood and guts come from the local butcher and are stored in the icebox until used. Only urine stinks, when used on very hot days, and even then temporarily.

6. Maureen Dowd, "Jesse Helms Takes No-Lose Position on Art, " *New York Times*, July 18, 1989.

7. "The Nigger Drawings" was an exhibition of abstract drawings by Donald Newman (using only his first name) held at Artists Space, New York, in 1979. The title, which

had nothing to do with the drawings themselves, was intended as pure sensation-
alism. The show was deeply offensive to the black art community and was protested
by artists of color and progressive groups. It became a watershed in the art world's
confrontation with racism and artists' assumed exemption from social responsibility.

8. Serrano, quoted in William H. Honan, "Artist Who Outraged Congress Lives Amid
    Christian Symbols," *New York Times*, Aug. 16, 1989.
9. Serrano, quoted in Susan Morgan, "Interview with Andres Serrano," *Artpaper*
    (Minneapolis), Sept. 1989.

■ Association for Independent Film and Video (AIVF) Advocacy Committee, The Attack Against the Arts Has Intensified — Help Fight Back!, mailing, May 10, 1990

*The AIVF is a national organization providing advocacy and professional
services for the independent media community.*

D ear AIVF member,

The National Endowment for the Arts is not out of danger yet. To the
contrary, the NEA is facing stepped up attacks from the well organized religious
right. The Reverend Don Wildmon's American Family Association (which led
the protest against *The Last Temptation of Christ*), Pat Robertson's *700 Club*, and
Phyllis Schlafly's Eagle Forum are besieging Congress with letters and phone
calls. Some congressional offices report their mail going 45 to 1 against the NEA.
The religious right's letters, leaflets, and ads — often filled with distortions and
misrepresentations about NEA-funded projects — not only attack what they
consider obscene art, *they seek to eliminate the NEA entirely.*

The bill reauthorizing the NEA will probably emerge this month from the
congressional committees clear of language that would restrict the NEA from
funding "obscene" art. However, Congress' primary opponents of the NEA —
Sen. Jesse Helms and Rep. Dan Rohrabacher — will undoubtedly introduce
restrictive amendments when the bill is debated by the full Senate and House
sometime in June. And they are threatening to use this as a campaign issue next
fall. *Don't let your representatives be cowed by Helms and his right-wing backers. Let
them know where you stand* — and that if they want your vote, you want their vote
in support of full funding for the NEA without any content restrictions.

We need your help immediately! Here's what you can do:

1) MEET IN PERSON WITH YOUR SENATORS AND/OR REPRE-
    SENTATIVE. A good time to do this is over Memorial Day recess (May
    25 – June 4), when most legislators will be in their home districts. They'll
    also be more relaxed and able to focus on your concerns. Call for an

appointment now; their schedules book up quickly. *Remember, a personal visit has much more weight than letters, telegrams, or phone calls.* See the back of this sheet for some commonly asked questions and possible responses.

2) WRITE IMMEDIATELY TO:

a) Your representative in the Senate and House. Be sure to remind them of President Bush's opposition to content restrictions. If you don't know who your representatives are, find out by calling: 1-800-836-6975. Or call your local chapter of the League of Women's Voters. Be sure to include your name and full address on any correspondence, which should be sent to:

The Honorable _____ or The Honorable _____
United States Senate   U.S. House of Representatives
Washington, DC 20510   Washington, DC 20515

b) WRITE ALL OF YOUR STATE'S REPRESENTATIVES. As a group, they constitute the state delegation, which must be responsive to the concerns of constituents throughout the state. For example, if you live in New York City, you might urge upstate representatives to remember the leading role New York State plays in the arts.

3) DROP OFF OR INCLUDE WITH YOUR LETTER A RECENT POLL OF PUBLIC ATTITUDES TOWARDS FEDERAL SUPPORT OF THE ARTS. This survey shows widespread support for federal funding of the arts without restrictions. For copies, contact People for the American Way, (202) 467-4999.

4) CALL YOUR REPRESENTATIVE to register your support for the NEA and opposition to content restrictions. Call the Capitol Switchboard, (202) 224-3121, to be connected with your Senators' and Representatives' offices.

5) SEND A TELEGRAM by calling 1-800-257-4900, operator 9681. When you call this number, set up by the People for the American Way, a pre-written Western Union telegram expressing your concern will be sent to Congress. $6.75 will be charged to your phone bill for the first telegram, and $6.00 for each additional one.

SOME QUESTIONS YOU MAY HEAR

When writing or speaking with your congressional representatives or with others in doubt about the NEA's funding practices and public support for artists and cultural institutions, you are likely to encounter several commonly asked questions. The AIVF Advocacy Committee has spent a great deal of time discussing these issues and formulating responses which we believe present a strong, principled argument in favor of continued government funding for the arts without any restrictions on the content of art eligible for such funding.

These statements may prove useful in drafting letters or doing interviews with Representatives or Senators.

1. *Why should taxpayers pay for art work that some consider offensive?*

In a representative democracy, we rely on small groups to make decisions for the majority. For instance, we do not take a popular vote on every taxpayer funded school curriculum or government brochure. Nor do we vote on which books should be purchased by public libraries; we assume that librarians will make these judgments based on literary and educational criteria. Most important, we do not attempt to defund or dismantle entire library systems just because some books may offend. By the same token, there is no reason to abandon the NEA's 25-year-old peer panel review method for awarding grants. It is a tried and true process that calls upon the expertise of individuals from a variety of regional, aesthetic, ethnic and racial backgrounds.

In a true democracy, some art work is bound to offend. Controversy sparks dialogue and debate — the healthy outcome of passionately held beliefs that inevitably come into conflict. Defunding work on the grounds that it might offend only stifles artistic expression, while effectively squelching opportunities to exhibit and debate the issues raised by the work.

2. *If language prohibiting grants to art work deemed "obscene" merely restates existing laws on obscenity as defined by the Supreme Court, what's wrong with incorporating it into legislation governing the Arts and Humanities Endowments?*

The law governing NEA and NEH grants adopted in 1989 and the one now before Congress are at the very least redundant, because these laws would have the panelists who judge NEA grant applications duplicate the process that police, prosecutors, and courts must apply — without any safeguards of the judicial process. Worse, these laws go beyond the Supreme Court language by singling out "homoeroticism" as a form of obscenity, breaking new ground in a disturbing way. The obscenity language is especially objectionable because it intrudes non-artistic judgement into the grant-making process for the first time in the Endowment's history. This is the road that inevitably leads to banning of movies and books and other, cruder forms of censorship. Already, the chilling effect of this language is becoming evident.

3. *Why should the government fund the arts at all?*

The U.S. lags well behind other western nations in its support for the arts and culture. While our federal government spends a paltry 68 cents per capita on the arts (compared to $1,200 on defense), West Germany spends $38.80, France spends $12.37, and even Thatcher's Conservative government in the U.K. spends $7.74. Yet even this modest sum has made a critical difference in the lives of millions of Americans, making possible a range of cultural experiences. Just in the past several years, federal funding has supported media activities conducted by groups like the Guadalupe Cultural Center in San

Antonio and Appalshop in eastern Kentucky, as well as the National Film and Video Preservation Center's programs for rescuing films and tapes stored in archives around the country. Also, the agency has enabled production, distribution and exhibition of numerous independent media works covering myriad topics and displaying a diverse range of techniques and ideas that challenge the conventional offerings of Hollywood and broadcast television. With increased support for federal arts funding, the variety of work could be expanded even further, serving even wider audiences, and moving closer to the realization of democratic participation in the cultural life in this country.

■ Rowland Evans and Robert Novak, The NEA's Suicide Charge, *Washington Post,* May 11, 1990

Rowland Evans and Robert Novak are nationally syndicated columnists. .

Ignoring danger signals from friends, the National Endowment for the Arts is poised to approve several grants this weekend that will either trigger Congress to cripple its independence or force George Bush into a no-win battle to preserve that independence in the great culture war raging from Capitol Hill to the hinterland.

Only a few exhibits up for approval inhabit the shadowy realm of controversy about true artistic merit. NEA Chairman John Frohnmayer has been advised to veto them, including the performance of a nude, chocolate-smeared young woman in what an NEA memorandum calls a "solo theater piece" and what the artist herself, Karen Finley, describes as "triggering emotional and taboo events." An administration insider calls the exhibit "outrageous."

But a disapproval would infuriate the formidable arts lobby. A powerful segment of that lobby seems unwilling or unable to distinguish between laudable promotion of the arts and artists by the private money of private benefactors, no matter how controversial the art, and promotion of the arts by the federal government —meaning all taxpayers.

A veto would ease President Bush's deepening troubles with conservatives on his suspect cultural agenda. The Mapplethorpe photographic exhibit funded by NEA last year has generated more angry mail than the abortion issue. Approval of all the exhibits up for grabs this weekend would compound Bush's effort to defuse the hottest cultural-and-taxpayer issue out in the land beyond the Beltway, where taxpayers think their tax dollars should be working for defense or highways or education — in short, for them.

Frohnmayer is a respected arts connoisseur from Portland, Ore., whose experience with the politics of Pennsylvania Avenue and Main Street is limited. This weekend in Winston-Salem, where the NEA Council meets to decide on the latest batch of exhibits recommended by special NEA arts panels, he is being watched closely by Washington politicians who worry about the size of the stakes.

Insiders in the sometimes-elitist world of the arts say privately it is inconceivable that the 24-member council would risk the outrage of arts intellectuals by imposing a veto on any of the recommended exhibits. A veto would cast aspersions on the critical faculties of panel members recruited from the art world to appraise and decide on the requests for taxpayer funding. Second-guessing artistic peers may be a no-no in the tightly intertwined realm of the arts.

Thus Frohnmayer is the lonely custodian of the veto. Just before the Friday evening convocation at Winston-Salem, he was said by White House sources to be adamant against disapproving any of the recommended exhibits. If so, the small first step taken by Congress last October to end NEA grants for what was vaguely called "obscene" art will be dwarfed by a new congressional attack on taxpayer-financed art. That will squeeze Bush into an uncomfortable corner: side with Congress and the voters or be swayed by the spurious charge of betraying freedom of the arts.

The Finley exhibit, praised by some but damned by others in terms of its artistic value, could become the Mapplethorpe case of 1990. Finley's theme is described admiringly by *Minneapolis Star-Tribune* reporter Mike Steele as "victimization, especially women as victim, women as underclass," "tough stuff... she casually peels off her dress and pours gelatin into her bra... slathers chocolate over her body... sticks blobs of bean sprouts over her body and calls it sperm."

Tough stuff instead, and particularly so for members of Congress, liberal or conservative, Democrat or Republican, old or young, man or woman.

Last Christmas, when feisty, liberal Sen. Barbara Mikulski (D-Md.) was asked by a constituent why on earth it was unconstitutional to place a nativity scene — or a Hanukkah menorah — on or near the steps of a U.S. courthouse, her answer spelled out the real mood on Capitol Hill: "If you could put those symbols in a container and fill it with urine or some other repugnant substance, you'd get a federal grant to pay for putting it up."

Mikulski told us on Tuesday that her voters are puzzled by the kind of exhibits and programs their federal tax dollars pay for. "Imagine!" she said. "My constituents don't get it!"

She might have added that if there is any resemblance between the constituents of Barbara Mikulski and the NEA panelists who chose art-worthy projects for her taxpayers to finance, it is purely coincidental.

■ Karen Finley, Letter to the Editor, *Washington Post,* May 19, 1990

Karen Finley is a performance artist. She was one of the "NEA Four," a group of artists who were denied NEA grants, and who sued the agency.

To the Editor:

I am outraged by the column by Rowland Evans and Robert Novak ["The NEA's Suicide Charge," op-ed May 11], which attacked my grant application to the National Endowment for the Arts. My performance was taken out of context, and I was presented in an inaccurate and maliciously misleading way.

I am a serious artist who performs throughout North America and Europe. I am committed to significant social theater and art, but I am now the latest victim of the attacks of the extremist right on freedom of expression. I see this attack as part of a larger trend of suppressing artists — especially those whose work deals with difficult social issues — by playing on society's fears, prejudices and problems.

I would like to set the record straight. First, I did not request support from the NEA for the performance, "We Keep Our Victims Ready," as Evans and Novak alleged. I received no funding for that piece; the grant would help me with future work.

As to my work being "outrageous," many of the people who seem to be outraged have never even seen me perform. Evans and Novak describe me as "a chocolate-smeared young woman," which suggested that my work is sexual or sexually explicit. Actually, my work speaks out against sexual violence, degradation of women, incest and homophobia. When I smear chocolate on my body, it is a symbol of women being treated like dirt. The same Minneapolis review that the columnists quoted called my work "moving" and "heartfelt."

Let me briefly describe my work: In the first act, I sit in a rocking chair, fully clothed, and talk about women as the underclass and society under patriarchal rule. In the second act, I talk about the daily oppression of women, people with AIDS and minorities and about how society ignores and suppresses these people. In the third act, I am shrouded in a white sheet at a bed, symbolizing a death bed. There I talk about the survivors of death in the wake of AIDS, the "Black Sheep" of our culture who are related by their diversities and are all part of our large extended family. By the end, the audience is usually moved to tears.

A sculpture incorporating my "Black Sheep" poem is on public display in New York City. I have performed this work across the United States and Europe and am scheduled to perform it at Lincoln Center in July.

American artists, writers, theater makers, musicians, poets, dancers and filmmakers have led the world in the arts because of our right to free expression. But if it weren't for the help provided by the NEA, art would be only for the rich and powerful.

I know that the witch-hunt of the arts does not truly represent the wishes of the American people but merely those of a fanatic faction. Americans want controversial artists to be funded, and the evidence is there in a new nationwide poll. I hope American citizens of different backgrounds will be able to continue to express themselves freely without fear of censorship.

Karen Finley

■ Kathleen Sullivan, A Free Society Doesn't Dictate to Artists, *New York Times,* May 18, 1990

Kathleen Sullivan is a constitutional law scholar and a professor at Harvard Law School.

The National Endowment for the Arts comes before Congress for reauthorization this year in the midst of a political firestorm generated by a few works — especially some nude photographs by the late Robert Mapplethorpe. Many are clamoring for restrictions on what publicly-funded artists may express through their art. But they are forgetting about the First Amendment. In a free society, such "content" restrictions have no place.

Advocates of restrictions commonly make three arguments. All three are wrong. First, they say, "It's the taxpayers' money and we may discriminate we like with it!"

The Supreme Court has long since rejected that plea. Rather, the Court has held, the First Amendment applies whether the Government is wielding its checkbook or its badge.

It is easy to see why. It would obviously be intolerable to make it a crime to vote Republican. But it would be just as unconstitutional to offer cash bounties to those who vote Democrat. Either way, the world would be skewed impermissibly in favor of the Democrats.

Likewise, bribing Warhol to copy Wyeth would have had the same effect as outlawing pop art. Either way, the world would be made safe only for landscapes. But as Chief Justice William Rehnquist wrote for the Supreme Court in a unanimous 1983 opinion, neither by penalty nor subsidy may the Government "aim at the suppression of dangerous ideas."

Indeed, the First Amendment has never been held to disappear just because the taxpayers are paying the tab. If you are a public school teacher, you cannot be fired for speaking out against the school board on matters of public concern — even though the taxpayers pay your salary.

If you wish to hold a rally or concert in a public park, you cannot be denied a permit because your ideas or songs are controversial — even though the taxpayers pay for the police who keep order at your event and for the sanitation workers who clean up the litter you leave behind. And editorials, however controversial, may not be banned from the public airwaves — even though the taxpayers foot the bill for the Corporation for Public Broadcasting.

The second argument often heard in favor of restrictions is that "government should not put its seal of approval on controversial art by paying for it." Wrong again. To make art possible is not to condone it. Consider, by way of analogy, recent events in the public spaces of the nation's capital.

Last autumn, pro-choice advocates filled the Washington Mall. A few weeks ago, anti-abortion demonstrators took the same ground. Both times, taxpayers paid the bill for the police and grounds keepers. But no one would seriously argue that Government was thus "approving" either side. Rather, the only "message" conveyed by such neutral and even-handed public subsidies is that, in the Government's house, all ideas are welcome.

Third, restrictions advocates often say, "If obscene art may be banned, we may make a grant recipient promise not to produce it." Not so fast. A nation that has long distrusted loyalty oaths should not be quick to impose conformity oaths.

We have long resisted such prior restraints on the ground that they exert an intolerable chilling effect. An artist who receives a check in the mail with a hit list of forbidden ideas attached will forego too much valuable and innovative expression for fear it will come too close to the line. As Justice Thurgood Marshall once put it, the problem with "a sword of Damocles is that it hangs — not that it drops."

Does this mean that Government can exercise no control whatsoever over publicly funded art? Of course not. Obviously, the Government may make sure that artists, like military contractors, use the money for what they are supposed to; some accountability is required. Moreover, the Government cannot fund everything; some selectivity is essential.

But quality, not political palatability, must be the touchstone. Except for neutral and nonpartisan requirements of esthetic excellence, Federal support for the arts should come without strings. In a free society, artists should not be the Government's puppets but should dance to their own tune. A free society can have no official orthodoxy in art any more than in religion or politics. And in a free society, such orthodoxy can no more be purchased by power of the purse than compelled by power of the sword.

■NEA Artists' Projects: New Forms Panel, statement, May 25, 1990

This public statement was written collectively by a NEA peer panel, and addressed to NEA chairperson John Frohnmayer, the members of the National Council on the Arts, and the Hon. Pat Williams.

As a particularly strong and diverse cross-section of art professionals at work today, this year's Inter-Arts Artists' Projects: New Forms panel wishes to express our concern and opposition to those who maintain that government should not provide public support for the arts, as well as to those who believe its support should be conditional on the satisfaction of restrictive language requirements of any kind whatsoever.

The arts community is confronted by an imminent danger: an attempt to fragment our sense of national will and identity through the dismantling of the federal government agencies that most crucially represent us. In this the National Endowment for the Arts is not the only targeted scapegoat: educational, housing and social service agencies are equally endangered. As committed art professionals we hereby make common cause with all Americans — the poor, the old, the sick, the homeless, the unschooled, and the unemployed — who are being systematically disempowered. We wish to signal our awareness that this agenda effectively deprives us of our civil rights to freedom of expression, just as it deprives others of their civil rights to equal opportunity, life, health and the pursuit of happiness.

Recently it has been argued that artists have no business involving their work in the social or political arena, but instead should concentrate on creating "pure art." This view expresses an ignorance of art history. Artists such as Michelangelo, Mark Twain, Brueghel, David, Courbet, Goya, Picasso, Paul Robeson, James Baldwin and Martha Graham often expressed social concern in their work; and through their work have influenced society. Artists frequently target new, unspoken or unresolved social issues for examination. Such content is often familiar, challenging, and disturbing. This is precisely what shows us that it is worthy of serious consideration. And it is a truism that art that is considered offensive and unacceptable at one historical juncture often evolves into a revered artistic treasure at a later one. Only a society that understands and strongly encourages creative freedom can ever produce these treasures.

We will see more such innovations in content, as previously disenfranchised social groups give artistic expression to their unique world views in response to the constantly changing demographics of the United States. That public funding is needed to support them is demonstrated by the insistent, burgeoning annual increases in applications to the National Endowment for the Arts from an ever-widening range of artistic communities in this country. Public support for the arts is being threatened at the very moment when more and more cultural communities are publicly gaining their artistic voice.

Scapegoating is not the way to resolve our differences as Americans, or to build national unity. As a democracy we face the danger of democratic fascism: the tyranny of the majority. Against this tyranny, mutual tolerance, respect and support for unfettered creative expression is necessary as a safeguard, both of individuality and of diversity. And we are nothing if not a nation of diverse individuals.

The panel selection process of awarding grants is a microcosm of the democratic process. Panelists are selected for their knowledgeability and diversity of viewpoints as well as their professional expertise and achievements. We each represent different constituencies, tastes and interests. The selection process is one of mutual dialogue, exchange and sharing of viewpoints. And the outcome represents our considered judgements, balanced with what we have

213

learned from our fellow panelists, as to that art most deserving of support among the applications submitted. To undermine the integrity of this process through the imposition of external constraints or restrictive language regarding what counts as acceptable art would be to deal yet another blow to the democratic process which this country can ill afford.

The National Endowment for the Arts is absolutely necessary. Its disappearance would be a profound loss to American culture. The National Endowment for the Arts democratizes and decentralizes the arts.

> Roberto Bedoya, Los Angeles, CA
> C. Carr, New York, NY
> Carl Cheng, Santa Monica, CA
> Marie Cieri, Cambridge, MA
> Jerry Hunt, Canton, TX
> Kahil El'Zabar, Chicago, IL
> Tiye Giraud, Bronx, NY
> John Kelly, New York, NY
> Victor Masayesva, Phoenix, AZ
> Adrian Piper, Washington, DC
> Ellen Sebastian, San Francisco, CA
> Liz Thompson, Brooklyn, NY
> M.K. Wegmann, New Orleans, LA

■ Samuel Lipman, Backward and Downward with the Arts, *Commentary*, May 1990 (excerpt)

Samuel Lipman is a music critic and the publisher of The New Criterion. *He served as a member of the NEA's National Council on the Arts from 1982 to 1988.*

Since the inception of the National Endowments there has been little serious discussion, not just of how the agencies should be run from day to day, but of what national policy should underlie their activities. Americans in any case tend to think of "cultural policy" as something slightly illegitimate, the sort of thing that gets promulgated not in a democratic society but by totalitarian regimes like Nazi Germany and Bolshevik Russia; and many Americans also still tend to think of culture as essentially a private matter. But now, for better or for worse, the issue of such a cultural policy, and of its place in our national life, is very much on the public agenda.

Where, then, do we stand? I would begin with two contradictory assertions. The first is that in the United States today, we have no national cultural policy; though we spend public money, the purposes for which it is spent are random, aimless as to desired outcome, and subject to no accountability either as expenditure or as result. The second assertion is that, on the contrary, we do have a national policy — one that is consciously formed, specific as to desired outcome, and strictly accountable for its results. As I shall try to show, the contradiction is actually more apparent than real: in fact, our present situation is characterized less by contradiction than by a dangerous unity.

We have no national cultural policy: a quick look at the past decade would appear to bear out this contention. There was, to begin with, an effort by the incoming Reagan administration actually to eliminate both Endowments. Then, in 1981, William J. Bennett — by my lights, an excellent choice — was named chairman of the National Endowment for the Humanities in a bruising political fight with no questions asked (by the administration) about the possible fate of the humanities under his stewardship; his replacement, Lynne V. Cheney, also an excellent choice, has been unsupported by White House policy under two Presidents, and has been left alone to fend off congressional marauders and sniping from the intellectual and academic communities. Under both Bennett and Cheney, the NEH has clung to a strongly held idea of intellectual mission, yet nowhere in the federal government has there been an attempt to apply, say, to educational policy the rigorously reasoned and powerfully written NEH reports on the state of education and of the humanities. The voice of the President in the service of the humanities, or even in the service of a philosophy of humanistic education, has been totally lacking.

The story at the NEA reflects the same absence of policy — but without the redeeming feature of strong agency leadership. In 1981, a chairman, Frank Hodsoll, was chosen for the NEA who lacked a background in art or the arts; the battle for his replacement in 1989 was marked by unseemly competition among various old-boy networks, with the final selection of John Frohnmayer being made on the basis primarily of political patronage. From the beginning, during Hodsoll's regime from 1981 to 1989, a series of wise and far-reaching administrative reforms — most, now, under Frohnmayer, a thing of the past — was unfortunately wedded to a refusal to make distinctions between programs and grants, between transience and permanence, between high art and entertainment. Even arts education, for some a quasi-religious cause undertaken on behalf of the nation, ended up after a promising start as a program to hawk the electronic media to our most media-corrupted generation.

Overall, the cry at the NEA has been "presence": the demand that every activity being supported bring the agency to the notice of as many influential people as possible. As was true in the first fifteen years of the NEA, it was felt in the 80's that public support could only be achieved by yoking the agency to the wagons of the glamorous, the famous, and the successful. The White House has abetted this tendency by sponsoring on its premises a mixture of glitz and gloss, Michael Jackson, and now country music. But neither in the Bush administration nor during the two relatively high-minded Reagan administrations that preceded it did anyone ever think that the public "presence" which the agency sought through an orientation to celebrity could be achieved overnight through notoriety. Ironically enough, it has been the function of the now-famous Serrano, Mapplethorpe, Artists Space, and Annie Sprinkle cases to bring the

215

NEA a presence in American life it was unable to win in the first twenty-four years of its existence.

Perhaps the clearest sign of the lack of a cultural policy has been the remarkable inability of the NEA and its supporters to undertake an effective defense of these objectionable grants, as well as of the presumed general purposes of the agency. Faced with public outcry, neither agency bureaucrats nor arts advocates at large could do anything more than assert lamely that the NEA, because it relied entirely on peer-panel review, in fact exercised no control over its grant-making. This response was so weak, and ultimately so lacking in philosophical weight, that even seasoned arts administrators — including leading voices at the NEA itself — were soon panicked into claiming that in making provocative grants the NEA was only fulfilling its proper function, since art itself was in its essence provocative. This line of argument, so far from improving matters, merely had the effect of reducing not only the NEA but art itself to being the handmaiden of anger, violence, and social upheaval.

And so for the last several months the struggle over the NEA has been waged entirely in terms of accusation and counter-accusation. Tons of ink and myriad strident voices have been employed in answering Senator Helms and his supporters, who no more have a coherent policy than do those whom they criticize. Neither side, in fact, has made clear just how and for what purposes NEA money should be spent, if it is to be spent at all. Even more significantly, the President of the United States has been all but silent, close in name only to the activities undertaken on his behalf.

So much for the first assertion. Now for the second: *we do have a national cultural policy*. This policy, some years in the making but now fully discernible, is based on three elements: affirmative action, that is, the preferential hiring of women and minorities to fill both administrative and non-administrative positions in the humanities and, especially, the arts; a bias toward "multicultural-ism"; and finally, public advocacy and financial support of so-called cutting-edge art. Each of these elements has been, and is, advanced by different forces in American life, and for different purposes, but they partake of a common function and have a common importance.

By affirmative action I do not mean the hiring of highly qualified candidates, who are in fact to be found in all of the groups that make up American life. Nor do I have in mind an actual quota system, though the hand of Congress has been heavy in attempting to enforce just such a system on both Endowments. I am concerned with something even more dangerous: the predisposition to require that for each position that becomes vacant, every conceivable candidate of the proper gender or color be sought out. In the area of government arts administration, it is now clear that even minimum qualifications, which often amount to no more than limited acquaintance with a field, are presumptive reasons for hiring. For the most important cultural positions in government, only a record of gross partisan political opposition now serves as a disqualification, and even here the standard is ever more rarely upheld.

Outside government, affirmative action is no longer primarily applied for the limited purpose of bringing minorities and women into traditional activities (as in the case of the hiring of a black bassist by the Detroit Symphony Orchestra last year). Instead it is implemented, from above, as a painless means of winning favor from well-organized and demonstrative groups, while from below it is deployed as a means of altering the traditional activities themselves, in order to transform them into activities for which no social or intellectual consensus now exists. This twin movement, impelled on the one hand by the desire to win immediate popularity, and on the other hand by the principled determination to mount a long-term cultural revolution, is now the most immediate of the factors eroding the life of traditional cultural institutions.

The name of that revolution is multiculturalism, a widespread assault on what is variously called Western, or European, or white-dominated or male-dominated civilization. To see the multiculturalist bias at work one need go no further than to the pages of *An American Dialogue*, a report on artistic touring and presenting put together by arts bureaucrats and paid for by a powerful public and private consortium made up of the NEA, the Rockefeller Foundation, and the Pew Charitable Trusts. According to this document, the purpose of the arts is overridingly socio-ideological: to make "a profound impact on American society and the changes that are shaping it."

The exact nature of this "profound impact" becomes clear in the way *An American Dialogue* treats the hitherto exalted status of European-based high art. These imperishable masterpieces, along with the artistic traditions derived from them, are now to be regarded as no more than one kind of ethnic manifestation; in preserving and extending those traditions on the American shore, European immigrants of the past, like peoples everywhere, were merely indulging old instincts and tastes, having brought "with them their hunger and demand for European-style performing arts events." But, the report tells us, we should not grant favored status to this kind of cultural and artistic expression, for we now know that art is itself made up of a "breadth of genres, styles, sources, venues, artists, art forms, and expressions," and that the art of all peoples is equally worthy of preservation and presentation.

It would be tempting to characterize all of this as blather. But I well remember a (failed) attempt several years ago to change the music program of the NEA from one concentrating on classical music and jazz to one open equally to all "world musics," without reference to any serious aesthetic consideration or discrimination; today, the new administration at the NEA gives every sign of implementing just such a change as part of its widely proclaimed multicultural agenda. In light of budget limitations, such a policy can only be paid for by taking money away from the large institutions that have been concerned with the transmission of great, albeit "European-style," art.

Nor should we be deceived by the egalitarian rhetoric of the advocates of multiculturalism. Beneath the slogans of equality lurk implicit, and sometimes, explicit, hierarchies of favored cultures, often chosen with political ends in mind. According to *An American Dialogue*, art is the product of "cultures and people... scarred by centuries of violence against them... these histories, and the images and the expressions that have grown from them, must be recognized and supported." Here we come to the true heart of multiculturalism: the frankly instrumental use of culture and art as a device of political consciousness-raising. In the private nonprofit sector, this thrust is already fully internalized. Both the Rockefeller and Ford foundations, to name only the two giants of American cultural funding, have made it clear that they intend to downgrade and even eliminate support for art based on traditional European sources, and instead will encourage activity by certain approved minorities in the United States and abroad. Where they lead, the public sector will surely follow.

The final element in our national cultural policy is the promotion of the so-called cutting edge (once known as the avant-garde). This takes many forms. Sometimes the cutting edge is a fringe movement in such traditional art forms as painting, music, opera, theater, photography, or dance. Sometimes it is a new aesthetic hybrid, such as multimedia art, multidisciplinary art, interdisciplinary art, or performance art. In these latter hybrid activities, the place reserved in multiculturalism for racial or ethnic or national minorities is filled instead by the claims of political radicalism, gender redefinition, and "life-style" — the latter perhaps now little more than a euphemism for florid and variant sexualities.

It hardly needs saying that what gives the cutting edge its current vitality in cultural policy is not the degree of artistic achievement it has displayed but rather its extra-artistic, social content. When I recently asked the woman responsible for arts grants in a great foundation whether she had any idea of just how bad was the cutting-edge art she supported, her answer was swift: "Listen," she said, "I've seen a lot more terrible work than you'll ever see."

The simple fact is that this cutting-edge art, flagrantly exemplified in the Serrano, Mapplethorpe, Artists Space, and Sprinkle cases, more subtly presented in the genre as a whole, is concerned not with art but with advocacy, not with the creation of permanent beauty but with the imposition of hitherto rejected modes of behavior and ways of living. At a conference just this past March on culture and democracy, the art critic Donald Kuspit put it well: the Mapplethorpe photographs, he remarked approvingly, for all their classicizing, half-ironic aspects, serve the purpose of "ultimately sanctifying the perverse subject matter." That being so, it was inevitable that cutting-edge grants would come to be defended by the arts establishment not in terms of artistic achievement but in terms of free speech.

Congress is now beginning to consider the statutory reauthorization of the National Endowments. The real battle, it seems plain, will initially be over the NEA, not the NEH. At this moment, the defenders of the NEA, an uneasy coalition drawn equally from establishment notables and from political and artistic radicals, spend little or no time talking about civilization and permanence, about the past and the future. They certainly spend no time talking about policy, about the large issues that properly underlie any consideration of what should be supported, and why. But neither do those who have the greatest interest in pursuing just such questions. In particular, the great institutions which in the past have been regarded as national treasures, and richly supported by government funds, everywhere stand timorous and silent.

218

Here is the point of dangerous reconciliation in the contradiction with which I started. For we both do not have, and yet do have, a cultural policy. Until now, our not having a cultural policy has meant no more than the tendency of our national leaders, both public and private, to regard art and culture as trivial, diversionary pastimes, at best mildly amusing or sentimentally uplifting. It has been consistent with this trivializing attitude to use the National Endowment for the Arts as a political cow, ripe for milking. But precisely in this way, our not having a national cultural policy has served to facilitate and consolidate the cultural policy we do have — namely, the effort to exploit the vestigial prestige of art and culture to accomplish radical social and political goals.

What, in the present environment, is the course that should be followed by those concerned with the stability of traditional political institutions, and committed to the preservation and transmission of the great traditions of art and learning and the values they embody? It seems to me there are essentially two options.

The first option is to reject *in toto* the entire apparatus of government support for the arts and, with the arts, the humanities. This would mean an end to the National Endowments, and an abandonment of the idea that one of the tasks of the federal government is to foster a common civilization. Because the rejection of direct government support would now be based not on a theoretical conception of the proper limitations on government, but rather on a gathering perception of the artistic and moral degeneration such support implies, the result would likely be a reexamination of indirect governmental support, in the form of tax deductions, as well. This in turn might lead to a reconsideration of the entire structure of tax deductions for charitable contributions, for the purpose of ascertaining whether such contributions are still today in the widest public interest. What we end up contemplating, in short, is a fundamental change in a whole series of longstanding American arrangements.

The second — and in my judgment the better — option is to refuse to abandon public life to those hostile to the cultural traditions, and the social norms, by which we continue to define — and defend — ourselves. Pursuing this option means continuing to fight, within government and without, in public and in private, for the preservation and extension of our common cultural and artistic inheritance. It means pressing, openly and passionately, for a cultural *policy* — but a policy which, when linked to programs of government support, will help make possible, in Coleridge's great phrase, "the harmonious development of those qualities and faculties that characterize our humanity."

In any case the battle has begun.

Carole S. Vance, Misunderstanding Obscenity, *Art in America,* May 1990 (excerpt)

Carole S. Vance is an anthropologist at the Columbia University School of Public Health, and the editor of Pleasure and Danger: Exploring Female Sexuality.

On Oct. 7, 1989, arts advocates felt relieved, even elated. They had lobbied against and defeated the censorious bill proposed by Sen. Jesse Helms (R-N.C.), in which he had sought to punish and restrict the National Endowment for the Arts (NEA). Instead, Congress passed a compromise bill which removed most penalties against specific artists and institutions and merely required that the NEA observe legal bans on obscenity. This product of much negotiation was widely hailed as a victory for the arts and for the principle of free expression. The victory, however, now shows every sign of turning into a defeat. The intervening months have been characterized by increasing self-censorship and anxiety in the arts community, spurred by new episodes of formal censorship and McCarthyite witch-hunts. Rather than being a harmless restatement of existing obscenity law, the new NEA regulation now looms as a breathtaking cultural intervention, one which the right wing did not consciously engineer but from which it will surely benefit. How did this happen?

During the summer of 1989, Sen. Helms joined a growing campaign against government support for art, claiming that certain works funded by the NEA were "indecent or obscene." As his principal targets Helms chose photographers Robert Mapplethorpe and Andres Serrano, who both had works in exhibitions supported by the NEA. Helms denounced Mapplethorpe's photographs of homosexual erotica as obscene and railed against one of Serrano's photographs as sacrilegious. As a warning to the NEA (and a gesture which many regarded as the first step toward dismantling the NEA altogether), Helms proposed that Congress cut the NEA's visual arts program by $400,000, that it ban for five years all NEA grants to the two institutions that had sponsored the exhibitions of Mapplethorpe and Serrano and that it prohibit future grants for art that was deemed "indecent or obscene."[1]

In a climate of intense antisexual hysteria that persisted throughout the summer and early fall, arts supporters and lobbyists worked to defeat the Helms Amendment and to craft a compromise bill which would permit legislators to register the politically requisite disapproval of "offensive" and "blasphemous" art without doing irreparable damage to the endowment and its programs. By early fall these arts advocates were making headway. Led by Rep. Sidney Yates (D-Ill.), they had successfully fought against almost all of the punitive proposals of Helms and other conservative legislators and had engineered a more temperate substitute bill.

When this compromise was passed on Oct.7, the sting had been reduced. The offending arts institutions, the Institute of Contemporary Art in Philadelphia and the Southeastern Center for Contemporary Art in Winston-Salem,

220

were placed on probation for one year; an outside panel was appointed to study NEA grant procedures; the NEA budget was cut by $45,000 (the exact amount of the grants related to the Mapplethorpe and Serrano exhibitions); and finally, the NEA was prohibited from funding "obscene" art. Although this bill marked the first attempt to control content in the NEA's 25-year history, arts advocates reasoned that the prohibition was meaningless. If obscenity was already illegal, what harm was there in prohibiting the NEA from funding it? The comment of Anne G. Murphy, executive director of the American Arts Alliance, reflected the dominant view in the art world: she said she could "live with the compro- mise" because it "only restated the law of the land."[2]

When the House and the Senate voted to prohibit the use of NEA and NEH money to fund "obscene" art, the intent of Congress was to apply the current legal definition of obscenity, spelled out in Miller v. California, a 1973 Supreme Court case. The Miller ruling provided a narrow definition of obscenity and made clear that only a small portion of sexually explicit material would fall within its boundary. According to what has come to be known as the "three prongs" of the Miller standard, work can be found obscene only when it meets *all three* of the following criteria stated in the ruling:

1) the average person, applying contemporary community standards, would find that the work, taken as a whole, appeals to prurient interest [transla- tion: "prurient interest" here means that the work leads to sexual arousal], and

2) the work depicts or describes, in a patently offensive way, sexual conduct specified by the statute, and

3) the work, taken as a whole, lacks serious literary, artistic, political, or scientific value.[3]

The Miller ruling does not prohibit specific sexual subjects or depictions and takes into account intent and context. And although parts of the definition are problematic and far from crystal clear (what are "contemporary community standards," for example, and how do you assess them?), winning an obscenity conviction under Miller is difficult. The most explicit, prurient and offensive image, for example, cannot be found obscene if it can be shown to have serious value. As a result, obscenity prosecutions directed at literature and art have virtually disappeared. Even prosecutions against X-rated material found in adult sex shops have dwindled, conservatives and fundamentalists lament, because convictions are so expensive, time-consuming and difficult to obtain.

For all these reasons, the crafters of the compromise legislation believed that the obscenity regulation would have no impact on the NEA and NEH. In practice, nothing that either agency has ever funded, including the photographs of Robert Mapplethorpe, could ultimately be upheld as obscene by a higher court. Indeed, it can be argued that the very choice of an endowment panel to award funds in a competition based on artistic excellence or the decision of an arts institution to show a particular work indicates a priori that the work in question has serious artistic value and thus could not be found obscene.

Despite the protective stringency of the Miller definition, the actual effect of this new regulation has been alarming, chilling and far from meaningless, even in these few months since its passage. The regulation has lifted the discussion of obscenity out of the public scrutiny of the courts and landed it in private rooms, where anxious arts administrators, untrained in law, worry about what obscenity *might* mean and perhaps decide to play it safe and fund landscapes this year.

One evident problem with the new regulation is that the procedures used to implement it operate entirely outside the structure of the court system. The determination of obscenity is made by NEA panelists and administrators — not by judges or juries — in private, following procedures that are totally unspecified. Since few arts administrators are attorneys, the "three prongs" of the Miller standard are replaced by gut feelings and vague intuitions. The injunction to avoid funding art that "*may* be considered" obscene, for instance, can suggest that panelists should reject any work that *might* offend any group, no matter how small. The phrase "may be considered" also creates a linguistic elasticity that conservatives exploit, since they already call any act or image that exceeds their notions of propriety "obscene." Moreover, the "may be considered obscene" phrase implicitly acknowledges that definitions of obscenity will not be legally tested. Ultimately, applicants whose work is deemed obscene have no right to defend their work before the persons judging them and no right of appeal. By contrast, in a legal obscenity trial, the prosecutor would have to prove beyond a reasonable doubt that a work or image was obscene; the defendant would be informed of all charges and be able to answer them in open court; expert witnesses could be called if necessary to challenge prosecutorial assertions that a specific work was obscene; and, even if convicted, producers of obscenity have full rights of appeal.

A second problem with the new regulation is the confusion that its language has sowed, even among those most friendly to the NEA. Serious misunderstandings exist about the precise legal definition of obscenity. Despite the rarity and difficulty of Miller-defined convictions, many well-meaning people now seem to believe that obscenity lurks everywhere. Consider two examples. An artist I know, who has already served on NEA panels, recently articulated to me her concern about whether or not she will be able to tell what is obscene when she serves on an upcoming panel, apparently anticipating difficult and wrenching deliberations over what is in fact a null set. (Question: Is there any reason for those who serve on an NEA panel to act any differently given the new obscenity regulation? Answer: A resounding "no," because serious art by definition cannot be obscene.) In another case, a sympathetic article in the liberal *Village Voice* nevertheless expresses some doubt about the legality of recently attacked art works, saying that "Robert Mapplethorpe's homoerotic photographs, and even Andres Serrano's 'Piss Christ,' might well pass" the Supreme Court's Miller test.[4] Of course they would pass. Both have serious artistic value, and "Piss Christ" is not even sexually explicit.

The various misreadings of "obscenity" can be traced to the peculiar wording of the compromise regulation, patched together in conference committee. The compromise bill states: the NEA is prohibited from funding "obscene materials *including but not limited to* depictions of sadomasochism, homoeroticism, the sexual exploitation of children, or individuals engaged in sex acts" (my emphasis). This phrasing derives almost word for word from the Helms amendment introduced by the senator at the height of the furor over the Mapplethorpe show. (Helms originally proposed to prohibit, among other things, the funding of "obscene or indecent material, including but not limited to depictions of sadomasochism, homoeroticism, the exploitation of children, or individuals engaged in sex acts."[5]) The purpose of this sexual laundry list was to provide specific examples of what Sen. Helms and, more generally, conservatives and fundamentalists find indecent. Although in the course of negotiations arts advocates succeeded in removing the term "indecent," the laundry list remained. And many now take this list as an explanation of what obscenity means.

What does the wording of the current compromise legislation really mean? The trick here is to understand that the list of sexual acts simply gives examples of depictions that *might* fall under the legal definition of obscenity, *after* the three prongs of the Miller test are met. But these sexual depictions or acts are not by themselves obscene. (Or, to take another example, more easily understood because it is not about sex, consider the phrase "obscene material including but not limited to black-and-white photographs, color slides and Cibachromes." We grasp immediately that the terms here are not interchangeable: obscenity may include black-and-white photographs, but not all black-and-white photographs are obscene.) Yet when the sexual laundry list is attached to the word "obscenity," many carelessly read the phrase to mean that any depiction of sadomasochism or homoeroticism is in itself obscene. This is no accident, since the original Helms list contains typical right-wing linguistic ploys that play on the readers' own sexual prejudices. It is a list that mixes up acts that are stigmatized (homoeroticism and sadomasochism), illegal (child pornography) and conventional (any individuals engaged in sex acts, the unspecified form of sex here being heterosexuality). Typically the stigmatized acts appear first and are intended to set off the readers' anxiety, their negativity about sex and homophobia. Critical thinking stops, and the sexual red alert flashes. Although many readers would realize that the mere depiction of (hetero)sexual acts is not necessarily obscene, the placement of the topic so late in the list makes this realization less likely.

The NEA regulation, then, contains a prejudicial sleight of hand, and it comes as no surprise that this language promotes conservative goals. The wide-ranging use of the term obscene has been an important and consistent ploy of conservative and fundamentalist sexual politics, familiar from recent debates over pornography and abortion. Frustrated by their limited ability to attack sexually explicit material through existing obscenity law, conservatives have pioneered new ways of expanding the rhetorical meaning of obscenity. In their own rhetoric, conservatives now routinely equate premarital sex and homosexuality with obscenity. Indeed, the list targets not just homosexual sex but the even broader category of homoeroticism, thus constituting an attack on all gay and lesbian images. If it were stated explicitly, this viewpoint would not be very convincing to the mainstream public. It is not difficult to imagine the fate of conservative legislation which attempted to define representations of premarital relations or homosexuality as obscene. Yet the almost unnoticed migration of conservative language into the widely circulated compromise legislation plays havoc with people's ability to think critically about obscenity.

How else do we understand the actions of *both* John Frohnmayer, head of the NEA, and Susan Wyatt, executive director of Artists Space, who each believed that the ban on funding obscene art somehow applied to "Against Our Vanishing," a 23-artist exhibition about AIDS that contained images of homosexuality?[6] Or, how do we explain a recent feature in *Art News*, "What is Pornography?"[7] which responded to the NEA crisis by providing ample evidence of widely differing subjective definitions of pornography, art and obscenity without ever informing readers that obscenity has a specific legal meaning? Or a recent *New York Times* article about the "loyalty oaths" that NEH grantees are now required to sign? Writers must swear that they will not produce obscene works with endowment funds, but many erroneously believe that the oath prohibits them from *writing* on specific sexual or erotic topics. The *Times* never corrects the error, but compounds it by stating: "grant recipients are now being asked to refrain from producing artworks that include, but are not limited to, 'depictions of sadomasochism, homoeroticism, the sexual exploitation of children, or individuals engaged in sex acts. ...' "[8] In this morass of confusion, the folk definitions of obscenity — though legally mistaken — are dismayingly compatible with the views and political goals of the right wing, though the vehicle which now endlessly circulates them — the NEA regulation — is no longer identifiably right wing.

The equation between obscenity and sexuality has already achieved wide currency. Consider the distribution of the NEA regulation with no effort to provide guidance about the legal meaning of obscenity or to clarify the relationship between the sex laundry list and that legal definition of obscenity. The unvarnished regulation is now routinely included in all NEA and NEH application packets. Each grant recipient must sign a form agreeing to the terms of the new law, under the threat of not receiving funds. Members of peer-review panels are also instructed to consider in the course of their evaluations whether the art works are obscene. For all concerned, the terms of this regulation are sobering, freighted with a foreboding sense of responsibility and imagined legal penalties for mistaken judgment. What is most fantastic about this regulation, however, is that it covertly circulates and legitimizes conservative definitions of obscenity among liberal, educated people who would, in other circumstances, indignantly reject them.

The past few months have already made clear that the chief effect of the new NEA regulation will be self-censorship by the arts community, both individuals and institutions, encouraged by sporadic episodes of formal censorship and sensationalized witch-hunts. Last November the *Los Angeles Times* reported that the NEA had held back five literature fellowships because of the sexual or political nature of the projects.[9] In January the *Los Angeles Times* obtained letters written by Sen. Helms to Frohnmayer demanding information about eight arts groups and nine artists over a seven-year period beginning in 1982; the demand seemed motivated by suspicions about the political or sexual biases of the works of those artists and groups.[10] In March, the indefatigable

224

Sen. Helms announced "compelling" evidence that the NEA had violated the ban on funding obscene art: it had awarded grants to "three acknowledged lesbian writers."[11] And most recently, last month, prosecutors in Cincinnati threatened to use the police to remove works that they considered obscene from an exhibition of photographs by Robert Mapplethorpe following unsuccessful conservative attempts to induce the Contemporary Arts Center to censor itself.

From the censor's viewpoint, self-censorship is an ideologue's dream, since it is cheap, self-policing and doesn't require a large bureaucracy to administer. It is more effective than legal regulation, since fearful individuals, trying to stay out of trouble, anxiously elaborate the category of what is likely to be prohibited. Best of all, self-censorship occurs privately, without contentious and unpleasant public struggles.

There is no question that a serious degree of self-censorship is already taking place. Acting on distorted definitions of obscenity, many artists and writers are simply deciding not to apply for NEA grants because they believe their work cannot be funded. Or they expand the scope of the regulation: one writer I know who signed the "loyalty oath" now wonders if her promise to avoid producing obscene work would be in effect forever or just for the duration of her NEH fellowship. Arts administrators and curators face similar decisions: curator Dana Friis-Hansen of MIT's List Gallery (on Helms's investigatory list for suspicion of having exhibited work with sexual content) remarks, "Now we would not consider trying to fund [controversial and difficult art] through the NEA."[12] Others decide that sexual topics are too risky altogether.

Artists and artists' organizations have responded vigorously to attacks on the NEA by lobbying, rallying and protesting these assaults. Artists must mount an equally aggressive effort to educate their own community about what obscenity is and what this new regulation means. A long-term goal, of course, includes defeating any regulation controlling the content of NEA- or NEH-funded work (an effort recently given an unexpected boost by the Bush Administration's support for removal of restrictions of federal grant recipients).[13] But in the short term, it is imperative to minimize the damage caused by the existing regulation, to publicize and to insist on strict Miller definitions of obscenity and to unveil current loose definitions of obscenity for what they are: right-wing pressure tactics that have no legal status or force.

The NEA must join in this effort, too, by issuing clear guidelines about what is and is not obscene. A simple paragraph of explanation would go far in clarifying the distorted belief that any depiction of specific sexual acts, including homosexuality and homoeroticism, is obscene and therefore prohibited.

Arts organizations can afford to take even more vigorous steps to educate their members. They can start by providing very specific information about obscenity and the new NEA regulation. Groups must take the initiative and prepare NEA panelists with hypothetical scenarios they may encounter in this (art and) sex panic, along with appropriate responses. Basically, organizations must communicate the message that the ban on "obscene art" has no meaning; to act as if it does is a capitulation to Jesse Helms, not any legal requirement. Similar scenarios and instructions need to be given to prospective NEA grant applicants, artists, museum administrators and curators — continue to apply for grants and refuse to be intimidated. Insist on the right to produce and distribute art with erotic and sexual content.

These educational efforts must address not only legal definitions of obscenity, but the way sex panics work, because the assault on the NEA — and its defense — takes place in an emotional and sexual climate. Right-wing concepts and definitions migrate not only because liberals and the arts community are uncertain about the law, but because even they harbor primitive and inchoate ideas that equate sexuality, especially its less conventional varieties, with obscenity. Right-wing politicians acquire power not only through their ability to mobilize votes and constituencies, but through their ability to mobilize sexual anxiety and reduce opponents to silence. In our culture, few people are immune. Sex panics work only because "regular" people, not just zealots, get caught up in their chilling dynamics: self-censorship, caution and the perception that the domain of sexuality is increasingly marked by penalty and danger. In this battle for the NEA, the legal definition of obscenity is on our side, unless our own residual shame and fear about sexuality immobilize us.

Thanks to Frances Doughty, Lisa Duggan, Nan Hunter, Gayle Rubin and Ann Snitow for helpful conversations.

1. Martin Tolchin, "Congress Passes Bill Curbing Art Financing," *New York Times*, Oct. 8, 1989, p. 27, and "Congress Bans Funding of Obscene Art," *New Art Examiner*, Dec. 1989, p. 10. For accounts of earlier legislative efforts, see "Congress Votes for New Censorship," *Art in America*, Sept. 1989, p. 33; Carole S. Vance, "The War on Culture," *Art in America*, Sept. 1989, pp. 39-43; Michael Oreskes, "Senate Votes to Bar U.S. Support of 'Obscene or Indecent' Artwork," *New York Times*, July 27, 1989, pp. A1, C18; William H. Honan, "Helms Amendment Is Facing a Major Test in Congress," *New York Times*, Sept. 13, 1989, pp. C17, C19; William H. Honan, "House Shuns Bill on 'Obscene' Art," *New York Times*, Sept. 14, 1989, pp. A1, C22; Nichols Fox, "Helms Ups the Ante," *New Art Examiner*, Oct. 1989, pp. 20-23; "House Passes Compromise on Federal Arts Financing," *New York Times*, Oct. 4, 1989, p. C19.

2. William H. Honan, "Debate Deepens Over Artistic Costs of Art Subsidies," *New York Times*, Mar. 18, 1990, p. 4E.

3. 413 US 15 at 24 (1973). See also Franklin Feldman, Stephen E. Weil and Susan Duke Biederman, *Art Law: Rights and Liabilities of Creators and Collectors*, New York, Little Brown, 1986, pp. 2-108.

4. Richard Goldstein, "Crackdown on Culture," *Village Voice*, Oct. 10, 1989, p. 29.

5. Oreskes, "Senate Votes to Bar U.S. Support," *New York Times*, July 27, 1989, pp. A1, C18.

6. It is clear that the motivations of Frohnmayer and Wyatt were not identical. Wyatt first alerted the NEA about the show because she did not want the agency to be "blindsided" by a new, suddenly erupting arts controversy. In response, Frohnmayer first expressed concern about the sexual content of the show but then claimed he rescinded the NEA grant because its content had become "political." For accounts of the controversy, see William H. Honan, "Arts Endowment Withdraws Grant for AIDS Show," *New York Times*, Nov. 9, 1989, pp. A1, C28; "NEA Recalls, Then Returns Artists Space Grant," *New Art Examiner*, Jan. 1990, p. 11; John Loughery, "Frohnmayer's Folly," *New Art Examiner*, Feb. 1990, pp. 20-25; Carl Baldwin, "NEA Chairman Does Turnabout on AIDS Exhibition," *Art in*

America, Jan. 1990, pp. 31–33; Allan Parachini, "Arts Groups Say NEA Future at Risk," *Los Angeles Times*, Nov. 10, 1989, pp. F1, F30.

7. "What Is Pornography," *Art News*, Oct. 1989, pp. 138–143.

8. "Artists, Accepting Federal Grants, Worry About Strings," *New York Times*, Mar. 10, 1990.

9. Allan Parachini, "Ex-NEA Head Requests Sessions of Arts Advisors," *Los Angeles Times*, Nov. 13, 1989, pp. F1, F6.

10. Allan Parachini, "Helms Letters Add Fuel to the Arts Controversy," *Los Angeles Times*, Jan. 29, 1990, pp. F1, F3.

11. Barbara Gamarekian, "White House Opposes Restrictions on Arts Grants," *New York Times*, Mar. 22, 1990, pp. A1, B4.

12. Parachini, "Helms Letters Add Fuel," p. F3.

13. Gamarekian, "White House Opposes Restrictions," pp. A1, B4.

■ Hon. William Dannemayer, Christianity Under Attack by "New Bigotry," *AFA Journal*, May 1990 (excerpt)

William Dannemeyer is a Republican member of the House of Representatives, representing the state of California.

My good friends, Christianity is under attack in America. The attack is mostly subtle, a sprinkling of local complaints and subsequent court decisions which serve to slowly squeeze the religious life out of our national heritage. Sometimes the attack is brutally offensive.

The Disguise of the Attackers

The attackers come at us in many disguises. They are secular humanists, or who Judge Robert Bork refers to as "moral relativists," people who believe at the very least that man is the highest form of life or, at the very most, that man is god.

Most of the attackers are atheists. If some do believe in God, they do not believe that their god intervenes in the affairs of men — and any god that does not intervene in the affairs of men, as we know, is no God of any salt. Hence, these attackers are left to themselves void of external standards, transcendent duties, or divine imperatives. They live by their rules, and their rules alone.

Our American attackers are a particularly virulent strain. The law of the land, founded on the Judeo-Christian ethic, is also the same law which gives them aid and comfort to subvert and work their mischief. Life, the same life which was given them by the sweat of the brow, has been much too easy for them. Ample discretionary time and a vibrant, prosperous economy has proved their greatest boon.

These American attackers are unlike their counterparts throughout the world. The evil empire of communism, the humanist prototype, is crumbling

227

right before our eyes —almost as if the Lord has stayed his hand no longer. No doubt the blood of Israel has saturated the Iron Curtain.

You will not hear the good people of recently freed Eastern Europe, both Jew and Gentile, bickering over the contents of a sincere and heartfelt prayer. They will no longer tolerate blasphemous assaults on the core of their existence. They have lived and died under the idiotic banner of "Man is god." And now they have had enough.

It is both marvelous and sad that Mikhail Gorbachev has been forced to admit, "Now we not only proceed from the assumption that no one should interfere in matters of the individual's conscience; we also say that the moral values that religion generated and embodied for centuries can help in the work of renewal in our country."

And yet, at home, a national crusade by the rhetorically perverted name of "People for the American Way" would choke and suffocate on such an utterance.

Let's be clear at least on one aspect of our attackers. They are full of hate. Life for these oppressors is chaotic and insecure. Their refusal to recognize a Supreme Being, one with efficacy, leaves them with the sand foundation of the words of men. This is not much to count on. So through civil and judicial means these lost souls attempt to justify the social contract of men — they seek passage of laws and court decisions which coerce both behavior and thought. Free agency is destroyed in the process and the iron yoke of oppression is the unspeakable, but governing, rule of the land.

New Bigots Hate Accountability

The object of hate for these moral eunuchs is anyone who believes that right and wrong or good and evil transcend any code of standards which the feeble mind of man can fabricate. You can now understand why these people hate accountability. Accountability means the existence of a standard.

So it is not difficult to fathom why those of us who profess the Judeo-Christian ethic are the primary targets for destruction by the counterculture. In fact, Jesus told us this would happen. He taught his disciples, "Blessed are ye, when men shall hate you, and when they shall separate you from their company, and shall reproach you, and cast out your name as evil, for the Son of Man's sake." (Luke 6:22)

How often have we heard the plaintive cry of humanists that the Judeo-Christian ethic, and particularly Christianity itself, are responsible for the woes of America?

Homosexuals, they say, would be happy if only society would condone sex acts between two men or two women; women would be happy if only they could kill their own offspring without the burden of guilt; kids would be happy if only society would recognize the inevitability of the pre-marital sexual relations; and Hollywood's elite would be happy if only society would properly care for its poor, thereby relieving the guilt associated with multi-million dollar incomes and 20,000 square foot homes acquired by the "hard work" of shedding one's attire on the big screen.

Christianity is the most oppressive external influence upon mankind, according to the new bigots. Hollywood, homosexuals, abortionists, family planners, the sexually promiscuous, failed spouses, failed parents, failed kids — all would be happy minus the Judeo-Christian ethic. Those Ten Commandments and that Sermon on the Mount can be so burdensome and restrictive. The best solution to relieve this burden is to get rid of it, or second best, put an amoral spin on it.

To pursue these solutions the new bigots have sought and nearly succeeded in taking control of our government and our educational system.

Control of the government is necessary to oppress adults who believe in personal accountability, self-sufficiency, and religious freedom. Control of our educational system is necessary to oppress the children of these adults and offset familial influences.

The result in government is a monstrous welfare state whose tentacles stretch far and wide sucking every last bit of liberty from the populace. The result is also direct assaults on the religious sensibilities of citizens.

Consider, for example, that taxpayers have managed to fund through the National Endowment for the Arts the creation of a crucifix of Christ dipped in urine, the "anal retentive" works of Robert Mapplethorpe, another picture of Christ injecting heroin into his arm, and Annie Sprinkle, the porn-star who will let you come up on stage and look in her vagina for $5 (the government subsidy must account for the bargain price)....

Homosexual Movement

A microcosm of the new bigotry we are exposed to today is the homosexual movement. They have published in their pages that under the homoerotic order "the family unit — spawning ground of lies, betrayals, mediocrity, hypocrisy, and violence — will be abolished," and that, "All churches who condemn us will be closed. Our only gods are handsome young men."

They have stormed churches, most recently St. Patrick's Cathedral in New York City. Defiantly unapologetic they respond, "We're not here to make friends. If you want me to apologize, I'm not going to. We're prepared to leave the Catholic Church alone when they leave us alone."

A revealing introspection of the homosexual lifestyle was recently published in book form title *After the Ball*, written by two avowed homosexuals. At one point, they lament over the atheism and amorality which is rampant in the homosexual community. Here are a few passages of interest:

"The explicit root-and-branch rejection of morality by gays has been real, pervasive, and baleful in its effect on both the quality of life that we create for ourselves within the community, and our p.r. with straights."

"There's a simpler, darker reason why many gays choose to live without morality: as ideologies go, amorality is d—ned convenient. And the mortal enemy of that convenience is the value judgment."

And one last one:

"Without morality, there can be no compelling basis for responsibility to others."

Let me close with an extension of that thought. It was spoken in George Washington's Farewell Address. He said:

"Of all the dispositions and habits which lead to political prosperity, religion and morality are indispensable supports. In vain would that man claim the tribute of patriotism, who should labor to subvert these great pillars... Whatever may be conceded to the influence of refined education... reason and experience both forbid us to expect that national morality can prevail in exclusion of religious principle."

Ladies and gentlemen, we should begin to call a spade a spade. The excesses of secular humanism, of the ACLU, of the People for the American Way, all the media such as *The Last Temptation of Christ*, all the laws and court decisions which have kicked God out of our public schools, and all the venomous politics of the left are all examples of anti-Christian bigotry. They are not claims for justice or a defense of civil liberties. It is the voice of bigotry — the new bigotry — and we should call it that from now on.

■ C. Carr, War on Art, *Village Voice*, June 5, 1990

C. Carr is a frequent contributor to the Village Voice.

We're not talking about artistic nudes.
—press secretary to Representative Dana Rohrabacher

Martha Wilson, director of Franklin Furnace, a major downtown venue for experimental art, came to work on May 21 to find large white stickers fixed to the front door: "VACANT — DO NOT ENTER. THE DEPARTMENT OF BUILDINGS HAS DETERMINED THAT CONDITIONS IN THIS PREMISES ARE IMMINENTLY PERILOUS TO LIFE."

After 15 years as an archive and performance showcase, the Furnace has been charged with not having an illuminated exit sign or emergency lighting, and with keeping the front door locked during a show. The action, however, had been prompted by another kind of emergency.

It started the day Karen Finley's installation opened, one week after syndicated columnists Evans and Noyak ridiculed the performance artist as "a chocolate-smeared woman." Wilson says "Karen's show triggered it. I don't think there's any doubt about it. People For the American Way told us we could expect something from the religious right because this has been going on all over the country."

According to Franklin Furnace, a man who'd attended Finley's opening got into an argument with staff members later that evening, when he wanted to leave and couldn't figure out how to buzz himself out. "He's not a performance goer," says Wilson. "He was there for another purpose." The man decided to report the Furnace. As spokeswoman Barbara Pollack put it, "We're operating in an atmosphere where people feel if they don't like art, they can call in the authorities."

Franklin Furnace is open again, but the basement performance space remains closed. Of course, it was the fire department, not the vice squad, that shut them down. But when people send the law after art, there's always some hidden agenda. That's true form here to Sincinnati.

I grew up in Fundamentalist Land, that theme park of guilt and transgression. I knew little of art, but lots about the God who could smite. Lately, I've wondered whether the National Endowment for the Arts didn't fund the experience that opened some door — no, some fire exit — in *me*. I was stuck in the glue of depression out in the heart of Illinois when I happened to see the Bread and Puppet Theater on cable television. In this play of shrouded, masked characters — all moving at a foghorn's pace — a dead man rises. A river is a very tall character. The narrator whispers. I still can't quite articulate what moved me, but the piece said: "Possibility." Eighteen years later, I can still remember nearly every line and image.

So, as the zealots force their scarlet letters on the art world, I know they're desperate to hold the fire exits shut. They see boundaries breaking. They see libidos play prime time. Porn walks in and out of the video store. Abortions are still legal, women who want sex aren't necessarily "bad," and gay people keep popping out of their closets. "Secular" can't even describe such humanism.

The Saved are always a minority among the Damned. Practicing zealots don't feel powerful, but beleaguered. That's why they're obsessed with policing the boundaries of the permissible. For a while in the '80s, it looked as if the right might sell their moral majority idea and transform the culture into some Heritage Park version of *The Handmaid's Tale*. But the Saved lost their Ronnie; their grip on prime time, if not Congress; even their moral high ground. How will they erase those sex-crazed Jimmies (Bakker/Swaggart) from our minds? Regroup around some unseen enemy. And wouldn't ya know, fresh outta godless Communists, they've discovered the art world — a rich new motherlode of sinners.

And deconstructionists. Jesse Helms hasn't lashed out at artists "deconstructing representation," but that's how a lot of this "pornography" got into the museums to begin with. Artists were pulling labels apart, questioning the God-given basics, like what it means to be a "man" or a "woman." They defiled the sacred barriers around "high art," and soon the "low" — from carnival to rock — rushed in. They acknowledged the Other and soon a few "others" dared to intrude. Isn't that what the post-modern lingo boils down to in the end; loss of authority for all powers-that-be?

In the good old days of modernism, the boundaries artists attacked were formal. Riots broke out when "Nude Descending a Staircase" was first exhibited, and "The Rite of Spring" was first performed, and "L'Age D'Or" was first screened. These works opened doors by expanding the parameters of perception. Now, there's all this *content* in art, all these dangerous messages — that you can become a *different* sort of man, a *different* sort of woman.

When Jesse Helms brought those "disgusting" Mapplethorpe photos to the Senate chamber, he asked the women and adolescent pages to leave. Representing sexuality; that's for grown men to decide, to judge, to control. That's why they're waging this war on difference. At stake is the sexual order.

Every artist attacked so far has challenged that hierarchy. (In Andres Serrano's case, it's the patriarchy implicit in church hierarchy.) And each is guilty of working with primal imagery, trafficking in the unclean, forcing contact with the body as it is; the coolly unregenerate s&m images in Robert Mapplethorpe's "XYZ Portfolios"; urine, semen, and menstrual blood in Serrano's photographs; the demystified female body in Annie Sprinkle's performances; the frankly homosexual body of David Wojnarowicz's paintings/writings; the documented "body modifications" in *ReSearch* magazine's "Modern Primitives" issue; and the exteriorized female body in the work of Karen Finley.

The far right often discusses this work in metaphors of chaos, dissolution, sewage, engulfment: "the river of swill" (representative Dana Rohrabacher); "stinking foul-smelling garbage" (an American Family Association coordinator); "a polluted culture, left to fester and stink" (Patrick Buchanan). The heightened emotions and uncontrolled sexuality of the Other threatens each of these wrathful Dads. It threatens their identity, their separateness from women and gays, their very sense of self.

There's an apocalyptic quiver at the heart of the religious right's anti-NEA campaign. For in this art, they see the decline of civilization. It's an old story. "Theater, art, literature, cinema, press, posters, and window displays must be cleansed of all manifestations of our rotting world.... Public life must be freed from the stifling perfume of our modern eroticism.... The right of personal freedom recedes before the duty to preserve the race." The author of these words: Adolf Hitler. And though the jackboot will not be televised, its imprint is evident in the current rhetoric of reaction. At Pat Robertson decried "tax-supported trash" on his *700 Club* one day, his co-host Sheila Walsh gravely concluded, "It's just a hellish plot to destroy this nation."

The American Family Association, the 700 Club, the Eagle Forum, and so on: let's call them the Gang of Fear. They'll pounce on Pepsi, circle the cineplex, picket 7-Eleven — wherever the obscene and the blasphemous show their faces. But when "art" is at stake, the gang grows larger and more genteel, as blue-chip conservatives enter the fray. Too highfalutin to be bothered with pop culture imagery, these critics and columnists *do* care about canon, about intrusions of the Other into their hallowed halls. The difference between these groups is one of class: blue-chippers *do* hate to dirty their hands among the "yahoos" (as William Safire has called them) — and they're no less condescending to transgressive artists. The artist they've chosen to attack is Karen Finley, known henceforth in the ivory tower as "a chocolate-besmeared nude live performer."

Safire claims he isn't for censorship but wants the NEA abolished because "Federal support ultimately conflicts with freedom of expression." This is exactly the point made by the Reverend Donald Wildmon of the AFA, who calls the Endowment a censor because it determines what art the government should fund. And they don't fund Christian art, do they? Rohrabacher told the *New Art Examiner* that most art "produced by the NEA [is] ugly and grotesque." Phyllis Schlafly, former ERA opponent turned NEA opponent, makes an inevitable connection between sexual hierarchy and the right kind of art: "Why didn't they give a grant to have a statue of Rocky on the steps of the museum in Philadelphia?"

The NEA isn't even the issue, just the first target. Ultimately, the Gang of Fear wants to control what's presented. Destroying the Endowment would cripple much that's marginal and developing, while helping to keep the Other confined to large cities. Barry Blinderman, who curated Wojnarowicz's retrospective in Normal, Illinois, told me, "The NEA made the difference between us being an outpost and us being connected to all the major art institutions. People in Normal are proud of that." NEA grants are the most prestigious available, emblems of an artist's worth or a venue's seriousness, and they attract corporate funding.

Tim McClimon, vice-president of the AT&T Foundation, a major corporate arts funder, points out that an "arts ecology" has developed among corporations, private foundations, and the government over the last 25 years. "We're partners. Restrictions on the NEA have a ripple effect. [The private sector] starts looking at the same issues. You can't view parts of an ecology in isolation." If the NEA collapsed, he says, "we might continue to support the arts, but we can't pick up where the government leaves off."

The war's already spread beyond the Endowment. Thanks to AFA pressure (55,000 letters), the Southeastern Center for Contemporary Art (SECCA) lost their funding from Equitable after exhibiting Serrano's "Piss Christ." Corporations have become nervous. One New York presenter heard from a private funder: "The arts used to be safe, used to be good PR. They aren't safe now."

"The change in the atmosphere in the last few months is striking," says Laura Trippi, a curator at the New Museum who worked on "The Decade Show," cosponsored by the Studio Museum of Harlem and the Museum of Contemporary Hispanic Art. "A year ago, 'The Decade Show' was extremely popular with corporate and private funders, because of the cachet around multiculturalism," she said. "Now, even with funders still committed to the project, we're finding a lot of caution and concern. We've had to give a lot more detailed information about any political or sexual content. Everything's been scrutinized to an extent that's unprecedented."

The Gang of Fear smells blood. When New York's John Simon speared the Mabou Mines version of Lear, he listed all their funders and asked: "Jesse Helms, where are you when we need you?" Could it be a coincidence that this was a gender-reversed production, with a drag queen for a Fool? They were "raping Shakespeare," Simon wrote.

Mississippi senator Trent Lott will reportedly seek "disciplinary action" against the Kitchen for presenting Annie Sprinkle. Says Bobbi Tsumagari, the Kitchen's executive director. "All we can do is to continue to honor the mission of this institution. If that means that the environment can't support a place like the Kitchen — better to close than to compromise."

You'd think the Helms Amendment had passed. One Helmsman (Senator Warren Rudman) gloated in defeat: "We have fired a warning shot across their bow." I don't think the military metaphor is accidental. The right has designated art as an area to be patrolled, even pacified. As John Killacky of Minneapolis's

Walker Art Center told me, after two members of the vice squad came to monitor a performance there by Karen Finley last January, "People on the right now feel empowered to stop art. They don't just want to disagree with it. They want to stop it."

The impulse has filtered down to the streets. Last month, a pack of roving art critics appeared at Max Fish, a bar on the Lower East Side, to "review" Allen Frame's double image of men touching, Boys on the Couch. While one connoisseur distracted the bartender, the others took the offending picture from the wall, went outside, and smashed it. One of them explained, "This isn't art."

Suddenly we're a nation of critics-at-large. (Some very much at-large, since they haven't even seen the work that so offends them.) We're caught up in a struggle between two sensibilities, two moralities, two kinds of critique — one that separates good art from bad, another that separates good from "evil."...

The Gang of Fear has found an ideal transgressor in Annie Sprinkle, the ex-porn star. She goes to the very crotch of the matter for them. Of course, Sprinkle has never received government funding, nor has she applied for any, but it isn't like the Gang to let a fact stand in its way.

The religious right feasted on Sprinkle's piece, *Post Porn Modernist.* They repeatedly described it as alive sex show. In fact, the performance was about Sprinkle coming to terms with her years of work in the sex industry. Porn, after all, has its own conventions about what should and shouldn't be seen in order to arouse the audience. In one segment, "Bosom Ballet," she manipulated her large breasts in time to music, subverting any turn-on with silliness. The point for Sprinkle is to do a show *she* enjoys, something sex-positive for grim times, something...well, educational. One bit that roused ire and umbrage in the Gang (only one of whom actually saw the show) featured Sprinkle inserting a speculum and inviting people to look at her cervix. "Demystifying the female body," she called it. This action also impressed me as the moment when a woman who's been ogled all her life says, in effect: You wanna look at me? Go ahead and look — all the way inside.

It nearly landed Sprinkle in jail on Easter weekend. She'd opened the Cleveland Performance Art Festival with the vice squad in attendance at both show. Sprinkle changed her act when police implied that the cervix piece would be grounds for arrest. The irony is that Sprinkle used to perform in Cleveland during her porn-star days, at a burlesque theater she describes as the "wildest" place she's ever worked. She actually *did* live sex shows them, and the vice squad never even showed up. "As long as it was in the porn ghetto. As long as it was *their* pleasure arena. But now that it's something for me...."

Sprinkle onstage is sweet, sometimes coy. There's a part of her porn persona she can't or won't drop — the part there for men. She who drops it, after all, risks monstrosity by embodying a female energy that men fear or hate.

During the '80s, however, a sort of rude-girl network developed in the downtown clubs. Performers like Lydia Lunch, Dancenoise, and Karen Finley had edges instead of softness. They allowed themselves to be monsters. Finley can be disturbingly confrontational in subverting images of the female body, as defined by male desire.

A few years ago, I wrote a *Voice* cover story praising Finley's work and Pete Hamill denounced her in the next week's paper, after days of interoffice uproar and graffiti sprayed across men's rooms. Like Evans/Novak and Safire, Hamill mocked Finley by focusing on food. He said her work was all about stuffing yams, just as the others say it's all about smeared chocolate. None of these Wrathful Dads has ever seen her. They write in that vacuum called male entitlement.

Obscenity is Finley's subject — not four-letter words but the emotion propelling them. Her monologues expose unspeakable acts and unforgivable feelings, deconstructing relationships into the most primal urges. She holds the mirror to what people try to hide, and for those things there are no polite words: rape, AIDS, incest, abandonment, brutality, emotional damage. She transforms food into an emblem of catharsis. It's where the boundary breaks, the boundary of the body. Inside goes outside. No doubt the reaction to that moment, and to her work in general, has to do with male terror when "primal" meets "female." Herstory is the history of such instincts kept under control.

"We Keep Our Victims Ready," the show criticized by E/N and Safire, is more straightforwardly political than anything Finley has done. Here, she uses food ritualistically, smearing on chocolate as she talks about female victimization. Because women are treated like shit. Slowly, she recreates herself, applying sprouts, red candy, and tinsel. By the end, she seems to be wearing a strange and beautiful costume. That is the heart of her work: to take some horror on, then turn it over. This show moved people to tears.

To those fretting over the social/sexual order, gender traitors take on this quality of monstrosity. So, it's a short step from rude girl to rude queer.

The Gang plays steadily and lucratively on the fact that homos are asserting themselves. Jesse Helms, who augments his NEA attacks with fulminations against *any* spending for AIDS, informed his Senate colleagues last fall that "Mapplethorpe's obscene photographs were an effort to gain wider exposure of, and acceptance for, homosexuality." The American Family Association, which has consistently attacked any television program with a positive take on homosexuals, runs anti-NEA newspaper ads that rail about such innocuous-sounding exhibits as "At Home with Themselves: Gay and Lesbian Couples" — confident that any tax money going to queers will trigger outrage.

The Corcoran Gallery's decision to drop "Robert Mapplethorpe: The Perfect Moment" sanctioned homophobia. And other artists have been encountering the fallout ever since. During a gig in Philadelphia, "I felt like people were gonna jump up on the stage and lynch me," says Holly Hughes, an openly gay playwright/performer. Recently, she says, presenters at venues that might ordinarily book her have been saying, "There's a problem with you coming, because it's lesbian material." Hughes feels the homophobia has "mushroom-clouded."

Last summer, Creative Time distributed an AIDS education card by Gran Fury, "Kissing Doesn't Kill: Greed and Indifference Do," and as director Cee Brown told me, "We got three complaints following the Corcoran thing. One artist from Boston called and said, "My daughter could pick this up and it's promoting homosexuality. I want to talk to every one of your funders.""

Performance artists Anne Iobst and Luxy Sexton (Dancenoise) appeared at the University of Massachusetts, and had their own problems when the young Puritans there complained about a sneak preview they did, because *these two women appeared in their underwear!* But in describing the campus mood, Sexton told me that the university's gallery had recently been vandalized (smashed windows, shaving cream) because an exhibit there included gay images. In the school newspaper, she says, young Helmsmen-in-training were declaring that their tuition money shouldn't have to pay for such art.

Obviously the NEA-bashers are horrified to discover that grants actually go to gay artists who make gay art. No wonder the Gang of Fear targeted David Wojnarowicz. A "Dear Colleague" letter from Representative Rohrabacher described the artist's NEA-funded retrospective at Illinois State University as "sickeningly violent, sexually explicit, homoerotic, anti-religious and nihilistic." The Gang just doesn't want to see the body through gay eyes. The AFA's Reverend Wildmon, master of the mail-order Judgment Day, went on a penis-hunt through Wojnarowicz's catalogue and diligently sent the xeroxed results to every member of Congress, 3200 Christian leaders, 1000 Christian radio stations, 100 Christian TV stations, and 178,000 pastors.

Wojnarowicz's work — political, emotional — is quite a contrast to Mapplethorpe's formal, depersonalized studies. But both insist on homoeroticism as a valid subject of art. It so obviously informs Wojnarowicz's worldview that deleting it would leave a shell, while Mapplethorpe's work is either hardcore transgression or lilies — art that could "pass." The antiporn diehards in Cincinnati kept proposing something to the tune of: *just take out those bad pictures; the other ones are nice.*

The Mapplethorpe pictures for which museum director Dennis Barrie will stand trial include five from "The XYZ Portfolios" plus two showing children with their genitals exposed. The work may not be benign, but neither is it pornographic. The stark images of sexual extremes in the Portfolio (fistfucking, water sports, rubber fetishists) don't reinforce fantasy, which is porn's job. They confront fantasy, which is art's job. They admit to the multiplicity of sexual experience, and pass no judgment on it.

What happened in Sincinnati is the culture war in microcosm: Your Patriarchy at Work. It had nothing to do with the NEA, everything to do with Dads who claim to know best.

The rest of the country may get to read *Hustler*, or hear N.W.A., or see ... *Equus.* But the town fathers in Cincinnati like to think this smut won't get past *them.* Since 1974, the city's had no adult bookstores, no X-rated videos or cable, no massage parlors, and no strip joints. *The Last Temptation of Christ* didn't play there either. (And don't try renting the video.)

"There's always a posse here to protect people from what we artists might perpetrate on the public," says Worth Gardener, artistic director of Cincinnati's Playhouse in the Park. Last year, the vice squad requested a police preview of *Equus*, because it includes a brief nude scene. "I've never lost my amazement at gestures like this. The banners are in the basement ready to come out."

There are gay people in Cincinnati, and I found them the old-fashioned way. Surreptitiously. At least, that's what it felt like when someone handed me a name written on a napkin: "He'll be able to tell you things." Once I got to that name, though, I plugged into a huge phone-tree of people offering to help — most of them closeted.

Others I met talked about the local chapter of Planned Parenthood: "a fort," constantly besieged by pickets. National Right to Life president and "founding father," Dr. John Willke, lives in Cincinnati. So does the Reverend Jerry Kirk, founder or chairman of: the National Coalition Against Pornography, People United Against Pornography, STOP (Stand Together Opposing Pornography), and the National Consultation on Pornography. (The AFA's Donald Wildmon was part of the latter group's "leadership team.")

The group that went after Mapplethorpe, Citizens for Community Values, is another creation of the ubiquitous Reverend Kirk. CCV's letterhead lists some of the city's wealthiest and most powerful businessmen, along with church leaders and the coach of the Cincinnati Bengals, while its literature boasts of "close working relationships" with police and prosecutors. Close it seems to be. Long before the offending photographs arrived in town, the group had finalized a "Mapplethorpe strategy" aimed at "turning public sentiment against the exhibit." They were confident that the campaign would succeed. A memo that fell into the hands of a reporter reads: "Since prosecution of the most objectionable and possibly obscene photographs will occur, CCV should take a passive role in this situation...."

Cincinnati's antiporn ardor was born in the mind of a single fearless crusader for morality: Charles Keating. He is better known today as the symbol of the savings and loan crisis; the man who sold uninsured and now worthless bonds to 23,000 Californians, most of them elderly and investing their life savings; the man who forked over generous campaign contributions to several U.S. senators with the power to influence banking examiners; the man who will eventually cost taxpayers an estimated two to three *billion* dollars.

Charles Keating lived in Cincinnati for 55 years, and there began his war against "diabolical and evil" pornography. One local woman, who did not wish to be named, recalled going to a meeting for teens at a friend's house in the early '60s. Keating arrived, she told me, with a briefcase full of *Playboy*s, much to the chagrin of her friend's father. She herself had never before seen a *Playboy*.

Keating — known locally as Mr. Clean — declared "holy war" on such threats to morality as the Ramada Inn that offered adult cable programming to guests. According to *The Cincinnati Post*, Keating also declared that "homosexuals should be prosecuted and put in jail." When Richard Nixon appointed him to the Presidential Commission on Obscenity and Pornography in 1969, an outraged Keating filed suit to hold up publication of the group's report, which encouraged sex education and found that pornography did not cause sex crimes. "Such an advocacy of moral anarchy!" he fumed in his dissent, where he linked pornography to infidelity, divorce, abortion, and suicide. Keating's obsession didn't die when he moved to Phoenix in 1978. "You could be discussing annexation or a zoning matter," Phoenix mayor Terry Goddard told the *Post*, "and somehow pornography would come up."

Cincinnati is a town where moral terrorism has worked. Where the men who control sex run everything else. Things are tidy. Simon Leis, the county sheriff, keeps it that way. He carries a terrible swift sword when it comes to "filth." Leis is the one who nailed Larry Flynt back in the '70s. And, as one of the locals put it, "There seems to be a common umbilical cord between the sheriff and the CCV."

But it was Charles Keating's old business partner at American Financial Corp., Carl Lindner, Jr., and his son, Carl Lindner III, who reportedly exerted much of the behind-the-scenes pressure against the Mapplethorpe exhibit. No one in the Cincinnati business community would talk about the Lindners, either on or off the record. They control United Brands, Penn Central, the United Dairy Farmers chain, Great American Broadcasting, Chiquita Banana, Provident Bank, one Cincinnati television station and two radio stations.

Carl Three, as he's often called, is a CCV board member. According to the *Post*, he was behind the pressure applied to the Central Trust bank, whose vice-president happened to be chairman of the museum's board. Central Trust was told it could lose 300 accounts if the Mapplethorpe exhibit opened. The veep resigned from his museum post. Soon, letters were circulating in corporate offices garnering support among employees to fight the show. Employees were advised to stop contributing to the city's Fine Arts Fund. The museum hadn't even uncrated the pictures yet.

This was the climate in which attorneys for the museum filed suit against the law enforcers. A "preemptive strike" they called it — to keep the police from closing the show or confiscating work. They wanted a jury to determine whether the work was obscene. A day before the exhibit opened to the public, a municipal judge dismissed the suit without comment or explanation. This seemed strange to me, but not to the locals. One interested party told me he'd spoken to a CCV member who seemed certain the suit would be thrown out of court.

On the morning the show opened, the police "investigated" "The Perfect Moment." They brought a grand jury right along with them. They had their warrants by midafternoon. And then the police bulldozed into the Contemporary Arts Center, all purpose and force, trampling over the velvet rope in their fever to arrest the spirit of Robert Mapplethorpe. Here were the ultimate wrathful Dads. They were about to tell us what we could and couldn't see.

And here were their designated children. I could hear them outside, chanting, "Not the church! Not the state! *We* decide what art is great." They were the newly formed anticensorship group and the small Cincinnati ACT UP chapter and the hundreds who'd been waiting to get into the museum. They yelled for as long as the police stayed inside. And whenever one of the blue uniforms appeared, fingers pointed and a thousand voices cried, "Shame! Shame! Shame!" The officers looked stunned.

Had they thought they were saving us? From evil?

The night of the opening, over 4000 people stood in line for hours to see those photographs. There was a gravity to it, an urgency. And once into the galleries, they weren't schmoozing. They were drinking in the pictures that, they all suspected, might be gone tomorrow. Some people approached me, the out-of-towner, wondering "What are people going to think of Cincinnati?" From local reporters to local artists to the clerk behind the desk at the hotel, they expressed their embarrassment. For some, though, the shame had begun to mutate into something more useful. They were *outraged*. I recall a woman active in the fledgling anticensorship movement telling me that they'd been putting up with this stuff for years. And why? Why?

A week later a poll conducted by the *Post* found that 59 per cent of those surveyed in the county thought the museum should be permitted to display the pictures. This could be the Perfect Moment for Cincinnati, the first crack in that patriarchal wall.

Far from Sincinnati, but all too near — Karen Finley recently dedicated another project made possible by government funding, an outdoor sculpture with a monologue from her recent show cast in bronze, "The Black Sheep." It sits at the corner of First Avenue and Houston, across the street from a small park filled with the homeless.

The day she installed it, someone from the Parks Department worried that people would tip the work over, hit it with sledgehammers, throw paint on it. But as one sallow, sunken-cheeked local said, "You'd have to be a lowlife to do that." He said he'd help her plant flowers in the few remaining patches of dirt in what could only pass in New York City for a park. And the next day, when it rained, someone came out and draped a coat over the sculpture.

"I just know all these people are black sheep," said Finley, as scores stopped to read her text. *We are sheep with no shepherd/we are sheep with no straight and narrow/we are sheep with no meadow....*These were the homeless, and people in ties, workers leaving the subway, and one guy who lived *in* the subway, "under the rock," as he put it.

Finley's piece for the black sheep of the family describes everyone the American Family Association will always hate and fear. The people who see things differently because they honor the reality of their own identities. As she says: *Black sheep's destinies are not in necessarily having families/having prescribed existences like the American Dream/Black Sheep destinies are to give meaning in life — to be angels, to be conscience, to be nightmares, to be actors in dreams.*

■ Hon. Edolphus Towns, statement to the House of Representatives, June 19, 1990 (excerpt)

Edolphus Towns is a Democratic member of the House of Representatives, representing the state of New York.

M r. Speaker, I stand today to lend my unequivocal endorsement for the work of the National Endowment for the Arts. In providing encouragement and assistance to individual artists, this incredible organization has enriched the society....

In recent years, the National Endowment for the Arts has come under attack by self-appointed arbiters of taste, decency, and decorum. I believe the American people can make their own decisions about the art they value and want to see. I have not become more qualified to critique art by virtue of holding public office. I don't know anyone who has. Many people are saying that because this art is publicly funded, a public consensus of acceptability is required. Art should not be held to any standard different from other governmental expenditures. We do not require a consensus for defense spending; funding for education; nor healthcare spending. We do not require a consensus because there are some projects which we fund because it is the right thing to do, it is the business of government to do it; it is necessary; and as a nation, we need it.

Art allows us to look into our hearts, see beyond ourselves and rise above the everyday mundaneness of the world. We expand the horizons of the innerself to learn to understand the life and experiences of others. You may never see Tahiti, but if you have seen Paul Gaughin, you have a feeling of knowing the people and customs of this place. You may never have been to Harlem, but you can begin to understand the life and dreams of these people by reading the works of Langston Hughes; you may never have known anguish or despair but if you see the works of Munch, you will understand the pain of those who do; you may never have known the tranquility of water lilies on a pond, but if you have seen Monet, you may understand.

In essence, art allows us to overcome, transcend, and be made sublime. Those who oppose art oppose openness, and new ideas. To oppose art is to oppose the potential inherent in each of us. To oppose art is to oppose yourself.

■ Hon. Major Owens, statement to the House of Representatives, June 19, 1990 (excerpt)

Major Owens is a Democratic member of the House of Representatives, representing the state of New York.

I am proud to speak this evening in strong support of reauthorizing the National Endowment for the Arts without any restrictive language or changes in the funding formula. I quote from one of our former Presidents:

"Artists stretch the limits of understanding. They express ideas that are sometimes unpopular. In an atmosphere of liberty, artists and patrons are free to think the unthinkable and create the audacious.... Where there's liberty, art succeeds. In societies that are not free, art dies."

From whom do I quote, Mr. Speaker? Not from one of our liberal Presidents, but from one of the most conservative Presidents of our time, Ronald Reagan.

I stress that point because the debate over the relative merits of the NEA has been centering on the wrong issues. It has been centering on what a very few artists have been doing with their grants and whether or not the works of art they have created are appropriate or decent. We are not artists. Very few of us would claim to be experts on art. So how can this body sit in judgment over the country on art and even attempt to deem it appropriate and inappropriate or good or bad.

As Mr. Reagan and thousands of other people who are knowledgeable about art assert, artists create art to reflect society, to explore societal ideas and concepts. They do not choose only those ideas which are comfortable and acceptable to us. If they did art would be universally boring; there would be nothing new, nothing daring, nothing to make us think about the art itself and about what it is reflecting.

A person who grew up in the savage ghettos of an inner-city, who lived in run-down housing projects and went to school in a crumbling, rat-infested school, whose family was left out of the trickle-down economics theory of the Reagan era, is not going to paint a pretty portrait of the former President. That artist is also not going to paint pretty pictures of landscapes and fruit bowls, and frolicking kittens. That artist's portrayals are more likely to reflect the experiences of his or her life and the anger of being shut out from the prosperity apparently being realized elsewhere in society.

When that artist paints pictures of ugliness and despair and we condemn that art as bad or inappropriate, what are we saying about that person's life? Are we saying it was bad, not legitimate, and not worthy of a true portrayal? Yes; we are. And what are we then saying about that person?

These are some of the human dynamics of this debate. I do not see how we can condemn art which is ugly, art makes us think about realities that we may not have experienced. This art is reflecting things that are happening in our society, and closing our eyes will not make those things go away. Such art can help us recognize other influences in our culture, and even help us understand them. And if it does not help me or you specifically, you can be sure that it is helping someone, somewhere, who can relate to it.

This is what the freedom of expression is all about.

■Robert Anbian, Bigots, Not NEA, Promote Social Decay, flyer, San Francisco/Bay Area Coalition for Freedom of Expression, June 22, 1990

Robert Anbian is a poet and the editor of Release Print, *the monthly newsletter of the Film Arts Foundation.*

The long-playing rape being perpetrated by right-wing Congresspeople and their religious fundamentalist allies on the integrity and very existence of the National Endowment for the Arts is part of a larger assault on

241

freedom of thought and expression in the United States. It is correspondingly an attempt by legislative coup to impose on all Americans moral and political orthodoxies.

The far right ideologues want to step on First Amendment protections, sanctify political symbols, break down the separation between church and state. They want to repress sexuality generally, persecute homosexuals specifically, suppress women's reproductive rights, and put down voices of political dissent. In the service of these ends, they want to wipe out the last wan vestiges of allegiance to the public interest in the halls of government.

These demagogues, with their crude baiting of the public, will shamelessly wrap themselves in the flag (even as they reify it as an authoritarian object), in the welfare of children (even as they let more children slip into poverty and ignorance), the taxpayer (even as they flack for tobacco subsidies and defense contractors), and scream bloody "pornography" at every exposed genital their ardent hearts can locate.

As such, they represent the most extreme threat to the American democratic heritage, as it has been forged by both liberals and conservatives, since "Tailgunner Joe" McCarthy waved his spectral lists of communists. The irony is that their own virulent attack on the American social center is a prime carrier of the decay they decry. The knife of censorship, aimed at the throat of the artist, lands in the chest of the body politic.

The attack on NEA has especially dangerous characteristics because the agency is the nation's flagship for the principle of public support of the noncommercial arts. So-called "content restrictions," political intimidation, and threats to the peer panel process at NEA constitute a Trojan horse of censorship meant to let loose the forces of repression in every burg and town. One only has to think of Cincinnati, where a museum director has been thrown into the judicial dock for showing Robert Mapplethorpe; or of the seizure by FBI agents of the works and equipment of San Francisco photographer Jock Sturges because of slides of innocent nude beach scenes sent to a lab for processing; or of the taking from the shelves of school libraries in Empire, California of Little Red Riding Hood, because in the original a bottle of wine is among the goodies being brought to Grandma.

The tactical advantage is with the demagogues. The tar of "pornography" is more easily applied than the clarities of artistic allegiance to truth explained. That, therefore, is the wrong battle. What has to be exposed are the real intentions of NEA's critics, and what must be defended and explained is the principle of public support of the arts.

One of the curious aspects of this struggle has been how easily confounded even many artists can be about public support of the arts. Out of a kind of anarchist, individualist reflex — which can both energize and hobble the arts community — they agree with the more sophisticated of NEA's critics that "government funding" of artists is antithetical to the idea of artistic freedom.

This, in fact, is the only principled argument that can be made against NEA. It is, nonetheless, a false argument, inasmuch as it has logic and validity only in the abstract. It must assume that the artist exists first in a dimension of freedom, and then the government comes along to distort that freedom through the inducement of funding.

Nonsense! Obviously, the artist — and the arts appreciating public — exists first in a cultural environment severely constricted by the requirements of mass production and consumption on the one hand, and the very specific needs of corporate image-makers on the other. In this actual environment, diversity is limited, controversy avoided, minority tastes and points-of-view ignored or watered down, and innovation takes a back seat to the formulaic. The major freedom afforded the artist concerned with any of the foregoing is the freedom to starve. But the travail of the artist is not the most significant aspect; in such an unleavened environment the whole culture is impoverished, and the range of substantive knowledge offered Americans narrows.

It is into this real environment that public support for the noncommercial arts enters. Such support is entirely consonant with notions of artistic freedom when that support acts to broaden diversity, encourage innovation and the airing of controversial issues, and give voice to minority and dissident points-of-view. These values are prima facie in the public interest not only because they are vital to a richness of culture, but because they are part of the very fabric of political democracy. The importance of these values not only outweighs the inevitability that certain art works will offend some or a majority of people, but is composed in part of that very inevitability. The public interest is served not by supporting certain kinds of art over others, but by supporting the field of noncommercial artistic endeavor.

Let's put it concretely: the marketplace can give us Teenage Mutant Ninja Turtles but it takes public support to give us Sesame Street; corporate sponsorship can give us evenings at Lincoln Center, but it takes public support — as well as the grit of the artist — to bring us frank expositions of race, sexuality, politics and other controversial subjects.

This was the clear-eyed realism that led to the creation of NEA in the best checks and balances tradition of American polity. The peer panel process has produced, if anything, a cautious funding record. Indeed the paucity of truly controversial projects funded by NEA prompted Garrison Keillor — whose own "A Prairie Home Companion" could not have gotten off the ground without a NEA grant — to tell Congress that it was "a remarkable testament to how timid, how self-repressed we all are." Evidently, even such "self-repression" is not enough for the dogs of censorship.

Any attempt to burden NEA support for the arts with "content restrictions" is to create an oxymoronic institution, one that restricts rather than opens up the cultural field. In regards to sexuality in particular, it is to say, in effect, that sex is a subject fit only for the pornographic peep show. Already, the "no obscenity" pledge required of artists getting NEA money has seriously if not fatally compromised the NEA mission, and is helping undermine the foundations of free speech and thought.

The destruction of NEA will hurt artists, but they will survive and work as they always have. It is the public, and the public's right to know and to choose, that will be hit hardest and most enduringly. We will descend into a long dark night of mutant turtles and self-righteous bigots.

■ Tim Miller, statement, July 4, 1990

Tim Miller is a performance artist, and one of the "NEA Four," a group of artists who were denied NEA grants, and who subsequently sued the agency.

An Artist's Declaration of Independence to Congress

When, in the course of cultural events, it becomes necessary for this artist to get pissed off and dissolve the political bonds which have connected me with the censorship of the state and the dishonesty of my government, ya gotta explain why you're stomping mad.

I hold these truisms to be self-evident: that all women and men should be created equal; that they should be endowed with certain inalienable rights; that among these should be life, liberty of expression, and the pursuit of happiness. This pursuit is not easy, especially for the homeless, lesbian and gay people, latinos, women and african-americans... who this society screws over and would like to make invisible. That to secure these rights, an artist has a big responsibility in these troubled times, and when a government gets too big for its own wing tips and tries to tell its citizens what to think and feel, it is the job of the artist to speak truth to King George Bush in a challenging and angry way. To prove this let facts be submitted to a candid world.

He has allowed artists that confront their society to be censored, distorted, and used by right wing demagogues to advance their political careers.

He has allowed his sleazeball appointee to cowardly undermine the cultural freedoms that are the root of our life as a nation.

He has allowed a cynical politicization of the 1st Amendment's freedoms to distract attention from his dishonest tax increases and his own son's billion dollar Saving and Loan bailout.

He has constrained our fellow-citizens with the ugly revival of a blacklist.... the bad dream of McCarthyism forty years later. Haunting us even now as cultural freedom breaks out all over the world.

He has conspired to make gay artists, artists who are people of color, feminist artists, artists who are dealing with AIDS, anyone who speaks their mind in an outraged and clear voice, to be considered unsuitable for the cultural support that any democracy should provide. He would have us silenced and invisible.

I therefore declare that this artist is, and of right ought to be, a free and independent citizen and have the full power to create art about my identity as a gay person, art that confronts my society, art that criticizes our government and elected officials, and maybe even some art that deserves a few tax dollars from the 20 million lesbian and gay men who pay the IRS... even more next year thanks to King George. Surprise! And for the support of this declaration, with a firm reliance on the protection of Divine Providence, the Goddess, Jesus, the

African Deities and others, I pledge to my society my life, my creativity, and my freedom of expression.

Signed and in challenge to the Congress,

Tim Miller, Performance Artist

■ Christopher Reeve, Rev. Pat Robertson, Mike Kinsley, and Patrick Buchanan, The NEA: Art or Outrage?, *CNN Crossfire*, July 16, 1990

Christopher Reeve is an actor, and a spokesperson for the Creative Coalition, a pro-NEA lobby group. Rev. Pat Robertson is the head of the Christian Broadcasting Network (CBN), a television evangelist, and the director of the Christian Coalition. Mike Kinsley is a television commentator. Patrick Buchanan is a nationally syndicated columnist and television commentator.

MIKE KINSLEY: Good evening. Welcome to Crossfire. Any day now the House of Representatives will vote on whether to restrict or even abolish the National Endowment for the Arts. The arts endowment is mired in controversy over grants it has made for works of art that many regard as obscene. In a newspaper ad, religious broadcaster Pat Robertson has thrown down the gauntlet to members of Congress. Quote, "You may find that the working folks in your district want you to use their money to teach their sons how to sodomize one another. You may find that the Roman Catholics in your district want their money spent on pictures of the Pope soaked in urine. But maybe not." A voice of sanity or cultural Kryptonite, Pat?

PAT BUCHANAN: Christopher Reeve, let me ask — let's take the picture of that — the Pope that is dipped in urine. Why should Roman Catholics be required to subsidize this kind of assault on their fundamental beliefs?

CHRISTOPHER REEVE: Well, I haven't seen that picture. But the point is that any citizen of this country as a part of the price you pay for living in this free society, is that our government should subsidize art. And with any subsidized art, with any kind of society that encourages art, there's a risk that certain things are going to be deeply, deeply offensive. The number of issues that are deeply offensive are minuscule. I mean, the — the NEA has given out 85,000 grants over 25 years and had maybe 20 controversies. This whole thing is very blown out of proportion.

BUCHANAN: All right. Christopher Reeve, let me follow up right there. Let's say this was not only controversial, but the crucifix in urine and the picture of the Pope in urine are deeply offensive. What is the matter with the arts community that they cannot do as other communities, come forward and say, "We really blew it. We made a mistake. We were given this money to a photographer. He did something that was really profoundly offensive. We should not have done it. We apologize. We'll keep an eye out for those mistakes in the future." Why don't they do something like that instead of defending these outrages?

REEVE: Well, the problem with an artist is you can't guarantee the results ahead of time. I mean, if you order up a Stealth bomber you know pretty much what you're going to get. But if you ask an artist, please, go create and here's some money to do it. You can't legislate or demand a priori what that creation should be. Unfortunately, sometimes an artist is going to come up with something deeply upsetting and disturbing. I personally think this picture which I haven't seen of the Pope in urine or whatever it is, that's — that's horrible. I find that deeply offensive. But I support to the death the artist's right to — to be funded to go and create. And I think a large percentage of his work may be very acceptable.

BUCHANAN: All right. Christopher Reeve, let's — we all would support an artist's First Amendment right to be free to produce or replicate the thought we hate. The question comes, why is he using my tax dollars? We can't use his tax dollars for my thoughts he doesn't like, and for my expression he doesn't like.

REEVE: Right.

BUCHANAN: Why should the tax dollars of the American people be used to fund this character?

REEVE: Because the problem is that many, many of the great things in the arts in this country are brought to you by your tax dollars and couldn't be brought to you any other way. When the NEA gives out a grant to a dance company or to a theater or to a writer, whatever, or — I mean, the NEA, for example, gave the money for the Vietnam Memorial. It provided the money for "A Chorus Line," it provided the money for "Driving Miss Daisy." It brings you symphony orchestras. It brings you arts education in the school. It brings you all of these things, many of which could not have happened, would not have happened without federal funding, because federal funding leads the way. It gives a certain legitimacy to creative groups. And then the private sector matches. And if you take away the federal funding, many of these artists just aren't going to be able to survive. And you're going to end up with a very sterile country.

KINSLEY: Okay, Let's get Pat Robertson in here. Pat, I'm a little bit confused about your position. Are you against all government help to the arts or only government help for art that you don't like?

PAT ROBERTSON: Neither, Michael. It's not a question of what I don't like. It's what is fundamental. You know, Thomas Jefferson said it very well, "to compel a man to provide contributions of money to propagate concepts of which he disagreed is sinful and tyrannical."

KINSLEY: Okay. But let's —

ROBERTSON: There's something wrong with the government taking my money, my taxes and using it to attack my savior, Jesus Christ, put him in a vat of urine and say, piss Christ. And that's what it said.

KINSLEY: Okay, okay. But only as Christopher Reeve pointed out, only a very few of the many, many grants made every year by the National Endowment for the Arts are in any way offensive to even a hair-trigger offense-taker like yourself. So, is it okay with you if the National Endowment for the Arts cleans up its act or are you just saying we should be out of this business?

ROBERTSON: Well, my position all along has been — clean the thing up. Of course, read my lips, we're going to pay more taxes. People out there don't want to pay more taxes to show two men engaged in anal intercourse. For instance, they just don't want to do that. And it's my money and I don't want it going for that. Now, if we've got surpluses in the federal till, we've got plenty of money, no raised taxes, well, of course —

KINSLEY: Wait a minute. If there were surpluses in the federal till, then it's okay to use the money to fund two men going at it —

ROBERTSON: That's right. As soon as you get — Michael, as soon as you get surpluses where you don't have to raise my taxes, then by all means, let's have a little surplus for art. My companies are spending —

KINSLEY: So, in other words, as long as there's a federal deficit, you're against any — even a single penny for art, offensive or otherwise? Is that your position? I mean, you're purposely ambiguous about that.

ROBERTSON: No, my position is not that way. I'm just telling you. If you read Naisbitt's book, Megatrends, he tells that more people go to art galleries, museums and plays and spend more money than they do on all the professional sports in America. We funded the private sector six and a half billion dollars. My companies are producing in co-production over $100 million worth of motion pictures this year. And —

KINSLEY: Pat, are you or are you not for government funding of the arts?

REEVE: May I interject something, please?

KINSLEY: It's a very simple question. Leaving aside —

REEVE: May I interject something?

KINSLEY: — the things that offend you, yes or no?

REEVE: May I —

ROBERTSON: I do not think the federal government can afford it right now. I think we're wasting money. And I think with six and a half billion dollars being spent on art in America, the $175 million of the NEA grants amounts to about 2.6 percent. We can do without it. But if the guys — I will not oppose it, Michael. I will not oppose it if Congress will put adequate safeguards so they won't be used to attack my religion. I don't think that's —

REEVE: May I please —

ROBERTSON: — too unfair.

BUCHANAN: Chris Reeve.

REEVE: May I please respond to that? Please let me respond to this tirade we've just heard for the last three minutes. Now, first of all, in terms of the money, $175 million that goes to the NEA. That is the same amount of money that we spend on military bands in this country, annually. And if you think that the arts aren't as important as military bands, then I think we're just in other — light worlds apart. Now, in terms of, quote, "cleaning up the act," let me again say this. You cannot legislate, you can't have a bunch of legislators, Jesse Helms or anybody, even a politician you like, you can't have any politician legislating what obscenity is because this creates a chilling affect on the artists of this

247

country. The Supreme Court in 1973 ruled what obscenity is. It's a definition that has to do with community standards. And the money should be given, as it has been given successfully for 25 years by a group which is driven by a peer panel review system, artists deciding about art, not politicians deciding about art.

BUCHANAN: Okay.

REEVE: It is —

ROBERTSON: Christopher, I want to ask you this question — let me ask you this —

REEVE: It's been operating successfully for 25 years and if the community —

BUCHANAN: Let Pat Robertson respond now, Chris.

ROBERTSON: Is it art — is it art to have one man urinating into the mouth of another? Is that creative art? It was one of the things we paid for, do you agree with that?

REEVE: No. It is probably not art. But the other work —

ROBERTSON: But we paid for it with my money.

REEVE: Well, unfortunately we also paid for a Stealth bomber. I happen to think the Stealth bomber is obscene. So, we all have our different definitions of what's obscene.

ROBERTSON: Well, one at least keeps us free. The other one may destroy young people. Do you think that child porn is good use of the money? There were pictures of young children naked in those Mapplethorpe's exhibit.

REEVE: No, I don't think it's good for children to see it. I think responsible parents and I think community leaders obviously need to protect children from that kind of influence. I understand where the concern comes from. The problem is you — you are going to end up with a country which is second-rate culturally if you go ahead with this chilling deadening of the whole artistic life of the country. We've already given away our position in the world as an economic leader, let's not become a second-rate cultural culture and end up with nothing but — you know, very — you know, productions of *The Student Prince*. Art has got to be on the edge of society. It's at the cutting edge. Artists have got to be the leaders and, if I may finish, they have to bring up points which often are uncomfortable to us. Let's take the case of Karen Finley who, you know, got an NEA grant and then it was pulled —

BUCHANAN: All right. Chris, we're going to cut you off right there. We're going to take up the case of Karen Finley when we come back, the young lady, semi-nude, who smeared herself in chocolate as a form of moral statement against what she called sexism. We'll be back with that and other artistic objects when we come back.

[Commercial break]

BUCHANAN: Welcome back. Congress is about to take up the refunding of the embattled National Endowment for the Arts. NEA subsidies of such work as the homo-erotic photos of the late Robert Mapplethorpe and the crucifix in urine of the photographer Andres Serrano have given it a year of grief and may yet ring down the curtain forever on the $175 million-a-year Great Society jewel. Our guests: the host of the "700 Club," CEO of the Christian Broadcasting

Network, and a 1988 candidate for the GOP nomination for president, Pat Robertson. And up in Albany, New York, Christopher Reeve, an actor on stage, screen and television for more than two decades whose most famous or most popular work was perhaps the film "Superman" and its several sequels.

Christopher Reeve, now, I want to ask you what Clark Kent would have said about something. This is Karen Finley. What she does and she admits it, she has — in one sequel, she, I guess, smears chocolate on herself, she's half nude and it's a form of artistic protest, as she calls it, a social statement against sexism and all the rest. Now, these are political views, Chris, and like my political views. Why in heaven's name, should we be required to subsidize Karen Finley's political statement?

REEVE: Because you're also required to subsidize all the millions of wonderfully diverse and interesting and rewarding and educational things that the NEA brings you. And the fact that you don't like Karen Finley's work is a very small price to pay for all the things you —

BUCHANAN: All right, Chris. Let me follow up on that. You are going to — now, you've mentioned a lot of things that have been done. "Driving Miss Daisy," symphony orchestras, some other terrific things that have been done.

REEVE: Many, many, many —

BUCHANAN: But let me suggest the reason the NEA is really the spotted owl of American politics right now is the refusal of the arts community to come forward and say, "We are sorry, this, that and the other is, as you said yourself, disgusting. We made a mistake; we didn't know beforehand what we'd get. We are going to try to avoid that sort of thing in the future." If the arts community would do that, my guess is you would not be in the kind of problem you are now which is defending this and even demanding funding for it from a public which is really fed up with it.

REEVE: Well, let me respond to that. What's going to happen, as a matter of fact, is if the legislation goes through with the authorization, the appropriation language, with politicians trying to define what is obscene, a lot of wonderful people like, for example, the producer Joe Papp who has run one of the best theaters in this country for 25 years, he isn't going to take the money that he's entitled to, as a protest. And what will happen, there will be a ripple affect. People who deserve the money, who aren't controversial, are going to say, no, because my brothers, my sisters, my fellow artists are being asked to apologize to politicians or to Pat Robertson or to anybody you care to name who is exercising this kind of limited tyranny of a minority point of view. And I prove to you why it's a minority point of view in a minute if you'll give me a chance.

BUCHANAN: But, Chris, it's not a minority point of — the point of view Pat Robertson's expressing about Mapplethorpe and Serrano and the other things we've discussed is not minority. It's about 99 or 96 or 97 percent majority.

REEVE: I disagree. May I read you some statistics? There was a poll conducted by research in Forecast, Incorporated. It came out on July 13. It has surveyed 1200 people and a cross section of this country, which is about standard for most polls. And the results show that 93 percent of the people say that even when they find a particular piece of art offensive, quote, "others have the right to view it." Goes on to say that the public —

249

BUCHANAN: Does it say that we have — we have the obligation to subsidize and if the art is not —

REEVE: I was about to get to that — I was about to get to that point, if I may continue. The poll also found that the public sides with National Endowment for the Arts in the current controversy. According to the survey, when asked to choose between the sides favoring and opposing NEA funding cuts and content restrictions, 61 percent chose the pro-NEA side opposing cuts in restrictions. Only 13 percent favored cuts and restrictions.

KINSLEY: Pat Robertson —

REEVE: That poll came out three days ago.

KINSLEY: Pat Robertson, have you been to see Karen Finley, the chocolate lady? Have you been to see her performance?

ROBERTSON: No, I have —

KINSLEY: How do you know it's obscene if you haven't seen it?

ROBERTSON: I didn't say anything about the chocolate lady. This is my first time of hearing about it. I've heard about Annie Sprinkle, though, that masturbated on stage, urinated —

KINSLEY: Did you see that? Did you see that?

ROBERTSON: Well, no, I didn't —

KINSLEY: How do you know it's obscene?

ROBERTSON: How do I know masturbating on stage is obscene in a theater in New York? Are you kidding?

KINSLEY: Don't you understand, Pat, that I could describe to you some of these great paintings by Raphael and those people as a bunch of naked little babies flying around with their genitals showing. And you'd say, gosh —

ROBERTSON: Michael, I want you to —

KINSLEY: — that sounds obscene. We don't know — we don't know what's great art from a description. We don't even know what's great art when we see it. It takes time. You have to be tolerant.

ROBERTSON: Michael, I want you to know this. I've been to the major galleries of the world and I have never in my life seen two men conducting anal intercourse in any one of them, nor have I seen obscene pictures of Jesus Christ, or Jesus Christ shooting heroin in his arm. Now, come off it. If you —

KINSLEY: My point is —

ROBERTSON: — guys don't know what is obscenity, then you shouldn't be talking about it.

KINSLEY: Why should you decide what's — who is to decide? You say, well, Raphael's fine with me, Andres Serrano's over the line. Someone else may come along and say, wait a minute, I don't want to see a lot of naked little babies; I want all that stuff out; I don't want to see these naked pictures of Christ on a crucifix, that you may find very religious, someone else may say is dirty.

ROBERTSON: Well, that's somebody's opinion. The question is —

KINSLEY: Christopher Reeve is saying we have to be tolerant of art. Doesn't he have a point?

ROBERTSON: Michael, the question is who's going to pay for it? Six and a half billion dollars in private money for art in America. The American people like art. They like to see art, no problem. I don't know, Christopher, how much did Superman cost, about $60 million for that production? You grossed about 180 or 200 million or more.

REEVE: That's totally irrelevant. That's a private —

ROBERTSON: It's not irrelevant at all. I mean, why didn't one of your studios give that money and make up the difference for the National Endowment for the Arts. I'm willing to do that with our company.

REEVE: That's ridiculous.

ROBERTSON: We sponsor — we sponsor art. I sponsor sculpture, I sponsor painting, original painting. We sponsor an art gallery in Jerusalem.

REEVE: Do you give your artists absolute carte blanche to do whatever they want? Do you give them total freedom of expression?

ROBERTSON: I never saw any of them —

REEVE: Do you give them total freedom?

ROBERTSON: The ones in Jerusalem, yes. I sponsored a gallery in Jerusalem for struggling Israeli artists and I didn't see one painting they put up. I don't know what they've got in it.

KINSLEY: Pat, I'm absolutely shocked. You funded a gallery in Jerusalem and you gave them carte blanche —

ROBERTSON: Absolutely.

KINSLEY: How do you know they don't have pictures of naked people pissing in jars or whatever is upsetting you so much?

ROBERTSON: Because the Israelis wouldn't allow it to happen because they are a moral people. They wouldn't allow this outrage. It seems like just in America we want this kind of thing. This goes against the grain and you can't tell me that 60 percent of the American people want their taxes raised in order to pay for people urinating in the mouth of another one. Come off it.

KINSLEY: All right. All right. Excuse me, Pat. We have to take a break. When we come back, we're going to come back to discuss one of Pat's other complaints which is that great — this art is teaching people how to commit sodomy.

[Commercial break]

KINSLEY: Pat, we only have a couple of minutes left. And I want to get into what's really going on here, which is, of course a cynical fundraising exercise by people like yourself. Now, your ad said that the NEA is teaching our sons how to sodomize one another. That's presumably a reference to these Mapplethorpe — Mapplethorpe photos. Now, you don't seriously think someone's going to go to this exhibit, turn to his buddy and say, "Hey, so that's how it's done. Let's go try it ourselves." Is that what you mean?

ROBERTSON: It's very possible. You know, Michael, what I said in that ad, and I'll say it again, if Congress wants to vote for this, if they want to go home, if they want to make sure there are 100,000 of those photographs passed out to voters in their district, then they can take the chance and let the voters decide. But I think it will be overwhelmingly against. The voters are fed up with what's going on. As I said in my ad, the savings and loan problem, some of these other problems, they're going to have to meet people at the polls and do they want to be in favor of funding homo-erotic —

KINSLEY: Pat, you spent more money on that ad than these obscene — these allegedly obscene art things actually cost. So, don't talk about the money. That's ridiculous.

ROBERTSON: I was willing to make a statement and to pay for that ad because I think Congress has to know that there are people in the grassroots who don't like their money used for these purposes any longer. What I can't understand is why the NEA won't say this stuff is horrible, let's ban this little bit and go ahead with the funding, and I would be quiet and so would be most everybody else who's objecting to it.

BUCHANAN: Chris Reeve, why not?

REEVE: Yeah, I've tried to explain that before. It's because you can't tell an artist what to create ahead of time. You don't seem to understand that because you're not an artist. The artistic impulse cannot be legislated or contained, it has to be encouraged. And Congress is not paying for obscenity. And it is wrong of you to suggest that as being the truth. It is not the truth.

BUCHANAN: Christopher Reeve, it is not — we are not telling the artist what to create. When they come in with this piece of trash, why don't you artists have the awareness —

REEVE: Sir —

BUCHANAN: — and the guts to get up and say, this is garbage, it's not what we expected, we're sorry.

REEVE: If you — if you have this authorization to go through with restrictive language, you are telling artists what to create. You are having politicians tell artists what to create. That's unacceptable. Now, the NEA provides money for the cultural diversity and life of this country. If every now and again something obscene comes up, that's the price you have to pay. And the other point I wanted to make is without —

KINSLEY: Very quickly, please.

REEVE: Without the NEA, this country is going to culturally go down the drain and I certainly don't want to see that happen.

KINSLEY: Okay. We're out of time. Thanks very much, Pat Robertson, Thanks, Christopher Reeve. And you're coming to us from Albany because you're up there at the Massachusetts — the Williamstown, Mass. Theater Festival. And Pat and I will be back in a moment.

■ Leila H. Little, Mapplethorpe: Art for Art's Sake, *The Pilot,* July 27, 1990

Leila H. Little is an editor for The Pilot, *the official newspaper of the Archdiocese of Boston.*

A group was standing before a modern painting. The viewers did not know what the picture was about, but one person was overheard defending the bewildering work: "Well, after all, art is a language, and why shouldn't a man be permitted to speak his own language?" A bystander responded incisively, "If art is a language, this artist is talking to himself."

Art for art's sake may be taken to mean, "Embody beauty wherever found, or realize to the full your ideal." Such a meaning is fruitful unless excessive individualism insists upon expressing its own perverted ideas of beauty and its own deviated ideals. To talk to one's self—or exclusively to one's colleagues—is excessive individualism. And to ignore the world addressed through artistic composition allows individualism to triumph.

Robert Mapplethorpe's photographs present a dramatic individualistic interpretation of art for art's sake. He was an extraordinary skilled artist, but 25 of his pictures depict extremely offensive sexual aberrations. Some are violent, none is subtle. The public is being forced to suspend all conventional sensibilities to affirm this individualism — under the guise of artistic license — that debases universally accepted moral standards.

"The flaw is not with a public that refuses to nourish the arts. Rather, it is with a practice of art that refuses to nourish the public," writes Frederick Hart in the fall issue of *Arts Quarterly*. "The public has been so bullied intellectually by the proponents of contemporary art that it has wearily resigned itself to just about any idiocy that is placed before it," Hart adds, saying, "but the common man has limits... and they are reached when these things are put in public places, when the public is forced to live with them and pay for them."

"What is at issue is that some artists apparently believe they can have it both ways: They want to engage in wanton destruction of a nation's values, and they expect that same nation to pay their bills," wrote David Gergen in the July 30 *US News & World Report*, warning that the society is being asked to pay for its own demise.

Mapplethorpe and his supporters have become their own dogmatists and moralists. Everybody being his own dogmatist means, ultimately, everybody is his own god. In art, individualism aims in principle and production not only to free art from restrictions but even to exempt the artist from responsibility. But the artist may not permit evil, because no artist has omnipotence and infinite wisdom and justice and mercy, like God, governing the permission of evil and guaranteeing good as a final result. May a man who owns a wild tiger of surpassing beauty, trusting in the right of property, parade down a crowded thoroughfare with his jungle pet tethered to a thread?

Ignoring the larger world around themselves, artists such as Mapplethorpe have failed to distinguish between the purpose of the artist as one thing and the purpose of art as another. Art resides in the soul. It is not a deadening of artistic impulse for an artist to be ruled by high purposes, but rather it is a stimulus and an inspiration. The madonnas of Italian art received from the painter a solemn beauty not only because they depict divine maternity, but because they were to grace a religious shrine. That may be one reason why the madonnas of the Renaissance are far superior to the prettiness and sentimentality of more recent ones.

The French poet Baudelaire warned against an exclusive passion for art, in that it progressively destroys the human subject and finally destroys art itself.

Art for art's sake would be better read: art for the sake of God, and for everybody's sake. Art for art's sake, with this reading, will temper the triumph of individualism. It clearly opposes a Mapplethorpe exhibit, which attempts to recreate society in a pagan image and thus risks society's own demise.

■ Holly Hughes and Richard Elovich, Homophobia at the N.E.A., *New York Times*, July 28, 1990

Holly Hughes and Richard Elovich are playwrights who perform their own works. Hughes was one of the "NEA Four," a group of artists who were denied NEA grants, and who subsequently sued the agency.

John Frohnmayer, chairman of the National Endowment for the Arts, has taken the unprecedented step of overturning four solo performance art fellowships that had been strongly recommended for funding by the peer panel.

The artists whose fellowships were denied — Karen Finley, John Fleck, Holly Hughes and Tim Miller — all create works that deal with the politics of sexuality. Three are highly visible gays.

The overturning of these grants represented Mr. Frohnmayer's and President Bush's attempt to appease the homophobic, misogynist and racist agenda of Senator Jesse Helms and company.

Mr. Frohnmayer apparently believes he can make sacrificial lambs out of gay artists and that no one will care, that no one will speak up for us. Unfortunately, he may be right.

Where was the outcry when the word "homoerotic" was included in the list of restrictions attached to National Endowment for the Arts funding contracts by Congress. No other group was so blatantly and prejudicially targeted.

There was no outcry. For there to be one, the gay and lesbian community would have to speak up with an informed voice. Nobody else will do so on the community's behalf.

Even well-intentioned arts organizations leading the anti-censorship battle are reluctant to speak up for us. They are afraid of turning off Middle America by embracing these artists' unapologetic effort to make their sexual orientation visible.

And because we gay artists, particularly lesbian artists, are so invisible, our problems are invisible as well. So we must demand visibility, or the issue will be lost. This is a First Amendment issue that affects all Americans.

The overturning of the N.E.A. grants must be understood in the context of the Government's continued indifference to the AIDS crisis and inaction toward it — and the 128 percent increase in reported gay-bashing incidents in New York City this year. The homophobes in the Government don't think we're being killed off at a fast-enough rate.

The gay and lesbian community must embrace the endowment defunding issue, because there is no direct-action group in the cluster of arts organizations to do this work with us.

We two writers don't claim to represent the gay community, or even all lesbian performance artists who live on St. Marks Place. But the right wing sees us — and artists like us — this way.

By attacking the lesbian poets Audre Lorde, Minnie Bruce Pratt, and Chrystos through Jesse Helms's direct-mail campaigns, and by defunding the four performance artists, the right is trying to blacklist all gays. The right wants to force all of us back into the closet, where it hopes we will suffocate and die in silence.

Gays and lesbians need to direct their outrage at Jesse Helms and anyone else who would cater to his agenda — and that means Congress, the President, Mr. Frohnmayer and fundamentalists.

The gay and lesbian community knows from its experience in the AIDS crisis that lobbying — letters, postcards, telegrams to Congress — is not enough. Jesse Helms must be confronted through demonstrations in Washington.

Gay men and lesbians must confront the nation's arts institutions — from the galleries to the theaters, from the downtown alternative spaces to the mainstream museums — and demand that they publicly support these black-listed artists, that they increase their presentations of open lesbian and gay artists, that they condemn Mr. Frohnmayer's actions and demand their reversal. To do anything less would be complicity.

The gay and lesbian community has insisted again and again that homophobia be specifically addressed when dealing with the endowment crisis. Such support must come primarily from the gay and lesbian community. The community must get behind the various anti-censorship organizations and insist that they openly include the homophobia issue in their efforts.

■ David Gergen, Who Should Pay for Porn?, *U.S. News and World Report,* July 30, 1990

David Gergen is a columnist and television commentator. He was the White House Director of Communications during the Reagan administration.

As Congress prepares to vote on new funding for the National Endowment for the Arts (NEA), leading artistic figures are angrily protesting any and all restrictions on federal moneys. A recent rejection of four grants, they claim, means that America is retreating into a dark age of censorship and Stalinist-style art.

What rubbish. Amidst all the pieties coming from people who know better, there has been very little talk about exactly what the four "artists" in question would do with their cash. Let the protesters call off their press conferences and hold a town meeting in Main Street America where they explain why taxpayers should pay to support these four.

Karen Finley, Nyack, N.Y., whose avant-garde performances include an act in which she coats her nude body with chocolate and bean sprouts representing sperm. She also openly rubs canned yams across her vagina. Outspoken in her denunciation of her rejection by the NEA, Ms. Finley makes clear that her work is intended to advance her aggressive feminism.

John Fleck of L.A., whose work includes a scene in which he urinates on a picture of Jesus in a toilet bowl.

Holly Hughes of New York, a playwright who wants to advance lesbianism and whose performance on stage includes a scene in which she places her hand up her vagina, saying that she saw "Jesus between Mother's hips." Apparently fixated by the subject, Ms. Hughes moved to New York a decade ago, where, she said, she wanted to "arrange a giant quartz-and-steel vagina in Federal Plaza that would topple the military."

Tim Miller of Santa Monica, Calif., a man who has been described by the NEA's theater-program director as "always political. As a member of the gay community, his work presents this vantage of the world to encourage education, understanding and eventual acceptance."

Their buddies are free to call this art. They are free to hold public exhibits. No one is trying to shut them down, because this country has a robust tradition of allowing freedom of expression. Censorship simply isn't an issue here.

What is at issue is that some artists apparently believe they can have it both ways: They want to engage in wanton destruction of a nation's values and they expect that same nation to pay their bills. Grow up, friends. No society, even one as tolerant as this one has usually been, is willingly going to pay for it own demise. The American people are rightly concerned about moral decay in our public life, from the thievery at savings and loans to the suppression of prayers in school. To argue that in the name of freedom they must send in money for smut perverts the idea of freedom itself. Taxpayers have rights, too, although they are often neglected.

The protesters answer that art has always pushed on the perimeters of social convention and that only by seeing in new ways will we advance. That's a fair point. But works of decadence and blasphemy have been around a long time; we don't need a new round to learn old lessons. If we can't draw a line here, where can we? Who will say no to the next applicant to the NEA who wants to attack blacks or Jews or gays? Andrew Dice Clay anyone?

If artists insist upon a wholesale denial of any standards, they will wind up wrecking the very institution they claim to need. The controversy over the NEA has already prompted some congressmen to believe the quickest solution is also the best: Off with its head. But that's wrong, too. The NEA has played a highly constructive role in the past quarter-century, and it deserves to be fully funded for the next five years. Its thousands of grants, all but a handful above controversy, have helped us spawn a flowering of the arts across the country. Since the mid-1960s, the number of major dance companies has reportedly jumped from 37 to 240; opera companies, from 27 to 125; orchestras, from 58 to 165. The NEA has been a wonderful catalyst for this explosion.

In its laudable desire to maintain standards of decency, Congress should leave in place its current rules against funding obscene works but should avoid imposing new restrictions that would handcuff the NEA. By rejecting the four controversial grants this summer, the NEA has shown a sufficient sensibility that it should now be allowed to run its own show. It knows where to draw the line.

■ Sarah Schulman, Is the NEA Good for Gay Art?, *Out Week*, August 8, 1990

Sarah Schulman is the author of several books, including the recent **People in Trouble.**

The government is using homophobia again as an instrument of social control. We need to focus on homophobia and not on "saving the NEA." Of course, museums and boards of directors find it easier to articulate "Save the NEA" than to engage in fighting the oppression of gay people. This euphemism might even make the fight more palatable, but when the crisis over the NEA is resolved one way or another, no political impact will have been made on our behalf.

At the same time, the organized arts community has a lot of soul-searching to do about its own history of exclusion. Before Helms, many other biases existed in the funding and presentation of artwork. Historically, the reward system in the arts has been reserved primarily for white people from the middle and upper classes whose work fits the aesthetic agenda of critics and arts administrators. Yet the majority of artists previously admitted to the reward system never spoke up about the institutionalized discrimination until it affected us. Obviously, it is not acceptable for artists who are gay (or whose work has explicit sexual content) to be excluded from federal funding. Nor is it acceptable for rewards to be demanded by one group at the expense of another.

For any minority artist, part of being admitted to the reward system is that while the benefits are great for the individual, the price for the community is tokenism. I know this first-hand, having personally benefited from the "exception" distortion because I fit the criteria for tokenism. It is important to remember that people get rewards, like grants, gigs and reviews, not necessarily because they are the "most deserving" but also because of things like personal connections and how well they play the art-game. Of course, recognition doesn't always equal betrayal, but I think that it is important not to blindly accept someone as our representative simply because she or he has been selected by a government agency, publishing company or corporate-funded art venue.

Up until about five years ago, lesbian artists were almost completely excluded from the reward system. In fact, some of the gay men currently involved in the NEA scandal participated in that exclusion. Lesbians were not reviewed in mainstream publications, were not presented in prominent art venues and almost never received funding for explicitly lesbian projects. As a result, the work remained invisible, and many women were unable to develop their talents, while others could, and their work thrived. This is still the case, with the small exception of the 30 or so out lesbian artists, across all genres, who have access to the new tokenism. However, before funding, work was supported by the audience and determined by the lives, needs and experiences of the community.

Now, through the new tokenism, a few political and apolitical sensibilities are permitted to be contained within the dominant culture. Individuals are even easier than political movements to contain. As a result, a single style is declared to be representative of a hugely diverse community that it cannot represent. At the same time, racism, class bias and the emphasis on trendy, marketable genres (like detective novels and stand-up monologues) keep other voices from the public arena. When the frustrated community pressures the token to be more accountable to its needs for expression, she often declares herself "independent," puts down the community as "p.c.," or "narrow," and disengages herself for her own artistic and career development. In the end, the permitted aesthetics encourage new artists to work in precisely the same styles so that they, too, can be rewarded. In this manner, much of the development of lesbian arts are taken out of the hands of the audience and given instead to a small group of critics and administrators. This year, the NEA panel that recommended the artists whose grants were later rescinded was composed of six arts administrators and one artist.

Media reporting on the NEA scandal further distorts the picture. A *Village Voice* cover story by critic Cindy Carr entitled "The War on Art" focused only on the exclusion of artists whose work she had previously supported. Although I deeply respect and admire the work of Karen Finley, there are entire communities of artists who have been systematically silenced. They too deserve C. Carr's attention, even if they don't meet her aesthetic agenda. Attaching the "censored" label to artists whose NEA experience is bringing in publicity and audiences far beyond what they might have naturally achieved takes the underdog position away from everyone who really is. It accepts the distortion that the art world is *the world*. When Karen Finley stands up at a national press conference and says, "A year ago I was in a country of freedom of expression; now I'm not," there is a refusal or ignorance about the history of this country in which most people have been systematically denied expression. I find a disturbing subtext to some of these arguments that white artists "deserve" to retain our race and class privileges even though we're gay. Artists could, instead, use this attention on funding as an opportunity to discuss a real democratization of the reward system, as well as the passive complicity with the state that has dominated North American arts.

The *Village Voice* ran photos of the four artists whose grants were rescinded over the caption "Defunded," even though they receive more funding, exposure and institutional support than 99 percent of the artists in this country. When Cindy Carr said, in a second article, that she "may now be forced to conceive of a new demimonde —a bohemia of the unfundable," I got really angry. Doesn't she know that 99 percent of the artists in this country already live in the world of the unfundable? And that this invisibility is due, in part, to the role played by critics like her? I certainly think that these artists should receive the grant money that they were awarded, but I do object to a kind of fetishized egomania that depoliticizes the events. We are living in a city of 90,000 homeless people. No one is getting the services and funding that they need. I wish that these artists could see themselves in relation to their own society and place the NEA event in a broader political context.

While we must support lesbian and gay arts, we must also refuse the distortion of calling "censorship" of the rewarded while ignoring the thousands who are systematically excluded from support because they don't fit the profile for privilege. Every out gay artist loses grants, gigs and opportunities and faces bias and limitations throughout her or his career for being gay. This needs to be addressed politically with a recognition of how homophobia works on all levels, not only in the case of the most visible.

Obviously artists want recognition. I apply for grants, and I like getting approval. But the NEA scandal is giving us all an opportunity to rethink the values we've created as well as the ones we've been handed. At the same time that we won't lie down for a homophobic, anti-sex NEA, neither can we roll over for elitist exclusionism in our community. The fact is that there is a huge backlash going on against the gay visibility generated by AIDS. This includes increased street violence, restrictive immigration and continued negligence in the face of the AIDS crisis. In response, a variety of grass-roots, community-based movements like ACT UP and Queer Nation are arising. Despite the historically apolitical stasis in which many artists have festered, we can still rise to the occasion and participate as activists in these movements, working in community to end the oppression of gay and lesbian people, instead of working to maintain an exclusive, tokenizing NEA.

■ Hilton Kramer, There Is Only One Magazine That Tells You What Is Right..., direct mail for the *The New Criterion*, August 1990

Hilton Kramer is the editor of The New Criterion, *and the art critic of* The New York Observer.

D ear Reader:

Do you have the feeling nowadays that something has gone terribly wrong with the arts? Do you sometimes have the impression that our culture has fallen into the hands of the barbarians?

Does it make you angry when you see museums putting on shows that are trivial, vulgar, and politically repulsive? Are you appalled when leading universities abandon the classics of Western thought for the compulsory study of "third world" propaganda?

Are you offended by the claim — recently supported by the Rockefeller Foundation and the National Endowment for the Arts —that the Western tradition of classical music (Bach, Mozart, Beethoven, et al.) is now to be considered nothing more than the narrow "ethnic" interest of a remnant of European immigrants?

Are you apprehensive about what the politics of "multiculturalism" is going to mean to the future of our civilization?

Well, there is a lot happening in our culture today that inspires such feelings of apprehension and dismay, and there is only one magazine devoted to the arts and the current cultural scene — *The New Criterion: A Monthly Review* — that addresses these issues with the criticism and candor this grave situation calls for.

I write today to ask you to join us as a subscriber in this critical effort to combat the mounting pressures that we all face from forces now determined to deconstruct our culture and dismantle the values that once made our civilization the envy of the world.

Nearly a decade has passed since I left my job as chief art critic of *The New York Times* to start *The New Criterion* with Samuel Lipman, the well-known pianist and music critic for *Commentary*. We said at that time that what was "urgently needed in our artistic and cultural life is criticism that asks hard questions, challenges reigning orthodoxies, speaks up for quality, and upholds a sense of standards." The need for such a tough-minded criticism is, if anything, even greater today than it was then.

What is different, however, is that *The New Criterion* now has a solid record of delivering on the promise we made then to provide "a critical perspective that is at once serious, high-minded, and disinterested — capable of producing criticism of such integrity that it stands apart from the blizzards of publicity and the unacknowledged social scenarios that today dominate the arts and traduce their objectives."

In this endeavor we have attracted many new writers to our pages — among them Roger Kimball, now our managing editor and author of *Tenured Radicals*, the best book yet written on the crisis in the universities.

At the same time, many established writers have rallied to our cause — Joseph Epstein, William Jay Smith, Karen Wilkin, C.H. Sisson, Renee Winegarten, Maurice Cowling, Joseph Frank, Creighton Gilbert, Elie Kedourie, Gloria G. Fromm, David Pryce-Jones, Deborah Solomon, and James W. Tuttleton.

Our regular roster of critics — Jed Perl and Eric Gibson on art, Samuel Lipman on music, Bruce Bawer on Literature, and Donald Lyons on theater — offers the most brilliant coverage of the arts to be found in any magazine or newspaper today. In the critical attention that Samuel Lipman has given to the NEA and government policy on the arts, our readers were given a preview of the uproar that has now divided opinion on these matters throughout the country. And you will also find that our poetry editor, Robert Richman, brings you the best poets now writing in English — among them, Elizabeth Spires,

Brad Leithauser, Dana Gioia, Donald Hall, Herbert Morris, Jane Kenyon, Louis Simpson, and Donald Justice.

It is no wonder that Julian Symons, writing in the London *Times Literary Supplement*, concluded that "As a critical periodical *The New Criterion* is probably more consistently worth reading than any other magazine in English."

Won't you join us as a subscriber to this indispensable publication? We need you, and I think you will find that you need *The New Criterion*. Today there is no criticism and commentary on the contemporary cultural scene more informative, more provocative, more independent, or more readable than what we regularly publish in our pages.

Sincerely,

Hilton Kramer

■ The Independent Commission, Recommendations on the Issue of Obscenity and Other Content Restrictions, from a report to Congress on the National Endowment for the Arts, September 11, 1990

This report offered the final opinions of the Independent Commission, a body created by Congress to study the NEA's grant-giving procedures.

---

1) *The Independent Commission affirms that freedom of expression is essential to the arts.*

As the Commission has earlier noted, public funding requires accountability and sensitivity. But the Commission also urges all to remember that the clash of ideas and visions is a vigorous and sometimes difficult process, in which all participants — artists, commentators and citizens — have the right to express their views fully and freely and should respect the views of others.

2) *The Independent Commission recognizes that obscenity is not protected speech and that the National Endowment for the Arts is prohibited from funding the production of works which are obscene or otherwise illegal.*

The current definition of obscenity was set forth by the United States Supreme Court in *Miller v. California*, 413 U.S. 15 (1973). The Court, citing previous decisions, reaffirmed in that case that obscenity is not a form of speech protected by the First Amendment.[1]

The Commission also notes that the issue of standards for public funding of the arts raises constitutional considerations beyond that of obscenity.

Although public debate and Congressional action have focused on "obscenity," the term is ambiguous. In a narrow, legalistic sense, "obscenity" involves the exacting standards of proof prescribed most recently by the United States

Supreme Court in *Miller v. California*. So far as we know, no NEA grant has ever been judicially found to be "obscene" in this sense.

The other meaning of the term, in common parlance, involves grossly "offensive" matter, usually of a sexual nature, to which different persons and groups react and describe as "obscene." Even without the specific proscription on "obscenity" which was directed at the Endowment in the appropriations legislation, the Endowment could not lawfully fund art which was "obscene" in the technical sense. Existing state and federal law criminalizes such obscene matter. We stress this point in order to make clear that although the re-enactment of a ban on obscenity in the Endowment's authorization statute may serve the legitimate objective of emphasis, such a ban has no talismanic capacity to encapsulate and eliminate the problems that are actually involved in the present controversy. These involved difficult questions of First Amendment law.

The Commission, therefore, convened a Legal Task Force of distinguished constitutional lawyers and sought their advice on this matter.[2] The Commission asked the Legal Task Force both to testify and to draft a statement of principles that would address the legal and constitutional issues involved in the support of art by the federal government, particularly those issues raised by the question of "standards for grant-making other than 'substantial artistic and cultural significance...'" The Legal Task Force endorsed the following statement:

LEGAL TASK FORCE CONSENSUS STATEMENT

1. *There is no constitutional obligation on the part of the federal government to fund the arts. That is a policy decision to be determined by Congress based upon its views as to whether it is useful and wise for the federal government to play a role in the arts funding process. The Constitution offers no guidance as to whether the arts should be funded by the federal government.*

2. *If federal funds are used to subsidize the arts, however, constitutional limitations on how the arts are funded may come into play. The most important of these is that while Congress has broad powers as to how to spend public funds, it may not do so in a way that the Supreme Court has said is "aimed at the suppression of dangerous ideas." Congress plainly may, for example, determine to spend all federal funds designated for the arts on music and none on the visual arts. Or vice versa. It may expend funds to celebrate American history or American diversity, even though spending for one purpose naturally means less money is expended on others. And, of course, it may insist on artistic excellence as a prerequisite for any funding. What it may not do, however, is to choose those to be funded — and, often more important, those not to be funded — in a manner which punishes what Congress views as "dangerous content." When funding denials are the product of invidious discrimination with the aim of suppressing a particular message and for no other reason, a particularly powerful case might be made that the decision was unconstitutional.*

3. *Obscenity is not protected speech under the First Amendment and Congress is under no obligation to fund obscene speech. In fact, under both state and federal laws, obscenity is a crime. The definition of what is and is not obscene*

was set forth by the Supreme Court in the 1973 case of Miller v. California, *which concluded that:*

> [W]e now confine the permissible scope of [obscenity] regulation to works which depict or describe sexual conduct. That conduct must be specifically defined by the applicable state law, as written or authoritatively construed....
>
> The basic guidelines for the trier of fact must be: (a) whether 'the average person, applying contemporary community standards' would find that the work, taken as a whole, appeals to the prurient interest; (b) whether the work depicts or describes, in a patently offensive way, sexual conduct specifically defined by the applicable state law; and (c) whether the work, taken as a whole, lacks serious literary, artistic, political, or scientific value...

4. *Unless a work fits within each of the prongs of the definition stated above, it is not obscene under the* Miller *standard. For example, any work which, "taken as a whole," has "serious... value" cannot be obscene under* Miller, *whatever its sexual content.*

5. *The NEA currently requires all grant recipients to certify, under oath, that they will adhere to and enforce a ban on any use of NEA funds for purposes which the NEA "may consider" to be obscene. Some of the legal advisors to the Independent Commission believe this requirement is unconstitutional; all believe the insistence on such a requirement is unwise and all recommend against it.*

In their appearance before the Commission, members of the Legal Task Force voiced differing views on a number of points raised by Commissioners and in their own comments on each other's testimony.

3) *The Independent Commission believes that the National Endowment for the Arts is an inappropriate tribunal for the legal determination of obscenity, for purposes of either civil or criminal liability.*

The Commission believes it inadvisable for the Endowment to attempt to make determinations of what constitutes legal obscenity. The nature and structure of the Endowment are not such that it can make the necessary due process findings of fact and conclusions of law involved in these determinations. The Endowment must, of course, make grants that comply with federal and state law but the appropriate forum for the formal determination of obscenity is the courts.

4) *The Independent Commission recommends that the National Endowment for the Arts rescind its current requirement that grantees certify that the works of art they propose to produce will not be obscene.*

The statement of policy and guidance issued by the National Endowment for the Arts for the implementation of Section 304 of the Department of the

263

Interior and Related Agencies Appropriations Act of 1990 (effective July 5, 1990) declared that:

> grant recipients, in order to receive funds, must agree that they will not use those grant funds to promote, disseminate or produce materials that are "obscene" under the well-settled legal definition employed by the Supreme Court in Miller v. California.

This requirement is presently under court challenge.

As Professor McConnell observed in testimony submitted to the Commission:

> *As a matter of law, it is unnecessary to call attention to any particular restriction, since grant recipients are already bound by all restrictions applicable to the program. Self-certification will be perceived, rightly or wrongly, as implicating the artist in what many artists believe to be improper restrictions on artistic freedom. There may be a public interest in governing their use of public funds, but there is no public interest in forcing them to sign their names to it. It is a recipe for resistance and conflict.*

Recognizing that the constitutional and other legal issues involved in the certification requirement will be decided by the courts, the Commission believes that as a matter of public policy, the requirement should be rescinded.

5) *The Independent Commission recommends against legislative changes to impose specific restrictions on the content of works of art supported by the Endowment. Content restrictions may raise serious constitutional issues, would be inherently ambiguous and would almost certainly involve the Endowment and the Department of Justice in costly and unproductive lawsuits.*

Although there was disagreement among the Legal Task Force members about the constitutionality of certain proposed restrictions, all agreed that specific legislative restrictions were unwise and should be avoided. As Professor McConnell said

> *...[A]dditional criteria for selection, if any, should be incorporated as part of the selection process (perhaps as part of a definition of 'artistic excellence'), rather than isolated and treated as exogenous considerations.... Whenever a process is set up so that controversial judgments are superimposed on a system, those judgments are legally and popularly vulnerable .... While a work of meager artistic quality should be disallowed because of inappropriateness for public funding, a work of great importance might warrant funding despite the same qualities of inappropriateness. It is better to treat all these factors as aspects of the ultimate aesthetic judgment [by the NEA] rather than to make the additional factors, whatever they may be, absolute prohibitions.*

Mr. Olson warned that

> *separating quality and offensiveness into separate categories may invite litigation and may inaccurately imply viewpoint discrimination where there has been none.... [E]xplicit definitions of 'offensiveness' and 'obscenity'... may be open targets for claims of viewpoint discrimination.*

The NEA Chairperson obviously has discretion to reject grant applications for reasons other than obscenity. As Mr. Abrams stated

Constitutionally, the Chairman has great powers, and may be given great powers if he doesn't have them already, to make anything that may reasonably be called an aesthetic judgment. And if he is genuinely making an aesthetic judgment that he believes this just isn't art, or that it is so vulgar that [it] cannot be described as excellent art, I don't think he has to fund it.

Indeed, the Chairperson of the Endowment has not only the discretion to reject grants for reasons other than obscenity but the obligation, when, for example, he judges projects to be of mediocre quality, to do so. Congress has, after all, enjoined the Endowment to foster excellence in the arts. The Chairperson must constantly make judgments about the nature and content of projects. Yet if the standards for making these decisions are codified as explicit content restrictions, it seems clear that the result will be not more elevated art but debilitating administrative and legal difficulties.

In recommending against specific content restrictions, the Commission by no means endorses all of the Endowment's operations. On the contrary, the Commission's recommendations are based on a judgment that the Endowment is not, in setting policy and making grants, adequately meeting its public responsibilities at the present time. We have thus called for basic structural and procedural reform of the Endowment at every level.

We have asked Congress to reaffirm, in its "Declaration of Purpose," that the Endowment serves all of the people rather than artists and arts institutions alone, that it must be aware of the nature of public sponsorship and that it reflects the high place the nation accords to the fostering of mutual respect for the disparate beliefs and values among us.

The Commission believes that if these recommendations are adopted, the intent of Congress for the future operations of the Endowment will be clear and should effectively govern the Endowment's decisions. We believe this comprehensive approach preferable to specific content restrictions. The practical obstacles to such restrictions are, as we have explained, great and the constitutional questions troublesome.

Maintaining the principle of an open society requires all of us, at times, to put up with much we do not like but the bargain has proved in the long run a good one.

---

1. If Congress chooses to reenact a specific prohibition against the use of Endowment funds for the production of obscene works, Congress will no doubt wish to use the definition of obscenity in *Miller* rather than a paraphrase.

2. The Legal Task Force, a group of six constitutional lawyers, were chosen for their expertise as well as the diversity of their philosophical views, ranging across the spectrum from conservative to liberal. The members of the Legal Task Force were: Floyd Abrams of Cahill, Gordon & Reindel; Professor Michael McConnell of the University of Chicago Law School; Professor Henry Monaghan of the Columbia University Law School; Theodore Olson of Gibson, Dunn & Crutcher; Dean Geoffrey Stone of the University of Chicago Law School; and Professor Kathleen Sullivan of the Harvard University Law School.

Debate in the House of Representatives, statements by Hons. Pat Williams, Bob Carr, Peter Kostmayer, and Robert Dornan, October 11, 1990 (excerpts)

Pat Williams is a Democratic member of the House of Representatives, representing the state of Montana. Bob Carr is a Democratic member of the House of Representatives, representing the state of Michigan. Peter Kostmayer is a Democratic member of the House of Representatives, representing the state of Pennsylvania. Robert Dornan is a Republican member of the House of Representatives, representing the state of California.

M R. WILLIAMS: Mr. Chairman, we Americans have a pluralistic society. We place great value on the variety of our origins, the hues of many colors, our cultures, our politics. Our differences of those things are very important to us. We understand that America's pluralism is our bulwark against tyranny.

The arts embody our differences, our individual viewpoints, our varied aspirations as a people. The arts and artists explore the many layers of our society.

Almost exactly 25 years ago the Congress, on behalf of the American people, found and declared that while no government can call great art into existence, it is necessary and appropriate for the Federal Government to help create and sustain not only a climate encouraging freedom of thought, imagination and inquiry, but also the material conditions facilitating release of creative talent. And so the National Endowment for the Arts was created.

A small and lovely revolution has resulted. Prior to the revolution America had 58 symphony orchestras, we now have close to 300. Prior to this small and lovely revolution, America was graced with 27 opera companies. We now have more than 150. There were, prior to this small revolution, 22 non-profit regional theaters in America. It is now approaching 500. And with regard to dance companies, we have gone from 37 to now close to 300. There were, back in the 1960's prior to the creation of the National Endowment for the Arts, only 5 State arts councils, and now 56 States and territories have State arts councils. There were only 55 local art agencies in America, and now this small and lovely revolution has caused more than 3,000 local art agencies.

Equally and perhaps more important is the encouragement that has been given to new artists, young, vital, unknown artists, who are exploring, alive and perhaps dangerous; perhaps dangerous. This little agency has so encouraged access to the arts, so enlarged cultural opportunities throughout this land, that it has, in fact, changed the way Americans think about the arts.

The artist Garrison Keillor from that little mythical town called Lake Woebegone has said:

Today no American family can be secure against the danger that one of its children may, indeed, decide to become an artist.

America likes art and artists as never before in its history. Cultural opportunities for all of our citizens have been enlarged. Art is accessible no longer to the wealthy and the few who live in the great large cities on both coasts, but now all Americans in the great large cities and in the great small towns have increased access to the arts, and we are all better off for it and for the small and lovely revolution created by the National Endowment for the Arts.

Mr. Chairman, I reserve the balance of my time.

Mr. CARR. Mr. Chairman, I thank the gentleman for yielding me this time.

Mr. Chairman, this is an important debate. A lot of people think that it has been trivialized, and I agree with them.

Our country stands for liberty and freedom. You know, I think it is very fitting that the symbol of liberty and freedom in this country sits in New York Harbor. It is a sculpture. It is a statue, the Statue of Liberty. Freedom and liberty are the core value of our society. Inherent in freedom and liberty is the notion that we are going to take some risks. We are going to take some risks that some are going to exercise their freedom and liberty in ways that we might regard as irresponsible. We take a risk that someone is going to exercise freedom and liberty and expression in ways that we certainly would not want and we would not do ourselves, but there are some people in our society, and some of them are represented here in the Congress, who do not want too much liberty and too much freedom. The thought police of America are represented in this Congress. The thought police are represented here and are trying to restrict artistic expression in America today.

As Maya Angelou, the outstanding artist, writer, and woman of letters stated: "Art poses the question of conscience and morality. It does not answer it."

Mapplethorpe may have posed questions. He did not answer them.

Serrano may have posed questions. He did not answer them.

The American public opinion will answer them and the American public opinion is strong enough, free enough, with liberty to make its own decisions about works of art.

The NEA cannot control creativity. It can only foster it....

All governments have given medals to artists when they are old, saintly, and almost dead. But 25 years ago the Congress boldly decided to boldly support the arts, support the art of creation, itself, to encourage the artists who are young, vital, and unknown, very much alive and probably, therefore, very dangerous. This courageous legislation has changed American life and ought to continue.

MR. KOSTMAYER: Mr. Chairman, what we are talking about and what we are seeing in the House today is very simple: this is book burning in America in 1990. This is what this is all about, and this amendment is brought to you by the book burners in the country and in the Congress.

The Congress cannot set standards for someone who is going to paint or dance or write or sing or compose. These are acts which are creative and occur independently of any rules we may write. We cannot set out preconditions for artists.

The NEA has made about 85,000 grants in its history. About 20 of them have been controversial. Only about 20. Our country, unhappily, has a dark side to it sometimes, a mean side. This amendment appeals to the darkest and the very meanest side of America. It appeals to ignorance and to bigotry and to fear and to prejudice. That is what this amendment is all about. It is brought to you by the very people who want to deregulate everything that ought to be regulated, and want to regulate everything that ought to be deregulated.

It is not the art that is offensive, it is the amendment that is deeply offensive. This country finds itself in the grip of an economic crisis. A fourth of the students who graduate from high school cannot read. Thousands of people sleep on our streets each night. And what are we talking about? Dirty pictures.

I think this amendment demeans my country. Let us reject it for the mean spirited and narrow effort that it is.

MR. DORNAN: The problem is not the peer review process, as some of my colleagues claim, or some other institutional flaw within the system. It is the attitude of the NEA and the arts community in general to those few times the process results in an Andres Serrano or Robert Mapplethorpe. If the NEA had said of Serrano and Mapplethorpe, "Oops. Sorry. We made a mistake. It won't happen again," and if the arts community had said, "Serrano's blasphemy against the crucified Christ and Mapplethorpe's homoerotic photographs and child pornography are garbage which should never have been funded," then I am sure we would not be going through this exercise.

But the arts community, instead of decrying the Serrano and Mapplethorpe outrages, turned both of them into heroes, martyrs of the first amendment. Quite frankly, if that is the attitude of the arts community then I don't think they deserve a dime of the taxpayers' money. Serrano's loathsome picture of Christ was both blasphemous and bigoted. The controversial Mapplethorpe photographs were clearly pornographic, as in child pornography. For the arts community to claim otherwise just illustrates how cut off they are from traditional American values. But the arts community did more than defend this so-called art, they demanded that the taxpayer continue to fork over money to pay for it — with no strings attached. Talk about arrogance....

It is clear, Mr. Chairman, that America is engaged in a kulturkampf, or culture war. From flag burning to abortion to capital punishment to public funding for the arts, America is struggling to define its moral and ethical foundations. On one side are the moral relativists, whose philosophy can be summed up with the credo "If it feels good do it." It is a philosophy based on nothing more substantial than whim and fancy. On the other side are those who find their moral direction in the Judeo-Christian tradition.

The moral relativists have led this country to excuse — indeed sanction — drug abuse, sodomy, casual sex and its concomitant diseases, abortion-on-demand for any reason, and a host of other acts the traditional community has always deemed immoral. It is hard for me to see how our culture has progressed by tolerating such immoral, indeed barbarous, acts.

Regarding the dangers of moral relativism, Paul Johnson wrote in his masterwork Modern Times, "when legitimacy yields to force, and moral absolutes to relativism, a great darkness descends and angels become indistinguishable from devils." That is exactly what has happened in this debate, Mr. Chairman. Those of us defending the values which form the moral foundations of our way of life and which gave rise to the democratic institutions we do cherish, are accused of being censors and fascists. Those moral relativists who have produced bigoted, blasphemous, and pornographic art are portrayed as persecuted champions of freedom....

Mr. Chairman, this Member has had it. In fact, I've had a belly full of the whining of the arts community, particularly by those people who earn several million dollars to act in a single motion picture. It is time to strike a blow for traditional values and economic responsibility. It is time for average Americans to take their country back from the amoral elites — in the universities, in the dominant media culture, in certain sectors of the arts community, and elsewhere — who have nothing but contempt for them and their way of life. It is time to put the NEA out of business. Heaven knows we could use the money elsewhere.

Let me sum up my view of the NEA, Mr. Chairman, by quoting that famous *New Yorker* cartoon of 1928. "I say its spinach, and I say the hell with it."

■ Elizabeth Hess, Art on Trial: Cincinnati's Dangerous Theater of the Ridiculous, *Village Voice,* October 23, 1990

Elizabeth Hess is an art critic for The Village Voice.

It's Friday afternoon, day 10 of the Mapplethorpe trial, and the jury has been out for just two hours. The optimists — and there only are a few — are hoping at best for a hung jury. So when word passes from reporter to reporter that the verdict is in, everyone rushes the courtroom, prepared for the worst. All the actors take their places, and the curtain goes up for the last time.

"Not guilty."

When these two little words roll off the clerk's tongue four times, on all four counts, Dennis Barrie's team shouts, applauds, hugs and finally allows some tears to flow. Two elated supporters jump up to embrace, but Judge Albanese, apparently furious in defeat, throws them out of his court.

Judge David J. Albanese has done everything in his power to convict the Contemporary Art Center and its director, Dennis Barrie. His honor has allowed the prosecution to turn his court into a house of "smut"; the courtroom drama over which he presided would ordinarily be illegal within city limits. There aren't any adult book stores, X-rated video stores, or newsstands with skin magazines (in theory) in Cincinnati. But there's a court of law here where... anything goes.

The Case

Fear has been the driving force in River City's artistic community ever since April 7, 1990, when Barrie and the CAC were each charged with two misdemeanor counts; pandering obscenity and the use of minors in nudity-oriented materials. The indictment cites seven works from "Robert Mapplethorpe: The

Perfect Moment" (the retrospective that was first censored by the Corcoran Gallery of Art in Washington, D.C.); five sadomasochistic photographs and two portraits of nude, or partially nude, children.

In a ruling on September 6, Albanese ruled that each of the five (sadomasochistic) photos would be treated as a "whole" and tried separately, out of context of the rest of the show, against the Supreme Court *Miller v. California* decision defining obscenity. During the trial, Albanese did not allow any testimony concerning the 168 other works in the exhibition.

To get a conviction in Ohio on the portraits of the minors, the prosecution must demonstrate "lewd exhibition" or "graphic focus on the genitals." To get a conviction in Ohio or anywhere else on the five sadomasochistic photographs, the jury must apply all three prongs of *Miller*: that the average person, using contemporary community standards, would find that the work, taken as a whole, appeals to "prurient interests"; that the work must be "patently offensive" as defined by state laws; and, most crucial in this case, that the work lacks "serious artistic value."

Jury Selection

The attorneys on both sides begin by apologizing to the 50 potential jurors for the questions they are about to ask. Each side has six peremptory challenges, which means they can remove six potential jurors without explanation. If the judge agrees, however, an unlimited number of jurors can be removed for bias. It's a game of chess; the attorneys try to get the judge to kick off potential candidates so they can save up their peremptory challenges. The case, ultimately, will be tried during this procedure, which is called *voir dire*.

In a metaphor that will stick throughout the trial, H. Louis Sirkin, the attorney representing Barrie, compares the Supreme Court *Miller* ruling to an apple pie. Pouring on the down-home charm, he says, "If I tell you that my apple pie has to have three ingredients in it, or it isn't an apple pie. And you only taste two ingredients in it — then it's not an apple pie. Right?" The jurors all nod and smile. From the beginning Sirkin has them eating out of his hand.

Frank Prouty, the prosecutor, a short, balding man who wears his suits on the tight side, is a stark contrast to Sirkin and Marc D. Mezibov, who represents the CAC. Prouty feeds them a restricted diet of one-liners: "You don't need an expert to tell you what art is, do you?" "You know obscenity when you see it, don't you?" They always agree. They agree with everything.

Dennis Barrie watches the whole show with amazing calm. He's either an extremely reserved person, or his lawyers have told him to remain deadpan at all times. The truth lies somewhere in the middle. His wife, Diane Barrie, is more responsive, yet she shuns the press outside of the courtroom. She looks miserable.

Mezibov has put a pretty face on the CAC, which is represented in court by Amy Bannister, the prim director of development. Bannister wears a conservative suit and high-collared blouse each day. She looks like the type who would rather die than go to a peep show, let alone hang one in her own gallery.

270

As voir dire begins, the chosen citizens of Hamilton County are raked over the coals about their art habits. Most of these jurors have never been in a contemporary art gallery and have not been in a museum since high school; they do not read newspapers regularly or watch much TV. (I wonder what they *do* do.) One juror has not been to a movie in 10 years. "Why should I spend $3.75 when the movie will be on cable?" he says.

Whenever anyone admits to having gone to a museum, Prouty asks "Why did you go?" Or, "Did you go voluntarily?" Meanwhile, the defense is also pushing telling questions: "Do you think art can be educational?" "Should museums get public funding?" "Can education be provocative?"

When a prospective juror tells the court his son drew portraits based on photographs published in *National Geographic*, the prosecutor asks, "Did he ever paint any nudes, or anything like that?" No way. When one of the defense attorneys asks him whether or not he would pay money to see an exhibition by a homosexual artist, he says, "No. But I know there are plenty [of homosexuals] around and I've probably shaken hands with some." The defense knocks him off.

A young black woman takes the hot seat. She's so shy we can barely hear her voice. Early in the interview, Prouty asks if she's ever seen a rap concert? Nope. Has she ever heard of 2 Live Crew? Nope. She looks like she's never heard of rock and roll, but Mezibov wants to find out what she really thinks. "Are you a member of a church?" he asks.

"Yes."

"Does your church have a position in regard to homosexuality?"

"We don't support it. But we are not against homosexuals."

"Are you personally offended by homosexuals?"

"Yes."

"If you were on this jury and you had to make a decision with regard to a homosexual, would you obey God's law, or man's law?"

"God's law."

This woman is not a minority in this courtroom. When another potential juror is asked by Sirkin if homosexuality should be off-limits, she says a definitive, "Yes." Sirkin continues, "Should the state pass laws against homosexuality?"

"Yes."

"Have you ever heard of AIDS?"

"Yes."

"Is AIDS an appropriate topic for a museum show?" The potential juror looks confused. But, before she can say anything, the judge jumps in: "I don't see how you can get AIDS in an art museum." Sirkin clears up the confusion as best he can.

Protest

Outside the courtroom, roughly 150 people have come to show their support for Dennis Barrie. The group comprises contingents from the city's Gay and Lesbian March Activists, ACT UP, and members of Voices Against Censorship, a collection of Cincinnati activists. ACT UP members want to get arrested, but the dozens of deputies hanging around don't wish to get too close, despite the fact that they're wearing rubber gloves.

The rally ends in the streets, with two men having mock sex, banging against each other and kissing. After spending all day in a courtroom where the word *homosexual* sounds like *insect* and the words *gay* and *lesbian* have not been uttered by either side, seeing this street theater is startlingly refreshing. The performers have succeeded in turning sex into a spectacle that literally stops traffic.

Police officers video the demonstrators and issue 35 warrants with the names Jane and John Doe attached to most of the photo identifications.

More Voir Dire

"Pornography and obscenity are not synonymous," says Sirkin. "Only obscenity is against the law." But what is obscenity? "Well," says Sirkin, "every time the Dodgers win a game — that's obscene." Everybody laughs and relaxes a little. For a second, the courtroom feels like a living room. Then we are brought back to the business at hand. "Robert Mapplethorpe's lifestyle isn't on trial here," says the defense attorney. "Dennis Barrie's conduct is."

Jury selection is moving along, and both sides are building their cases, giving the jurors ground to stand on as they prepare to consider the evidence. "Robert Mapplethorpe was exploring a lifestyle that no longer exists from the late '70s," says Sirkin, "for better or worse." Sadomasochism, we are led to believe, is a form of sex between consenting homosexuals that has become obsolete. It's as if Mapplethorpe's s&m pictures were created exclusively as education tools to combat AIDS.

AIDS is the silent witness throughout this trial.

A switchboard receptionist in a law firm, maybe thirtysomething and overweight, steps into the spotlight. She tells us that she does not visit museums "by choice." However, she has followed this controversy in the papers and seen the seven photos, partially blacked out, on CNN. The woman is nervous; she covers her face for a few seconds to regain control and says, apologetically, "I'm not sure I can look at these pictures [without sections blacked out]." The jurors must, obviously, be able to look at, if not study, these pictures. In fact, it's only a matter of time before either the prosecution or the defense introduces them in court. (The press can't wait to see the reaction.)

Prouty: "Do you understand that there is nothing wrong with being repulsed by these pictures?"

"Objection!" Both defense attorneys pop up together like pieces of toast.

"I guess I could try to look at them," says the woman, mustering up all the courage she seems to have.

Mezibov takes over the interrogation. By this time, the woman looks miserable, like she's going to burst into tears. "I'm uncomfortable. I don't know if I can be fair," she says. She's having trouble speaking.

Mezibov turns to the judge to say only what is obvious: "Your honor, she has expressed a clear belief that this is not the case for her." He asks the judge to respect her request. Nooooo way. Albanese doesn't want to let her go. "You didn't ask for this job," he says to his fragile captive, "and we don't expect you to know all the answers. But, do you think you can sit on this jury and deliberate and discuss with an open mind?"

"Yes," she answers, to everyone's amazement, pulling herself together to give the judge the answer he wants.

Mezibov continues, "Can you imagine any legitimate reason for anyone to see or display these pictures?"

"Not really," she says, frankly.

"Do you believe homosexuality violates God's law?"

"Yes."

"Knowing that Mapplethorpe was a homosexual, can you still be fair to him?" asks Mezibov?

"... Yes," she whimpers.

Visions of a mistrial dance through the air. The press is almost ready to start a defense fund for this woman if she's forced to be a juror.

When she finally says, "I really feel I should disqualify myself," Prouty jumps in without missing a beat. "Are you saying you can't keep an open mind?" he asks.

"I feel unsure," she says.

"Many people are unsure of themselves," says the judge, who seems determined to get this bundle of Jell-O on the jury. "The question is, can you be a fair and proper juror?"

"I don't think so," she says, as if it is a crime.

"I'm not trying to rake you over the coals," says Albanese. "The fact is that I just want to see if we're on the same wavelength. Do you feel," he asks *again*, "that you can give the defendant a fair trial?"

"No. I want to be fair," she tells him, finally figuring out that she must just say no.

The judge dismisses her.

Waves are rippling through the jury pool. The process is about as appealing as rancid meat.

Pinocchio

When Carol Murphy takes the voir dire seat, the theater really begins. Murphy works in a church and hasn't been to a museum since she was a child. She admits she looked at copies of *Playboy* and *Hustler* "once" 15 years ago "to make a judgment" about them.

It turns out that Jerry Kirk, director of the National Council Against Pornography, was Murphy's pastor and mentor. (Kirk is one of the "spiritual" forces behind Citizens for Community Values, the right-wing organization that has lobbied the citizens of Cincinnati to stop this show.) According to Sirkin, the National Council Against Pornography has been training jurors for obscenity trials.

Murphy is clear about her belief that adults should not be able to see sexually explicit materials. Has she seen any of the pictures involved in this case?

273

"One of my coworkers brought in a xerox of the man urinating in another man's mouth." Murphy describes the photograph with a little too much ease. It's as if she's been rehearsed.

When Mezibov asks her if she has formed an opinion about the photo, she says, "Yes." Nevertheless, the attorney cannot get the judge to dismiss her.

Under further questioning. Murphy reluctantly reveals that she met with Kirk last month, when the controversy was in full swing and the reverend was an outspoken player. She also attended a conference against pornography in Cincinnati during which Mapplethorpe was discussed.

Everybody smells a rat. Murphy is getting excited. It's not only painfully obvious that she has strong feelings about the material, which she characterizes as "not morally decent," but she has close ties to the folks who fueled this controversy. She's one of *them*, and she's determined to get on this jury.

The odd thing is, as Murphy continues to make the absurd argument that she's capable of objectivity, she begins to break out in a rash. It seems like every time she reiterates that she can give Barrie a fair trial, another crimson blotch appears on her neck. Pinocchio!

When Sirkin finds out that Murphy is on the mailing list of the CCV, the organization that has campaigned against Barrie and put pressure on local businesses to stop the show, she says, "But I'm not a member. Just a supporter."

Taking a different approach, Sirkin asks, "Why do you want to be on this jury so badly?" Murphy, her neck a summer sunset, fires back, "I don't have a burning desire to sit on this case, but I want justice served!" She catches herself and stops short of giving a speech.

The judge refuses to dismiss her for bias, so the defense has to do his work for him.

Finally, a man who actually subscribed to *Playboy* takes the stand. (There's one in every crowd.) The prosecution dismisses him quickly.

On the Waterfront

The days are long in Cincinnati, and the nights are even longer. Val Beck-Sena, a social worker who has been helping the CAC staff "get through this ordeal," invites a bunch of reporters out to dinner. "I want you all to enjoy Cincinnati," she says. She is one of many residents who is embarrassed about the fact that this trial is happening here. An attractive woman by any standards, Beck-Sena bops around in her husband's red Porsche. She invites us to the latest waterfront restaurant, partly owned by Pete Rose.

Even the cabdriver (who, incidentally, thinks that "Robert Mapplethorpe is innocent") is impressed by our classy destination. I arrive accompanied by Joy Silverman of the National Campaign for Freedom of Expression, who has come from L.A. Silverman and I sit down at the bar to have a drink. When we look up at the waitress, both of us are stunned: she's wearing a bathing suit, the kind with the large arches cut out over the thighs to the waistline, and a tight T-shirt. To us, she might as well have been naked. But, then again, this isn't Cincinnati. We're over the Ohio river, 10 minutes from the courthouse, in Kentucky.

"How can you let yourself be exploited that way," says Silverman, not adverse to exerting a little moral pressure herself. "Tell your boss you won't wear that outfit. This is 1990, you don't..." The waitress interrupts her. "Listen, honey, if you had my body you'd wear this outfit too."

After an excellent dinner of grilled fish, we go upstairs to the ladies room. Inside this chamber is a fully stocked bar and a small dance floor; a Chippendales-style male dancer serves the drinks and keeps the ladies happy. Unfortunately, he's on a break.

The Pictures

Jury selection takes four days. Eventually four women and four men are enpaneled. They look proud, like they've just won the lottery together. One young woman, engaged to be married, works in an athletic-clothing store; she has said that she believes homosexuality should be illegal. Another woman, who is separated from her husband (a musician in a country-western band), is a secretary for a technical-supply company. Another woman is an X-ray technician (the prosecution asked her if she'd ever X-rayed a child in the nude). The only black juror works at Procter & Gamble; she had the occasion to flip through the Mapplethorpe catalogue at work. When asked by the prosecution what she thought of the sexual photos, she said she "was more interested in the flowers."

Among the men, there's an electrical engineer, a data processor, a warehouse manager, and telephone-repair worker. One is a Purdue man (the only college graduate on the jury) who once took an art-appreciation course, primarily because he thought he could "get a good grade." The warehouse manager wears all black one day and brings a Stephen King novel to read.

The first witness for the prosecution takes the stand. Officer Don Ruberg is on the vice squad. He's one of the cops who was invited by the CAC to visit the gallery five days before the show opened. (When Hamilton County sheriff Simon Leis publicly called the show "criminally obscene," Barrie, in an attempt to get him to put up or shut up, invited the vice squad to preview the show.) Ruberg returned on April 7 with a search warrant to videotape the entire exhibition for evidence. (But the jurors are not allowed to see this tape because Albanese has ruled that the other photographs will poison them.)

Prouty introduces each photograph into state's evidence as Ruberg limns its content. Number one is the portrait of "a minor, a boy with his genitals showing"; number two is a portrait of "another juvenile wearing a dress which is lifted so that her genitals are visible"; number three is a photograph of "a man urinating into the mouth of another man"; number four shows "a man shoving his arm and fist up another man's rectum."

Ruberg is not enjoying this process. He takes a deep breath and continues to describe the pictures as if they are rudimentary traffic accidents. Number five "is a man [actually a self-portrait of Mapplethorpe] with a bullwhip inserted in his rectal area"; number six "is a man with a cylindrical object inserted in his rectal area"; number seven is "a man with a finger inserted into the head of his penis."

This list will soon be as familiar to jurors as the backs of their hands.

275

The prosecutor returns to exhibit number four and asks Ruberg to describe it again. "It's a picture of a fist and forearm inserted into the anal area," says the embarrassed officer.

"Have you ever heard of fisting?" asked Prouty.

"Yes."

"What is fisting?"

Sirkin objects. "Unless this witness is qualified as an expert I don't possibly see how he can answer the question." Everybody laughs, with the exception of Ruberg, who shifts uncomfortably in the witness chair.

Unfortunately for him, the judge instructs Ruberg to answer the question. "It's a form of sex where one man rams a fist up the anus of another man."

Prouty wants to know more. He wants to know why people do this weird thing. "For sexual gratification," says Ruberg, matter-of-factly.

Prouty puts two more vice on the stand and then, to everyone's astonishment, he rests his case. It's as if he's finished before he's even started. His strategy seems to be an antistrategy. There simply is no case.

The defense moves for an immediate acquittal. Mezibov argues forcefully that the "state has failed to demonstrate that the work does not have artistic value." The state has also not bothered to present any definition of "what constitutes community values." As far as the children's portraits are concerned, the state has not shown "lewd exhibition or graphic focus on the genitals." Mezibov wants to know "why the city is prosecuting this case?"

The judge takes off his glasses, rubs his eyes, and turns to Prouty for help.

"Materials, um, court, as far as the statute goes..." Prouty's having trouble getting a sentence out of his mouth. "There's no need to demonstrate community values," he says. "The bottom line is — the pictures."

After a long, embarrassing moment, the judge overrules the defense motion: "This court will not substitute its judgment for the jury's in determining the facts." Judge Albanese seems determined to give the Court of Appeals some work.

A Question of Stature

The New York Times publishes a profile of Judge David Albanese. It is truthful, not flattering. Isabel Wilkerson traces Albanese's relationship with Sheriff Leis, whom she has previously described as "Oliver North with a badge." It is common knowledge in Cincinnati that Leis orchestrated this censorious disaster. Wilkerson points out that the two men went to high school together and still "work out together at the Cincinnati Athletic Club."

Wilkerson also notes that when Albanese first ran for the bench in 1981, he was given the lowest possible rating, "Not Recommended," from the Cincinnati Bar Association. And, rubbing salt into the wound, she described the judge as a "short, thin, unimposing man."

The judge is gunning for the *Times* reporter. Members of the press are asked to sign in as we enter the courtroom — name, affiliation, and city. Tony Upton, the unctuous court assistant in charge of the press, has been given the assignment of finding Wilkerson. But he's having trouble. We are all Isabel Wilkerson.

A couple of days later we're waiting in court for the show to begin, but there's an inexplicable delay. Finally, word is passed to the press that Wilkerson has been summoned to the judge's chambers. A group of reporters marches out of court to the judge's door.

I knock and tell the bailiff, "If there's a press conference in the judge's chambers, we would all like to attend." The bailiff is confused. Wilkerson is not around. She's already out, but Upton has witnessed the private interview.

"The judge invited Isabel into his chambers to show her that he's human," says Upton. "She called him 'thin and short' in her article. Well, the judge put a pile of law books on the floor behind his desk and stood on them when she walked in." Upton finds this hilarious. So do I.

The Defense

Janet Kardon, who organized the Mapplethorpe show when she was the director at the Institute of Contemporary Art in Philadelphia, is the defense's first witness. It is important for the jury to see that an older, respectable woman put together this exhibition. The defense brings her to Cincinnati under a subpoena. Sirkin says it "was for her own protection so she couldn't get arrested." Was an arrest likely? "Well, no," he says. "But this is Cincinnati."

Kardon explains to the jury what a museum is, what a director does, what a "retrospective" means. She comes off as extremely knowledgeable, somewhat arrogant, and nervous; she twists a handkerchief in her hands. Kardon is watching the clock, and the judge finally comments that he is aware that she has a plane to catch.

"When I heard that Mapplethorpe was ill I thought it was imperative to give him a retrospective," says Kardon. "He was one of the most important photographers working in the '80s in a formalist mode." The expert gives the court a crash course in formalism.

So, Prouty asks her to give a "formalist" analysis of each of the seven photographs. The director describes the artist's self-portrait with bullwhip as an "almost classical" composition; she describes the "opposing diagonals" in the urination photo and the "centrality" of the forearm in another piece (you know which one).

While looking at the image of a man with a finger up his penis (an exceptionally excruciating work for most men I know), Kardon stops and says, "Oh yes, Robert thought the hand gestures in this one were particularly beautiful."

"Did you ever consider whether homosexual values were appropriate for the [Philadelphia] community?" asks Prouty. "We never discussed that," says Kardon, making it clear that the question is beneath her dignity.

Next, Jacquelynn Baas, director of the University Art Museum at Berkeley, which housed the exhibition without incident, takes the stand.

"Does the show as a whole focus on sexual practice?" asks Prouty. Baas doesn't think so.

"Well, what is the intent of the five [s&m] pictures?"

"To make a work of art."

"Just to make a work of art!" says Prouty, expressing shock for the first time.

"Well, it's hard to make a work of art," says Baas.

The CAC

"We went through hell and fought a very lonely battle in Cincinnati," says Barrie. "I would have gladly had a few more swords and shields." Barrie reluctantly agrees to a short interview halfway through the trial. He's tired of speaking and, it seems, tired of the press. He doesn't want to talk about his adversaries or the folks he can no longer count on.

Like Chad P. Wick, who was pressured to resign as chairman of the board by his employer, Central Trust. Wick is still on the board, but one member dropped off altogether for fear of losing his job. Barrie doesn't want to talk about it. "The onslaught was greater than we expected," he says.

According to CAC's Amy Bannister, "there were people on the board who wanted to eliminate certain photos from the show," but Barrie didn't edit. "It would have created havoc," says Bannister, "although the business community would have cheered us on." Barrie decided to go on with the show — not that he had much choice. Which is worse? Getting lynched by right-wingers in Cincinnati, or getting lynched by members of the art world? Christina Orr-Cahall, former director of the Corcoran, had adequately demonstrated that the latter route was suicidal. Regardless, says Barrie, "We could not alter our contract with the ICA" to drop the controversial works.

Why did this show upset the right wing so much? Bannister looks at me as if I've asked a dumb question. But I want to know what she thinks; she's been with the CAC for 16 years. "People are afraid of AIDS, because you can't cure it," says Bannister, "but that's not the only problem with Mapplethorpe. [The work] incenses these old men — when they look and see all those beautiful bodies. Mapplethorpe empowered women and blacks. Look at [body builder and Mapplethorpe subject] Lisa Lyon! It's not just AIDS and homophobia that's the problem here — but the power of women and blacks. That's why I have to wear a suit and a shirt buttoned up to my neck every day in court. Look at these pearls," says Bannister pulling on a string around her neck as if it were noose.

Aliens

All sorts of people show up in court. One day two jurors who were bumped come back to see what they've been missing: a priest comes to watch a morning session, along with a man on crutches who describes himself as "an expert on sadomasochism." One day all three wives of the attorneys show up, as well as Page, Mezibov's 13-year-old daughter. "My eight-year-old wanted to come too," says Ann Mezibov, "but I thought he was too young."

One morning, Judge Albanese addresses the press: "Some of you are strangers in Municipal Court in Cincinnati, but this is my house. My bailiff and I had to clean up in this courtroom — cigarette butts, newspapers. Nobody should read newspapers in my courtroom. We're not here to enjoy ourselves." I'll say.

"I recognize that we are inundated with aliens," says Albanese, "but there will be no more press conferences in this courtroom."

A number of reporters have requested a larger courtroom because there aren't enough seats in Albanese's "house": the spillover sits in a nearby room and watches the events on a TV moniter.

Robert Sobieszek, then senior curator of the International Museum of Photography at the George Eastman House, gives a video deposition. He's particularly good, unruffled and articulate. The defense pushes the association between the Eastman museum and Kodak, its founder. If Baas represents innocence, Sobieszek represents the corporate man.

Sobieszek explains that "Mapplethorpe wanted to document what was beautiful and what was torturous — in his personal experience."

"Can art be pornographic?" asks Prouty.

"I don't believe so," says the director.

"Can it be obscene?"

"If something is truly obscene or pornographic," says Sobieszek, "then it's not art." He goes on to say that Mapplethorpe's desire to cope with his problems "is not unlike van Gogh painting himself with his ear cut off." This quote makes it to the nightly news.

The Brass Ass

As the trial proceeds, Phil Donahue does a show about the strip joints and go-go clubs in Newport, Kentucky, an area just over the river from Cincinnati; the mayor, a bunch of city officials, and a couple of strippers are all on the air. One night, one other intrepid reporter and I climb into a cab to find the Brass Ass.

The place looks like a set out of *Twin Peaks*. We each pay two bucks to Joe, the hefty proprietor, who looks at me and says, "Don't worry, there's two other women in there." But they're wearing black lace lingerie.

As we walk in, Eelise LaShay, who appeared on *Donahue*, is dancing on a runway, the kind that Miss Americas get to walk down. We think that LaShay is outfitted with what has been the focus of the controversy in the local press — transparent tape on her nipples. (Actually, it's hard to tell, but we know she has something pasted onto her.) LaShay grins out at us as she rubs her body against a pole. Eventually, she puts a sheet on the floor and lies down to do a horizontal performance. There are a dozen sleepy-looking people in the place.

We have a drink at the bar, and then leave. On the way out we ask Joe if it's always so dead. "No," he says, "when the Reds are playing the place is packed after the game." How come nobody has managed to close this place down? "The politicians need us. Every time there's a reelection, we give them something to talk about."

279

The Mothers

Two depositions from the mothers of the children in the photos are read by a young female attorney who sits in the stand. Both mothers were not only present during the shoots, but delighted with the outcomes; they express their dismay over the whole controversy and their personal affection for Mapplethorpe.

All Prouty can do in the cross is point out that both women are divorced, and that neither of the fathers were present when Mapplethorpe took the pictures.

Jerry Stein, the art critic for the *Cincinnati Post*, is a little rattled, but he seems really to want to speak about the work. He gave it a rave review in the paper and on the stand compares the two photos of children to "Renaissance putti." It's a nice idea and the jury is buying it, whether or not they are familiar with putti.

"Are you acquainted with formalism?" Prouty asks the critic. The prosecutor suddenly wants to discuss the light and lines in each picture. "Are the [little boy's] legs spread apart?" he asks.

"His appendages are balancing him," says Stein.

"Don't the lines [his legs make] move up toward the penis? Don't they point right toward the penis?" says Prouty, in a last-ditch effort to demonstrate, as the law requires, "graphic focus on the genitals."

"Objection," shouts Sirkin in disgust. "The only person who seems to have that opinion is Mr. Prouty." In an unusual moment, the judge sustains an objection from the defense.

Dennis Barrie is the last witness for the defense. But, by the time he takes the stand, what he has to say about Mapplethorpe has already been said.

Prouty is getting tired. He begins to asks Barrie whether or not he would allow his children to be photographed in the nude, but stops in the middle of his sentence. "I'll strike that," he says. Instead, predictable Prouty tries to get Barrie talking about the dirty pictures, but everyone's fed up with this tactic. Both defense attorneys rest their cases.

Captain Kangaroo Court

In a kamikaze effort to save his case, Prouty puts a rebuttal witness on the stand. The trial turns into a circus when Judith Reisman, a former songwriter for *Captain Kangaroo*, begins discussing the artistic merits of "Robert Mapplethorpe: The Perfect Moment."

Reisman argues that nude pictures of children on museum walls are part of a "standard codified technique" that "child abusers use to seduce vulnerable kids."

The perky, gray-haired woman then investigates the photographs in detail, using her hands to outline the configurations in each; she sculpts the air as if this is a performance, demonstrating, for instance, the placement and the angle of the forearm in the fisting opus. A CAC supporter later describes her testimony as "pornography for the hearing impaired."

"She's Dr. Ruth's evil twin," comments Nancy Bless, one of several artists regularly attending the trial. Reisman clearly loves to talk and give advice, but it is painfully obvious that she does not have the credentials to testify as an expert. Prouty spends 10 minutes going through her resumé, which is so long that the witness refers to it during her testimony to refresh her memory.

Mezibov and Sirkin demolish her in seconds. Reisman never taught at one university with which she was associated; during a pretrial hearing she testified that she received a research grant from the Department of Justice resulting in work that was not published by the department, but during the trial she claims it was; it turns out that, according to the defense's tally, the art "expert" has less than 30 hours of art education.

But the big secret finally comes out. Reisman is the former research director of the American Family Association. Director Donald Wildmon paid her more than $23,000 in 1989.

The New Critics

Jesse Helms, among others, must have believed that there was no better place in America than Cincinnati for the first obscenity trial against a museum to take place. If you can't get a conviction here, where can you get one? So this victory is especially sweet. But it will have to be built upon, protected.

Now that the House of Representatives wants the courts, rather than the National Endowment for the Arts, to distinguish art from obscenity, prosecutors across the country may soon be getting an art education. Could Prouty have made a convincing case that Robert Mapplethorpe is not an artist, or that his retrospective was unsuitable for a museum? I don't think so, but he certainly could have tried. Where was Hilton Kramer? Why wasn't Christina Orr-Cahall subpoenaed to explain why her Corcoran board voted unanimously to censor "Robert Mapplethorpe: The Perfect Moment"?

The irony is that Mapplethorpe's worst art-world adversaries consider him a fashion photographer, not an artist. This debate might have intrigued the jurors. It might also have made their job a good deal harder. The fire in the courtroom could have been much hotter.

The trouble in River City isn't over. Last week, Sheriff Leis announced that he would be previewing *Henry & June*, the new film about Anaïs Nin and Henry Miller that portrays sex between women. Leis will determine whether NC-17-rated films play in Cincinnati. There wasn't even a battle over Scorsese's *The Last Temptation of Christ* because none of the theater owners wanted to play it. When a production of *Equus* was scheduled to open at the city's Theater in the Park, the director *invited the vice squad in* to get its approval. The police are the new critics of Cincinnati.

Robert Mapplethorpe was born in a predominantly Catholic suburb of New Jersey that's not unlike Cincinnati. The artist once described home as "a good place to come from and a good place to leave." But hometown Cincinnati might be changing. Mike Campbell is the portly superintendent of buildings and grounds for Hamilton County who helped the crowd flow out of the courthouse at the end of the trial. "Well," he said, "it looks as though Cincinnati is going to make it into the 20th century."

■ Karen Finley, It's Only Art, *Village Voice Literary Supplement,* October 1990

Karen Finley is a performance artist. She was one of the "NEA Four," a group of artists who were denied NEA grants, and who subsequently sued the agency.

I went into a museum but they had taken down all the art. Only the frames were left. Pieces of masking tape were up with the names of the paintings and the artists stating why they were removed. The guards had nothing to guard. The white walls yellowed. Toilets were locked up in museums because people might think someone peeing is art. Someone might think that pee flushing down that toilet is art. Someone might think that the act of peeing is a work of art. And the government pays for that pee flushing down the toilet. There were many bladder infections among those who inspected the museum making sure that there was no offensive art. They might lose their jobs. It's a good life when no one thinks that you ever piss or shit.

In the empty frames were the reasons why art was confiscated.

Jasper Johns — for desecrating the flag.

Michelangelo — for being a homosexual.

Mary Cassatt — for painting nude children.

Van Gogh — for contributing to psychedelia.

Georgia O'Keeffe — for painting cow skulls (the dairy industry complained).

Picasso — for urinating, apparently, on his sculptures, with the help of his children, to achieve the desired patina.

Edward Hopper — for repressed lust.

Jeff Koons — for offending Michael Jackson.

All ceramicists were banned because working with clay was too much like playing with your own shit.

All glassblowing became extinct because it was too much like giving a blow job.

All art from cultures that didn't believe in one male god was banned for being blasphemous.

We looked for the show of early American quilts, but it had been taken down. A guard said that a period stain was found on one, another guard said he found an ejaculation stain on a quilt from Virginia. In fact, they closed all of the original thirteen states. You can imagine what happened under those quilts at night!

After the Confiscation of Art occurred, an Art Propaganda Army was started by the government. Last month the national assignment for the army artists was to make Dan Quayle look smart. The assignment for the army writers was to make the Stealth bomber as important as the microwave oven. Musicians were asked to write a tune, how the HUD scandal was no big deal, like taking sugar packets from a cafe. Dancers were to choreograph a dance showing that the Iran-contra affair was as harmless as your dog going into your neighbor's yard. And filmmakers were told to make films about homelessness, poverty, and AIDS, saying that God has a plan for us all.

But no art came out.

No art was made.

Newspapers became thin and disappeared because there was no more criticism. There was nothing to gossip about. Schools closed because learning got in the way of patriotism. No one could experiment, for that was the way of the devil.

There was no theory. No academia. No debate teams. No *Jeopardy*.

Everyone became old overnight. There were no more reasons for anything. Everything became old and gray. Everyone had blue-gray skin like the color of bones, unfriendly seas, and navy bean soup. And then the Punishers, the Executioners, the Judges of Creativity grew weary, for there was no creativity left to condemn. So they snorted and they squawked, but they held in their boredom. All that was printed in newspapers, journals, and magazines was the phrase "I don't know."

All actresses and actors were gone from TV except Charlton Heston. Charlton did TV shows 24 hours a day (with occasional cameo appearances by Anita Bryant).

One day Jesse Helms was having some guests over from Europe. A dignitary, a land developer, and a king. Mrs. Helms asked them where they'd like to go in America. The king said, "Disneyland."

Mr. Helms said, "Oh, that was closed down when we saw Disney's film *Fantasia.*"

So the guests said, "Nathan's Hot Dogs on Coney Island."

Mr. Helms answered, "Sorry, but hot dogs are too phallic. In this country we don't eat anything that's longer than it's wide. Nathan's is history. In this country we don't even eat spaghetti. Bananas aren't imported. Tampon instructions are not allowed."

"Well," the guests said, "we'd like to go to the Museum of Modern Art, and if we can't go there, then why come to America?"

Mr. Helms was stuck. He wanted everyone to think he was cool, having Europeans visit him. Then he had an idea. He'd make the art himself to put back into the empty museums. He'd get George Bush and William Buckley and Donald Wildmon and Dana Rohrabacher and Tipper Gore to come over and make some art on the White House lawn. So he called all of his cronies. And everyone came because it was better than watching Charlton Heston on TV.

Mr. and Mrs. Helms looked all over for art supplies. They came up with old wallpaper, scissors, and house paint, and laid it all out for their friends to express themselves.

When the friends arrived they were scared to make art because they never had before. Never even used a crayon. But then a child picked up a crayon and drew a picture of her cat having babies. Then she drew a picture of her father hitting her. Then a picture of her alone and bruised. The mother looked at the picture and cried and told the daughter she didn't know that had happened to her. The child screamed out: "DRAW YOUR DREAMS! DRAW YOUR NIGHTMARES! DRAW YOUR FEARS! DRAW YOUR REALITIES!"

Everyone started making pictures of houses on fire, of monsters and trees becoming penises, pictures of making love with someone of the same sex, of being naked on street corners, of pain and dirty words and things you never admitted in real life.

For 13 days and nights everyone drew and drew nonstop. Some started telling stories, writing poems. Neighbors saw the art-making and joined in. Somehow, pretend was back. Somehow, expression sprang up from nowhere.

But then the Confiscation Police arrived and they took everyone away. (The father of the child who drew the father hitting the child complained.) Everyone was arrested. They even arrested Jesse Helms, for he was painting his soul out, which was HATE AND ENVY AND CRIME AND DARKNESS AND PAIN. They threw him into the slammer. He was tried for treason and lost. And on his day of execution his last words were: "It was only art."

■ Public Law 101-151, November 5, 1990 (excerpt)

This law provided a new set of restrictions for NEA grants based on the definition of obsenity in the Supreme Court case **Miller v. California.**

TITLE I — AMENDMENTS TO THE NATIONAL FOUNDA-TION ON THE ARTS AND HUMANITIES ACT OF 1965

SEC. 101. DECLARATION OF FINDINGS AND PURPOSES.
    Section 2 of the National Foundation on the Arts and the Humanities Act of 1965 (20 U.S.C. 951) is amended to read as follows:
    "DECLARATION OF FINDINGS AND PURPOSES
"SEC. 2. The Congress finds and declares the following:

"(1)   The arts and the humanities belong to all the people of the United States.

"(2)   The encouragement and support of national progress and scholarship in the humanities and the arts, while primarily a matter for private and local initiative, are also appropriate matters of concern to the Federal Government.

"(3)   An advanced civilization must not limit its efforts to science and technology alone, but must give full value and support to the other great branches of scholarly and cultural activity in order to achieve a better understanding of the past, a better analysis of the present, and a better view of the future.

"(4)   Democracy demands wisdom and vision in its citizens. It must therefore foster and support a form of education, and access to the arts and the humanities, designed to make people of all backgrounds and wherever located masters of their technology and not its unthinking servants.

"(5)   It is necessary and appropriate for the Federal Government to complement, assist, and add to programs for the advancement of the humanities and the arts by local, State, regional, and private agencies and their organizations. In doing so, the Government must be sensitive to the nature of public sponsorship. Public funding of the arts and humanities is subject to the conditions that traditionally govern the use of public money. Such funding should contribute to public support and confidence in the use of taxpayer funds. Public funds provided by the Federal Government must ultimately serve public purposes the Congress defines.

"(6)   The arts and the humanities reflect the high place accorded by the American people to the nation's rich cultural heritage and to the fostering of mutual respect for the diverse beliefs and values of all persons and groups.

"(7)   The practice of art and the study of the humanities require constant dedication and devotion. While no government can call a great artist or scholar into existence, it is necessary and appropriate for the Federal Government to help create and sustain not only a climate encouraging freedom of thought, imagination, and inquiry but also the material conditions facilitating the release of this creative talent.

"(8)   The world leadership which has come to the United States cannot rest solely upon superior power, wealth, and technology, but must be solidly founded upon worldwide respect and admiration for the Nation's high qualities as a leader in the realm of ideas and of the spirit.

"(9)   Americans should receive in school, background and preparation in the arts and humanities to enable them to recognize and appreciate the aesthetic dimensions of our lives, the diversity of excellence that comprises our cultural heritage, and artistic and scholarly expression.

"(10)   It is vital to a democracy to honor and preserve its multicultural artistic heritage as well as support new ideas, and therefore it is essential to provide financial assisstace to its arts and the organizations that support their work.

"(11)   To fulfill its educational mission, achieve an orderly continuation of free society, and provide models of excellence to the American people, the Federal Government must transmit the achievement and values of civilization from the past via the present to the future, and make widely available the greatest achievements of art.

"(12)   In order to implement these findings and purposes, it is desirable to establish a National Foundation on the Arts and the Humanities."...

(c) DETERMINED TO BE OBSCENE; FINAL JUDGMENT. — Section 3 of the National Foundation on the Arts and the Humanities Act of 1965 (20 U.S.C. 952), as amended by subsection (a), is amended by adding at the end the following:

"(j) the term 'determined to be obscene' means determined, in a final judgment of a court of record and of competent jurisdiction in the United States, to be obscene.

"(k) The term 'final judgment' means a judgment that is either —

"(1) not reviewed by any other court that has authority to review such judgment; or

"(2) is not reviewable by any other court.

"(l) The term 'obscene' means with respect to a project, production, workshop, or program that —

"(1) the average person, applying contemporary community standards, would find that such project, production, workshop, or program, when taken as a whole, appeals to the prurient interest;

"(2) such project, production, workshop, or program depicts or describes sexual conduct in a patently offensive way; and

"(3) such project, production, workshop, or program, when taken as a whole, lacks serious literary, artistic, political, or scientific value.".…

(b) ARTISTIC EXCELLENCE AND OBSCENE MATTER. — Section 5(d) of the National Foundation on the Arts and the Humanities Act of 1965 (20 U.S.C. 954(d)) is amended to read as follows:

"(d) No payment shall be made under this section except upon application therefor which is submitted to the National Endowment for the Arts in accordance with regulations issued and procedures established by the Chairperson. In establishing such regulations and procedures, the Chairperson shall ensure that —

"(1) artistic excellence and artistic merit are the criteria by which applications are judged, taking into consideration general standards of decency and respect for the diverse beliefs and values of the American public; and

"(2) applications are consistent with the purposes of this section. Such regulations and procedures shall clearly indicate that obscenity is without artistic merit, is not protected speech, and shall not be funded. Projects, productions, workshops, and programs that are determined to be obscene are prohibited from receiving financial assistance under this Act from the National Endowment for the Arts.

The disapproval or approval of an application by the Chairperson shall not be construed to mean, and shall not be considered as evidence that, the project, production, workshop, or program for which the applicant requested financial assistance is or is not obscene."...

(h) LIMITATION ON RECEIPT OF FINANCIAL ASSISTANCE — Section 5 of the National Foundation on the Arts and the Humanities Act of 1965 (20 U.S.C. 954), as amended by subsection (g), is amended —

(1) by redesignating subsections (l) through (p) as subsections (m) through (q), respectively, and

(2) by inserting after subsection (k) the following:

"(l)(1) If, after reasonable notice and opportunity for a hearing on the record, the Chairperson determines that a recipient of financial assistance provided under this section by the Chairperson or any non-Federal entity, used such financial assistance for a project, production, workshop, or program that is determined to be obscene, then the Chairperson shall require that until such recipient repays such assistance (in such amount, and under such terms and conditions, as the Chairperson determines to be appropriate) to the Endowment; no subsequent financial assistance be provided under this section to such recipient.

"(2) Financial assistance repaid under this section to the Endowment shall be deposited in the Treasury of the United States and credited as miscellaneous receipts.

"(3)(A) This subsection shall not apply with respect to financial assistance provided before the effective date of this subsection.

"(B) This subsection shall not apply with respect to a project, production, workshop, or program after the expiration of the 7-year period beginning on the latest date on which financial assistance is provided under this section for such project, production, workshop, or program."...

"(c) The Chairperson of the National Endowment for the Arts shall utilize advisory panels to review applications, and to make recommendations to the National Council on the Arts in all cases except cases in which the Chairperson exercises authority delegated under section 6(f). When reviewing applications, such panels shall recommend applications for projects, productions, and workshops solely on the basis of artistic excellence and artistic merit. The Chairperson shall issue regulations and establish procedures —

"(1) to ensure that all panels are composed, to the extent practicable, of individuals reflecting a wide geographic, ethnic, and minority representation as well as individuals reflecting diverse artistic and cultural points of view;

287

"(2) to ensure that all panels include representation of lay individuals who are knowledgeable about the arts but who are not engaged in the arts as a profession and are not members of either artists' organizations or arts organizations;

"(3) to ensure that, when feasible, the procedures used by panels to carry out their responsibilities are standardized;

"(4) to require panels —

"(A) to create written records summarizing —

"(i) all meetings and discussions of such panel; and

"(ii) the recommendations made by such panel to the Council; and

"(B) to make such records available to the public in a manner that protects the privacy of individual applicants and panel members;

"(5) to require, when necessary and feasible, the use of site visitations to view the work of the applicant and deliver a written report on the work being reviewed, in order to assist panelists in making their recommendations; and

"(6) to require that the membership of each panel change substantially from year to year and to provide that each individual is ineligible to serve on a panel for more than 3 consecutive years.

In making appointments to panels, the Chairperson shall ensure that an individual who has a pending application for financial assistance under this Act, or who is an employee or agent of an organization with a pending application, does not serve as a member of any panel before which such application is pending. The prohibition described in the preceding sentence shall commence with respect to such individual beginning on the date such application is submitted and shall continue for so long as such application is pending."

■ Richard Goldstein, Doowutchyalike: In the Brave New World, Sex Sells, *Village Voice*, November 6, 1990

Richard Goldstein is a critic for The Village Voice.

Who'd have thought juries in Cincinnati and Fort Lauderdale, two cities not known for their tolerance, would refuse to find work by Robert Mapplethorpe and 2 Live Crew obscene. Who'd have thought a judge would force the New York Archdiocese to go to *tenants court*, for crissakes, in order to close a sacrilegious show performed on church-owned property. I remember when a grumble from the archdiocese was enough to close a play or yank a film from the screen. (As a child, I was an avid follower of films "condemned" by the church, and once snuck into the movies to hear the forbidden word *virgin* uttered in a tepid comedy called *The Moon is Blue*.)

Who figured that any elected official — not to mention a member of Congress in an election year — would vote against a provision barring grants to art works "that depict or describe... sexual or excretory activities or organs." But that's what happened last week, as Congress removed statutory barriers to art enacted only a year ago. The question of obscenity will now be left to the courts where, apparently, it takes more than a bullwhip up the ass to faze a jury these days. This "compromise" on the National Endowment for the Arts was hardly a victory for truth and transgression. A hip Congress would have condemned NEA chairman John Frohnmayer to appraising macramé in Oregon. But I never imagined I'd see Jesse Helms rise on the Senate floor to deliver a ringing attack on "slime and sleaze," then sink back in his seat, scared of the effect a filibuster might have on his lagging reelection campaign.

Until last month, an X rating was enough to prevent a film from being advertised in many newspapers. Now, movies that feature a stick of butter applied to more than bread will be rated NC-17. It'll be hard to raise hell over a rating that sounds more like a license plate than an emblem of the devil. Of course, Christian soldiers can still converge on the Cineplexes of Sodom. For that matter, the legions of Tipper Gore will still ride herd on rock 'n' roll. And the cops in Cincinnati and Fort Lauderdale are still trying to keep hardcore music out of the racks. But the people have spoken, and so far their verdict is: DON'T TREAD ON ME.

Sounds trad. But for someone like me, who grew up on dirty Polaroids passed from hand to boyish hand; who dog-eared the meager smutty parts of *Peyton Place* ("Is it hard yet, Rod?"); who devoured every novel or poem ever declared obscene, and trekked down to Greenwich Village from the Bronx to buy *Tropic of Cancer* when it was finally cleared by the courts: For someone my age, this is a brave new world. Even in Cincinnati, Henry Miller is shtupping onscreen — in Dolby no less.

Why would a jury of ordinary Americans, who could always be counted on to see a threat to law and order in whatever turned them on, suddenly turn tail on history, giggling over what the Man calls dangerous? The answer has a lot to do with another honorable American tradition: contempt for authority. But there's a more subtle reason why many people have come to resent the policing of erotica. And that has more to do with marketing than with morality.

It's been nearly 20 years since porn came out from under the counter. In that time, smut's gotten cheaper than a six-pack, and videotape has made filth a fixture of the home entertainment center for millions of Americans. Some of these folks, inevitably, end up on juries. (Even the good people of Cincinnati can cross the river into Kentucky to get their dose of dirt: no wonder they weren't particularly shocked by Mapplethorpe's tableaux.) A generation has grown up with access to erotica in the form of mass-circulation slicks like *Hustler*, as well as slasher films, music videos, and advertising that flashes sexual desire as an iconic strobe. A touch of lingerie, a glimpse of bondage, a quick crack of the whip: this is the hot sauce of American entertainment. And most of us have become accustomed (if not addicted) to a market economy that serves up an ever more specialized menu of sexual fantasies, as fresh and hot as a delivery from Pizza Hut.

The Bakker/Swaggart syndrome notwithstanding, most fundamentalists live outside this pornocopia. But that isolates them from most Americans, and makes their champions seem quaint, if not threatening. What we've learned from the Mapplethorpe and 2 Live Crew cases is that right-wing repression is a paper tiger in America today. There may be 40 million of *them*, but there are five times as many of *us*. And though true believers can wreak havoc with a business that stocks dirty records or videotapes, the market for such commodities is too diverse to be permanently suppressed. There's big money in sex — and in the end, Americans usually go for the gold.

The demise of the X rating, the exoneration of the NEA, the Mapplethorpe and 2 Live Crew verdicts — all create a climate in which erotica can be mass-marketed in ever more elaborate venues and varieties. As a mechanism to insure some balance between profiteering and decency — whatever we may take that term to mean — the new system will create a hodgepodge of "community standards" and empower all sorts of pressure groups. Not just fundamentalists, but feminists, advocates for children, and civil rights groups all may gather their forces to protest offensive works. In the short run, boycotts will proliferate, as the line between permissible and forbidden games is drawn in the marketplace, rather than in Congress and the courts. But in the long run, sensation will create its own demand, pushing the limits of representation toward the actual contours of the imagination. For better or worse.

Some of my colleagues are convinced that, despite the string of acquittals, the fix is in on raunchy rock (not to mention films and TV fare). But as *Married... With Children* proved, even an advertiser boycott can't stop a sitcom with legs (not to mention cleavage). And who's to say the same public that acquitted 2 Live Crew won't find a new way to receive such product: maybe through the mail or, as telecommunications become more advanced, over the phone lines. Once you privatize the reception of erotica, you remove the stigma and assure its ubiquity. In that regard, the recent failure of the right to enact a federal ban on phone sex is another sign that they've lost the war on smut.

But the free market is a poor provider, in culture no less than in the rest of life. The new economy of desire could well end up restricting the fine arts even as it liberates mass culture. The vital interests of entertainment conglomerates don't usually extend to the arts, so it's unlikely that these industries will bring their political clout to bear on government grant-giving. Radical artists can survive without public support, but the venues that distribute and exhibit their work cannot. Who'd have thought you could see full frontal nudity on television but not in a performance space. Because it doesn't move megabucks, the Kitchen is now more vulnerable to censorship than Tower Records. Though Congress backed away from a confrontation with the arts, no one really thinks the NEA is out of the water — and at the rate Frohnmayer is moving, next year's grants could well be given out by Al D'Amato's cousins and the editorial board of *Commentary*. Museums that dare to show erotica (or even politically provocative works) could find themselves embroiled in an exhausting battle with terrified bureaucrats.

In such a climate, porn-art could be confined to private galleries and their elite clientele, while mass-cult smut is readily available. The difference is not only a matter of complexity, but of sensibility. In America today, the most popular entertainment reinforces orthodoxies, while the most powerful art is a weapon of dissent. When it comes to eroticism, suppressing Karen Finley and David Wojnarowicz while allowing the Diceman and Ice Cube to bray virtually assures that the most brutal aspects of human sexuality will prevail. This is how the new freedom could foster a rigid, regressive society. To strengthen the connection between desire and humanism, the fine arts must be as free as mass culture. That's the real struggle now: to lift all content restrictions on public funding, so art can "compete" in the erotic marketplace.

This is a crusade you'd think sex radicals and neocons would jointly wage. But don't expect William Safire to defend an artist who speaks truth to male power. A more likely alliance is between the libertarian left and the army of just plain folks who wanna get off. Folks who fancy that other American dream — not the house and car and world-dominance thing, but a vision of instant ecstasy, fed by a technology that puts fantasy at their fingertips.

Pleasure, in all its particularities, has always been an American obsession — inscribed as "the pursuit of happiness," implicated in Whitman's democratic vista; incarnated in Vegas, Hollywood, and lately, porn. Now, as our other industries falter, fantasy may be our most important product. A hunch that desire is big business might be what motivates juries, judges, and even senators to loosen the reins on erotica.

Digital Underground know what it takes for America to remain competitive: "Saywutchyalike... wearwutchyalike... doowutchyalike." No wonder the puritans are on the run.

■ Andy Grundberg, Art Under Attack: Who Dares Say That It's No Good?, *New York Times*, November 25, 1990

Andy Grundberg is a photography critic, formerly with the New York Times. *He is the director of programs for the Friends of Photography in San Francisco.*

One consequence of the uproar over art labeled obscene, blasphemous or otherwise offensive is that the careers of the creative artists whose work is at issue have been given a rocket-powered boost. This was surely not intended by those who have taken the artists and the National Endowment for the Arts to task, but it should not have surprised them. In today's culture, notoriety often equals fame, and fame passes for success.

Unfortunately, the increased attention these artists and performers have gained makes it nearly impossible to evaluate their work. The prevailing critical response has been to circle the wagons. Instead of arguing about esthetics, critics now spend their time defending the notion that artists can do and say whatever they please. To argue about the merits of artists who have been attacked is, in certain circles, tantamount to heresy, no matter how mediocre their work.

In an era when "political correctness" has become a criterion for judging art, this response is doubly dangerous. For one thing, it plays into the hands of those who equate the outer edges of art with a radical political agenda. And it encourages artists of limited talent to take a shortcut to success by cultivating outrageousness for its own sake.

Two years ago, the names Karen Finley, Holly Hughes, Andres Serrano and Jock Sturges were little known, and the 2 Live Crew was just another rap-group-come-lately. But in becoming the focus of controversy, these artists are now in the enviable position of having their every move watched with intense interest. Even those who already enjoy celebrity benefit from such limelight. The latest example is the novelist Bret Easton Ellis; this month Simon & Schuster abruptly canceled plans to publish his violence-filled new work, creating invaluable publicity.

For the most part, the artists whose work is at the center of controversy are by no means representative of the best talents in their fields. Karen Finley, who wears chocolate as a costume as part of her performance art, is not in the same league as Laurie Anderson or Spaulding Gray, who have honed their individual gifts into unmistakable styles. The photographs by Mr. Serrano, who specializes in images of bodily fluids, and Mr. Sturges, whose subjects are nude teenagers, have yet to inhabit the distinctive and personal terrain of Cindy Sherman or William Wegman. The 2 Live Crew has not shown the talent for musical innovation exhibited by other rappers of equally disputable taste, like the Geto Boys.

Robert Mapplethorpe's sexually explicit photographs, which seem like the first spark in a fire now raging out of control, at least provoked arguments about his importance as an artist. To some his work embodies the essence of contemporary beauty; to others it is simply fashion photography extended to new territory. Once Senator Jesse Helms rendered an opinion about it, however, disputes about the value of Mapplethorpe's work all but stopped. It seemed essential to protect all art, not just unarguably good art, from heathen attackers.

Only recently have critics broken the silence and begun to examine the photographer's artistic legacy with some reasonableness. One such critic is Ben Lifson, a writer and photographer, who takes a dim view of Mapplethorpe's contributions in the fall issue of a newsletter published by Curatorial Assistance Inc., an exhibition service based in Los Angeles. Mr. Lifson sums up the situation quite neatly by saying "In this climate, whatever is said about Mapplethorpe largely, if not entirely, degenerates into propaganda."

Propaganda is hardly a form of art criticism, and it does nothing to reconcile the growing tensions between those who believe that cultural life is the ultimate measure of a society and those who feel threatened by what they see as culture's increasingly political agenda. Nor can propaganda make distinctions that can stimulate the emotions and the mind, which is what the arts and criticism are ultimately all about. What is needed at this moment is esthetic judgments, not political ones.

Suspicions about the agenda of the arts and attempts to limit artistic expression are not unique to our time, of course. Works like James Joyce's "Ulysses" and D.H. Lawrence's "Lady Chatterly's Lover" were kept out of circulation in the United States for much of the first half of the century because of their erotic content. In the 1950's anti-communist ardor resulted in the blacklisting of several screenwriters and authors, effectively halting their careers.

(Paradoxically, controversy often pays for today's artists. In the case of Mapplethorpe's photographs, which were the focus of a much publicized obscenity trial in Cincinnati, more people entered the museums where the exhibition was shown in a month than normally pass through their gates in a year. Sales of the 2 Live Crew album that led to the obscenity conviction of a record store owner in Florida have surpassed two million copies.)

One could argue that the urge to suppress artistic expression is a cyclical part of American life, as predictable as artists' urges to violate conventional taste. What makes it different now — as well as surprising — is that it comes after 25 years of governmental advocacy for the arts. The National Endowment has been more than a grant-making agency, after all; its mission, and the mission of local and regional arts councils, has been to spread the word that the arts are good and good for America.

Today this supposition is under attack, and cultural life consequently needs to be defended with passion and political savvy. But this should not mean that every artistic utterance that defies convention merits praise, or that art that raises hackles is necessarily more vital than work that does not.

Notoriety not only impairs our ability to judge art on its merits. As the case of Andres Serrano suggests, it can also befuddle an artist. Mr. Serrano, 39, is best known for his image of a plastic crucifix in a tank of urine, and has become something of an art-world hero for having provoked considerable ire from Christian fundamentalists, among others. But his most recent work, which is on view at the Stux Gallery in the SoHo section of Manhattan (155 Spring Street, through Saturday), marks a radical departure from the images that brought him to public attention, which featured combinations of milk, blood, urine and other naturally occurring fluids.

The artist's most recent pictures are portraits of homeless men and women (a series he calls "Nomads") and of members of the Ku Klux Klan — subjects that seem to reek of chic. The subjects are as fixed and monumental as the New Guinea tribesmen found in Irving Penn's series "Worlds in a Small Room" and no less exotic. The homeless seem like figures from a far-off land, and the Klansmen, in their hoods and gowns, resemble a perverse version of Vatican fashions. If Mr. Serrano's subject was once the irreconcilability of the spirit and the flesh, his new photographs seem to about the mutability of cultural representation. There's nothing inherently wrong with changing artistic direction. But Mr. Serrano's present preoccupations seem fueled by a desire to prompt the kind of controversy that his earlier work caused.

For all the interest of their openly "political" subject matter, though, Mr. Serrano's new pictures are not always as beautiful to behold as they could be. His large prints are sharp enough, but their colors are acidic and their tonalities are unpleasantly contrasty; in some places, the blank surface of the paper is all that one sees. This is especially true of the Klan pictures, which are the most recent, suggesting that the artist took too little time in the darkroom supervising their production.

Jock Sturges, the San Francisco photographer of nude adolescents, is another artist who has acquired a major reputation despite his relatively minor work. In May, the Federal Bureau of Investigation raided his San Francisco studio and confiscated its contents. The F.B.I. acted after being contacted by a photo processing lab, which suspected that the Sturges pictures it was developing were pornographic.

(The F.B.I. has urged processing labs to report to the police the names of customers whose pictures might be pornographic; under California law, such labs are legally obligated to do so.)

The abrupt seizure of the photographer's work set off shock waves in California and across the country. Although Mr. Sturges's work was not widely known — in addition to making pictures intended to be seen as art, he does commercial photography for a living — the implications for artists were clear, as was the specter of Big Brother.

The pictures that sounded the alarm at the processing lab in San Francisco have not been seen publicly, but some inkling of what the fuss might be about can be gleaned from Mr. Sturges's exhibition at the Vision Gallery in San Francisco, which closed yesterday.

The more than 50 images in the show were exquisitely printed enlargements, made from large-format black-and-white negatives, of naked young women and a few naked young men. These subjects have been photographed in a direct, candid portrait style that suggests the influence of Jack Welpott and Judy Dater, at places like northern California communes and French nudist colonies. They have names like Danielle, Marine and Misty Dawn.

In a sympathetic review in The San Francisco Chronicle, the art critic Kenneth Baker concentrated on responding to allegations that Mr. Sturges's pictures constituted pornography. "What decisively absolves this work of the suspicion of pornographic intent is its absence of shame," Mr. Baker concluded, as if intention were the bone of contention.

But if the work is not child pornography, neither is it good art. Mr. Sturges seems too caught up in the Lolita-like qualities of his subjects to be able to fashion an original picture; as a result, the work seems to be one long leer. The history of photography is full of pictures that document the male urge to possess what is otherwise forbidden or untouchable — Bellocq's portraits of New Orleans prostitutes come immediately to mind — and Mr. Sturges's pictures certainly fit into this tradition. But whatever the forces of moral rectitude make of them is ultimately less important than the tired way they repeat a thoroughly discredited genre.

As was true in the controversies surrounding Mapplethorpe's and Mr. Serrano's pictures, the defenders of Mr. Sturges's First Amendment freedoms seem reluctant to discuss artistic values. Perhaps this is because those artistic values are so meager, or perhaps it is because no one wants to be seen as a supporter of Humbert Humbert. In any case, the result is an uneasy silence about the very issues that would be at the center of discussion in a healthy, less politicized, cultural climate.

Artistic freedom should always be defended. But abandoning esthetic discourse means capitulating to the very forces that seek to politicize, and thus control, all artistic activity.

■ Dennis Barrie, Freedom of Expression Is the Issue, *SITE sound* , November/December 1990 (excerpt)

Dennis Barrie is the director of the Contemporary Arts Center in Cincinnati.

Something like eight months ago, my museum, my staff, my board, and I entered into a battle for the survival of our museum, and ultimately for the survival of free expression in this country.

About two years ago we decided to take the Robert Mapplethorpe exhibition "The Perfect Moment" which was organized by the University of Pennsylvania. When we took the exhibition it was not a controversial exhibition, and not very different than anything we had done over our 51-year history. We have a long history of doing provocative and challenging exhibitions. Mapplethorpe was in our eyes another exhibition.

That changed in June of 1989, when that wonderful senator from North Carolina launched his campaign against the NEA, specifically against the Mapplethorpe exhibition as an example of misuse of federal funds. I sat in a meeting in Providence, Rhode Island of museum directors, and at that meeting it was announced that the Corcoran Gallery in Washington had withdrawn from the exhibition. There was absolute silence in that room. People couldn't speak because we knew at that point the door was open to all museums across the country. The six or seven of us in the room who knew we were taking the Mapplethorpe show were particularly disturbed. I really couldn't sleep that night thinking about what the consequences might be somewhere along the line.

When I went back to Cincinnati we convened our board and I told them that what was just another exhibition was no longer just another exhibition, and that we'd have to be prepared for a perhaps very rocky road. At that meeting of our board, thirty people sat in the room, looked at all the photos, looked at what had happened at the Corcoran, and said "We are committed to this exhibition" — much to their credit. These were people who were very vulnerable, as you'll soon hear, in terms of their professions and their livelihoods and their lives in Cincinnati. But they agreed that we would go forward, that we had a moral, ethical right to go forward, and we would have this exhibition.

Months passed, and it became cocktail conversation in Cincinnati about the Mapplethorpe show coming. We did a very large educational program, trying to explain to people who Mapplethorpe was, why his art was important, why the Center was doing it, why there were difficult works in the exhibition. We had meetings with clergymen, with City Council, with civic leaders, with business-men, with art groups — and there was a consensus in the city that this was okay. In fact one of the funniest moments — this is actually true — was the mayor of Cincinnati walking up to me at a Christmas party, and he walked up and he said, "Do I have to be concerned about this exhibition?" And I said, "No." And he said, "This Mapplethorpe guy, he's the guy that has the peeing on the Christ, right?" And I said, "No, that's Andres Serrano." And he said, "Well, what does this Mapplethorpe guy do?" I said, "He's known for his homoerotic photogra-phy." And he said, "Oh, that homoerotic stuff. We can handle that." I think that's the first time our mayor said "homoerotic" anywhere, but since then everybody uses it in our town.

Things were pretty calm. And then in February of this year one of the local television stations did a three-part series on censorship in the arts — a rather conscientious series, quite honestly, detailing what Helms had done, what was going on with the Reverend Donald Wildmon, and what was going on in preparation for Mapplethorpe in our city. In that series they interviewed me and they interviewed lots of people. Among the interviews was the sheriff, who has built his reputation on leading anti-porn crusades in Hamilton County. His name is Simon Leis. And the Reverend Jerry Kirk, who has been an anti-porn leader nationally. He happens to be based in Cincinnati. He's the head of something called the National Coalition Against Pornography, which was co-founded at least in its earlier form by a wonderful moral man, Charles Keating, whom you all should know. During this television series, Jerry Kirk said this was terrible and horrible stuff. Simon Leis, the sheriff, said, by his estimation, what he had seen in past years, his wide knowledge, this was not criminally obscene material (and they showed them all the photos).

Three days later the sheriff called a news conference and said he had reversed his decision and this indeed was criminally obscene and that actions would be taken. This is late February 1990, and this is when our roller-coaster ride began. What followed was like nothing I've ever had happen in my life, and I think few arts organizations have ever experienced. There was in Cincinnati an organized campaign by this anti-porn coalition, funded to some degree by outside money, certainly in connection with the Reverend Donald Wildmon. They began a letter-writing campaign — something like 18,000 letters went to the heads of various corporations, they went to the archbishop, they went to City Council, and they attacked the employers of our board. It was a very effective campaign, because nobody had ever experienced a campaign like this before. They managed to disrupt our city. They managed to literally halt in mid-drive our annual fine arts fund drive. Our institutions are funded by an annual drive which raises about $5 or $6 million each year. They halted that drive, telling everybody that the drive was bringing in pornography, child pornography, and that no one should give, and if this meant the symphony, the art museum had to go down with the Contemporary Arts Center, that was fine. They got major corporations to follow their lead, and literally things came to a halt in our city. It became so bad that the chairman of our board was severely attacked, and he had to resign as chairman of our board. He also finally resigned from his position at the bank. So the fallout from this is very, very real and the consequences are very, very real. The onslaught was unlike anything they expected or even could handle.

This battle had already disrupted our city by the beginning of March, and the show did not open until April 7.

Early in March the sheriff, the police chief, and the county prosecutor made statements in the paper and to the news media that they were going to review the exhibition. We had a private phone call from a city official, very high up, saying that it wasn't going to be a review; it was going to be seizure and arrest, and that we should be prepared for that, and there was nothing he could do to stop it. We decided to take the bad guys to court and say, "If you think these works are obscene, let's have it decided before a judge and a jury before the exhibition opens." We filed suit in March for this very purpose. We named the city and county as defendants. There were literally thousands of demonstrators outside that courtroom, both pro and con. There were moments of confrontation but nothing serious happened outside. Inside the courtroom, we had a one-hour hearing in which the city and county stated that moves against us were mere hearsay in the newspaper and the media, that the media had created the sensation, and that there was no reason to believe they were going to act against us. The judge took them at their word and dismissed the case without ever hearing the essentials, and on April 6 we walked out of that courtroom with the assurance that no one would move against us.

By now we were a media event of unbelievable proportions in that city. Everybody was there — ABC, NBC, CBS, the *New York Times*, *Washington Post*, *Village Voice* — they were all there. We were deluged with media. They camped out, literally. It was a circus at all times. The next morning they were there at the crack of dawn.

That morning at ten o'clock when we opened, the sheriff's deputies came in with members of the grand jury to look at the photographs. The media followed them around as they looked at each photo and asked them what their opinion was. I got to know the one officer very well, by the way, and he came to see the show several times. He's a photographer, and he loved the show. Anyway, they went back, the grand jury reconvened, and it became common knowledge in the media that they were going to indict us. Now, the media followed their every move. At twelve o'clock the vice squad and the sheriff's deputies left the courthouse, and the media followed them as they went to McDonald's before they came to the Contemporary Arts Center. It looked very certain that there were going to be arrests, which is a very scary thought when you think about it. I mean, I'm willing to do many things for my institution, but the thought of going to jail was a very scary one. And it was announced that I was going to jail; I didn't know about the rest of my staff, but I certainly was going to jail. My attorneys thought that I should surrender rather than be led out in handcuffs.

They came into the gallery at two o'clock in the afternoon wearing their dress uniforms. There were something like twenty officers. We knew they were coming in because you could hear the boos as they came up the escalators into our space, and it was a very frightening moment.

They did announce that there would be no arrests, there would be no seizures; that they were indicting us on a misdemeanour rather than a felony, on two charges against me and two charges against the museum, but that everyone would have to leave while they videotaped the work for evidence.

Now what happened is that our gallery space is in this atrium building, and our sort of lobby area is below. They had forced everybody out but they hadn't figured out how to deal with crowd control, and at that moment, one of the city councilmen was in the space viewing the exhibition, and he said, "We're about to have a riot out here. Would you go talk to the people and calm them down."

There were two thousand or more people in that space, and at this point they are chanting and singing and it became a very dangerous moment for all of us.

I loved the sign: "If you give artists freedom of expression soon every American will want it." In that crowd — there were a lot of students in the front — but in that crowd there were ladies 80 years old, priests, city council-men, business people; it was a real cross-section of Cincinnati. I saw a lot of them that day, talked to them afterward, and the outrage of those 2,000 people, knowing what was going on, was incredible. It really was a dangerous situation. People were getting physical, the police were getting physical, they were pushing reporters around. It got to be very dangerous, but fortunately we were able to calm everybody down and tell them they could come back later in that day.

What happened was after that we went to a federal judge, got an injunction to keep the exhibition open, and the exhibition remained open. There were 81,302 people who saw the exhibition in seven weeks, a record for any exhibition in the city of Cincinnati. If we could have kept it there ten weeks, we could have broken all records in that city for all time. People came in just by the thousands each day — incredible numbers, waiting in line for hours to see the exhibition.

Mapplethorpe has been called the best classical photographer of the late 20th century. Some people don't like his work, some people call him a second-rate artist. I've heard all these debates in the eight months I've been involved with this battle. I think it's a really good body of work, but his standing, good or bad, is not the issue here. The real issue is freedom of expression.

There are lots of issues at work here. There are issues about "pornography" or "obscenity," but there are other issues about homosexuality and also about racism. Many of Mapplethorpe's subjects were black men, and certainly this was an issue with Helms and this was an issue with some of the people who reacted against us.

The indictments: there were two. One was for pandering obscenity, and the other was for the use of children in nudity-oriented material. If you read the rest of the law, which I can't quote precisely, it's with lewd focus on the genitalia for prurient interest, and without the permission of the parents.

When people heard about these photos they thought the worst.

The two photos that touched off the furor in the arch-conservative world were both taken with parental permission. Both families were friends of Mapplethorpe's. You can find matching photos in family albums everywhere. If you look at the work of most photographers in the 20th century, you'll see photos like this. It was ironic that when the thousands filed in to see these photos they could never find them. They kept coming up saying, "Where are the photos of the children?" And we said, "They're right there." "Well that can't be the photo." This is the reaction we got over and over and over again. Being a parent I was particularly bothered by this charge, that someone could find evil and lewdness in such photos. Both mothers, by the way, were outraged that anybody would think that these photos were evil, that they were dirty....

There have been numerous moments when this prosecution could have been dropped. Museums are protected institutions. Whether the work is "obscene" or not, if it is in the setting of a museum it is protected. In order to get around that the judge declared that after 51 years we were no longer a museum, because we didn't have the word "museum" in our name. So he got around it. He could have dropped it at that moment.

We maintain that you must judge the whole exhibition. That is a critical issue. It's a critical issue for all of you in the arts. The judge ruled that the five photographs cited for obscenity can be judged individually. So this is a very serious decision for us, and ultimately for all of you, if indeed work can be judged that way; if you can pull sentences out of a play or pages out of a book, this to me is the same concept. Even more so, the five images taken out of the portfolio are part of thirteen images. Why didn't they cite the other eight? If they were going to cite them, they might as well cite all of them.

Somebody asked me how I thought it was going to go. I don't think I'm going to jail, but I do think there is a concerted, serious effort to convict the Contemporary Arts Center, and I think our chances as of last Thursday became very bad, and I think we can wind up being convicted.

What are the consequences of that conviction? I think the consequences are for all museums. They've opened the door in our museum, and they can open the door here in Detroit, and they can open the door in Oklahoma, and in Tulsa, and in Toledo, and anywhere else that they want to open that door. They want this victory. The consequences are really consequences for freedom of expression and access to that expression. If we let them win here, they've scored a big victory. I'm starting to see self-censorship all over the place. You think twice about what you're going to put out: whether you're going to have Karen Finley perform, and whether you're going to have a work that makes political statements, and whether you're going to sign your NEA contract. These are all the consequences of this decision. I worry about a country that can tolerate things like this. You must maintain freedom of access to expression and the freedom of that expression.

So I guess I'm saying to all of you a kind of dire warning: You've got to get off your derrières, not just for the Contemporary Arts Center, and you've got to learn to be organized. You've got to learn to get active politically. It's sad that the art world sits here. We've got to get politically active.

So I guess I say to all of you: think about what's happened in Cincinnati and think about what you can do about it tomorrow — then do it, because the future of our society, not just the future of art; it's the future of our society that's at stake.

I'll leave you with an upbeat note. I don't want to paint Cincinnati in a bad way. What keeps me fighting is the support of people in that city. Every day someone comes up and tells me to keep up the fight, that you're doing the right thing.

I had to catch a plane and I was leaving late and had to get to my car. Cincinnati is not the loosest city in the world, but it's not the most rigid — but you're not supposed to jaywalk. They have very strict rules about jaywalking. I was standing there at the corner, very late, trying to get to my car, and the light was against me, and I thought, "Damn it, I've just got to go against this light." And I see a cop sitting there, and I thought, "I'm going to get arrested for jaywalking!" I thought about having another charge against me. Then I thought, well, the hell with it, I'll go for it. So I go across the street, and the police officer's car horn honks at me, and I just start like that. The officer reached his hand out of the car, and he said, "Dennis," and he raised his hand like this [in the V-for-victory sign].

■Margaret Spillane, The Culture of Narcissism, *The Nation* December 10, 1990

Margaret Spillane is a writer.

Do we not mystify the facts
And milk the taxpayer of his tax
   By the illusion
That our minds serve much higher ends
Than bending backs and blistered hands?
How much of common good depends
   On education?

—Seamus Heaney, "Versus for Fordham Commencement," 1982

When some people say that the NEA selection process in itself is censorship, they are wrong. Art is a profession and has experts, as do other areas. When one applies to a public university there are certain eligibility requirements of excellence. When people say the NEA should end altogether and that private business should fund the arts, they are

—Karen Finley, National Association of Artists' Organizations newsletter, 1990

Several weeks ago, a body was found in my New Haven neighborhood. At 7:30 on that Friday morning, a custodian discovered the corpse of a young African-American woman on the asphalt behind Wilbur Cross High School. A single bullet had been fired through her head. At 8:30, Principal John Courtmanche made the grim announcement to students over Wilbur Cross's P.A. system, while the local morning news announced the same story to all of New Haven. The next morning's paper provided her identity — Jacqueline Shaw, 21 years old, of 21 Kossuth Street — but no new information. And that was it. Not another word was said in the press or on television about who she was, no columnist meditated upon that round, radiant face appearing in her postage-stamp-sized obit photo.

In fact, for whatever police-blotter reason Shaw might have been killed, her murder was also her punishment for being a woman, as the condition of her corpse clearly displayed. Her shirt was yanked up over her face, all garments below the waist were gone, a handful of twenty-dollar bills were sandwiched between her thighs and more money stuffed into her clenched hand. This part of the story went unreported in the press.

The frequency with which the corpses of female homicide victims undergo some ritualized post-mortem degradation is common knowledge among police officers and hospital morgue personnel. Such degradation committed upon the bodies of living women is even more frequent. This is one of several reasons why I was certain, before I had ever seen "We Keep Our Victims Ready," that Karen Finley was taking on a vital and courageous task. When right-wing columnists Evans and Novak took sneering exception to that "chocolate-smeared woman," I knew that Finley was sending seismic shocks through those secure walls of denial and domination behind which woman-beaters carry out their favorite form of self-expression. Finley's chocolate-smearing sounded like no mere symbol, but straightforward social realism.

With that in mind I was willing to put up with the cute *épater-la-bourgeoisie* chitchat with which Finley opened her piece. I thought, no doubt she is making a serious effort to navigate her mostly white, educated audience away from the safe ground of their conventional aesthetic expectations to far more perilous places. If she indulges herself and her audience a little, it's not the end of the world.

At one point Finley provided just the sort of revolutionary ground I'd been waiting for. Standing in a ruby-red merry-widow corset, she talked about the availability of takeout containers of Jell-O from corner convenience stores. She held two such containers aloft, then unceremoniously dumped the contents of each into the cups of her bra. Finley nonchalantly strolled the stage while her Jell-O breasts jiggled with a life of their own. Like Chaplin's wrench in *Modern Times*, Finley's breasts become hilariously emblematic of the way a perfectly safe, normal element of everyday life can be transformed, in a culture of domination, into something whose meaning and destiny are controlled by outside forces.

But what was on both sides of that episode was awful. The awfulness had nothing to do with denunciations from the pulpit of right-wing journalism or censorship by decree of the National Endowment for the Arts. The truly unpleasant surprise about Finley's performance was its utterly conventional treatment of her subject matter. All the controversy seemed to promise a bare-knuckled assault on those barriers separating the privileged from the powerless. But while she seemed poised to indict the short-shrift chronicling of atrocity typified in the coverage of Jacqueline Shaw's murder, Finley presented a laundry-list, headline-formula reading of contemporary horrors. The individual victims she promised to evoke — the battered child, the exploited female service worker, the person with AIDS — turned out to be carelessly assembled amalgams of bourgeois Americans' cultural shorthand for those they believe exist beneath them. "Southern" accents at times suggested sadistic white male supremacists, at other times work-wearied women, and at still other times fulsome, ridiculous Bible-punchers. Then there were nonspecific "blue collar" women's accents, with none of the music of neighborhood or ethnicity but all of the stereotypes of gum-chewing and bad grammar.

This could have been written off as a disappointing evening at the theater. But Jesse Helms, John Frohnmayer and her own publicity machine have made Karen Finley a symbol. The arts community in general sees Finley and the other three artists who were denied N.E.A. grants as symbols of right-wing censorship. And so they are. But Finley also symbolizes — and collaborates in — censorship of a different sort, censorship that ought to be pondered by anyone concerned about the politics of art and the relationship of the arts community to the broader community. She is emblematic of the art-making population's troublingly restricted notion of who its audience needs to be, and its equally troubling lack of alarm at who is being entirely left out of the art-making, -consuming and -rewarding tracks.

It is easy to identify censorship when someone stands up in Congress and says that the creation of artistic works by certain sectors of the population will not be funded by the government. But no liberal defender of arts funding has seized this excellent opportunity to ask the most jarring questions of all: Who gets to make art; who even gets to imagine that they might become an artist? And who gets to have their story told through art?

Finley and three other artists got their grants cut by the N.E.A. specifically because their work contained representations of their minority cultures: lesbian, gay and confrontational feminist. But as their cases demonstrate, it's entirely possible to be a member of an oppressed minority and still participate in the privileges of the dominant culture. As white middle-class artists, they must begin to recognize the fact that they occupy a privileged place within the reward system.

If arts journalist Cindy Carr is to be believed, most white middle class artists accept as natural their place within the networking, promoting and rewarding system. Carr, a *Village Voice* staff member who sits on peer-review panels, provides disturbing testimony of the degree to which contemporary artists have felt immune from any responsibility to examine their corporate-funded dollars for any traces of blood. "In more innocent times, vanguard artists theorized and fantasized about integrating art with life.... [Nowadays] all of us are being faced with ethical questions we've never had to think about before. These days, along with their usual worry (how to get money), artists and presenters must add a new worry (whether to *take* the money)."

One wonders how those so quick to express moral outrage when they feel their own rights are violated could have felt so comfortable all those years taking multinational funny money. One long-time and generous contributor to the arts, United Technologies, builds attack helicopters used in Central America. Another generous funder, Philip Morris, has for some years now been aggressively dumping on the Third World the high-tar cigarettes health-conscious Americans have abandoned. And the list goes on. Karen Finley, herself, if the quotation above is any indication, understands the hand-in-glove relationship between Big Business and the endowment but utterly fails to question how the very crimes she rails against are created by those corporate patrons whose approbation she hopes to enjoy.

The status of these artists in the reward system makes them members of the affluent class of Caucasians serviced by both the N.E.A. and corporate donors — the Arts Producers and Consumers, or ArtPAC. It's a far cry from those radical artists — painters, poets, composers, actors, playwrights — associated with the Works Progress Administration in the 1930s, who saw government support as a way of integrating the work of artists into the rest of the working community. Artists were treated as salaried workers and paid out of the same budget as bridge builders and road crews. Unlike the W.P.A. artists, who imagined art itself as drawn from and returned to the broad stream of American life, ArtPAC elects to converse, select and reward within its own small pool, ratifying and perpetuating its community with peer-review panels drawn from its own ranks.

ArtPAC's specialized, class-bound notion of Those Who Know What Art Is — and those who get to make and judge that art — persistently undermines confidence in the popular creative spirit. What's more, the whole process of art making gets sealed off into a realm of magical, inscrutable secrets. To demonstrate what an effective bludgeon such mystification makes, let's look at the degree of intimidation felt by jurors in Cincinnati's Mapplethorpe obscenity trial. Interviewed after the trial, a number of jurors displayed profound mistrust of their own abilities to observe and analyze. Art is simply a subject on which they feel totally disqualified from holding any opinion, they explained, so they relied entirely on the expert witnesses called by the defense. No arts journalist or First Amendment expert seemed to find that irregular — even though similarly constituted juries make decisions on biological engineering, nuclear-waste disposal and transnational corporate mergers.

To even the most socially conscious members of ArtPAC, such admissions aren't evidence that there is something radically wrong with how and to whom contemporary American art speaks: It is simply a matter of taste, an example of the wonderful "diversity" that exists out there in America. Some people go to museums, they reason, and some people go to tractor pulls — and neither should presume to tell the other which is superior. This cultural laissez-faire attitude was probably best summed up by the late painter Jack Tworkov, who mused, "Those who enjoy baseball are lucky."

That is why someone like Finley can slap together a crude, broad-voweled bray, an occasional Southern twang and the revival-tent punctuation of a "Yea-uh!" to insure that both ArtPAC's journalistic chorus and audience are amply satisfied with her social commitment. The satisfaction that the performance community on both sides of the footlights has demonstrated for this dashed-off, broad-stroke portrait of The People cries out for an adaptation of "The Emperor's New Clothes" in which a child speaks clearly from the back of the theater, "But they aren't *saying* anything!"

Finley's superficial depiction of working people is, again, only one example of the broad condescension displayed by ArtPAC. Not long ago I received a mailing from the National Association of Artists' Organizations. Over the text of the N.E.A. anti-obscenity clause was emblazoned an American flag and the slogan, "Don't Sound Like America to Me." This is ArtPAC's idea of wrapping itself in the same flag that good ol' Americans love: Real Americans, it knows, are as ungrammatical as they are true blue. Real Americans may not know what art is — only peer-review panels and downtown audiences enjoy that privilege — but they shuuur know censorship when they smell it.

Clearly, alienation from ArtPAC is real — and well deserved. People in communities from East St. Louis to Staten Island sense that their lives and opinions are uninteresting to arts-world decision makers. Their rage was there long before it was tapped by tax-exempt right-wing churches. Is ArtPAC, when it assails these institutions as enemies of the First Amendment, going to continue to condescendingly characterize those anti-N.E.A. letter-writing citizens as dupes while it ignores the genuine exclusion they feel? I wrote support-the-N.E.A. letters to my senators and congressman in the lobby of Manhattan's Public Theater: While I had been sitting in the audience at the end of a performance of George C. Wolfe's *Spunk*, actress Danitra Vance came forward on the stage and urged people to write to legislators before they left the theater. Does that make me a dupe of Danitra?

Here is a golden opportunity for America's arts community to pause and mediate upon the reasons why such antipathy has flourished beyond their pale, and to learn some respect for that vast majority that's not the usual audience for art.

The arts community must also be concerned with the censorship that happens to people who are not artists, because there is absolutely no vocabulary in their environment to describe that aspiration. It's the experience I once heard James Baldwin describe about his early life: "Growing up in a certain kind of poverty is growing up in a certain kind of silence." You cannot name the sensations, fears, injustices and simple facts of daily life because "no one corroborates it. Reality becomes unreal because no one experiences it but you." When the young Baldwin read Richard Wright, he experienced the first shock of corroboration: "Life was made bearable by Richard Wright's testimony. When circumstances are made real by another's testimony, it becomes possible to envision change." People who grow up in that kind of silence don't know about the existence of a network of grant-giving, rewards-distributing,

show/performance/publication/exhibition-sponsoring colleague-rallying ratifi-
cation.

Like Baldwin before his Wright epiphany, they never see an art describing
what they eat, how they sleep, what they dream about, what they fear, what
might help them see their way to gather strength. The heartwarming mythology
of the American culture industry is that working-class and ethnic artists
"emerge" out of their "pasts" — leaving behind all that the culturati consider
cheap and ignorant, and striving to find their place in the understanding
community of other artists. While plenty of artists act out the swagger of
"working-class" macho as a battle against the effete, they really don't care to do
the slow, attentive, frustrating excavation through all the heaped-up rubble of
history beneath which so many poetic voices lie buried.

It is certainly true that great and successful artists like Baldwin emerge from
that silence. But as the novelist and lesbian activist Sarah Schulman wrote
recently in *Outweek*, "For any minority artist, part of being admitted to the reward
system is that while the benefits are great for the individual, the price for the
community is tokenism... [A] single style is declared to be representative of a
hugely diverse community that it cannot represent." In fact, says Schulman —
who cites her own success as an example — the token artist's isolated acclaim
helps "keep other voices from the public arena."

Tokenism may be a strange charge to level at an ArtPAC which throughout
the N.E.A. struggle has spoken regularly about multiculturalism. But this comes
from a community that so far has interpreted censorship to mean denial of
N.E.A. grants to their current and familiar recipients. Artists under attack for
being lesbian, gay or feminist can only honestly and effectively articulate their
position as silenced citizens by situating themselves squarely within that larger
history of silences in America, both past and present.

In the most practical terms, those who have benefited from the reward
system must relinquish their presumption to privilege in favor of those the
reward system has traditionally excluded. Schulman has proposed reconstitut-
ing the N.E.A.'s peer panels so that 80 percent of their members are drawn from
traditionally marginalized or excluded communities. That might be a start.

Meanwhile, performance artists searching for a role model might consider
the work of Franca Rame, the radical Italian playwright and actress. Like
downtown artists such as Karen Finley, Rame specializes in the one-woman play
in which she herself is the performer. The difference between Rame and these
performance artists lies in the broad audience she achieves and direct content
she provides. Rame performs in conventional theaters and in union halls, on
television and in stadiums. In her "Tutta Casa, Letto e Chiesa," for example,
Rame presents a serious, hilarious and sometimes devastating look into the
minute-to-minute limitations, responsibilities and exasperations of a working-
class woman. Her character must maintain heroic stamina to deal with endless
incursions of boss, husband, men in the street, children and appliances upon her
life. Rame has also made theater out of a horrific event; the night she was
abducted from the street by far-right-wing thugs and brutally gang-raped. She
spares nothing of the humiliation, the sexual slurs, the cigarette burns to her
thighs. Rame has forged her own agony into a passionate social declaration:

Those unspeakable details of a woman's brutalization, which a censorious society would quickly close the lid upon and bury, Rame propels into the spotlight of the stage.

Jacqueline Shaw will never be able to tell what unspeakable things were done to *her* soul and body before that bullet was fired through her brain. Even if she hadn't been murdered, it's unlikely we would ever have heard about the details of her life. She belonged to that large group of American citizens who neither get to tell their stories nor get their stories told. Any battle against censorship that fails to clamor in outrage against this massive smothering of voices has already torpedoed its own cause with narcissism.

■ Sen. Jesse Helms, letter to Rev. Jerry Falwell, 1991

Jesse Helms is a Republican senator representing the state of North Carolina. He was the leader of the anti-NEA campaign in the U.S. Senate.

Dear Jerry:

I know that you decided two years ago to relinquish your role as an American political leader to enable you to devote your time pastoring Thomas Road Baptist Church and leading Liberty University.

Jerry, since you made what must have been a difficult decision, many very disturbing things have happened on the American political scene.

The homosexual "community," the feminists, the civil libertarians, the pro-abortionists, the flag burners and many other fringe political groups are more active than ever in promoting their dangerous anti-family and anti-American agendas. They are battling us on every front!

I sometimes feel that I am fighting these groups by myself. The media have attacked me more strongly than ever in recent months for my stands.

I would not, of course, suggest that you abandon your church and university responsibilities. I realize you cannot do that —and you must not.

But I do hope that you will alert America's Christian leaders regarding the activities of the National Endowment for the Arts.

I believe that if you alert your friends and supporters regarding how the NEA is using American taxpayers' dollars, it will make a difference.

Jerry, America needs your help — again.

Your friend,

Jesse Helms

Illustrations

Andres Serrano, *Piss Christ*, 1987, courtesy of Stux Gallery

Tim Miller, performance, *Sex/Love/Stories*

Annie Sprinkle, performance, *Post Porn Modernist*, photo by Leslie Barany

John Frohnmayer and Reverend Donald Wildmon debate on CNN, photo by
Glen Stubbe

RELAX SENATOR HELMS, THE ART WORLD IS YOUR KIND OF PLACE!

- The number of blacks at an art opening is about the same as at one of your garden parties.

- Many museum trustees are at least as conservative as Ronald Lauder.

- Because aesthetic quality stands above all, there's never been a need for Affirmative Action in museums or galleries.

- Most art collectors, like most successful artists, are white males.

- Women artists have their place: after all, they earn less than 1/3 of what male artists earn.

- Museums are separate but equal. No female black painter or sculptor has been in a Whitney Biennial since 1973. Instead, they can show at the Studio Museum in Harlem or the Women's Museum in Washington.

- Since most women artists don't make a living from their work and there's no maternity leave or childcare in the art world, they rarely choose both career and motherhood.

- The sexual imagery in most respected works of art is the expression of wholesome heterosexual males.

- Unsullied by government interference, art is one of the last unregulated markets. Why, there isn't even any self-regulation!

- The majority of exposed penises in major museums belong to the Baby Jesus.

Please send $ and comments to:
Box 1056 Cooper Sta. NY, NY 10276 **GUERRILLA GIRLS** CONSCIENCE OF THE ART WORLD

Guerrilla Girls, poster, 1989

313

Are you going to let politics kill Art?

Art should be supported by government and protected from politics.
Until now that has been the enlightened principle that has guided all legislation affecting the Arts in America.
Art must live free to survive.

That is why it is crucial that every friend of the Arts send a message to Washington right now.

There is still time for cool heads and common sense to prevail over the Helms amendment to the appropriations bill for the National Endowment for the Arts.

But the Arts desperately need your help now. Today.

It is with a sense of the greatest urgency that we ask you to write to the people in Congress
who will be meeting in the next few days in a crucial conference between the Appropriations Subcommittees of
both Houses to resolve differences in the National Endowment for the Arts legislation.

The names and addresses of the Congressional people to contact are listed below.

You are probably aware of the controversy that inspired the devastating amendment by Senator Jesse Helms.
In a July 28 editorial, entitled "The Helms Process," the New York Times wisely urged Congress
to protect the legislation that insulates art from politics. It observed:

"The Helms process would drain art of creativity, controversy – of life... and would plunge one esthetic question after another into the boiling bath of politics. That's unlikely to be good for politics; it would surely be fatal to Art."

Don't let moral panic and political pressure kill the Arts.
Don't assume that "someone else" will fight this battle for you.

Write, call, fax, or telegram the Congressional leaders listed below *now* and urge them to delete the Helms provisions from the conference report on H.R. 2788.

Trustees of the Whitney Museum of American Art

WHO TO CONTACT:

SENATE SUBCOMMITTEE ON THE INTERIOR
TELEPHONE 202-224-7233
Address for Senators:
U.S. Senate, Washington, D.C. 20510

	Telephone	FAX
Sen. Robert Byrd (D-WV) Chair	202-224-3954	202-224-8070
Sen. Dale Bumpers (D-AR)	202-224-4843	NONE
Sen. Quentin Burdick (D-ND)	202-224-2551	202-224-1143
Sen. Dennis DeConcini (D-AZ)	202-224-4521	202-224-8698
Sen. Ernest Hollings (D-SC)	202-224-6121	202-224-3573
Sen. J.Bennett Johnston (D-LA)	202-224-5824	202-224-2501
Sen. Patrick Leahy (D-VT)	202-224-4242	202-224-4797
Sen. Harry Reid (D-NV)	202-224-3542	202-224-7327
Sen. Thad Cochran (R-MS)	202-224-5054	NONE
Sen. Pete Domenici (R-NM)	202-224-6621	202-224-7371
Sen. Jake Garn (R-UT)	202-224-5444	NONE
Sen. James McClure(R-ID)	202-224-2752	202-224-1006
Sen. Don Nickles(R-OK)	202-224-5754	NONE
Sen. Warren Rudman (R-NH)	202-224-3324	NONE
Sen. Ted Stevens (R-AK)	202-224-3004	NONE

HOUSE SUBCOMMITTEE ON THE INTERIOR
TELEPHONE 202-225-3081
Address for Representatives: House of
Representatives, Washington, D.C. 20515

	Telephone	FAX
Rep. Sidney Yates (D-IL) Chair	202-225-2111	202-225-3493
Rep. Chester G. Atkins (D-MA)	202-225-3411	NONE
Rep. Les AuCoin (D-OR)	202-225-0855	202-225-2707
Rep. Tom Bevill (D-AL)	202-225-4876	202-225-0842
Rep. Norman D.Dicks (D-WA)	202-225-5916	202-225-1176
Rep. John P. Murtha (D-PA)	202-225-2065	202-225-5709
Rep. Bill Lowery (R-CA)	202-225-3201	202-225-7383
Rep. Joseph M.McDade (R-PA)	202-225-3731	202-225-9594
Rep. Ralph Regula (R-OH)	202-225-3876	202-225-3059

Whitney Museum of American Art, advertisement, *New York Times*, September 7, 1989

1. The American Flag is not an object of worship.

2. The New York Times manufactures censorship.

3. The United States Senate dictates censorship.

4. The United States courts are partial to Government.

5. The United States Government destroys art.

6. The United States Government deprives artists of moral rights.

7. Support indecent and uncivil art!

8. No mandatory patriotism.

Richard Serra 8 Drawings: Weights and Measures
23 September-14 October 1989 Leo Castelli 420 West Broadway New York

Richard Serra, advertisement for exhibition, *Art in America*, October 1989

TO THE CONGRESS OF THE UNITED STATES

Ladies and Gentlemen:

You are being asked to appropriate funds taken from the American taxpayers in order to continue the National Endowment For The Arts.

In recent years the NEA has used funds provided by you to pay for exhibitions of paintings and photographs depicting:

- Two naked men engaged in anal intercourse
- Little children with exposed genitals
- One man urinating in the mouth of another

- Jesus Christ immersed in a jar of urine
- The Roman Catholic Pontiff immersed in a vat of urine
- Jesus Christ shooting heroin into his arm

This November you will face an electorate:

- Furious at being forced by you to pay for the greed of savings and loan manipulators
- Disgusted with your handling of your pay raise

- Shocked at the revelation that you have been looting the Social Security Trust Fund for years
- Discouraged at your inability to balance the federal budget

Do you also want to face the voters with the charge that you are wasting their hard-earned money to promote sodomy, child pornography, and attacks on Jesus Christ?

You could choose to fund the NEA while refusing public funding for obscenity and attacks on religion. But the radical left wants you to give legitimacy to pornography and homosexuality. So you are being asked to vote like sheep for $175,000,000 with no strings attached.

Of course, when you vote, you may not have any risk.

We may not be able to give out 100,000 copies of the Mapplethorpe and Serrano "art" to registered voters in your district.

There may be more homosexuals and pedophiles in your district than there are Roman Catholics and Baptists. You may find that the working folks in your district want you to use their money to teach their sons how to sodomize one another. You may find that the Roman Catholics in your district want their money spent on pictures of the Pope soaked in urine.

But maybe not.

There is one way to find out.

Vote for the NEA appropriation just like Pat Williams, John Frohnmayer, and the gay and lesbian task force want.

And make my day.

Sincerely,

Pat Robertson
President, Christian Coalition

Christian Coalition

825 Greenbrier Circle, Suite 202, Chesapeake, VA 23320   (804) 424-2630

Christian Coalition, advertisement, *Washington Post*, June 20, 1990

Robbie Conal, *Artificial Art Official*, 1990

Hans Haacke, *Helmsboro Country*, 1990, photo by Fred Scruton

Robert Mapplethorpe's work projected on the Corcoran Gallery of Art during
pro-Mapplethorpe rally, June 30, 1989, photo by Robert Preissler

Robert Mapplethorpe's work projected on the Corcoran Gallery of Art, June 30, 1989,
photo by Robert Preissler

Robert Mapplethorpe, *X Portfolio, Jim and Tom, Sausalito,* © 1977, Estate of Robert Mapplethorpe

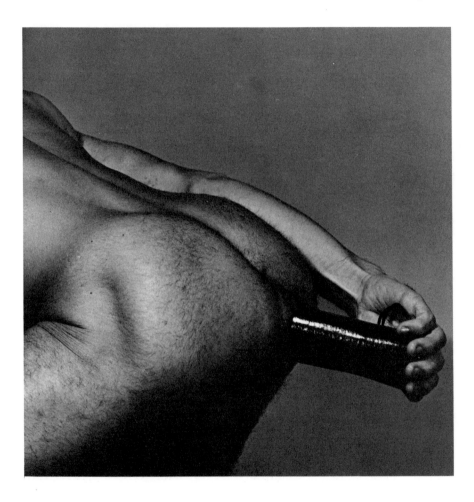

Robert Mapplethorpe, *X Portfolio, John*, © 1978, Estate of Robert Mapplethorpe

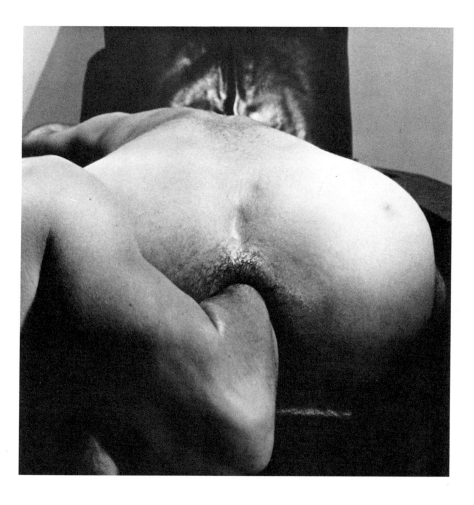

Robert Mapplethorpe, *X Portfolio, Helmut and Brooks, NYC*, © 1978, Estate of Robert Mapplethorpe

Robert Mapplethorpe, *X Portfolio, Joe,* © 1978, Estate of Robert Mapplethorpe

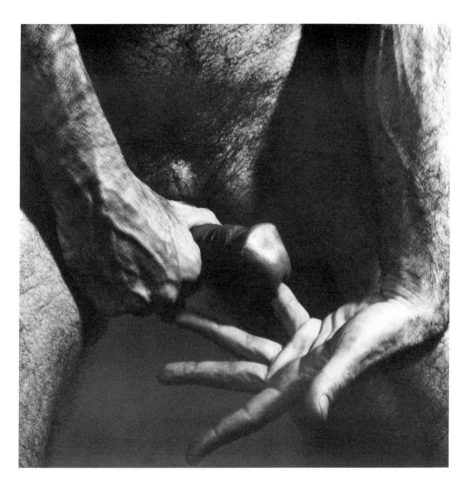

Robert Mapplethorpe, *X Portfolio, Lou,* © 1978, Estate of Robert Mapplethorpe

Robert Mapplethorpe, *X Portfolio, Self Portrait*, © 1978, Estate of Robert Mapplethorpe

Robert Mapplethorpe, *Ajitto*, © 1981, Estate of Robert Mapplethorpe

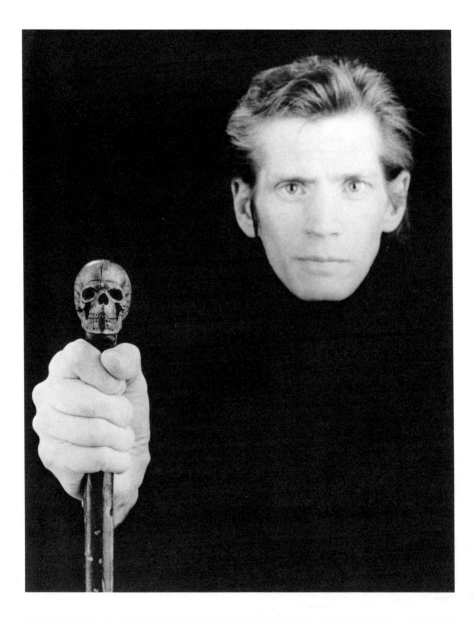

Robert Mapplethorpe, *Self Portrait*, © Estate of Robert Mapplethorpe

Chronology

CHRONOLOGY
Philip Brookman and Debra Singer

This chronology includes selected examples of major cases of censorship and controversy in American culture, beginning in 1962 with events leading up to the establishment of the National Endowment for the Arts (NEA) and continuing through 1990. It includes events related to the arts, media, obscenity, and cultural symbolism. Particular attention is devoted to events surrounding the problematic 1989–1990 congressional reauthorization of the NEA. For reasons of space, the frequent banning of textbooks and literature from school libraries, and specifics about the ongoing harassment of popular entertainers for using explicit language or images in their performances, videos, or record covers are not represented here (with the exception of the prominent 2 Live Crew case).

■ 1962

March: President John F. Kennedy appoints August Heckscher as his Special Consultant on the Arts to develop policy on federal involvement in the arts.

■ 1963

May 28: In his report to President Kennedy, entitled *The Arts and the National Government,* August Heckscher recommends the establishment of a Federal Advisory Council on the Arts and a grant-giving National Arts Foundation. Kennedy announces, "We are justly proud of the vitality, the creativity, and the variety of the contemporary contributions our citizens can offer the world of the arts. If we are to be among the leaders of the world in every sense of the word, this sector of our national life cannot be neglected or treated with indifference."

June 12: By executive order, President Kennedy establishes the President's Advisory Council on the Arts.

December 20: The Senate passes S. 2379, a bill creating a National Council on the Arts and a National Arts Foundation.

■ 1964

August 20: The House of Represenatives passes H.R. 9586 to legislate creation of a National Council on the Arts. The following day the Senate concurs with the House bill by a voice vote.

September 3: The National Arts and Cultural Development Act of 1964 (Public Law 88-579) is signed by President Lyndon B. Johnson, formally establishing the National Council on the Arts.

October 7: $50,000 in federal funds is appropriated for the National Council on the Arts.

■ 1965

March 10: President Lyndon B. Johnson asks Congress to pass legislation to establish a National Foundation on the Arts and Humanities.

September 15: The House passes legislation to create the National Foundation on the Arts and Humanities. The following day the Senate agrees, and the bill (S. 1483) is given to the president for signature.

September 29: Public Law 89-209, also known as the National Foundation on the Arts and Humanities Act of 1965, is signed by President Johnson. This law creates the National Endowment for the Arts (NEA) and the National Endowment for the Humanities (NEH). The law states that "the practice of art and the study of humanities requires constant dedication and devotion and that, while no government can call a great artist or scholar into existence, it is necessary and appropriate for the federal government to help create and sustain not only a climate encouraging freedom of thought, imagination, and inquiry, but also the material conditions facilitating the release of this creative talent." The law details the mission, structure, and operating guidelines for the endowments. It also authorizes the chairperson of each endowment to work with "panels of experts" to review grant applications, and it positions the National Council on the Arts to advise the chairperson of the NEA, requiring that the council review all grants before they are authorized. In its report on this bill, the Senate Labor and Public Welfare Committee insists that the law give "the fullest attention to freedom of artistic and humanistic expression. One of the artist's and humanist's great values to society is the mirror of self-examination which they raise so that society can become aware of its shortcomings as well as its strengths."

October 31: $2.4 million in federal funds is appropriated for the NEA during the final eight months of fiscal year (FY) 1966. The NEA begins operations with fewer than twelve employees.

■ 1966

July 1: The NEA is budgeted $7.96 million for FY 1967.

■ 1967

July 1: The NEA is budgeted $7.2 million for FY 1968.

■ 1968

July 1: The NEA is budgeted $7.8 million for FY 1969.

■ 1969

July 1: The NEA is budgeted $8.25 million for FY 1970.

■ 1970

July 1: The NEA is budgeted $15.1 million for FY 1971.

■ 1971

April 6: An exhibition by Hans Haacke is canceled by the Guggenheim Museum in New York. Two of the works created for the show are investigations of the real estate holdings of two New York City investment groups. The first, *Shalopsky et al. Manhattan Real Estate Holdings, a Real-Time Social System as of May 1, 1971*, documents the slum holdings of a Manhattan real estate corporation; the second, *Sal Goldman and Alex DiLorenzo Manhattan Real Estate Holdings, a Real-Time Social System as of May 1, 1971*, details the properties of Manhattan's largest private real estate corporation. The museum claims the works might subject them to legal action and that Haacke's descriptions of "social systems" represent "an alien substance that had entered the art museum organism." Edward Fry, the exhibition's curator, is fired.

July 1: The NEA is budgeted $29.75 million for FY 1972.

■ 1972

Having been subjected to criticism from two Public Broadcasting Service (PBS) news shows, *Thirty Minutes With* and *Washington Week in Review*, President Richard Nixon vetoes the entire budget of the Corporation for Public Broadcasting (CPB). CPB provides funding for PBS programming.

Erica Jong lists the NEA in the acknowledgments of her controversial book *Fear of Flying*. First-term Senator Jesse Helms (R–N.C.), among others, becomes concerned about government funding of this "reportedly filthy, obscene book."

July 1: The NEA is budgeted $38.2 million for FY 1973.

■ 1973

June 21: The U.S. Supreme Court rules on *Miller* v. *California*, an obscenity case. A new legal definition of obscenity results, superceding the *Roth* v. *United States* decision of 1957. A three-part test is established by the court, which rules that "a work may be subject to state regulation where that work, taken as a whole, appeals to the prurient interest in sex; portrays in a patently offensive way, sexual conduct specifically defined by the applicable state law; and, taken as a whole, does not have serious literary, artistic, political, or scientific value."

July 1: The NEA is budgeted $60.77 million for FY 1974.

■ 1974

July 1: The NEA is budgeted $74.75 million for FY 1975.

■ 1975

July 1: The NEA is budgeted $82 million for FY 1976.

■ 1976

July 1: The NEA is budgeted $34 million for the fiscal "transition quarter" period of July 1 to September 30.

October 1: The NEA is budgeted $94 million for FY 1977.

■ 1977

October 1: The NEA is budgeted $123.85 million for FY 1978.

■ 1978

July 3: In its ruling on *Federal Communications Commission* v. *Pacifica Foundation*, the U.S. Supreme Court overrules a U.S. Court of Appeals finding and agrees with the Federal Communications Commission that a radio broadcast is obscene. As part of a program about people's attitudes toward language, radio station KPFA in Berkeley, California, had aired a twelve-minute monologue called "Filthy Words," including a list of all "the words you couldn't say on the public...airwaves."

October 1: The NEA is budgeted $149. 58 million for FY 1979.

■ 1979

October 1: The NEA is budgeted $154.61 million for FY 1980.

■ 1980

October 1: The NEA is budgeted $158.79 million for FY 1981.

■ 1981

February 2: Reverend Donald Wildmon's National Federation for Decency and Reverend Jerry Falwell's Moral Majority join forces with about four hundred other Christian organizations (including the Eagle Forum, American Life Lobby, Pro-Family Forum, and Concerned Women for America) to form the Coalition for Better Television (CBT), with Wildmon as the director. The CBT announces that it will boycott television programs it deems offensive as well as the companies advertising on the programs. "No matter how well intentioned...such efforts amount to censorship," states CBS spokesman Gene Mater. "We are also concerned that this effort to restrict the individual's freedom of choice by having only 'approved' television programs available may bring on similar campaigns directed at other communications media."

June 5: President Reagan appoints the Presidential Task Force on the Arts and Humanities to review the activities of the NEA and NEH. The Heritage Foundation, a conservative think tank, independently offers recommendations for reforming government operations and agencies. Its report, *Mandate for Leadership*, calls for major changes at the NEA. President Reagan proposes a 50 percent budget cut for the NEA and NEH, as well as the elimination of the Institute of Museum Services, which provides general operating support for museums. Funding to the endowments is cut by only 10 percent in the final congressional appropriations, but the "Art Critics" funding category (a source of controversy because of the allegedly political nature of some grants) is suspended by the NEA, partly in response to the president's proposed cuts. The Reagan administration successfully eliminates the Comprehensive Employment Training Act (CETA) public service employment programs, which are responsible for an estimated $200 million in jobs nationwide, including support of many workers in the arts. The Presidential Task Force on the Arts and Humanities recommends that the NEA's structure of grant-giving be maintained, but also recommends a stronger Federal Council on the Arts and Humanities to oversee the Endowment.

June 15: Procter and Gamble withdraws its sponsorship of more than fifty television programs two weeks before the Coalition for Better Television was to begin a boycott of the company. "We've had dialogues with P&G over a period of many months. They hear what we've been saying and they share many of our concerns," says Coalition director Donald Wildmon (see February 2, 1981).

October 1: The NEA is budgeted $143.45 million for FY 1982.

■ 1982

October 1: The NEA is budgeted $143.87 million for FY 1983.

■ 1983

NEA chairperson Frank Hodsoll vetoes a panel-approved grant to the Heresies Collective and PAD/D in New York that would have supported a series of public forums featuring politically oriented artists Hans Haacke, Martha Rosler, Suzanne Lacy, and critic Lucy Lippard.

October 1: The NEA is budgeted $162 million for FY 1984.

November 18: The Reagan administration issues a booklet entitled *President Reagan on Peace, Arms Reductions, and Deterrence* in response to ABC-TV's controversial film *The Day After*, which depicts the destruction by nuclear attack of a Kansas community. White House officials say they are concerned that the film will advance the cause of the nuclear freeze movement. Reverend Jerry Falwell announces a boycott of the program's advertisers by the Moral Majority.

■ 1984

August 22: Gregory Lee Johnson is arrested for burning an U.S. flag at the Republican National Convention in Dallas in protest of the Reagan administration's Central American policies, the threat of nuclear war, and certain Dallas-based corporations. Johnson is later convicted of violating a Texas law against "desecration of a venerated object" (see June 21, 1989).

October 1: The NEA is budgeted $163.66 million for FY 1985.

October 9: Retired General William Westmoreland's $120 million libel suit against CBS is heard in court. Westmoreland claims that the network misrepresented him in a 1982 documentary entitled *The Uncounted Enemy: a Vietnam Deception.* The program reported that the general and other military commanders in Vietnam deliberately underreported enemy strength in 1967 and 1968 in order to convince the government and the public that the war was being won (see March 1, 1985).

■ 1985

January 21: In a letter circulated by the National Congressional Club, America's second-largest political action committee, Senator Jesse Helms urges conservatives to join together to buy the CBS television network. Helms and his supporters inform the Securities and Exchange Commission that they plan to buy enough CBS stock to "regain control of the airwaves" and that they would then request an end to the network's "liberal bias in news reporting and editorial policies."

March 1: General William Westmoreland and CBS-TV announce an out-of-court settlement in the former general's libel suit against the network. Westmoreland withdraws the case, and receives a statement from the network saying that "CBS respects General Westmoreland's long and faithful service to his country and never intended to assert, and does not believe, that General Westmoreland was unpatriotic or disloyal in performing his duties as he saw fit."

March 6: The New York regional office of the General Services Administration (GSA) begins hearings about relocating *Tilted Arc*, Richard Serra's abstract, site-specific public sculpture. The GSA had commissioned the sculpture for Federal Plaza in Manhattan. Two months after its 1981 installation, thirteen hundred people who worked in buildings adjacent to the plaza signed petitions calling for the work's removal.

May 31: In response to more than seven thousand signatures gathered on petitions, the GSA announced that it will move Richard Serra's *Tilted Arc* from Federal Plaza to an undetermined location. Serra says, "To relocate it is to destroy it. It was built specifically for that place."

June: The Reagan administration creates the Attorney General's Commission on Pornography (also known as the Meese Commission) to investigate the connection between pornography and antisocial behavior. The Meese Commission hearings are chaired by Henry E. Hudson, a district attorney from Arlington County, Virginia, who is well known for his zealous prosecution of pornography cases. Many invited witnesses testify to the negative effects of pornography.

September 1: Reverends Jerry Falwell and Donald Wildmon organize a march of five thousand protesters to challenge the sale of *Playboy* and *Penthouse* magazines by 7-Eleven convenience stores. The protesters march on 7-Eleven's Southland Corporation headquarters in Dallas, where they are met by five hundred counterdemonstrators.

September 10: Representative Steve Bartlett (R–Tex.) proposes an amendment to a FY 1986 appropriations bill that would prohibit NEA grants from going to artists whose work is "patently offensive to the average person" and lacks "serious literary or artistic merit." The House Committee on Education and Labor debates how criteria for "offensive work" could be established and how the term "average person" should be defined. Debate also focuses on NEA funding of allegedly obscene, gay-oriented poetry. Representative Tom DeLay (R–Tex.) complains about several NEA-supported projects, including Celia Condit's videotape *Possibly in Michigan*, poetry published by the Gay Sunshine Press, and Jean-Luc Godard's film *Hail Mary*, shown at the NEA-funded New York Film Festival. Representative Bartlett's amendment is subsequently defeated in committee, but Representative Richard Armey (R–Tex.) promises to reintroduce the amendment to the full House during their upcoming vote to reauthorize the endowment.

September 19: The Senate Committee on Commerce begins hearings addressing the regulation of music recordings that contain lyrics referring to sex and violence. The committee considers requiring companies to place warning labels on such recordings. Tipper Gore, wife of Senator Albert Gore (D–Tenn.), and her organization, the Parents Music Resource Center (PMRC), are instrumental in convincing this committee to hold hearings.

October 1: The NEA is budgeted $158.82 million for FY 1986.

October 10: The House of Representatives passes legislation reauthorizing the NEA. Going against the Reagan administration's recommendation to cut $20 million from the NEA budget, the House increases the budget by $3 million for FY 1986. Two amendments by Representative Richard Armey are also passed, requiring the NEA to fund only projects with "significant literary, scholarly, cultural, or artistic merit," and requiring financial reports to be filed by grant recipients within ninety days of the end of their grant period. Representative

Tom DeLay introduces an amendment to change the NEA's reauthorization period from every five years to every two years; it is defeated.

November 19: The U.S. release of Jean-Luc Godard's film *Hail Mary* triggers protests nationwide. The film offers a contemporary description of the birth of Jesus: Mary works in a gas station, Joseph is a taxi driver, and the angel Gabriel is a street-smart tough guy. The film includes nudity and profanity. Organizers of protests in New York and Boston include the Society for Tradition, Family, and Property, an international extremist group. Triumph Films, a subsidiary of Columbia Pictures and Coca-Cola, cancels its plans to distribute *Hail Mary*, and Sack Theaters cancels a scheduled run of the film in Boston after receiving numerous phone calls and threats.

December 6: The United States Information Agency (USIA) and its director, Charles Z. Wick, are sued in a Los Angeles federal court for interfering with the international distribution of several educational documentary films. The suit, filed by a group of independent filmmakers represented by the Center for Constitutional Rights in New York, charges that the USIA used political criteria to withhold duty-free export certificates for these films. It is argued that the USIA's action violates the First and Fifth Amendments of the Constitution, as well as the Beirut Agreement, a treaty simplifying the exchange by signatory nations of educational, scientific, or cultural materials. The six films named in the suit are: *In Our Own Backyards: Uranium Mining in the U.S.*, *Peace: A Conscious Choice*, *What Ever Happened to Childhood*, *Save the Planet*, *Ecocide: A Strategy of War*, and *From the Ashes...Nicaragua Today* (see October 24, 1986).

■ 1986

January 6: A sculpture by San Diego artist David Avalos is removed from public exhibition by U.S. District Court Judge Gordon Thompson, who claims that the sculpture is a security risk. Avalos's work, *San Diego Donkey Cart*, was installed in the plaza of the San Diego Federal Courthouse as part of an exhibition sponsored by Sushi, an alternative gallery. The sculpture, placed near the offices of the Immigration and Naturalization Service (INS), includes images of an undocumented worker being frisked and arrested by a U.S. Border Patrol agent. Although the General Services Administration had granted permission for *San Diego Donkey Cart* to be exhibited in the courthouse plaza, Thompson has GSA officials dismantle and remove it. The American Civil Liberties Union (ACLU) files a court action on Avalos's behalf.

February: The Meese Commission on Pornography sends a letter to retailers across the country who sell erotic magazines in their stores. The letter informs the retailers that they were named by an anonymous commission witness as distributors of pornography. The letter warns these retailers that they will be named in the commission's report unless they can disprove this testimony. A federal court later orders the commission to send letters retracting these allegations, but some retailers (including 7-Eleven and Rite-Aid stores) stop selling certain magazines, such as *Playboy* and *Penthouse*. It is learned that the commission's "anonymous witness" is Reverend Donald Wildmon, director of the American Federation of Decency.

June: The Meese Commission on Pornography issues its final report. The report argues that sexual imagery and sexual behavior are linked, and therefore calls for stricter regulation of the distribution and sale of erotic materials.

June 20: A federal appeals court rules that the U.S. Justice Department may require labels on three Canadian films in order to identify them as "political propaganda" when the films are imported into the United States. Justice Department rules may also require distributors to file reports naming the organizations and individuals who asked to see the films. The ACLU had sought to prevent the classification, which the distributors felt would inhibit distribution of the films in the United States. All three films — *Acid Rain from Heaven*, *Acid Rain: Requiem or Recovery*, and the Academy Award winning *If You Love This Planet* — were produced by the National Film Board of Canada. The court, in an opinion written by Judge Antonin Scalia, said the term "political propaganda" is not unconstitutional.

July 22: NEA chairperson Frank Hodsoll vetoes a NEA Inter-Arts grant, recommended by the panel, for a Washington, D.C., exhibition by artist Jenny Holzer, sponsored by Washington Project for the Arts. Holzer planned to show her own video works, as well as videotapes by ten other artists, on a billboard-sized video truck at public sites near the White House, the Capitol building, and the Supreme Court. Members of the viewing public were to be given an opportunity to use the giant screen to express their views about freedom of expression. In denying funding, Hodsoll cited his and the National Council on the Arts' concerns about "the intrinsic aesthetic value of the project; its actual 'interdisciplinary' nature and potential quality...and its artistic merit based on the material submitted."

September: Judge Martin S. Speigel, upholding a 1985 Immigration and Naturalization Service ruling, refuses to renew the U.S. citizenship of American-born writer and teacher Margaret Randall. The judge also refuses to reverse a deportation order pending against Randall. The writer had become a Mexican citizen in 1967 when she moved there to work and marry. She returned to the United States in 1984 to teach at the University of New Mexico, Albuquerque, and at that time petitioned the U.S. government to renew her citizenship. Speigel says that his opinion is based partly on the content of Randall's writing. "Portions of the respondent's various writing advocates the economic, international, and governmental doctrine of world Communism," he says.

September 3: Lynn Cheney, chairperson of the National Endowment for the Humanities, attacks the public television series *The Africans*, which had received $600,000 from the NEH during production. Calling the series an "anti-Western diatribe," Cheney asks that the NEH's name be removed from the program credits, and she rejects a request from producing station WETA-TV in Washington, D.C., for an additional $50,000 grant for program publicity. Cheney tells WETA, "Anybody in this country can, of course, produce any film with any bias he or she pleases. But when you seek funding from NEH — when you use taxpayer dollars to underwrite your efforts — then standards of balance and objectivity are demanded."

October 1: The NEA is budgeted $165. 28 million for FY 1987.

October 24: Judge A. Wallace Tashima of the U.S. District Court of Los Angeles, responding to a December 1985 suit filed against the United States Information Agency, rules that it is illegal for the USIA to refuse export certificates to six educational films. He decides that the USIA's guidelines for obtaining certificates "on their face value violate the First and Fifth amendments to the Constitution.... These regulations are not merely flexible, they are boundless and put the Information Agency in the position of determining what is the 'truth' about America, politically and otherwise" (see December 6, 1985).

■ 1987

April 28: The U.S. Supreme Court rules that it is constitutional for Congress and the Justice Department to label as "political propaganda" foreign films that might influence public opinion on U.S. foreign policy. The court also decides that the government can keep track of whoever distributes or receives such films in the United States. In a 5–3 decision on *Meese* v. *Keene,* the court upholds a lower court ruling, thereby allowing the Justice Department to label three Canadian films about nuclear war and acid rain. The court finds that "Congress simply required the disseminators of such material to make additional disclosures that would enable the public to evaluate the import of the propaganda." Justice John Paul Stevens said the required labels do not have to include the word "propaganda" but they must be labeled as registered foreign agent materials (see June 20, 1986).

August: A federal judge rules that the General Services Administration may remove Richard Serra's sculpture *Tilted Arc* from Manhattan's Federal Plaza. The judge says that even though the sculpture was originally commissioned as a permanent, site-specific work, "the government had the right to do what it wished with its property." At the request of the GSA, a NEA panel convenes in December 1987 and recommends that the work not be removed (see March 6 and March 31, 1985).

October 1: The NEA is budgeted $167.73 million for FY 1988.

■ 1988

January 2: San Diego artists David Avalos, Louis Hock, and Elizabeth Sisco place a poster addressing immigration issues on one hundred San Diego Transit District buses. The artists buy advertising space on city buses to display a poster, entitled *Welcome to America's Finest Tourist Plantation.* It addresses the city's consumer-oriented tourist industry, relating tourism to the problems of the many undocumented workers in this industry. Tourism and city officials de-

340

mand removal of the posters but transit officials refuse, saying that to remove them would be unconstitutional. Because the project received funding from San Diego's Combined Arts and Educational Council and from the NEA through this council, it is also requested that the legal aspects of the funding be investigated. The counsel for the state legislature determines that no funding laws have been violated.

January 13: In a 5–3 decision, the U.S. Supreme Court rules that the Hazelwood (Missouri) School District can delete two pages of articles from a student newspaper. These articles describe students' experiences with divorce and pregnancy. The decision increases the power of school officials to censor other "school sponsored expressive activities." In its decision of *Hazelwood School District et al.* v. *Cathy Kuhlmeier et al.*, the Supreme Court rules that the rights of students are not the same as those of adults "in light of the special characteristics of the school environment...even though the government could not censor similar speech outside the school." In his majority opinion, Justice Byron White says that schools can censor the speech of students that would "associate the school with any position other than neutrality on matters of political controversy."

January 15: Ignoring a 1986 federal court ruling, the USIA insists that the educational film *From the Ashes...Nicaragua Today* be labeled as "propaganda" before it can receive a duty-free export licence. Produced in 1981 by the Women's Film Project of Kensington, the film is critical of U.S. government policies in Central America (see October 24, 1986).

April 23: A Mighty Mouse cartoon by Ralph Bakshi is attacked by the American Family Association in Tupelo, Mississippi, and its director Reverend Donald Wildmon. Wildmon asserts that the cartoon depicts Mighty Mouse sniffing cocaine under the guise of sniffing a flower. He initiates a letter-writing campaign against CBS-TV, the network broadcasting the cartoon. Bowing to the pressure, CBS cuts the three-second scene from the cartoon.

May 11: A painting entitled *Mirth and Girth* by David K. Nelson is removed by a group of Chicago aldermen and the Chicago police from a student exhibition at the School of the Art Institute of Chicago. In Nelson's painting, the late Chicago Mayor Harold Washington is depicted wearing lingerie. The aldermen justify their actions by saying that the painting offends them and that it might fuel racist feelings in the city. The American Civil Liberties Union files suit in U.S. District Court, charging the aldermen and the Chicago police with censorship and with the violation of Nelson's constitutional rights.

July 14: The home of Arlington, Virginia, artist Alice Sims is searched by police and postal inspectors, who are investigating Sims for producing child pornography. The artist had sent a roll of film containing photographs of naked children to a local drugstore for processing. Sims had photographed her own children as studies for a series of drawings. Her children are taken away by investigators, and returned the next day, after Sims and her husband are granted temporary custody. The case is eventually dropped by the State of Virginia.

August 9: The House of Representatives passes a resolution (H. Res. 517) asking Universal Studios to cancel the release of Martin Scorcese's film *The Last Temptation of Christ.* The resolution claims that the film "exceeds acceptable bounds of decency in offending the Christian community," and it encourages patrons to boycott the studio and theaters showing the film. Several days earlier, Reverend Jerry Falwell also denounced the film and urged a boycott. Protesters picket the film nationwide.

October 1: The NEA is budgeted $169.09 million for FY 1989.

■ 1989

January 27: A concurrent resolution (H. Con. Res. 35) is passed in the House of Representatives, stating that the U.S. flag "should be treated with due respect," and that "public desecration of the United States flag is not considered symbolic speech under the First Amendment to the Constitution." The resolution calls for "prohibitions against the willful and knowing display of contempt" of the flag.

February 28: The Senate issues a resolution (S. Res. 72) condemning death threats against British author Salman Rushdie and the publishers of his book *The Satanic Verses.* The action is taken in response to a call by Iran's Ayatollah Ruhollah Khomeini for the assassination of the author and the officers of Viking Press. Khomeini considered Rushdie's book to be blasphemous to Islam. The Senate resolution declares "its commitment to protect the right of any person to write, publish, sell, buy, and read books without fear of intimidation and violence."

March 10: Artist Richard Serra files a legal action against the New York state government in a last-minute attempt to prevent the removal of his sculpture *Titled Arc* from its site in New York City. In response to Serra's appeal, Judge Robert P. Paterson of the U.S. District Court issues a temporary restraining order against dismantling the sculpture. Serra says that the removal of *Titled Arc* "is a death blow, it's thoughtless and barbaric. The U.S. government has never before destroyed a work of art it has commissioned" (see March 6, 1985 and August 1987).

March 14: A concurrent resolution (H. Con. Res. 72) is passed in the House of Representatives, condemning the Art Institute of Chicago and the School of the Art Institute of Chicago for "permitting the display of an exhibit that encourages disrespect for the flag of the United States and abuses the right of freedom of speech as guaranteed by the Constitution." The resolution is offered in response to an artwork entitled *What Is the Proper Way To Display a U.S. Flag?* by "Dread" Scott Tyler, an art student at the school. In this work, Tyler exhibits a collage of photographs depicting coffins draped with flags and South Korean protesters burning a U.S. flag. An actual U.S. flag is placed on the gallery floor in front of a ledger, where viewers can write comments and answer the question posed by the work's title — but must step on the flag in order to do so. Hundreds of people, led by Vietnam veterans, had marched on the Art Institute of Chicago to protest the display.

March 15: The General Services Administration dismantles and removes Richard Serra's *Tilted Arc* from Federal Plaza in New York City. Serra says, "*Tilted Arc* was not destroyed because the sculpture was uncivil, but because the government wanted to set a precedent in which they could demonstrate their right to censor and destroy speech."

April 4: In response to numerous complaints and boycott threats from religious groups, Pepsico, Inc., decides to withdraw Pepsi ads featuring the pop star Madonna and her song "Like a Prayer." The American Family Association and other organizations, offended by the use of religious imagery in the video version of this song, had called for a one-year boycott of all Pepsi products. The boycott is called off when Pepsico officials stop airing the commercial.

April 5: Reverend Donald Wildmon brings artist Andres Serrano's photograph *Piss Christ* to the attention of Congress and the media. *Piss Christ*, a large color photograph depicting a small plastic crucifix submerged in the artist's urine, is part of an ongoing series of photographs in which the artist combines various bodily fluids with other objects. In 1988 Serrano won a $15,000 fellowship from Awards in the Visual Arts (AVA), a program administered by the Southeastern Center for Contemporary Art (SECCA), Winston-Salem, North Carolina. This program is funded by grants to SECCA from a number of different sources, including the NEA. *Piss Christ* was included in a 1988 traveling exhibition of works by AVA award winners. The exhibition was shown at the Virginia Museum in Richmond, where *Piss Christ* offended some museum visitors. Wildmon was informed about the work at this time, and began a letter-writing campaign to Congress, Christian organizations, and the media, decrying the work as blasphemous and calling for an end to government funding of such art.

April 12: San Diego artists David Avalos, Louis Hock, Elizabeth Sisco, and Deborah Small install a billboard referring to a local debate about whether to name the new San Diego Convention Center after Dr. Martin Luther King, Jr. The billboard raises the issue of racism in the city. The problem of determining an appropriate dedication to King previously arose in a 1987 city referendum, when voters reversed a city council decision to rename a street after the civil rights leader. The artists' project, entitled *Welcome To America's Finest...*, is funded by city, state, and federal grants and is coordinated by Installation Gallery, a local alternative art space. In response, on May 31 the San Diego City Council's Public Services and Safety Committee vetoes a $42,000 operating grant for Installation Gallery. On June 29, reacting to accusations of censorship, council members reverse their decision and reinstate a grant of $37,525 to the gallery. A stipulation is added that these funds must only be used for an annual "Artwalk" event (see January 2, 1988).

May 18: Senator Alfonse D'Amato (R–N.Y.) expresses to the Senate his anger over the federal funding of Andres Serrano's *Piss Christ*. D'Amato tears up a copy of the Awards in the Visual Arts exhibition catalogue that reproduced Serrano's

343

work. Agreeing with Senator D'Amato, Senator Jesse Helms says, "I do not know Mr. Andres Serrano, and I hope I never meet him. Because he is not an artist, he is a jerk." Twenty-five members of the Senate cosign a letter written by D'Amato to acting NEA chairperson Hugh Southern, requesting that the endowment review and reform its grant-making procedures.

June 5: The U.S. Supreme Court refuses to hear an appeal by David Avalos in his ACLU-sponsored lawsuit against Judge Gordon Thompson, who removed Avalos's sculpture *San Diego Donkey Cart* from a federal building plaza in 1986 (see January 6, 1986).

June 8: Representative Richard Armey (R–Tex.) is joined by more than one hundred members of Congress in sending a letter to the NEA criticizing the endowment's support of an exhibition entitled *Robert Mapplethorpe: The Perfect Moment.* This retrospective exhibition, organized by the Institute of Contemporary Art (ICA), at the University of Pennsylvania in Philadelphia, contains more than 150 photographs by Mapplethorpe, including several images depicting explicit homosexual acts or nude children. The ICA had received a grant of $30,000 from the NEA to help underwrite the approximately $200,000 cost of organizing and touring the exhibition.

June 13: The Corcoran Gallery of Art in Washington, D.C., hoping to avoid controversy, cancels their scheduled showing of *Robert Mapplethorpe: The Perfect Moment.* Corcoran director Dr. Christina Orr-Cahall says, "Citizen and congressional concerns — on both sides of the issue of public funds supporting controversial art — are now pulling the Corcoran into the political domain."

June 20: In an attempt to limit debate over government funding of controversial art, Representative Sidney R. Yates (D–Ill.) offers an amendment to the House Appropriations Subcommittee requiring that no NEA funds may be regranted by other organizations. For example, the Southeastern Center for Contemporary Art had received funds from the NEA, which were then regranted to Andres Serrano through SECCA's Awards in the Visual Arts program. Yates's amendment passes the committee unanimously.

June 21: The U.S. Supreme Court rules that desecration of the flag is a protected form of free speech or "symbolic speech." The 5–4 decision in *Texas* v. *Johnson,* written by Justice William J. Brennan, nullifies flag desecration laws in forty-eight states. Brennan writes, "We do not consecrate the flag by punishing its desecration, for in doing so we dilute the freedom that this cherished emblem represents." The ruling overturns the 1984 conviction of Gregory Lee Johnson, who was fined and sentenced to jail for burning a flag in Dallas (see August 22, 1984).

The Senate, the Chicago City Council, and both houses of the Illinois state legislature all pass measures in response to a student exhibition at the School of the Art Institute of Chicago that included Scott Tyler's *What Is the Proper Way To Display a U.S. Flag?.* These various measures bar display of the American flag on the ground. The Illinois legislation makes such an act a felony, punishable by one to three years in prison and a fine of up to $10,000. The acts, however, are nullified by the Supreme Court ruling in *Texas* v. *Johnson*, decided the same day (see March 14, 1989).

June 26: Responding to the Corcoran Gallery of Art's cancellation of the exhibition *Robert Mapplethorpe: The Perfect Moment*, Washington Project for the Arts (WPA), an alternative arts organization in Washington, D.C., announces plans to show the exhibition. WPA's Board of Directors had voted unanimously on June 14 to host the show from July 21 to August 13 (see June 13, 1989).

June 27: Representative Matthew J. Rinaldo (R–N.J.) introduces to the Committee on Education and Labor a resolution (H.R. 2762) to amend the NEA's founding legislation the National Foundation on the Arts and Humanities Act of 1965, "to prohibit the use of certain grants for a project which desecrates or denigrates a religious or national symbol."

June 29: The House Appropriations Committee approves a proposal by Representative Sidney Yates, recommending that the NEA and NEH give subsidiary groups in regranting programs the authority only to recommend awards of federal money, leaving the power for final approval to each endowment (see June 20, 1989).

Reacting to controversy over *What Is the Proper Way To Display a U.S. Flag?*, the School of the Art Institute of Chicago issues new guidelines for "disruptive" student work on public display. The guidelines, developed by a committee of students, faculty, and administrators, allow the school to "relocate or remove" any exhibit that "may be disruptive to the educational process" or may be "hazardous to the health and or safety of viewers or participants."

June 30: President Bush and other Republican leaders propose a constitutional amendment to overturn *Texas* v. *Johnson*, the Supreme Court ruling that determined burning a U.S. flag to be a protected form of free speech.

July 3: Nine hundred people gather in front of the Corcoran Gallery of Art to protest the museum's cancellation of *Robert Mapplethorpe: The Perfect Moment*. Ten twenty-five foot images of Mapplethorpe's photographs are projected onto the facade of the museum. The protest is organized by the Coalition of Washington Artists and other local arts and gay-rights organizations.

July 7: President Bush announces his selection of Oregon lawyer John E. Frohnmayer as the new chairperson of the National Endowment for the Arts, replacing acting chairperson Hugh Southern. Frohnmayer says art that is "cutting edge is always an issue. I think the public arts agencies, be they state or federal, need to walk a very fine line between supporting that art which is really very meaningful, and protecting the public trust."

July 10: Ziff Sistrunk, executive director of the Chicago Sports Council, files a complaint with the Chicago Public Library Cultural Center about its exhibition of Eric Fischl's painting *Boys at Bat*, which depicts a naked man swinging a baseball bat as a young boy in uniform watches. The painting is part of *Diamonds Are Forever*, a traveling exhibition about baseball organized by the New York State Museum and the Smithsonian Institution Traveling Exhibition Service.

Sistrunk feels that the painting encourages homosexuality and child molestation. Sistrunk says that Fischl's painting "is not connected with baseball in any way. I have trained players in Little League and semi-pro baseball, and at no time did I train them naked."

July 12: The House of Representatives rejects Representative Dana Rohrabacher's (R–Cal.) proposal to defund completely the NEA, and passes an NEA appropriations bill that contains a symbolic cut of $45,000 from the NEA's budget. This figure reflects the amount that SECCA awarded to Andres Serrano ($15,000, funded in part by the NEA) plus that the NEA awarded to Philadelphia ICA, (a $30,000 NEA Museum Program grant for *Robert Mapplethorpe: The Perfect Moment*). The bill, introduced by Representative Sidney Yates, is approved by a vote of 361–65.

July 17: Reverend Donald Wildmon, director of the American Family Association and of Christian Leaders for Responsible Television (CLeaR-TV), initiates a boycott of the Mennen and Clorox Corporations because, he claims, these companies sponsor prime-time programs that contain "high levels of sex, violence, or profanity."

July 18: The Senate considers the Biden-Roth-Cohen Flag Protection Act of 1989, which aims to protect the physical integrity of the U.S. flag. This legislation is intended to counter the Supreme Court's ruling in *Texas* v. *Johnson*, which determined that burning the U.S. flag is a protected form of free speech. The Flag Protection Act of 1989 was soon passed and signed into law (Public Law 101-131) by President Bush. In an early test of the Supreme Court's *Texas* v. *Johnson* decision, a flag was burned in Seattle and protesters were arrested and charged with violating the Flag Protection Act. U.S. District Judge Barbara Rothstein, using *Texas* v. *Johnson* to declare the Flag Protection Act unconstitutional, dismisses the charges (see June 21, 1989).

July 20: Robert Mapplethorpe: The Perfect Moment opens at Washington Project for the Arts. Almost fifty thousand people visit the exhibition during its twenty-five day run.

July 25: The Senate Appropriations Committee votes for a five-year ban on NEA grants to the ICA in Philadelphia (which organized *Robert Mapplethorpe: The Perfect Moment*), and to SECCA in Winston-Salem (which gave a $15,000 fellowship to Andres Serrano). The measure also allots $200,000 from the NEA budget for a study by an independent commission of the NEA's grant-making procedures. The Senate accepts the $45,000 cut proposed by the House in the NEA appropriations bill, and also shifts $400,000 from the NEA's Visual Arts Program to Local Programs and Folk Art Programs (see July 12, 1989).

July 26: Late in the evening, Senator Jesse Helms introduces an amendment proposing new guidelines for the NEA in the Interior Department's appropriations bill. By a voice vote in the nearly empty Senate chamber, the "Helms Amendment" is added to the bill. The amendment prohibits the use of NEA funds for the "dissemination, promotion, or production of obscene or indecent materials or materials denigrating a particular religion." The limitations state:

"None of the funds authorized to be appropriated pursuant to this Act may be used to promote, disseminate, or produce — 1) obscene or indecent materials, including but not limited to depictions of sadomasochism, homoeroticism, the exploitation of children, or individuals engaged in sex acts; or 2) material which denigrates the objects or beliefs of the adherents of a particular religion or non-religion; or 3) material which denigrates, debases, or reviles a person, group, or class of citizens on the basis of race, creed, sex, handicap, age, or national origin."

August 8: Senator Jesse Helms sends four photographs from Mapplethorpe's exhibit, which he labeled "indecent," to House and Senate members who will be deciding the terms of the NEA reauthorization. Helms urges his colleagues to keep his amendment in the final legislation. Michael Stout, the lawyer for Mapplethorpe's estate, says that Helms may have violated copyright laws by distributing the photographs without permission.

August 30: Reacting to the Corcoran Gallery's cancellation of *Robert Mapplethorpe: The Perfect Moment*, several artists initiate a boycott of the gallery. A major show by Annette Lemieux is "indefinitely postponed" after the artist withdraws her work. Another exhibition entitled *Gallery One: Six Sculptors — The Resonance of the Odd Object* is canceled when artists Liz Larner, Donald Lipski, Patty Martori, Charles Ray, ZiZi Raymond, and Buzz Spector also withdraw their work.

September 7: The Whitney Museum of American Art places a full-page "open letter" advertisement in *The New York Times* and *The Washington Post*. Voicing the museum's objections to the "Helms Amendment," the advertisement shows a Mapplethorpe photograph of a wilted flower accompanied by the headline, "Are you going to let politics kill art?"

September 8: The Corcoran Gallery of Art asks the New York artists' collective Group Material to organize an exhibition about censorship. The exhibition, which may include work by Robert Mapplethorpe and Andres Serrano, among others, is planned to help the Corcoran reestablish its "reputation as a serious gallery in which to show contemporary and experimental art." Group Material, however, decides not to participate in the show because the Corcoran had yet to issue a public apology for canceling the Mapplethorpe exhibition.

September 13: In a 264–53 vote, the House of Representatives decides not to add the "Helms Amendment" to their version of the NEA appropriations bill. The move to add the amendment had been spearheaded by Representative Dana Rohrabacher (see July 26, 1989).

September 28: An attempt by Senator Jesse Helms to restrict federal funding of the arts by including his amendment in the NEA reauthorization bill is defeated in the Senate by a 62–35 margin.

October 1: The NEA is budgeted $171.22 million for FY 1990.

October 3: The House of Representatives passes the House-Senate conference committee compromise on the NEA appropriations bill by a vote of 381–41.

Opposing the compromise bill is Representative Dana Rohrabacher, who says it has "enough loopholes to drive a porno truck through." The bill establishes a twelve-member commission to study the NEA to determine if new standards should be adopted for federal funding of art. The bill also prohibits funding for projects that can be considered obscene according to criteria established by the 1973 Supreme Court case *Miller* v. *California*, and gives the NEA chairperson the power to determine if the merits of an application outweigh the agency's concerns over any sexually explicit content.

October 7: The Senate–House compromise appropriations bill for the NEA passes the Senate by a vote of 91–6 and is sent to President Bush to sign. The bill marks the first time Congress has mandated content restrictions for NEA grants.

October 19: The Senate votes against instituting a Constitutional amendment outlawing desecration of the U.S. flag. The bill was intended to circumvent *Texas* v. *Johnson*, the Supreme Court's ruling that defended flag burning as a protected form of free speech. President Bush and the Republican leadership in Congress continue to lobby for a constitutional amendment prohibiting flag desecration (see June 30 and July 18, 1989).

November 8: NEA chairperson John Frohnmayer revokes a $10,000 NEA grant awarded to Artists Space in New York City for *Witnesses: Against Our Vanishing*, an exhibition about AIDS. He also asks that the endowment not be listed as a sponsor of the exhibition. Frohnmayer says that his decision is not based on the content of the exhibition itself, which includes images of homosexual acts, but on the show's catalogue, which includes an essay by artist David Wojnarowicz that lambastes several prominent public figures, including New York Archbishop John Cardinal O'Connor, Representative William E. Dannemayer (R–Cal.), and Senator Jesse Helms. Frohnmayer says he would not make a distinction between the catalogue and the artwork presented in the show, and also complains that the exhibition was "political rather than artistic in nature."

November 13: NEA chairperson John Frohnmayer says that he regrets describing as "political" his reason for withdrawing endowment support for *Witnesses: Against Our Vanishing*. Attempting to clarify his position, he claims that his decision is based on "erosion of the artistic focus" of the exhibition.

November 15: Composer Leonard Bernstein refuses to accept the National Medal of Arts awarded to him by President Bush. He rejects the award to protest John Frohnmayer's decision to rescind NEA funding for *Witnesses: Against Our Vanishing*. Also, San Diego photographer Elizabeth Sisco, NEA Visual Artists Organizations panelist, resigns from the panel to protest Frohnmayer's decision.

November 16: Witnesses: Against Our Vanishing opens to large crowds at Artists Space in New York City. Following an outcry from the arts community, NEA chairperson John Frohnmayer restores the exhibition's NEA grant but stipulates that the funds cannot be used for the show's catalogue.

November 29: How Ya Like Me Now?, a billboard-size streetcorner painting by African American artist David Hammons, is torn down in Washington, D.C., by offended citizens. Hammons's work, sponsored by Washington Project for the Arts, portrayed Reverend Jesse Jackson as a white man with blond hair and blue eyes. The perpetrators believe that Hammons's painting is making fun of Jackson.

December 18: Dr. Christina Orr-Cahall resigns as director of the Corcoran Gallery of Art. Her announcement comes just before the museum's Board of Trustees is scheduled to vote on her future as director. Three weeks later she is named director of the Norton Gallery and School of the Arts in Palm Beach, Florida.

■ 1990

January 10: The performance *Post-Porn Modernist* by Annie Sprinkle opens at The Kitchen in New York City. On January 22, the *New York City Tribune* reports that Sprinkle's performances, in which she performs nude and discusses issues of sexuality, are partially funded by the NEA and the New York State Council on the Arts. In February, *Post-Porn Modernist* is criticized by Pat Robertson on his *700 Club* television program and is described by Representative Dana Rohrabacher (R–Cal.) in a "Dear Colleague" letter to other members of Congress. NEA chairperson John Frohnmayer denies that federal funds were used by The Kitchen to sponsor Sprinkle's show.

February 20: Representative Dana Rohrabacher composes another "Dear Colleague" letter to Congress condemning NEA support of artist David Wojnarowicz's exhibition *Tongues of Flame* at the University of Illinois at Normal.

March 3: Representative Dana Rohrabacher announces his intention to submit an amendment to the House of Representatives that will end all government funding for the arts.

March 5: A congressional hearing on the reauthorization of the NEA is conducted at the J. Paul Getty Museum in Malibu by the House Postsecondary Education Subcommittee of the Education and Labor Committee. Twenty-eight people are arrested in Los Angeles during a march in defense of the NEA and freedom of expression in the arts.

March 7: Citizens for Community Values, a Cincinnati-based organization focusing on issues of morality, sends their sixteen thousand members a letter detailing ways to halt the exhibition *Robert Mapplethorpe: The Perfect Moment*, which is scheduled to open in April at the Contemporary Art Center in Cincinnati.

March 9: The Washington Post reports that an antiobscenity clause has been added to the "General Terms and Conditions for Grant Recipients" that must be signed by all organizations and individuals receiving NEA funds. A number of writers, who were the first grant recipients to receive the new regulations, protest the new clause. It states:

> *Restriction on the use of FY 1990 Appropriated Funds.* Public Law 101-121 requires that: "None of the funds authorized to be appropriated for the National Endowment for the Arts...may be used to promote, disseminate, or produce materials which in the judgement of the National Endowment for the Arts...may be considered obscene, including but not limited to, depictions of sadomasochism, homoerotocism, the sexual exploitation of children, or individuals engaged in sex acts and which, when taken as a whole, do not have serious literary, artistic, political or scientific value."

Reverend Donald Wildmon, director of the American Family Association, sends a mailing to members of Congress, Christian organizations, and individuals nationwide, complaining of the NEA's support of pornographic, anti-Christian art. Included in the mailing is a page entitled "NEA-Funded Blasphemy" that reproduces details from works by David Wojnarowicz, including part of a work that depicts Christ with a hypodermic needle in his arm.

March 12: Representative Dana Rohrabacher distributes another letter to members of Congress, complaining about NEA support of *Modern Primitives: An Exhibition of Live Events on Contemporary Body Modification*, shown at Southern Exposure gallery in San Francisco.

March 15: A Broward County, Florida, judge bans local sale of the album *As Nasty as They Wanna Be* by the rap group 2 Live Crew.

March 20: Hundreds of people gather for Cultural Advocacy Day in Washington, D.C., to support federal funding of the arts without content restrictions. Meetings are held between lobbyists, administrators, artists, writers, actors, and members of Congress. Almost five hundred people attend a rally on the steps of the Capitol.

March 21: The Contemporary Art Center in Cincinnati holds a press conference and confirms its commitment to present the exhibition *Robert Mapplethorpe: The Perfect Moment.* At the press conference, representatives of some area educational, religious, and cultural groups express their support of the CAC's position.

The House Subcommittee on Post-secondary Education holds a second hearing on the reauthorization of the NEA. NEA chairperson John Frohnmayer submits the Bush administration's recommendations for the reauthorization bill, telling the committee that the administration will not seek content restrictions on NEA funding of controversial art.

Senator Jesse Helms asks the General Accounting Office (GAO) to investigate the NEA to determine whether taxpayer funds are being used in an acceptable manner. Helms sends the GAO several examples of controversial art funded by the endowment, urging that due to the nature of the work, "great care be taken to assure that your women associates not be exposed to the material."

March 22: Representative Dana Rohrabacher sends another "Dear Colleague" letter to members of Congress, summarizing his three previous letters, and again asserting that Annie Sprinkle's performances at The Kitchen were funded by federal tax dollars (see January 10, 1990).

Cincinnati's Citizens for Community Values declares *Robert Mapplethorpe: The Perfect Moment* to be "criminally obscene." Chad P. Wick resigns as chairperson of the Board of Directors of the Contemporary Art Center, attributing his action to pressures on his employer, the Central Trust Co., by conservative lobbying groups. The bank had received threats of a boycott because of Wick's affiliation with the CAC (see March 7, 1991).

March 23: Cincinnati law enforcement officials announce that they will review the Mapplethorpe exhibition for possible illegalities. Hamilton County Sheriff Simon Leis says, "the pictures I have seen certainly have been criminally obscene."

March 24: The General Accounting Office begins their investigation of the NEA, as requested by Senator Jesse Helms.

March 25: The Contemporary Art Center withdraws from the 1990 Cincinnati Fine Arts Fund drive, an annual campaign to raise general operating support for major cultural organizations in the city. CAC officials fear that the dispute over the Mapplethorpe exhibition would hinder the campaign.

March 27: Taking a proactive stance, Cincinnati's Contemporary Art Center, the Robert Mapplethorpe Foundation, and the Mapplethorpe estate together file suit to determine if any photographs in *Robert Mapplethorpe: The Perfect Moment* are criminally obscene under Ohio state law. "We want a decision on whether the work as a whole has serious artistic value," says CAC attorney Louis Serkin.

March 28: The American Family Association runs a full-page ad in *USA Today* to focus public attention on government funding of David Wojnarowicz's *Tongues of Flame* exhibition at the University of Illinois at Normal.

April 4: The National Campaign for Freedom of Expression (NCFE) is launched by artists and arts activists in Washington, D.C. Formed as an advocacy organization for the arts, the NCFE first targets the election districts of Senator Jesse Helms and Representative Dana Rohrabacher, two leaders in congressional actions against the NEA. Artists are asked to work to help defeat Helms and Rohrabacher in their upcoming elections. Charlotte Murphy, director of the National Association of Artists Organizations says, "This is the start of creating a mass constituency for the arts."

An emotional hearing is held by the House Subcommittee on Postsecondary Education on the question of reauthorizing the NEA. Representative Dana Rohrabacher again states that Annie Sprinkle's performance, *Post-Porn Modernist*, was an indirect recipient of federal tax support, since The Kitchen, which sponsored the performance, received money from the federally funded New York State Council on the Arts (NYSCA). Representative Pat Williams (D–Mont.) argues that the performance occurred after the last of the year's NEA funding had been given to the theater. NYSCA denies that any state funds went to fund Sprinkle's performance, even though it funded other shows in the same series at The Kitchen.

April 5: The National Association of Recording Merchandisers announces that legislation calling for the mandatory labeling of recordings with "explicit lyrics" had been dropped in many states. Instead, many record companies voluntarily agree to use a uniform label on potentially controversial recordings that states "Explicit Lyrics — Parental Advisory" (see May 10, 1990).

April 6: An Ohio judge rejects a request from Cincinnati's Contemporary Art Center to make an advance ruling on the photographs in *Robert Mapplethorpe: The Perfect Moment.* CAC director Dennis Barrie says he is afraid that county officials might now try to confiscate some of the photographs or close the show because of potential obscenity charges. The same evening, over three thousand people attend a preview of the exhibition at the Contemporary Art Center.

April 7: Robert Mapplethorpe: The Perfect Moment opens to the public in Cincinnati, drawing record crowds to the Contemporary Art Center. Visitors include nine members of a grand jury, who later indict the Contemporary Art Center and its director Dennis Barrie on misdemeanor charges of pandering obscenity, and of illegal use of a minor in nudity-oriented material. Cincinnati police temporarily shut the museum for an hour, forcing patrons to leave while they videotape the exhibition as evidence. County Prosecutor Arthur Ney asks the CAC to remove seven controversial photographs from the exhibition. Barrie refuses.

April 8: U.S. District Judge Carl Rubin blocks Cincinnati police from confiscating any photographs from the Mapplethorpe exhibition at the Contemporary Art Center. He orders Hamilton County and city authorities not to interfere in any way with the exhibition while charges against the CAC are under consideration. "You may not recover any photos, you may not close the exhibit to the public, you may not take any action that could be intimidating in nature to prevent the public from seeing the exhibit," says Rubin.

April 10: NEA critic Representative Dana Rohrabacher comes out against the indictment of the Contemporary Art Center in Cincinnati. He argues in favor of the center's First Amendment rights, and states, "My focus has been the federal subsidization [of art] and I am not advocating that these actions be taken by local governments."

April 12: The American Family Association again mails to Congress, Christian organizations, and individuals nationwide sexually suggestive details of larger images cropped from works by David Wojnarowicz. The AFA distributes thousands of copies of a pamphlet, urging Congress to "either clean up the NEA or abolish the agency altogether." The mass mailing, entitled *Your Tax Dollars Helped Pay for These Works of Art*, protests a $15,000 NEA grant to the University Galleries of the Illinois State University at Normal, for Wojnarowicz's exhibition *Tongues of Flame.*

April 14: Hamilton County Prosecutor Arthur M. Ney, Jr. withdraws from the obscenity trial against Cincinnati's Contemporary Art Center after a misdemeanor indictment is obtained against the center. Ney had sought felony charges against the CAC and its director Dennis Barrie, and Ohio law bars Ney as county prosecutor from trying misdemeanors. City Solicitor Richard Castellini takes over the case.

April 16: Dennis Barrie and the Contemporary Art Center enter "not guilty" pleas on obscenity charges related to exhibiting *Robert Mapplethorpe: The Perfect Moment.* Judge David J. Albanese of the Hamilton County Municipal Court is assigned to the trial. Albanese previously spent six years working for Hamilton County Sheriff Simon Leis, who has called Robert Mapplethorpe's photographs "criminally obscene."

April 16: The New York Times reports that the national publicity surrounding *Robert Mapplethorpe: The Perfect Moment* has inflated the prices of Mapplethorpe's work and enriched the artist's estate — a Mapplethorpe self-portrait sold at auction in New York for $38,500 in fall, 1989. Licensing agreements for Mapplethorpe's books, T-shirts, and posters have brought additional income to the Mapplethorpe Foundation. Much of the foundation's income will be donated to AIDS organizations, art museums, and libraries.

April 19: The Supreme Court rules 6–3 that states can pass laws against viewing or possessing child pornography. This ruling in the case *Ohio* v. *Osborne* upholds an Ohio law criminalizing possession or viewing of material depicting a minor "in a state of nudity" constituting "lewd exhibition" or "a graphic focus on the genitals." The law exempts material that is in the possession of a child's parents, or that which is used for "bona fide" artistic, educational, or scientific purposes.

April 24: The Motion Picture Association of America's X-rating for Pedro Almodovar's film *Tie Me Up, Tie Me Down* is upheld by a New York court. The filmmaker had appealed the rating, wanting neither to cut the film and receive an R-rating nor to release the film with an X-rating (see July 19, 1990).

April 25: Acting on a tip from a photography lab, San Francisco Police and the Federal Bureau of Investigation raid the home and studio of photographer Jock Sturges and the home of his assistant Joseph Semien, looking for "questionable photographs of juveniles." Sturges, known for his portraits of families in the nude, had hired Semien to reproduce some of his portraits depicting nude children. Semien delivered this work to a local photographic lab and was subsequently arrested on charges of possessing obscene material. California state law requires photo labs to report pictures that may violate child pornography laws. Charges against Semien are later dropped. Sturges says that all of these pictures were made with the permission of the children's parents, and that the photographs "could not be considered by any healthy mind, by any stretch of the imagination, to be pornographic."

April 27: Joseph Papp, director of the New York Shakespeare Festival, refuses to accept a $50,000 grant from the NEA. Papp states, "I cannot in all good conscience accept any money from the NEA as long as the Helms-inspired amendment on obscenity is part of our agreement." The New York Times Company Foundation and television producer Mark Goodson provide the Festival with enough funds to replace the refused grant. The festival had received $350,000 in grant funds from the NEA in 1989.

May 10: Representative Phil Crane (R–Ill.) introduces the "Privatization of Art Act," a bill that aims to abolish the NEA immediately.

The Recording Industry Association of America unveils its "Parental Advisory — Explicit Lyrics" warning, intended for labeling musical recordings that are potentially controversial (see July 1, 1990).

May 11: In a syndicated editorial, Roland Evans and Robert Novak claim that NEA chairperson John Frohnmayer has been advised to veto several Theater Program grants, including one to performance artist Karen Finley. After Evans and Novak break the story, Frohnmayer denies that he is under any pressure to veto the grants.

May 12: The National Assembly of State Arts Agencies (NASAA) recommends restructuring NEA procedures to increase the percentage of NEA funds distributed by state arts councils. NASAA director Jonathan Katz also recommends that all NEA grants be "substantially over $10,000" so larger grants could be given to nationally focused organizations, rather than to individuals.

May 13: The National Council on the Arts meets in Winston-Salem, North Carolina, to discuss strategies for dealing with the NEA crisis, and to respond to critics of the endowment. The Council also reviews current funding recommendations, and vetoes two of the three $40,000 grants approved by panels for the University of Pennsylvania's ICA, organizers of *Robert Mapplethorpe: The Perfect Moment.* The Council also defers decisions on eighteen other grants in the NEA Theater Program category, including a grant recommended for Karen Finley.

May 15: Representative Pat Williams introduces White House-backed legislation to reauthorize the NEA for five years without content restrictions. The House Subcommittee on Post-secondary Education hears testimonies and performances by Yo-Yo Ma, Jessica Tandy, Joseph Papp, Ruby Dee, Jane Curtin, Roy Lichtenstein, and Robert Rauschenberg, among others.

May 16: Representatives Steve Gunderson (R–Wis.) and Tom Coleman (R–Mo.) offer a new proposal that restricts the kinds of grants that can be offered by the NEA, and allocates 60 percent of the NEA's grant money directly to state arts agencies for regranting to regional programs and artists. With its remaining budget, the NEA would give grants to art of national and international significance, and to the development of institutional excellence.

The directors of all seven museums hosting *Robert Mapplethorpe: The Perfect Moment* gather at Washington Project for the Arts in Washington, D.C., to meet with NEA officials, members of the House of Representatives, and the press. The directors issue a joint statement, declaring that they are in Washington "to bear witness, to the Congress and to the public, that the right of freedom of expression must never give way to censors — to those whose standards are the lowest common denominator of accepted convention."

May 17: President Bush confirms the appointments of some members of the Independent Commission mandated by Congress to review NEA grant-making procedures. Committee members include: John Agresto, president of Saint John's College; John Brademas, president of New York University; Leonard Garment, lawyer and former Special Consultant to the President (under Richard Nixon); Joan Harris, commissioner, Illinois Department of Cultural Affairs; and Kitty Carlisle Hart, chairperson, New York State Council on the Arts.

May 21: David Wojnarowicz files suit in federal court against the American Family Association and its director, Reverend Donald Wildmon, seeking damages "in excess of $1 million" for copyright violation, defamation of character, and violation of a New York state law prohibiting unauthorized alteration and dissemination of an artist's work. The suit is in response to AFA mailings that reproduced fragments of Wojnarowicz's work without his authorization. These mailings stated the AFA's opposition to an exhibition and catalogue of Wojnarowicz's work, partially funded by the NEA (see March 9 and April 12, 1990).

May 22: Representative Pat Williams, chairperson of the House Postsecondary Education Subcommittee overseeing reauthorization of the NEA, withdraws his proposal to extend the life of the NEA without content restrictions. To help formulate new legislation, he convenes a summit conference of representatives from an array of arts organizations and relevant constituencies. Participants in the summit include the American Arts Alliance, the AFL-CIO Professional Employees in the Arts, the Coalition of Arts Educators, the American Design Council, the National Association of State Arts Agencies, the Coalition of Writers Organizations, and the National Association of Artists Organizations.

May 23: The New School for Social Research and lawyer Floyd Abrams file suit in New York City federal court, asking the NEA to stop requiring their "obscenity pledge," the promise that grant recipients must make declaring that they will not use federal funds to create or exhibit works of art that may be considered obscene. The suit names the NEA and its chairperson, John Frohnmayer, as defendants. The New School refused to sign the "obscenity pledge," turning down an NEA grant of $45,000 for sculptor Martin Puryear and architect Michael Van Valkenburgh to redesign the school's sculpture courtyard.

May 25: After three days of discussion, the summit meeting of arts organizations convened by Representative Pat Williams unanimously declares its support for a five year reauthorization of the National Endowment for the Arts without content restrictions of any kind. It calls for legislation that will place the burden for determining obscenity directly on the courts instead of on the endowment. The group also rejects a proposal from the National Association of State Arts Agencies to increase the amount of NEA support that is funneled directly to state arts councils.

June 1: A painting by artist Carlos Gutierrez-Solana, on view in a Richmond, Virginia, storefront window, is covered over by city officials who claim that the painting violates state obscenity laws. The painting is part of *Coastal Exchange 3*, an exhibition at the alternative gallery 1708 East Main, cosponsored by the Richmond Arts Council.

June 6: The White House asks Congress to reauthorize the NEA without any restrictions for one year while the Independent Commission mandated by Congress reviews the endowment's grant-making procedures. A White House official states that the administration wants "to let the noise level die down...let the commission do its work...and revisit this next year."

The General Accounting Office (GAO) discusses the results of its investigation of the NEA with the House Subcommittee on Post-secondary Education. The GAO report, requested by Senator Jesse Helms and disputed by Helms upon its completion, concludes that the NEA has not violated federal law by funding "sexually explicit" or "sacrilegious" art because the NEA had not judged this art to be obscene or sacrilegious.

In Miami, Florida, U.S. District Judge José Gonzalez rules that *As Nasty As They Wanna Be*, a new album by the rap group 2 Live Crew is "probably obscene." Gonzalez states, "It's an appeal to 'dirty' thoughts and the loins, not to the intellect and the mind."

June 7: Many institutions mark *Arts Day USA* with protests. The Metropolitan Museum of Art in New York City drapes paintings in black, 110 art museum directors stand on the steps of the Art Institute of Chicago behind a banner reading "Save the Arts," and the lights in the Kimbell Art Museum in Fort Worth, Texas are turned off.

June 10: Following a performance at a Florida nightclub, members of 2 Live Crew are arrested on obscenity charges by Broward County Sheriff's deputies. The lyrics of some of the group's songs describe sexual acts.

June 12: The Senate Subcommittee on Education, Arts, and Humanities unanimously agrees to send a five-year NEA reauthorization bill without content restrictions to the full Senate Committee on Labor and Human Resources.

June 13: Representative Paul B. Henry (R–Mich.) circulates a proposal banning federal funding of art that deliberately denigrates "the cultural heritage of the United States, its religious tradition, or racial or ethnic groups," or that violates "prevailing standards of obscenity or indecency." Senator Orrin Hatch (R–Utah) proposes to amend the NEA reauthorization bill so that artists who produced obscene works will be ineligible for federal grants for up to ten years.

June 19: The House Education and Labor Committee agrees to place the NEA reauthorization bill before the full House in mid-July. The Senate Labor and Human Resources Committee puts off sending its version of the NEA reauthorization bill to the Senate floor to allow committee members time to reach a consensus on the future of the endowment.

Judge David J. Albanese of the Hamilton County Municipal Court finds that the Contemporary Art Center in Cincinnati and its director Dennis Barrie must stand trial on two criminal charges related to their presentation of *Robert Mapplethorpe: The Perfect Moment.* The first complaint, for child pornography, stems from the exhibition of two photographs of nude children; the second charge, for obscenity, is related to the exhibition of five homoerotic images.

June 20: The House Judiciary Committee sends a proposal to the House floor for a constitutional amendment banning desecration of the U.S. flag. The committee sends the proposal with no recommendation because a majority on the committee cannot agree on the action.

June 22: Two literary journals, the *Paris Review* and the *Gettysburg Review*, refuse to sign the NEA's "obscenity pledge" and reject the grants awarded to them.

June 25: Federal Judge William C. Conner in the U.S. District Court of Southern Manhattan issues a temporary injunction barring further publication of the American Family Association pamphlet *Your Tax Dollars Helped Pay for These Works of Art,* which reproduces cropped portions of larger works of art by David Wojnarowicz (see May 21, 1991).

June 29: NEA chairperson John Frohnmayer vetoes NEA Theater Program grants to performance artists Karen Finley, John Fleck, Holly Hughes, and Tim Miller. These grants were approved by peer panel review, but the panel's recommendations were rejected by the National Council on the Arts. Each performer had created works dealing with issues of sexuality (see May 13, 1990).

July 1: Record companies begin to affix parental advisory labels to albums, tapes, and CDs that might be considered controversial because of lyrics about sex, violence, and drug use. Individual record companies and recording artists are responsible for determining which albums to label, and restrictions on the sale of recordings are decided by individual retailers (see April 5, 1990).

July 3: Formal obscenity charges are filed against members of the rap group 2 Live Crew and a record store owner. Bandmembers Luther Campbell, Mark Ross, and Chris Wongwon are indicted in Broward County, Florida, for an allegedly obscene performance in Florida on June 10. Charles Freeman, owner of E-C Records, is charged with selling copies of the group's album *As Nasty as They Wanna Be,* which previously had been ruled obscene by a federal judge (see March 15 and June 10, 1990).

July 6: Members of the NEA's Theater Program panel strongly urge the agency to reconsider its rejection of grants to Karen Finley, John Fleck, Holly Hughes, and Tim Miller.

July 11: The NEA publicly issues new guidelines to define obscene art. These guidelines are based on the legal definition of obscenity established by the Supreme Court in *Miller* v. *California.* The guidelines differ from the "obscenity pledge" that grant recipients still must sign. This creates a situation where grant recipients "are still asked to sign language which says one thing and simultaneously told that it means something else," says Lawyer Floyd Abrams (see June 21, 1990).

July 12: Bella Lewitzky of the Bella Lewitzky Dance Company files suit in U.S. District Court in Los Angeles against NEA chairperson John Frohnmayer and the endowment. The suit is filed to test the constitutionality of obscenity restrictions and "loyalty oath" requirements for artists accepting NEA grant funds. The company turned down an NEA grant of $72,000 because of the required "obscenity pledge." On January 9, 1991, a U.S. District Court in Los Angeles rules on *Bella Lewitzky* v. *John Frohnmayer* and declares the NEA's requirements to be unconstitutional.

July 19: New York state Judge Charles E. Ramos upholds a lower court's ruling and lets stand the X-rating placed on Pedro Almodovar's film *Tie Me Up, Tie Me Down.* But he also calls the rating system "a form of censorship" and advises the Motion Picture Association of America to revise the rating system or abolish it. The court suggests creating another rating for mature films that are not deemed pornographic (see April 24, 1990).

The Rockefeller Foundation in New York City opposes the NEA's "obscenity pledge." The NEA and the Rockefeller Foundation agree that grant recipients working on projects funded by both organizations may revise the NEA's "obscenity pledge" before signing it. Grantees can state that they will comply "to the extent that such terms and conditions, and the requirement to accept them, are lawful under the Constitution and the laws of the United States."

July 23: The NEA asks Franklin Furnace, a gallery and performance space in New York City, to prepare a complete description of its next season's programming. The gallery is told it must comply within thirty days or lose its NEA funding. The endowment requests "identification of the artists involved and the nature of the work to be performed or installed" so that a "final determination" can be made on their grant applications. An installation by Karen Finley is on view at the time of this request.

July 24: Scheduled debate on legislation to reauthorize the NEA is postponed until October by House Speaker Tom Foley (D–Wash.) to allow sufficient time to consider twenty-six amendments to the bill proposed by members of Congress.

July 30: In a public statement, NEA chairperson John Frohnmayer says art that is too confrontational or offensive to be exhibited in public places "would not be appropriate for public funding.... A photograph of Holocaust victims might be inappropriate for display in the entrance of a museum where all would have to confront it, whether they choose to or not."

July 31: On the *Ten O'Clock News,* Boston public television station WGBH shows viewers the controversial photographs in the exhibition *Robert Mapplethorpe: The Perfect Moment,* then on view at the Institute of Contemporary Art, Boston.

August 3: The National Council on the Arts recommends that the NEA and Congress rescind the requirement that grant recipients sign a pledge certifying that they will not create or show art that is considered obscene under the terms of the NEA's legislation; that two grants previously rejected by the council be restored to the ICA in Philadelphia; and that the endowment's legal counsel review five recommended Inter-Arts grants (to Karen Finley and Jerry Hunt, Holly Hughes and Ellen Sebastian, Adrian Piper, Wim Vandekeybus, and Daniel Martinez and Harry Gamboa) that might have been affected by conflict of interest problems on the review panel, and convene a new panel to reconsider them. Members of Out, a gay rights organization, disrupt the National Council on the Arts meeting and demand reconsideration of rejected grants to gay and lesbian artists. They are ejected by police.

August 8: A federal judge orders the American Family Association to correct and redistribute their pamphlet *Your Tax Dollars Helped Pay for These Works of Art.* Artist David Wojnarowicz had sued the AFA for $1 million for reproducing his images out of context and without his consent. Wojnarowicz was awarded only one dollar by U.S. District Judge William C. Connor, who said that Wojnarowicz could not prove any financial loss (see May 21, 1990).

A citizen's action case is filed by Boston's First Amendment Common Sense Alliance (FACS) against Boston's Institute of Contemporary Art (ICA) and its director David Ross for showing the exhibition *Robert Mapplethorpe: The Perfect Moment.* The ICA is charged with violating state laws against obscenity and child pornography. An obscenity complaint is also filed against artist Richard Bolton for his exhibition *The Emperor's New Clothes: Censorship, Sexuality, and the Body Politic* at the Photographic Resource Center (PRC), Boston University (see August 15, 1990).

August 14: A performance by San Francisco-based Survival Research Laboratories is canceled at Artpark in Lewiston, New York. In the performance, a twenty-foot-high earth-mover robot covered with donated bibles was to be ignited by a replica of a World War II rocket. (Survival Research Laboratories is known for pyrotechnic performances using complex robotic machines that destroy themselves and each other.)

August 15: The obscenity complaint against artist Richard Bolton and his exhibition *The Emperor's New Clothes: Censorship, Sexuality, and the Body Politic* is dismissed by Roxbury District Court Justice Charles Spurlock. The judge rules that Boston's Photographic Resource Center, where the show is held, is exempt from the state's obscenity laws because these laws do not apply to schools, museums, or libraries (see August 8, 1990).

The Federal Communications Commission (FCC) announces that it will investigate Boston television station WGBH for broadcasting certain photographs by Robert Mapplethorpe on their *Ten O'Clock News* program. According to the FCC, WGBH may have violated the commission's "obscenity" or "indecency" regulations (see July 31, 1990).

August 16: A West Hollywood, California, billboard painting by artist Robbie Conal is taken down by the owner of the billboard, the National Advertising Company in Chicago. Conal's painting depicts a portrait of Senator Jesse Helms superimposed on an artist's palette. The painting's caption says, "Artificial Art

Official." The billboard owner says that it was a matter of questionable taste that led them to remove Conal's statement.

September 5: Complaints filed by the First Amendment Common Sense Alliance against the Institute of Contemporary Art in Boston, and its director David Ross, are dismissed in Boston Municipal Court (see August 8, 1990).

September 6: In the obscenity case against Cincinnati's Contemporary Art Center and its director Dennis Barrie, Judge David J. Albanese rules that the prosecution can isolate individual photographs in *Robert Mapplethorpe: The Perfect Moment* for presentation to the jury. This means the defendants can be convicted even if only one of the photographs is found to be obscene. "This Court finds that each photograph has a separate identity; each photograph has a visual and unique image permanently recorded," said Albanese (see June 19, 1990).

September 11: The bipartisan twelve-member Independent Commission, mandated by Congress to investigate grant-making procedures at the NEA, unanimously approves and submits its final report to Congress. The report recommends that the NEA rescind its "obscenity pledge" requirement, and that no legislative restrictions be placed on the content of art funded by federal grants. The commission states that it considers the NEA to be "an inappropriate tribunal for the legal determination of obscenity." The report also calls for major reforms of the NEA's grant-making procedures (see May 17, 1990).

September 12: The Senate Committee on Labor and Human Resources approves the "Hatch-Kennedy-Pell-Kassenbaum" bill by a 15–1 vote. This bill calls for a five-year reauthorization of the NEA without content restrictions on grants, and includes a provision allowing the NEA to recoup grant funds from any recipient convicted of making federally subsidized art that violates local obscenity or child pornography laws. The bill adopts many reforms recommended by the Independent Commission, including increased funding to state arts councils, and increased power to the NEA chairperson and the National Council on the Arts.

September 14: The board of directors of Creative Time, a New York City arts organization supporting the public presentation of work by emerging and mid-career artists, votes to refuse the organization's 1990 NEA grants to protest "the current restrictive contract language disallowing funding for certain artistic content."

September 25: About two hundred demonstrators march in downtown Cincinnati in a show of support for the Contemporary Art Center and its director Dennis Barrie.

September 27: Performance artists Karen Finley, John Fleck, Holly Hughes, and Tim Miller file suit in Los Angeles Federal District Court against the NEA and its chairperson John Frohnmayer. The suit, filed through the National Campaign for Freedom of Expression Legal Defense Team, charges that the NEA violated the artists' constitutional rights by denying them panel-approved grants for political reasons.

October 1: The NEA is budgeted $174.08 million for FY 1991.

October 4: Representatives Pat Williams and Thomas Coleman reach a compromise on House legislation reauthorizing the NEA. Their joint proposal, like that approved in the Senate committee, shifts responsibility for judging obscenity from the NEA to the courts, and stipulates that artists be asked to give the NEA more details on their projects when applying for grants.

October 5: Dennis Barrie and the Contemporary Art Center are found not guilty of obscenity charges filed against them for showing the exhibition *Robert Mapplethorpe: The Perfect Moment.* The jury takes less than two hours to acquit the CAC and Barrie (see June 19, 1990).

The Robert Mapplethorpe Foundation in New York announces that it will donate 20 percent of its gross revenues for the next three years to AmFAR, the American Foundation for AIDS Research.

October 11: The House of Representatives votes 349–76 in favor of the Williams-Coleman compromise bill, reauthorizing the NEA for three years. The House bill imposes no content restrictions on works of art funded by the NEA, but it requires that grant recipients whose federally funded work is found in court to be obscene must repay grant funds to the NEA. The bill calls for major changes in the endowment's procedures, including new requirements for artists to provide more details about their proposed projects. Applicants would be required to submit interim reports detailing the progress of their projects, and artists' panels would be expanded to include "knowledgeable laypersons."

October 20: The rap music group 2 Live Crew is acquitted of obscenity charges after being accused of conducting an obscene performance in a Florida nightclub. Following a two week trial, the jury deliberated for two hours before reaching their verdict (see June 10, 1990).

October 22: The Institute of Contemporary Art in Boston announces that a NEA grant for an exhibition of work by Mike Kelly, approved by a Museum Program panel, has been rejected by the National Council on the Arts and by NEA chairperson John Frohnmayer. "The only reason that this grant was turned down after unanimous peer review approval was that the council and Frohnmayer fear that the work would be politically unacceptable," says ICA director David Ross.

October 24: The Senate passes its version of a reauthorization bill for the NEA by a vote of 73–24. Amendments to restrict public funding of sexually oriented art are defeated; a last-minute amendment by Senator Jesse Helms passes, denying funds for any work that denigrates religion. The Senate bill also requires grant recipients to return funding for work found in court to be criminally obscene.

October 25: As required by the court, Reverend Donald Wildmon mails a correction to recipients of the American Family Association's earlier pamphlet *Your Tax Dollars Helped Pay for These Works of Art,* which reproduced fragments of work by David Wojnarowicz. His letter acknowledges that the images reproduced in the pamphlet "do not constitute the entire work from which they were reproduced" (see August 8, 1990).

October 27: The House and Senate pass legislation reauthorizing the NEA for three years. The final compromise language eliminates explicit legislative restrictions on the type of art that may be funded. The bill does require that grantees take into consideration "general standards of decency and respect for the diverse beliefs and values of the American public." The bill allocates $175 million to the NEA in FY 1991 and increases the percentage of grant money funneled to state arts agencies from 20 to 27.5 percent. The bill also gives the NEA the right to recoup funds from grant recipients who create works with federal grant money that are found by the courts to be obscene.

October 29: The NEA announces that it is eliminating its "obscenity pledge" requirement that all grant recipients sign a contract promising not to use NEA funding for the creation and promotion of obscene art.

America's Finest?, a series of posters addressing the controversial use of deadly force by the San Diego police department, is installed on twenty-five bus benches throughout the city by artists Deborah Small, Elizabeth Sisco, Louis Hock, and Scott Kessler. Funded in part by a grant from the NEA, the poster depicts seven silhouettes representing victims of police violence. Feeling that this project was an inappropriate use of government funds, Representative Bill Lowery (R–Cal.) urges the NEA to investigate whether federal funds were used for commercial advertising, which is not permitted under NEA guidelines. In 1991 the NEA develops a strict policy on the purchase of advertising space with federal funds.

November 2–3: The National Council on the Arts meets in Washington. The five Inter-Arts grants previously postponed by the Council for potential conflict of interest problems are reconsidered and approved (see August 3, 1990).

November 6: In North Carolina, Jesse Helms is reelected to his U.S. Senate seat for a fourth six-year term, defeating Democratic challenger Harvey Gant.

November 13: Members of the 1990 NEA Literature Program's Literary Publishing panel resign to protest the new congressionally mandated "decency provision," which calls for "general standards of decency" to be considered in awarding grants.

November 16: NEA chairperson John Frohnmayer informs the Citizens Environmental Coalition in Houston, Texas, that he is rejecting an Inter-Arts Program grant for a project by New York artist Mel Chin. The project was recommended for funding by an NEA Inter-Arts panel and by the National Council on the Arts. Chin's proposed project, *Revival Field*, uses plants to "remediate an area contaminated with heavy metals." The endowment's rejection letter states, "the Chairman [Frohnmayer] was not persuaded...that the artistic aims as outlined in the application were sufficient to merit arts endowment funding."

December 14: NEA chairperson John Frohnmayer states that he will no longer reject panel-approved grants on the basis of the "decency provisions" placed in the agency's new authorizing legislation. "I am not going to be the decency czar," says Frohnmayer.

December 20: After meeting with artist Mel Chin, NEA chairperson John Frohnmayer announces that he will reconsider the rejected grant to Chin for *Revival Field*. Chin is asked to redraft his proposal, and on February 1, 1991, Frohnmayer reverses his decision and approves the grant. On February 22, 1992, Frohnmayer is forced by the Bush administration to resign his position as NEA chairperson.

About the Author

R ichard Bolton is an artist and writer whose work addresses a wide range of questions concerning mass media, popular culture, democratic participation, and the social function of art. He received an MFA in photography from Cranbrook Academy of Art in 1981, an MA in Liberal Studies from St. John's College in 1985, and is now an associate professor and the chairperson of the Department of Art Studio at the University of California, Santa Barbara. Bolton is also the editor of *The Contest of Meaning: Critical Histories of Photography* (Cambridge: The MIT Press, 1989). In 1991 and 1989 he received NEA Visual Artists Fellowships in the area of New Genres.